in the hands of the landed aristocracy and the very rich, and the unwritten rules that defined membership in this charmed, doomed circle, the like of which could never form again. Based on original research, interviews and much hitherto unpublished material, it could revolutionize our view of the serene Indian summer of Victorian England and the values upon which it rested.

ANGELA LAMBERT's interest in the aristocracy dates from the time when, as a little girl, she stayed in a medieval German castle and stared at the ancient, many-branched family tree that hung on one of its walls. Ever since then the aristocratic obsession with family and bloodlines has always intrigued her. Her passion for research and the unraveling of connections has its academic roots in a degree from St. Hilda's College, Oxford, and its daily professional use in her work as a current affairs reporter with Thames Television in London. For a decade or more she has been delving into politics and personalities at the turn of the last century. It became clear that no one had written the book she really wanted to read, so she set about writing it herself—and the result is *Unquiet Souls*.

UNQUIET SOULS

UNQUIET SOULS

*A social history of the illustrious,
irreverent, intimate group of
British aristocrats known as
"the Souls"*

ANGELA LAMBERT

1817

HARPER & ROW, PUBLISHERS, New York
Cambridge, Philadelphia, San Francisco, London
Mexico City, São Paulo, Singapore, Sydney

FIRST U.S. EDITION

ISBN: 0-06-015329-6

LIBRARY OF CONGRESS CATALOG CARD NUMBER: 84-47584

84 85 86 87 88   10 9 8 7 6 5 4 3 2 1

To my children
Binkie, Johnnie and Marianne

Contents

viii   Contents

List of Illustrations

Acknowledgements

My first thanks must go to the children, grandchildren and friends of the Souls who gave me their time and attention. Many of them answered intrusive questions; others must have realized, from the tenor of my enquiries, that they would not agree with the kind of book I was going to write. In spite of this, they were patient, helpful, often hospitable and always courteous, with a courtesy that enabled me to glimpse the lost world of their forebears, the Souls.

Lord David Cecil gave me what was, in effect, an extended private tutorial on the society, manners and language of his parents, the Marquess and Marchioness of Salisbury, and his friend, Lady Desborough and her circle. It was a delight, as were the letters which he wrote in answer to my queries and arguments. I know he will take issue with much that I have said in this book and I must stress that only his own quoted words represent his judgments.

Lady Alexandra Metcalfe, Lord Curzon's daughter, gave me several hours of her company and conversation. The tenderness and pride with which she cherishes the memory of her parents were evident in every word and I am grateful to her for sharing her feelings and recollections with me and for lending me some wonderful portraits of her mother.

Lady Diana Cooper has been a legendary figure all her life and is so still. She, too, talked to me for hours about her mother, the soulful Violet, Duchess of Rutland, and her friends, both among the Souls and the doomed generation of their children. Much of what I have written in the final chapters of the book was inspired by the tone of voice in which she said, 'They all died, you see.' I am very grateful to her for those conversations and for allowing me to search through her two great scrap books, mementoes of ninety years of crowded life, in search of illustrations for this book.

Lady Mary Lyon invited me, at short notice, to visit her beautiful house in Gloucestershire, close to the Elcho family home at Stanway; and there she talked with perfect recall and some sadness of the world of her youth. She generously allowed me to reproduce some pictures of her mother, Lady Elcho, and family. I am very grateful.

Lady Gage invited me to her London home, where she reminisced fascinatingly. In addition to this, through her kind introductions I gained access to others who could tell me about the Grenfell family – most notably her stepson, the Hon. Nicolas Gage. Thanks to him, I visited Firle Place on two occasions and leafed spellbound through several volumes of the Taplow Court Visitors' Books. Nicolas Gage has provided, in the end, most of my illustrations, and far more than he originally realized (or intended). I am extremely grateful to him for this kindness and for his warm hospitality.

Lord Crathorne saw me at the very beginning of my quest into the history of the Tennant family and their links with the Souls. His encouragement and patience towards a fledgeling historian were remarkable. He made available boxes of family papers, which he had painstakingly put in order, and answered my questions at an early stage of my research when I must have seemed distressingly ignorant. He, more than anyone, gave me the confidence and the stimulus to forge ahead, and for this I feel a particular gratitude.

Baroness Elliot of Harwood, a daughter of Sir Charles Tennant, demonstrated the energy and intellectual resources of her family, as well as their kindness to strangers. She proved an illuminating link with her sisters, Laura and Margot Tennant, and I much enjoyed talking to her.

The Hon. John Jolliffe, grandson of Raymond Asquith, whose letters he has so sensitively edited, saved me from many pitfalls while at the same time leaving me free to maintain opinions that were usually very different from his own. He answered my letters in great detail, encouraged me at a stage when my nerve was failing, and I owe him deep thanks.

By far the most enjoyable part of my work on this book has been talking, and listening, to all these people. I know that they will not share many of my conclusions and so I am doubly grateful for their tolerance.

There is one particular debt of gratitude that stretches back twenty years and which is beyond my power to express. This is to Elizabeth and Frank Longford, whose love and support, enthusiasm and example were the inspiration for writing this book. I am also most grateful to Lord Oxford and Asquith for allowing me to quote from the letters of his father, Raymond Asquith.

My greatest piece of luck was in meeting, almost by chance, Peter Scott of Bertram Rota, the antiquarian booksellers. With a truffle-hunter's instinct and persistence he managed to track down most of the rare or obscure books that I needed for my research. In addition, he turned out to be a leading expert on the First World War. His boundless generosity in offering me – by letter, in conversation, and over lunch – the fruits of years of expertise, while tactfully correcting my elementary mistakes, is more than a library of first editions could repay.

Mary Berger of Oxford spent many hours in the Bodleian Library, reading back numbers of century-old journals in search of contemporary detail, besides bringing a perfectly tuned ear to bear upon niceties of grammar. Antonia Summers ferreted through the archives of *Country Life* in search of illustrations of Souls' houses. I thank them both for their hard work.

And in the end, James Butler probably had more to put up with than anyone during the two years I spent writing this book. His superb cooking sustained me and my children through many weekends when we would otherwise have lived on scrambled eggs. His hospitality in Essex and Portugal, while I shut myself away to the sound of a clacking typewriter, was loving indeed.

The book would not, however, have been written at all if my three children had not been extraordinarily long-suffering during the many hours when they could not engage my attention, make a noise, play records or watch television because 'Mummy's working on the book.' They must often have been sick of the Souls, yet they hardly ever allowed me to realize it; instead, they were marvellously encouraging, patient and loving.

Thank you all.

Angela Lambert
London
May 1982–February 1984

Main Characters

This book is about a group of people, the Souls, and to a lesser extent about a second group, the Coterie, who were their children. For that reason, it has a great many characters in it, some of whom change their names by marriage or inheritance, and, in order to simplify matters for the reader, I have divided the main characters up between lists of these two groups. The first list contains MAJOR SOULS (whose full names are printed in capitals) and MINOR SOULS (whose surnames only appear in capitals at the start of their entries); the second lists the leading members of the *Coterie* (whose names are printed in italics).

Each person's name and dates are followed by a lightning sketch of their character, a suggestion of other main individuals to whom they were related or with whom they were chiefly involved and, where relevant, a brief summary of their career. When a person changes name, his or her history is continued under the new name.

These lists are not intended to be read *before* embarking on the book, but to serve as points of reference for the reader. Other characters not listed here will be found in the Index.

Souls

ASQUITH, Herbert Henry (1852–1928). Created 1st Earl of Oxford and Asquith 1925. Married (1) Helen Melland, by whom he had five children (the oldest being *Raymond Asquith*), and after her death (2) MARGOT TENNANT in 1894, by whom he had two more children. After a relatively modest beginning his career soared through Balliol and the Bar to the Home Secretaryship in 1892 and the Liberal Premiership 1908–16. During the First World War his attention was greatly distracted by his passionate love for *Venetia Stanley*.

ASQUITH, MARGOT (1864–1945). *Née* MARGOT TENNANT, she married H. H. Asquith in 1894. After this her sparkling originality and social boldness turned into something more bitter and highly strung and, although she remained at the centre of events and was always hospitable, she became an eccentric and sometimes unhappy woman, the scourge of her husband's political enemies. She had two children (Elizabeth and Antony ('Puffin')) and five stepchildren.

BALFOUR, ARTHUR (1848–1930). Aloof, detached, cerebral philosopher, Conservative politician and charming guest. Eton 1861–6; Trinity College, Cambridge, 1866–9. Inherited estate at Whittingehame and large fortune in 1869. Elected Conservative MP 1874 and represented East Manchester 1885–1906; Chief Secretary for Ireland 1887–91; Leader of the Conservatives in the House of Commons 1891–1911; Prime Minister 1902–5; Foreign Secretary 1916–19; created Earl of Balfour 1922. First love was May Lyttelton, sister of ALFRED LYTTELTON, but she died young. From early 1880s loved MARY WYNDHAM with constancy until his death, despite her marriage to LORD ELCHO.

BARING, Hon. John (1864–1929). Succeeded to title as 2nd Baron Revelstoke 1897. Devoted acolyte of ETTIE GRENFELL, he never married, but helped her protégés into his family's firm, Baring's Bank.

BLUNT, Wilfrid Scawen (1840–1922). Handsome, bearded, ardent, nationalistic, a poet and a lifelong seeker after passion and freedom. Married Byron's granddaughter, Lady Anne King-Noel, and had numerous other relationships with some of the loveliest women in society, including, briefly, with his distant relative MARY ELCHO, who bore him a child in 1895.

BRODRICK, St John (1856–1942). Succeeded his father as 9th Viscount Midleton, and created 1st Earl Midleton 1920. Married Lady Hilda Charteris, sister of LORD ELCHO, in 1880. Close friend of GEORGE CURZON until the two men fell out over policy in India 1902–5, after which they were never fully reconciled.

CHARTERIS, Evan (1864–1940). Brother of LORD ELCHO and Lady Hilda Brodrick. Another lifelong admirer of ETTIE GRENFELL until his belated (and frowned-upon) marriage in 1930.

CURZON, GEORGE (1859–1925). Proud, hard-working, travelled, witty, autocratic and warm-hearted. Eton 1872–8; Balliol College, Oxford, 1878–81; Fellow of All Souls, Oxford, 1883. Conservative MP for Southport, 1886–98; Viceroy of India, 1898–1905. Chancellor of Oxford University 1907; created Earl Curzon of Kedleston 1911; inherited father's title as 4th Baron Scarsdale 1916; KG 1916; Foreign Secretary 1919–24; created Marquess Curzon of Kedleston 1921. Married (1) in 1895 Mary Leiter, beautiful daughter of an American millionaire, who bore him three daughters. She died 1906 and after two years' intense mourning he began a long affair with romantic novelist Elinor Glyn. Married (2) in 1917 an American widow, Mrs Alfred ('Gracie') Duggan.

CURZON, Mary (1870–1906). *Née* Mary Victoria Leiter. Cultivated, intelligent, delicate, adored wife of GEORGE CURZON; his prop and stay while he was Viceroy of India, mother of his three daughters and go-between for innumerable colleagues, friends and hangers-on. Although Mary was never fully accepted by the Souls, the Curzons' marriage was perhaps the happiest of all in that circle. Exhausted by overwork and climate in India, she died tragically young.

CUST, HARRY (1861–1917). Handsome, romantic, journalist, poet, dilettante and lover of women; great-grandson of 1st Earl Brownlow and nephew and heir of 3rd Earl Brownlow, whose title he waited all his life to inherit: in vain. Eton, where he was Captain of Oppidans and tipped for even greater things; Scholar of Trinity College, Cambridge. Barrister; member of Crabbet Club; Conservative MP for Stamford Division of Lincolnshire 1890–5 and MP for Bermondsey 1901–6. Editor of *Pall Mall Gazette* 1892–6. Had numerous love affairs with Souls women, including LADY GRANBY, Pamela Wyndham and others, but was forced in 1894 to marry a young woman whom he had seduced but did not love, Nina Welby-Gregory. Father of *Lady Diana Manners*, and, by repute, many more.

CUST, Nina (1867–1955). *Née* Nina Welby-Gregory. A minor beauty, minor painter and sculptor, and minor Soul, her life was given centre and purpose by her unrequited passion for HARRY CUST. After nearly twenty-five years of neglect, he finally returned to her just in time to die. She spent the rest of her life making monuments to him.

DESBOROUGH, ETTIE (1867–1952). *Née* Ethel Priscilla Fane and the former Mrs Willy Grenfell until BALFOUR ennobled her husband in 1905. She was a tireless and magnetic hostess and fascinator of men, including GEORGE WYNDHAM, John Baring (later Lord Revelstoke) and Evan Charteris; later *Archie Gordon* and *Patrick Shaw Stewart*. Granddaughter and heiress of 6th Earl Cowper, from whom she inherited Panshanger in 1914. Mother of five children, including *Julian* and *Billy Grenfell*.

DESBOROUGH, Lord (1855–1945). Formerly Willy Grenfell, created 1st Baron Desborough by ARTHUR BALFOUR as a favour to his wife ETTIE in 1905. Spent his last forty years in the House of Lords, on various international sporting committees, and on the River Thames. Became increasingly taciturn, even eccentric; an object of respect and some alarm to his wife's unceasing flow of guests.

ELCHO, Lord (1857–1937). Formerly Hugo Charteris. Extravagant, impatient, witty husband of MARY ELCHO and heir to Earl of Wemyss and March. (Inherited title and money at last in 1914.) Stanway was the family home where his wife entertained despite their straitened circumstances in much-appreciated comfort and disorder. He was the lover of the Duchess of Leinster and Lady Angela Forbes, and father of five children including his heir, *'Ego' Charteris*.

ELCHO, MARY (1861–1937). *Née* Mary Wyndham. Generous, impulsive, unpunctual, unselfconscious, warm-hearted, kind. Popular hostess at Stanway. Married HUGO ELCHO in 1883 although ARTHUR BALFOUR was, and remained for the next fifty years, her real love. Had a short-lived romantic sojourn in the Egyptian desert with Wilfrid Scawen Blunt, as a result of which she bore him a daughter in 1895. Sister of GEORGE WYNDHAM and Pamela Tennant.

GLENCONNER, Lady Pamela (1871–1928). *Née* Pamela Wyndham. Youngest daughter of Percy and Madeline Wyndham of Clouds, she fell unwisely and too much in love with HARRY CUST, but was safely married to Edward Tennant, later Lord Glenconner, after a period of recuperation in India. After this marriage she had a long liaison with Edward Grey, later Lord Grey of Fallodon, whom she married in 1921 after her first husband's death. Mother of five children, including *Edward ('Bim') Wyndham Tennant*.

GLENCONNER, Lord (1859–1920). Formerly Edward Tennant, eldest son of Sir Charles Tennant and brother of MARGOT ASQUITH, CHARTY RIBBLESDALE, LAURA LYTTELTON, etc. Married 1895 Pamela Wyndham, sister of MARY ELCHO and GEORGE WYNDHAM, thereby rescuing her from disastrous aftermath of relationship with HARRY CUST. Created Lord Glenconner in 1906 thanks to MARGOT's intercession on his behalf with ARTHUR BALFOUR.

GRAHAM SMITH, Lucy (1860–1942). *Née* Lucy Tennant. Married Thomas Graham Smith, early and rashly, in 1879 and lived thereafter at Easton Grey, near Malmesbury in Wiltshire. Here her unhappy marriage was palliated by devotion to hunting, HARRY CUST, and the art of watercolour. Later in life became crippled with arthritis and was confined to a wheelchair. Childless herself but devoted to her many nephews and nieces.

GRANBY, Lord (1852–1925). Formerly John Henry Manners. Handsome, sporting, philistine heir to the 7th Duke of Rutland (whom he succeeded in 1906) and to at least 75,000 acres of prime agricultural land all over England, including the beautiful Vale of Belvoir, and several great houses, including Belvoir Castle. His wife's passion for the theatre was matched by his for actresses, which ensured mutual tolerance of one another's dramatic excursions.

GRANBY, LADY VIOLET (1856–1937). *Née* Violet Lindsay. Ethereal, artistic, bohemian, passionate, Soulful. Married Henry Manners in 1882; he became Lord Granby in 1888 and Duke of Rutland in 1906. She bore him two sons (one of whom died young) and a daughter before embarking on other liaisons, most notably with HARRY CUST, to whose daughter, *Diana,* she gave birth in 1892, though this could not prevent their affair from ending unhappily soon afterwards. She was looked at somewhat askance for her friendships with actor-managers like Herbert Beerbohm Tree and her fondness for backstage life, but she was genuinely creative and a skilled artist in pencil and stone.

GRENFELL, ETTIE (1867–1952). *Née* Ethel Priscilla Fane. Socially ambitious, brilliant hostess, good talker and even better listener; fascinating to men, particularly at arm's length; well-read but unmusical. Granddaughter of 6th Earl Cowper and thus wealthy heiress to Cowper–Lamb inheritance. Married, surprisingly, Willy Grenfell in 1887 and bore him three sons, of whom *Julian* (b. 1888) and *Billy* (b. 1890) grew up to become well-known. Enjoyed many long liaisons, possibly platonic, and did not allow them to interfere with her very happy marriage and close family life.

GRENFELL, William Henry ('Willy') (1855–1945). Tall, athletic: a perfect specimen of late-Victorian muscular Christianity. His years at Harrow and Balliol were remarkable more for his sporting than his intellectual achievements. Liberal MP 1882–6, Conservative MP 1900–5. The course of his life was largely determined for him by his marriage in 1887 to heiress ETTIE FANE, a powerful personality and social magnet to their contemporaries, whom she attracted to his large but ugly house, Taplow Court, set beside the Thames (his ruling passion after ETTIE) at Maidenhead. Willy tolerated his wife's emotional promiscuity and was a devoted father to their five children, all of whom looked just like him.

GROSVENOR, Lady Sibell (1855–1929). *Née* Lady Sibell Lumley. Her ailing first husband's death in 1885 made her the perfect young widow: rich, beautiful and much in need of masculine care and protection. From among her countless suitors, including GEORGE CURZON, she chose GEORGE WYNDHAM, eight years her junior, as her second husband in 1887 and bore him one son, *Percy Wyndham.* Other than this, alas, she soon bored him.

HORNER, Lady Frances (1858–1940). *Née* Frances Graham. Knowledgeable and discerning patron of the arts, she was the unrequited love for many years of Pre-Raphaelite painter Edward Burne-Jones and dearest friend of LAURA TENNANT, who met her various suitors under Lady Horner's hospitable roof at Mells Park, near Frome, in Somerset. Mother of *Edward,* Cicely and *Katharine* Horner.

HORNER, Sir John (1843–1927). Descendant of little Jack Horner of nursery rhyme fame, and still living at the centuries'-old family home at Mells Park. A kindly, bookish, classic country gentleman somewhat on the fringe of the Souls and many years older than his artistic wife.

LIDDELL, Adolphus ('Doll') (1846–1930). Tall, angular, goatee-bearded, serious young lawyer. Eton, Balliol and the Bar led him into the Lord Chancellor's office, whence he fell deeply in love with LAURA TENNANT. After being unhappily crossed in love by the more dashing, equally sweet-natured ALFRED LYTTELTON, he eventually recovered and fell in love with 'D.D.' Balfour: whereupon ALFRED LYTTELTON crossed him again! After the uniquely unfortunate experience of losing both the women he loved to the same man, he retired from the matrimonial fray and became only an occasional Soul.

LYTTELTON, ALFRED (1857–1913). Outstanding athlete, especially cricketer. Last son of the very large family of 4th Baron Lyttelton, Alfred was much-loved and something of an innocent all his life. Educated at Eton and Cambridge, called to the Bar 1881. Married (1) LAURA TENNANT and (2) D. D. Balfour (no relation of A. J.) 1892. Liberal MP for Warwick from 1895; Colonial Secretary 1903–5. Died after being struck by a cricket ball during an amateur match.

LYTTELTON, LAURA (1862–86). *Née* Laura Tennant, daughter of Sir Charles Tennant. Extraordinarily gifted, mercurial, mystical, passionately loving wife of Alfred. She died in childbirth in 1886, eleven months after her marriage. The deep sense of mourning after this early and shocking death drew her many friends together into the group that later became known as the Souls.

LYTTELTON, Edith ('D.D.') (1865–1943). *Née* Edith Balfour (but no relation to Arthur); second wife of ALFRED LYTTELTON and mother of *Oliver*.

PLYMOUTH, Countess of (1863–1944). Formerly Lady Gay Windsor; *née* Alberta Paget. Became Countess of Plymouth in 1905, but her long relationship with GEORGE WYNDHAM was the mainspring of her life, despite attempted flirtation by Wilfrid Scawen Blunt. Her long, stable and fulfilling liaison with GEORGE WYNDHAM ended appropriately when he died in her arms during a visit to Paris in 1913.

RIBBLESDALE, Lord (1854–1926). As Thomas Lister met, fell in love with and married CHARLOTTE TENNANT in 1877, by which time his father's death had made him 4th Baron Ribblesdale. A soldier, a courtier, but above all a hunting man, he was seen as the archetypal country gentleman, largely due to Sargent's full-length portrait depicting him as such: top-hatted, booted and spurred. He was less devoted to intellectual pursuits than his clever and popular wife, and only a peripheral Soul. After her death he lived for many years as a guest of Rosa Lewis in the Cavendish Hotel.

RIBBLESDALE, LADY 'CHARTY' (1858–1911). *Née* Charlotte Tennant. Elder sister of MARGOT and LAURA TENNANT, Lucy Graham Smith and Edward Glenconner. Tall, blonde, patrician, clever like all her sisters, and a gifted hostess and letter-writer. Mother of two sons (both killed in war) and three daughters, one of whom, *Diana*, married *Percy Wyndham*. She was a very close and lifelong friend of GEORGE CURZON. She died relatively young of hereditary tuberculosis.

RUTLAND, DUCHESS of (1856–1937). Formerly Violet Lindsay and then LADY GRANBY. Talented artist, ethereally slender and ultimately a sad figure due to her long, and finally disappointed, love for HARRY CUST. Became Duchess when her husband succeeded to the dukedom in 1906 and relished the title; the marriage less so. Her three daughters, *Lady Violet* ('Letty'), *Lady Marjorie* and *Lady Diana Manners* formed the centre of the Coterie.

RUTLAND, Duke of (1852–1925). Born Henry John Manners, then Lord Granby, he came into his splendid inheritance in 1906. He was known – not unkindly – as 'a dull, dumb Duke': probably because his glittering womenfolk so outshone him. He seems not to have minded, entertaining their many friends at Belvoir Castle and 16 Arlington Street and the actresses he preferred in rather more privacy elsewhere.

TENNANT, CHARLOTTE ('CHARTY') (1858–1911). Variously gifted, like all the Tennant sisters, and the most beautiful of them all, she married at the end of her first London season but continued to stay often with her parents at Glen, the family home in Peeblesshire, where, with MARGOT, LAURA and Lucy, she attracted the crowd of brilliant young men who were to form the nucleus of the Souls.

TENNANT, Edward (1859–1920). Eldest son of Sir Charles Tennant and the most aristocratic in appearance of a gifted entrepreneurial family. He married Pamela Wyndham in 1895 and became Lord Glenconner in 1906. Lived in an apparently amicable *ménage-à-trois* with his wife's devoted admirer, another Edward, later Lord Grey of Fallodon. Also in 1906, after his father's death, he became lord of Glen, the large, rambling family home.

TENNANT, Sir Charles ('Bart') (1823–1906). Not a minor Soul, nor indeed a minor anything, he was remarkable for his talent for making money, both by his business activities and by his shrewd collector's instincts. Equally remarkable, he fathered sixteen children over a span of 54 years: twelve by his first wife, Emma, and, after her death in 1895, four more by his second wife Marguerite. His older children were the centre of a group of young people who were welcomed under his hospitable roof at Glen in Peeblesshire and 40 Grosvenor Square in London.

TENNANT, LAURA (1862–86). The fourth of five Tennant daughters who delighted and astonished the most discriminating and unconventional young men of the 1880s by their defiance of *haut-bourgeois* behaviour. Although no beauty, Laura's sweetness of nature, her talents as a musician, actress and conversationalist, allied to a surprising but profound strain of religious mysticism, ensured that she fascinated everyone she met. The Balfour brothers competed with GEORGE CURZON and 'Doll' Liddell for her love, until she became engaged to ALFRED LYTTELTON in January 1885.

TENNANT, LUCY (1860–1942). A typical Tennant in appearance, and extraordinarily like her younger sister Margot. She was a talented artist, painting watercolours of all her friends and family, but an early marriage in 1879 prevented her personality from ever flowering as did her sisters'. Her husband, Thomas Graham Smith, was a boorish country squire, and Lucy's platonic passion for HARRY CUST could not console her for the failure of her marriage.

TENNANT, MARGOT (1864–1945). Youngest and most celebrated of the five sisters, Margot was the apotheosis of all that Tennant meant. Only five feet tall, and elegantly slender all her life, her energy and wit sent shock waves through London society when she came out in 1881. Her coruscating intellect (much admired by Gladstone and Jowett) was balanced by a passion for hunting, which led to an 8-year relationship with Peter Flower. She ultimately abandoned him in favour of the politically promising H. H. Asquith, whose wife she became in 1894.

WEBB, Godfrey (1832–1901). Oldest member of the Souls and the Crabbet Club and much-loved friend of the Tennant family. As a bachelor clerk of the House of Lords he was much in demand as a weekend and dinner guest.

WEMYSS, MARY, COUNTESS OF (1861–1937). The last name borne by Mary Wyndham/Charteris/Elcho when her husband finally succeeded to the earldom.

WEMYSS AND MARCH, EARL OF (1857–1937). Lord Elcho became the Earl in 1914 when his father finally died. Apart from the money, which he urgently needed after dissipating a small fortune in his youth, the title brought him little joy. His beloved sons, 'Ego' and Yvo, were both killed in the war.

WINDSOR, Lady Gay (1862–1944). *Née* Alberta Paget, one of the wistful, wide-eyed Souls beauties, and much wooed by many besides her husband, Lord Windsor, whom she married in 1883. They entertained at Hewell Grange in Worcestershire and, more romantically, at St Fagan's Castle in Wales. She became the acknowledged mistress of GEORGE WYNDHAM in the late 1890s, remaining so until his death. In 1905 Edward VII revived the defunct title of the Earl of Plymouth for her husband's benefit. Their son was one of the first casualties of the war, in August 1914.

WYNDHAM, GEORGE (1863–1913). Not only astoundingly handsome, but handsome in the manner that epitomized late-Victorian standards of masculine good looks: large dark eyes, soft dark hair and moustache, a dashing figure with an operatically melancholy expression – assets which he exploited to the full. First they earned him the hand of the richest and most beautiful young widow of his time, Sibell Grosvenor, in 1887; then a period of emotional masochism at the hands of ETTIE GRENFELL; and, finally, safe anchorage with Lady Windsor. Conservative MP for Dover 1889–1913, he shared A. J. BALFOUR's stormy passage as Chief Secretary for Ireland, and himself took on the job in 1900: without, however, the same success. In 1905 he had to resign, amid rumours of heavy drinking and neurotic lapses, and he died at fifty, a disappointed man.

WYNDHAM, MARY (1861–1937). The lovely, large-eyed daughter of the aesthetic but matrimonially ambitious Madeline Wyndham. Her mother, fearful that a potential earl might slip through her fingers, pressured her into marriage with HUGO ELCHO rather than letting her wait for ARTHUR BALFOUR to make up his mind to marry her. Remarkably, all three remained on close terms throughout their lives.

WYNDHAM, Pamela (1871–1928). Younger sister of MARY and GEORGE, she shared her family's disastrous propensity to be crossed in love. A youthful infatuation with HARRY CUST was transformed into a sensible union with Edward Tennant, later Lord Glenconner: eldest brother of MARGOT, CHARTY and LAURA.

The Coterie

Asquith, Raymond (1878–1916). Eldest son of H. H. Asquith and his first wife, Helen. After distinguishing himself at Winchester and Balliol College, Oxford, worked at the Bar for ten years. Universally regarded as the figurehead and leader of the Coterie, Raymond was in fact not typical of that reckless, pleasure-loving set. Tall, with chiselled good looks and perfect if somewhat distant courtesy, he was revered as well as loved by his own and also his father's contemporaries. In 1907 married *Katharine*, the clever but retiring younger daughter of Sir John and Lady Horner of Mells Park in Somerset. Shortly after the birth of their third child in April 1916, Raymond was killed at the Battle of the Somme in September 1916.

Charteris, Hugo ('Ego'), Lord Elcho (1884–1916). Son and heir of the EARL OF WEMYSS, 'Ego' possessed dark and dashing good looks and rather awe-inspiring nobility of character. In 1911 married *Lady Violet ('Letty') Manners*, second daughter of the DUCHESS OF RUTLAND, and they had two sons. A burgeoning diplomatic career was cut short by the outbreak of war, and Ego enlisted in the Gloucestershire Yeomanry. He was killed at Katia, in Egypt, on 23 April 1916.

Charteris, Yvo (1896–1915). Youngest son of the Charteris family, his intellectual range and promise were only just beginning to be recognized when he went straight from Eton into the Grenadier Guards. In September 1915 his regiment was sent to France, and six weeks later he died leading his men over the top and into battle.

Cooper, Duff (1890–1954). Born into the professional rather than the landed classes, Duff Cooper's unshakeable self-esteem more than compensated for this. After Eton and New College, Oxford, he was destined for a diplomatic career. One of the more raffish members of the Coterie, he ate, drank and gambled more than he could afford, and was as inveterate a partygoer as *Lady Diana Manners*, his eventual wife. Being a Foreign Office clerk, he was not sent to the Front until April 1918, which probably saved his life. Once there, his gallantry in action won him the DSO, and a year later he finally secured the consent of the Duke and Duchess of Rutland for his marriage to Lady Diana Manners.

Gordon, Archie (1884–1909). Third son of the 7th Earl of Aberdeen, he was an Oxford undergraduate when in 1904 he first met ETTIE GRENFELL, and was captivated by her social and emotional sophistication. Although not handsome, he was charming and devoted. In December 1909, however, he suffered a fatal car accident, and died three weeks later.

Grenfell, Billy (1890–1915). Younger son of Willy and ETTIE GRENFELL, Billy was a contradictory character: very tall and good-looking, he could also be a bully. He was intellectually outstanding, winning the Newcastle Scholarship to Eton and obtaining a Second in Greats at Balliol, as well as the Oxford–Cambridge heavyweight boxing championship. When the war began he followed his brother to the Front, and died six weeks after him, in July 1915.

Grenfell, Julian (1888–1915). Never really a Coterie member – he was too complex an individual to fit easily into any social set – but Julian was brought up among the children of the Souls and circulated assiduously around its well-born daughters by his socially ambitious mother. He fell deeply in love with *Lady Marjorie Manners*, but when she chose to marry the Marquess of Anglesey, Julian took refuge in an affair with an older, married woman, the beautiful Pamela Lytton: much to the indignation of his mother. To escape the ensuing complications, Julian joined the army in 1912 and served in India and South Africa before returning home with his regiment at the outbreak of war. He had six months in France, where he was among the few who actively enjoyed fighting and killing, before being wounded in April 1915. He died three weeks later.

Horner, Edward (1888–1917). Yet another conspicuously tall and handsome young member of the Coterie, though he too had a reputation for wild behaviour. But he was personable and much-loved, and is said by many to have been unofficially engaged to *Lady Diana Manners*. He was the only son of Sir John and LADY HORNER, and brother of *Katharine Asquith*, and was doing well in F. E. Smith's chambers when the war began. Edward was wounded three times, and finally died at Cambrai in November 1917, thereby ending the four centuries'-old lineage of 'little Jack Horner'.

Horner, Katharine (1885–1976). Unusually intelligent and well-read, it was her knowledge of classical literature rather than her high forehead and eyebrows and dark beauty which first captivated *Raymond Asquith*. After a long, slow courtship they were married in 1907, to the delight of both their families and all the Souls.

Lister, Charles (1887–1915). Second son of Lord and LADY RIBBLESDALE (their first son, Thomas, had been killed in South Africa in 1904), he was in many ways the most genuinely original of the Coterie. An Eton and Balliol contemporary of *Julian Grenfell* – who loved and respected him for his directness and reliability – he was a fervent socialist, who both collected money and worked for this political ideology, so foreign to the thinking of his parents and contemporaries. He was in favour of the Independent Labour Party, in favour of votes for women, and – for a while, until the outbreak of war – in favour of Bertrand Russell's pacifism. By 1913 he was Third Secretary at the British Embassy in Rome. Unfortunately for him, the war changed all that, and he went off to die with most of his friends: in his case, of wounds, at Gallipoli, in August 1915.

Lyttelton, Oliver (1893–1972). Son of ALFRED LYTTELTON's second marriage, to Edith ('D.D.') Balfour, he was never really a Coterie member. But the war brought him into contact with *Edward Tennant* and Osbert Sitwell, both of whom served in his regiment (the Grenadier Guards). He joined the army in August 1914 and was one of the very few young officers of his class who left it, completely unscathed, at the end of the war, having been at the Front almost throughout.

Manners, Lady Diana (b. 1892). 'Soulful daughter of a Soulful mother', as the popular press loved to say, she was the dazzling, daring, radiantly fair leader of the Coterie. Nearly all its young men fell in love with her – Denis Anson, George Vernon, *Edward Horner, Charles Lister, Duff Cooper*, to name but a few. Several older men also lusted after her shapely fair limbs and pale features, and she juggled happily with lovers and lechers alike, until the war made life grimly serious. Lady Diana overcame parental opposition to train as a nursing auxiliary at Guy's Hospital, and had to watch with deepening shock as one by one her friends and lovers were killed . . . all except *Duff Cooper*, whom she married in 1919.

Manners, Lady Marjorie (1883–1946). Oldest of the three Manners sisters and famous since childhood for the spectacular beauty of her liquid dark eyes. *Julian Grenfell* was deeply in love with her, but her ambitious mother hoped for a better match: hopes which were fulfilled when Marjorie and the young Marquess of Anglesey fell in love and married. Thereafter they lived somewhat apart from the frenetic Coterie, and were thus spared the most harrowing effects of the war.

Manners, Lady Violet ('Letty') (1888–1971). Second daughter of the DUCHESS OF

RUTLAND, her bold sculptured profile was not approved of by her mother; however, *Lord Elcho ('Ego' Charteris)* found it irresistible. Their marriage was a happy one; Letty adored her husband, and accompanied him to Egypt when his regiment was posted there in 1915. She nursed in Alexandria, and the first eighteen months of the war were thus relatively secure for them both. In April 1916, however, he was reported missing and three months later his death was finally confirmed.

Shaw Stewart, Patrick (1888–1917). Friend and contemporary of *Julian Grenfell* at Eton and Balliol, where his intellectual prowess was extraordinary, and he won every academic prize possible, ending with a First in Greats and Fellowship of All Souls. He became a leading light of the Coterie, and also succeeded *Archie Gordon* as ETTIE DESBOROUGH's young favourite. With her contacts and his talents he rose swiftly in Baring's Bank. His pallid appearance belied a ferocious ambition, and his success seemed assured, until the war put a stop to all his plans. After surviving Gallipoli, he was killed in France on the last day of 1917.

Stanley, Venetia (1887–1948). Independent, strong-minded, intelligent daughter of Lord Sheffield, her modern manners and strong good looks fascinated both the Prime Minister, H. H. Asquith, and his wealthy Private Secretary, Edwin Montagu. She vacillated between the two of them for over three years, an object of obsessional love to them both, until in 1915 she surrendered to the social need to be married and became Edwin's wife. The marriage was not a happy one; and it broke Asquith's heart.

Tennant, Edward Wyndham ('Bim') (1897–1916). Adored elder son of Lord Glenconner (Edward Tennant) and Lady Glenconner (*née* Pamela Wyndham), and thus nephew of both MARGOT ASQUITH and GEORGE WYNDHAM, 'Bim' was born into the innermost circle of Souls' children, and was richly gifted: not least with a responsive heart. He and his mother idolized each other; she was devastated when he went to France in August 1915 with the Grenadier Guards. His attempts to reassure her with almost daily letters proved ultimately to be in vain, for he was killed before he was twenty, in the Battle of the Somme in September 1916, just a few days after *Raymond Asquith*.

PART I

HEYDAY

1880–1900

– 1 –
All Souls

1889

On 10 July 1889, the young George Curzon held a dinner party at his club for a group of his closest friends. It was never intended to be more than an amusing evening and a means of returning hospitality before he set off for a 'cure' in Switzerland the following month. It might also be the last time he saw most of them for several months, for in September he planned to leave on yet another journey of exploration: this time to Persia. Yet somehow, the guests assembled for that dinner came to be regarded as the founding members of the Souls, so that the evening took on a significance that none of them could have anticipated at the time.

We know precisely who was there, partly because it was characteristic of Curzon's attention to detail that he should have kept a meticulous note; but also, in this particular case, because he wrote a set of verses to mark the occasion. They are the most dreadful doggerel, full of facetious references and private jokes. For all that, they are highly revealing, because they include at least a mention, often a few lines, about everyone assembled that evening. Curzon had the verses printed, and a copy was laid on each guest's empty chair. Margot Tennant kept hers for over thirty years, and in due course reproduced them in full in her *Autobiography*. By the time it was published, young George Curzon had become the Marquess Curzon of Kedleston, KG, and British Foreign Secretary, and may well have been mildly embarrassed by this reminder of his frivolous bachelor past.

Yet the verses, precisely because they were never intended for posterity, capture the light-heartedness, confidence and intimacy of that vanished evening and the glittering circle of friends. For a moment the Victorian era stops in its tracks. There, caught in close-up, are several frames displaying the very choicest blooms from the orchid house of society. They seem just as they did to H. G. Wells a few years later, 'like going to a flower show and seeing what space and care can do with the favoured strains of some familiar species'.[1]

Forty Souls were present that evening, seated around a long table laid with immaculate white linen and silver cutlery, and crystal bowls of flowers alternating with silver and deep blue glass cruet stands. Club servants waited deferentially to proffer the first of several elaborate courses, accompanied by fine French wines. Unlike most late Victorians, the Souls prized slenderness as a desirable attribute in female beauty. Gluttony was not their style. Few of them would have done more than toy with the eight or more courses presented in sequence, dark and light dishes alternately.

First, however, before the meal began, Curzon would have risen to his feet and hushed the animated conversation. Margot Tennant has described his appearance at this time, when he was thirty:

> A conspicuous young man of ability, with a ready pen, a ready tongue, an excellent sense of humour in private life and intrepid social boldness. He had appearance more than looks, a keen, lively face and an expression of enamelled self-assurance . . . and he added to a kindly feeling for other people a warm corner for himself. . . . He was chronically industrious and self-sufficing; and, though Oriental in his ideas of colour and ceremony, with a poor sense of proportion and a childish love of fine people, he was never self-indulgent. He neither ate, drank, nor smoked too much and left nothing to chance.[2]

Quite unabashed at being the centre of attention – he had, after all, already been a Conservative MP for three years – Curzon proceeded to harangue the assembled company. . . .

> Around him that night –
> Was there e'er such a sight?
> Souls sparkled and spirits expanded;
> For of them critics sang,
> That tho' christened the Gang,
> By a spiritual link they were banded.

This is bad enough, but it gets worse. He goes on to apostrophize the acknowledged leader of the Souls, Arthur Balfour:

> There was seen at that feast
> Of this band, the High Priest.
> The heart that to all hearts is nearest;
> Him may nobody steal
> From the true Common weal
> Tho' to each is dear Arthur the dearest.

Even dear Arthur's celebrated detachment might have winced at this; and he would have recognized the truth of the jibe, that each Soul thought himself – or herself – secretly Arthur's favourite.

Curzon carried on in the same style for a further twenty-five verses, with a few appropriate lines for each guest. Not a word of it has poetic merit, yet taken all together the artless verses are both charming and evocative. Everyone around the table must have been smiling as Curzon finally read his concluding peroration:

> Now this is the sum
> Of all those who have come
> Or ought to have come to that banquet.
> Then call for the bowl,
> Flow spirit and soul,
> Till midnight not one of you can quit!

> And blest by the Gang
> Be the rhymester who sang
> Their praises in doggerel appalling;
> More now were a sin –
> Ho, waiters, begin!
> Each soul for consommé is calling!

Curzon had invited fifty-three people to his dinner; and considering the nature of the occasion – both thanks and leave-taking – it is perhaps surprising that as many as fourteen declined. His choice of date was unlucky. It coincided with a state visit by the Shah of Persia, who was being entertained that same night by Baron Ferdinand de Rothschild at his Buckinghamshire home, the opulent Waddesdon Manor. In different circumstances Curzon would probably have hoped to be there himself, to establish some official contacts with the Persian court, and ask advice about protocol and travelling conditions during his imminent journey through Persia. Several leading Souls had been obliged to refuse Curzon's invitation because their attendance upon the Shah and his retinue was required. Curzon referred disparagingly to the inconvenient monarch in his lines about Lord and Lady Brownlow, who *were* present, having already done their duty as hosts to the grimly formal, autocratic Shah at their country house the previous evening:

> And Ashridge's lord
> Most insufferably bored
> With manners and modes Oriental.

The visit had evidently been something of an ordeal.

After Curzon's dinner ended the company were still in such high good humour that host and guests went back to the hospitable house at 40 Grosvenor Square belonging to Sir Charles Tennant, head of the Tennant family. It was a favourite venue, free from the constraints of chaperones and convention; and here they danced or played games or flirted, but above all talked half the night away.

During that London season of 1889 few of George Curzon's friends suspected that his health was causing him more than usual concern. In addition to a chronic spinal weakness that forced him to wear a heavy brace for most of his life, his doctors had recently diagnosed lung trouble. They had advised him to benefit from clear mountain air at a sanatorium in Switzerland before embarking on his next foreign adventure. This was why Curzon had gathered his friends around him for what might, for all he knew, turn out to be their last evening together. Only the previous year one of the Tennant sisters, the gentle and saintly Posie, had died of tuberculosis at Davos, aged just thirty-three. Tuberculosis was not to be taken lightly.

Where to hold the dinner presented a problem. Curzon had no town house of his own, and his country seat – Kedleston Hall, in Derbyshire – was more than usually uncomfortable, for all its vast marble splendour. Besides, it was still presided over by his austere father, a clergyman of the Church of England, the 4th Baron Scarsdale. When in London, Curzon could have stayed or dined in any one of half a dozen clubs. The Carlton was his favourite but, like most gentlemen's clubs, it did not admit ladies; and in 1889 it was still unthinkable for a lady of birth and breeding to dine in a public place such as a restaurant. All social life and hospitality among the upper classes was private, though on a lavish scale. In those days of spacious houses, scores of servants and unlimited means there was nothing unusual in entertaining several dozen people to dinner at home, and twenty would have been considered a small party. The great hostesses of the day rivalled one another with formal balls for hundreds of guests, and many private houses still had ballrooms to accommodate them: Grosvenor House, Stafford House, Londonderry House – the vanished palaces of London.

Curzon, however, possessed neither his own home, nor a wife to act as hostess. He had been accumulating social debts for years. As long ago as 1882 he had written to his old friend Dick Farrer – another who died young of tuberculosis: 'I have just had over four weeks' Season, which I have enjoyed enormously. During that time I have only dined at home once, and have been to a dance (excluding Saturdays and Sundays) every night but one.'[3] The meeting place he finally settled upon was the only one of his clubs that did admit ladies. It was too exclusive to be regarded as a public rendezvous, and it offered comfortable private rooms and excellent cuisine for young bachelors in just Curzon's predicament. Indeed, it was called the Bachelors' Club. It was accepted as a suitable place where a respectable young lady might meet her brother, perhaps, or even a male cousin, without being compromised and without endangering her all-important reputation. The club premises were at 8 Hamilton Place, next door to Apsley House and a stone's throw from Hyde Park and the fashionable residential areas of Mayfair and Belgravia, where most of Curzon's friends had their town houses.

The Bachelors' was a club designed for single men: so much so that it fined members £25 upon marriage. Its atmosphere was younger and more relaxed than the ambience of some of the traditional clubs, and it was said to be the original on which P. G. Wodehouse based the Drones' Club. The Bachelors' lacked the serious political overtones of the Carlton and the Reform, and even the theatrical raffishness of the Garrick, yet was not as unpredictable as the Travellers', a favourite haunt of Victorian explorers. It was, in short, a perfectly safe place to which to invite young women – who were themselves required to be ('it is almost needless to add' said the club rules primly) eligible for presentation at court. Wives and sisters might be brought there, but certainly not mistresses, or those ladies tucked away in villas in St John's Wood, on the wrong side of the Park.

London possessed a number of restaurants by 1889, though most were chop-houses or taverns, more appropriate for a City lunch or a rowdy evening. However, there were also Simpson's in the Strand; Rules, in Maiden Lane; the Café Royal, a meeting place for the bohemian and literary world; while the newly opened Savoy Hotel had been built to cater for the growing influx of American visitors. Gentlemen might find at any of these an acceptable alternative to dinner at their club; and could go on from there, if they wished, to enjoy the pleasures of the West End's night life. The Alsatians' Club in Oxford Street, as described by George Cornwallis-West, was typical: 'It consisted of one long room for dancing and a smaller room where a perfectly horrible supper was served at an outrageous price. The male members of it belonged to the *jeunesse dorée* of the period, while the lady members were taken from the oldest profession in the world.'[4] And thus, with the oldest euphemism in the world, the author dismissed London's reputed quarter of a million prostitutes.

In 1889 the double standard was still in evidence everywhere. Women of the upper classes were artificially preserved in a state of complete innocence until their marriage – an innocence designed to conceal from them, not only the most basic physical and sexual information, but also the fact that they were kept equally ignorant of the political, social and economic pressures which made their virginity essential. But their untouchability depended upon the liberty of their brothers to debauch women of lower social status than themselves. Only thus, it was believed, could their sisters' virginity be preserved. Society remained a small, cohesive group whose membership had changed remarkably little for centuries, and one of the things that kept it unchanged was the purity of its bloodlines. The great English families could not risk having their daughters seduced, or the paternity of their heirs suspect.

The English upper class consisted, in 1889, of around ten thousand people, drawn almost entirely from a core of fifteen hundred families. They all knew each other, or, if not personally familiar, they knew 'of' each other. They knew all about one another's marriages, scandals, lunatics, roués and misfortunes. Their tribal characteristics were either an ancient name and lineage, or a title – and an ancient title was better than a recent one. The title would have been acquired by royal or political patronage, perhaps in return for loyalty to the winning side in some far-off dynastic struggle; or for services rendered, in terms of men, money or hospitality; or it might even have been straightforwardly bought, though in due course the passage of time would discreetly blur such origins. The aristocracy owned great estates and houses and works of art – but, above all, they owned land. Well over ninety per cent of the acreage of Britain was theirs. The only other way into the highest society – since no one ostracizes the really rich – was to have a very great deal of money: like, in fact, Baron Ferdinand de Rothschild, for whom even the xenophobic, anti-Semitic British upper classes were prepared to make an exception. The foremost members of the aristocracy displayed all these tribal characteristics and thus enjoyed every worldly advantage.

Lady Frances Balfour, sister-in-law of Arthur Balfour, wrote nostalgically about the calm superiority of the denizens of that world:

> Social life was centred in the home and its interests. Outward distractions were few, and 'entertainment' meant by the gifts and talents of the hosts and guests. It was a circle intimately interwoven. . . . They were all known to one another, to be left out or forgotten was an unthinkable misfortune. The old were established facts, and over all was the grace and beauty of the best manners and the ease which accompanies people who are sure of themselves, and need no advertisement.[5]

It was as a reaction to this pattern of late Victorian society that the Souls developed their new and distinctive style. They were not satisfied with the entrenched, ineffable, unchanging manners and modes of the upper-class world. They were faster, keener, more animated; they chattered and sparkled and laughed amid the heavy and stolid formality of their contemporaries.

The leading set in society was composed of the courtiers and hangers-on who surrounded the Prince and Princess of Wales. They were known as the Marlborough House Set. Slavishly supplying and aping the tastes of the middle-aged, indulgent, amiably tyrannical heir to the throne, the men and women of his circle devoted their lives to gargantuan meals, to the wholesale butchery of game animals and birds, to racing and playing cards and gambling and adultery; in short, to the constant (and frequently unsuccessful) pursuit of pleasure. They loved and feared the Prince of Wales. He was fatally easily bored, and so the mainspring and purpose of the Marlborough House Set was to stave off his *ennui*. Secretly, they were all waiting for the old Queen to die.

The second group, emerging gradually during the 1880s, and in complete contrast to the Prince of Wales's set, was the one that had been christened the Souls. It never counted among its innermost ranks more than forty or fifty people, though the same number again might have been considered as 'occasional Souls'. It was not easy for an outsider to gain full acceptance. The Souls prided themselves above all on their intellect, their aesthetic sensibility, their unique interpretation of the taste and manners of their time. These were the qualities that secured entry to the charmed circle. Their houses, their clothes, but above all their conversation were different from the rest of their class. Only twice during the previous history of the English aristocracy had *intelligence* been regarded as a desirable, let alone an essential, attribute. The first time was during the reign of Elizabeth I. The second was the heyday of the Holland House Set, a century before.

Nobility was not an absolute condition of membership of the Souls. Wit was. Many of the Souls would have been considered intellectually brilliant by any standards, though mere intellect was not enough. George Curzon had been elected a Fellow of All Souls, Oxford, at the age of twenty-four: but it was his swift, glancing, vivacious wit that endeared him to the Souls, and made him a leading light. Arthur Balfour could have been an academic philosopher had he not chosen to play the game of politics instead, and throughout his life he divided his time between philosophy and his parliamentary duties. Yet his wit, soft-voiced yet rapier-sharp, was what entranced his friends. Many of the women of the Souls were also remarkable: the more so in that this was not an era that admired clever women. Margot Tennant and her sisters were celebrated for being exceptionally well read; for being talented musicians or painters or writers; and not least for their unorthodox wit. Lady Granby and Frances Horner were also gifted amateur artists; while those who lacked such expertise concentrated their energies into being superb hostesses. Lady Elcho and Ettie Grenfell were said to have elevated hospitality into something close to an art. Visitors to their country houses enjoyed a lost perfection of comfort, conversation and cuisine.

Many outsiders, jealous of this exclusive circle, felt that the brilliance of the Souls was overblown, decadent, even suspect. The Souls remained unconcerned with what others thought, and saw no need to court society, being almost self-sufficient in their own company. Forty years later, Ettie Grenfell wrote a letter to *The Times* defending her vanished group of friends:

Never can there have been people less desirous of forming a clique, in any sense of the word, or of posing in any way. They were great friends – the men all hard at work in various ways, the women occupied and busy – who often met together to talk and play, and who enjoyed every moment of their pastimes. . . . Many are gone from sight, and it is for their sakes that one would like to recall the joys, imponderable as gossamer and dew, the laughter and delight, and the steadfast loyalty of friendship, that those far-off days enclosed.[6]

The marital ambitions of Victorian mothers for their daughters were such that George Curzon must always have been a sought-after guest. He was a young bachelor with expectations of a title; personable, amusing, widely travelled and ambitious enough to appeal to the mothers – but in addition, with his cameo profile, finely textured skin and hair, and penetrating dark eyes, highly attractive to their daughters. Small wonder that, after a decade in society, he had built up a considerable backlog of obligations. In spite of this, he was neither married, nor showing any signs of an imminent intention to marry. It was generally known that his heart had been broken two years earlier, in 1887, by the lovely young widow of Earl Grosvenor, the sickly heir to the Duke of Westminster. After her husband's death, and months of vacillation, the sweet-faced Sibell had finally rejected George Curzon's suit in favour of his rival, the handsome George Wyndham. Curzon's heart, and his pride, had begun to recover from the blow; though he was human enough to derive some small satisfaction from noting that Sibell chose to retain her former husband's name, and was known for the rest of her life as Lady Grosvenor rather than as plain Mrs Wyndham!

Sought-after though he was, George Curzon's financial means were relatively modest. In 1889, at the age of thirty, he had to manage on a private income of less than £1,000 a year, supplemented by whatever he earned from the sale of books and journalism about his extensive travels. If that figure is inflated by a factor of around thirty-three, to bring it in line with the contemporary value of money, it appears that Curzon had roughly £33,000 a year to spend. George Cornwallis-West described in his autobiography how it was possible to exist on this:

A bachelor in London with a thousand a year was comparatively well off. He could get a very good flat in Mayfair, to hold himself and his servant, for a hundred and fifty pounds per annum. Dinner at his club cost him about four shillings, and any good restaurant would have been prepared to provide an excellent dinner, if he chose to give one to his friends, at ten and sixpence a head. The best tailor in Savile Row would make a suit of evening clothes for eleven guineas, and a morning suit for about eight guineas; dress shirts could be bought for ten and sixpence.[7]

For an aristocratic young man of expensive tastes, accustomed to the best of everything, it would not have been regarded as excessive. Some of his friends, such as Balfour (who had inherited a fortune when he came of age), would have had ten times as much money at their disposal. Clearly, the best thing George Curzon could do was to find a rich wife. Meanwhile, a Tory colleague said of him: 'Long before leaving Oxford the name of George Curzon had become a household word in London society, and for ten or twelve years past he has been a welcome guest in the best literary, political and social circles.'[8]

If the Souls were beginning to attract attention by 1889, George Curzon himself had evidently been doing so for years. He cannot have been too disconcerted to read a paragraph in *The World* – a popular journal of social gossip and fashion – which drew its readers' attention to his dinner at the Bachelors' Club:

> Mr George Curzon was the most privileged host of last week, for on Wednesday he entertained that select circle best known as 'the Souls'. . . . This highest and most aristocratic cult comprises only the youngest, most beautiful and most exclusive of married women in London. Its high priest is Mr A. J. Balfour and its Egeria is Lady Granby. . . . Very few have been initiated into its mysteries. . . . Certain intellectual qualities are prominent among 'the Souls', and a limited acquaintance with Greek philosophy is a *sine qua non*.[9]

Envy and inaccuracy are the keynotes of this paragraph. The Souls were not by any means all young. Godfrey Webb, 'dear old Webber', always one of their central figures, was fifty-seven. Lady Pembroke was fifty and her husband – one of the handsomest men in Society – forty-nine. Lord Cowper, the uncle of Ettie Grenfell and the person who had brought her up after the early deaths of both her parents, was fifty-five. Nor were all the Souls aristocratic. Seventeen out of the forty people present at the dinner were titled: a high proportion, certainly, but not even a majority, let alone a unanimity, of titles. Nor was it true that all the women were married. One, at that first dinner, was still single. The fact that she could accept the invitation reflected Curzon's long and reputedly platonic friendship with the Tennant sisters, of whom Margot, the youngest, was the only one still without a husband. Evidently the presence of two married sisters was accepted as chaperonage enough. Another single woman, Miss Betty Ponsonby, daughter of Queen Victoria's private secretary, had also been invited but had declined. But the article was right in singling out intellectual qualities as worthy of comment. The Souls were already making their mark.

The Tennant brothers had been Eton contemporaries with Curzon, and through reading parties at their home in Scotland he came to meet their sisters. Later, all the girls had been half in love with the polished yet warm-hearted young undergraduate when he came to their Border home, Glen, for long vacations. In the unusually liberated atmosphere of the Tennant household, Curzon had flirted with more than one of them at once, and would send them all long, devoted letters from San Francisco or Constantinople or Teheran. Of all the sisters he loved Laura best – 'that brilliant child,' as he called her – while Charty, in spite of being married, was deeply in love with him. Their friendship earned a special mention in his verses that July night in 1889:

> Here a trio we meet,
> Whom you never will beat,
> Tho' wide you may wander and far go;
> From what wonderful art
> Of that gallant old Bart
> Sprang Charty and Lucy and Margot?
>
> To Lucy he gave
> The wiles that enslave,

> Heart and tongue of an angel to Charty;
> To Margot the wit
> And the wielding of it,
> That make her the joy of a party.

The Tennant family, and in particular the Tennant sisters, formed the nucleus of the Souls. Margot was never beautiful – though a stranger passing her in Rotten Row would have been struck by the wild, crinkly hair, intense gaze and upright carriage – but her wit, the quality in her that Curzon singled out, was as spontaneous and unpredictable as though she were totally unaware of society's rules for decorum. It flashed like lightning, often bizarre, occasionally brilliant, and apparently surprising her as much as it did her hearers. In later years she said of herself, 'Truth has never been a virtue, it has been a temptation.' It was a temptation she seldom resisted, and many people feared her accurate, sharp tongue. But she was, and remained all her life, a genuine social original.

Charty (or Charlotte), the oldest of the sisters, was also the most beautiful. Tall, slender, blonde, with the proud, vigorous step that characterized them all, she reigned within society as one of its most accomplished young hostesses. For all her love of Curzon, she was perfectly at ease in her rôle as wife to the sporting and patrician 4th Baron Ribblesdale. Lucy Graham Smith, another Tennant by birth, was the saddest member of the family. She had married impulsively at seventeen, and soon lived to regret it. She had no children, but occupied herself with hunting and watercolours: both pursuits that she excelled at. The miniatures which she painted of all her family and friends show that she would, a century later, have been capable of making a living by her brush. As it was, hers was a life of frustration. It may or may not have been helped by her hopeless and silent devotion to Harry Cust.

Cust was a notorious, and plainly irresistible, lover of women. He too was at Curzon's dinner, and must have sent a *frisson* round the table, since at least four of the ladies present had reason to avoid his eye in the company of their husbands. Harry Cust's pictures show a fair, chiselled face, good-looking certainly, but there must have been more than that to explain his extraordinary appeal. Curzon's verse about him said:

> Harry Cust could display
> Scalps as many, I lay,
> From Paris as in Piccadilly.

He was another who had been friendly with Curzon since their Eton days. His tutors then believed, not only that he could choose to be scholar, statesman, diplomat or poet, and adorn any rôle, but that, of all his contemporaries, he was most likely to be Prime Minister. In the event, Harry Cust chose to be Don Juan, with a singlemindedness that left him little time for anything else. He did, briefly, edit the *Pall Mall Gazette*; but he treated it – like everything else other than his philandering – as little more than a sideline. Yet he was a lively, iconoclastic journalist, and the magazine was widely read during his editorship.

George Wyndham, another young Soul, had a great deal in common with Cust; though in 1889 he was still resting on his laurels after marrying Sibell Grosvenor against competition from – it was said – no fewer than eighty-three rivals! She was immensely wealthy, thanks to the Grosvenor Estate; but her portraits also show a kittenish face with a sweet and gentle expression. Her eyes always looked faintly wistful – but perhaps that was due to short sight. At any rate there could be no clearer proof of young Wyndham's sexual attraction and charm than the fact that Sibell chose him to end her short widowhood, even though her father-in-law, the Duke of Westminster, strongly disapproved – perhaps because Wyndham was eight years her junior. Curzon had evidently forgiven his former rival; but although he invited the young couple to dinner, neither attended. Sibell was ill, or so she claimed; while George was contesting a by-election at Dover.

The table dazzled with young beauties nonetheless. The Elchos were there and the Horners were there and the Grenfells were there; and so were the Americans, Harry and Daisy White – a popular couple from the Legation. Possibly the most dazzling of all was Millicent, Lady Stafford, just twenty-two, whom the future Duke of Sutherland had married on her seventeenth birthday. In time she became one of the most celebrated beauties of the nineties, and one of the few women to be equally at home with the Marlborough House Set. Another lovely young future duchess, Lady Granby, was certainly one of those avoiding the eye of Harry Cust. Her husband Henry, later the Duke of Rutland, was probably thinking wistfully of after-theatre romps with the jolly actresses whom he found more congenial than the cerebral Souls. He must have winked gratefully at Curzon when he heard the tactful lines about his already faithless young wife:

> Is there one of the Gang
> Has not wept at the pang
> That he never can Violet's man be?

The Drummonds were there, and three Charteris brothers and two Lyttelton brothers – in short, seated around that dinner table one summer night over a century ago were most of the galaxy of distinguished people who still preferred to call themselves the Gang, though society – with its usual mixture of envy and sarcasm – had dubbed them the Souls. That dinner, though none of them realized it, was in effect their inaugural meeting. How had they formed themselves into this group?

The majority of the men were Etonians, and Curzon, Cust and Wyndham had all been at the school together. They were also linked – as were a number of other occasional Souls – by membership of an iconoclastic, irreverent bachelor set called the Crabbet Club. It was defined by its founder, Wilfrid Scawen Blunt, as 'a convivial association which had for its object to discourage serious views of life by holding up a constant standard of its amusements.'

The Crabbet Club met only once a year, on the first weekend in July, when its twenty or so members would gather at Blunt's Sussex home to play 'tennis, the fool, and other instruments of gaiety'.[10] On these occasions the composition of humorous verses was a prime object and they were expected to reach a higher standard than the doggerel in which Curzon had addressed his friends. Each annual Crabbet meeting culminated in a banquet, at which members would read out their poem on a prearranged theme, and elect a prizewinner, known for that year as the Crabbet Laureate. Among the few lines that have passed into posterity are those which Curzon wrote about himself in 1891 – the year he was placed second:

Charms and a man I sing, to wit – a most superior person,
Myself, who bears the fitting name of George Nathaniel Curzon,
From which 'tis clear that even when in swaddling bands I lay low,
There floated round my head a sort of apostolic halo.

Curzon was declared the winner in 1893 with a rollicking ode of sixteen verses on the chosen subject of Sin. It tries half-heartedly to shock, and ends up laughing at itself and the company:

In times so unromantic
And vulgarly pedantic
That history will style it a reproach to live therein,
We need some new Society
For the stamping out of piety
And the rehabilitation of uncompromising Sin!

. . .

The juvenile and tender,
Without regard to gender,
Shall be handed up to Godfrey's* indiscriminate embrace.
And Oscar[†] shall embellish
In a play that all will relish
The gradual and glorious declension of the race.

Self-assurance and good fellowship shine out of these facetious lines, but they do not reach any remarkable heights of wit. On the page they merely seem self-consciously boastful; aiming at decadence and ending in foolishness. But, like all conversational gifts, wit needs a live audience to develop its savour. Encouraged by laughter, capped by rhymes suggested by other members, honed by the fast riposte of men practised in verbal dexterity, the wit of the Crabbet Club, and of the Souls, is too evanescent to survive the passing of the only coterie it was ever intended to amuse.

Just occasionally, something remains to convey that tone of voice which kept society envious and scandalized by turns. *This* has the authentic touch of the Souls in those confident early days, mocking both themselves and the Victorian respectability they saw all around them. It is a parody that George Curzon wrote after dinner one evening at Stanway, the country home of the Elchos:

I sing of the attractions of the Belles,
London Belles,
Society Belles.
Of the manifold allurements of the Belles:
Oh, what rhapsodies their charm deserves;
How delicious and delirious are the curves
With which their figure swells –
Voluptuously and voluminously swells –
To what deeds the thought impels.
How their image in me dwells
And inspires the inmost cells
Of my agitated brain;
Till it whirls and whirls again

---

*Godfrey Webb ('Webber').   [†]Oscar Wilde.

> With the captivating vision of these Belles,
> > Country Belles,
> > Stanway Belles;
> With the vision of these most seductive Belles;
> > But most of all they capture,
> > And with fiery warmth enrapture,
> The vulnerable bosoms of the Swells,
> > London Swells,
> > Society Swells;
> The palpitating bosoms of the Swells,
> > Country Swells,
> > Stanway Swells;
> The wild and wanton bosoms of the Swells.

Deeply susceptible to one another's charms, within their magic circle the Souls interwove the ties of blood and marriage, threading in and out of relationships with the skill of dancers in some elaborate minuet. But their dance was also more than that; an intricate maypole dance, some amorous ritual whose measure they all knew. In the end, after thirty or forty years, there was nobody who was not linked by some strand, licit or illicit, erotic or platonic, with several other Souls. Wit may have brought them together, but love and affection kept them bound to one another.

Were they important? Did they influence society . . . did they change anything, even influence any changes? Did they deserve their extraordinarily privileged position at the apex of a social and economic pyramid which dominated not just the British Isles but the British Empire? For these were the halcyon days of the ruling classes, when a few hundred, or perhaps a few thousand, scions of the aristocracy and the gentry administered the greatest political and financial unit in the world in the name of an elderly white Queen. The masters of one quarter of the globe could probably all have been assembled for a single Buckingham Palace garden party, where they would have felt quite at ease recognizing and greeting one another, exchanging anecdotes about the 'native problem'. Yet for most people, those so-called halcyon days were not in reality prosperous, or secure, or leisured, let alone frivolous and carefree. In 1890 the population of the British Isles was 32 million, and of the British Empire around 400 million. The upper classes numbered ten thousand; the Souls, perhaps a bare hundred of those.

What would happen when the artificial conditions – the hothouse – in which the pampered Souls flowered and displayed themselves so gorgeously was exposed to the cold winds of a new social order, fanned by deep draughts of poverty and discontent? What would be their response when they were propelled into catastrophe by the apotheosis of all the ideals they had been taught to cherish, the First World War?

In 1889 the Souls took it for granted that they were the élite and deserved that pre-eminence. They could not foresee, and would not have believed in, a time when their power and privilege and wealth might be curtailed. They imagined that their sons, and their sons' sons, would live just as they did. They were not accustomed to questioning their delightful world. If they examined their consciences at all, it was in the light of Christianity rather than political ideology.

The lessons of the French Revolution were lost upon them; the imminence of the Russian Revolution inconceivable; the rise of socialism unregarded. Theirs was the world of lawns and drawing-rooms, boudoir and billiard table; the world of Art Nouveau and the Pre-Raphaelites and the new Liberty style . . . a world of the dragonfly and iris and peacock feather.

George Curzon played host on that evening of 10 July at the Bachelors' Club, but the one person whose character proved the magnet that drew the Souls together into hoops of friendship that lasted many of them a lifetime was a woman – a young, unmarried woman. In 1889 Margot Tennant was only twenty-five. With her prominent nose, angular chin and rapid step she was a dynamo of energy, moving, thinking and speaking with vigour and speed. Yet she was lovable too: a piquant social eccentric such as only occurs once or twice in any generation. With the backing of her father's vast wealth and her brothers' social connections from Eton and Oxford, she was able to fascinate and galvanize a brilliant circle. She changed the course of at any rate a tributary of society, turning it aside from the sluggish flow of the mainstream. Her salient characteristic was, as Desmond MacCarthy recalled, 'that dangerous, graceless, disconcerting, invigorating, merciless, shameless, lovable candour'. Such words were not often applied to young women from rich families. But Margot was not alone. She was further blessed in having been brought up among four almost equally remarkable sisters. Their arrival in London in 1881, scarcely noticed at the time, was to prove the catalyst that created the Souls.

- 2 -

Their Own Good Hearts

1881–1888

In 1881 Mr Charles Tennant bought himself a large house in the most fashionable part of London, and that purchase led to the dinner which George Curzon gave for his friends at the Bachelors' Club eight years later. The connection may seem obscure, and yet it was, more than anything else, the arrival in London of the Tennant family and, in particular, the Tennant sisters, which was the first step towards the eventual emergence of the Souls as a new and distinct group within society.

The house was at 35 Grosvenor Square (renumbered a few years later to become 40), a substantial Georgian house in the heart of Mayfair, then, as always, the most sought-after residential area in London. Charles Tennant's business interests – he was on the board of nearly thirty companies, fifteen of them as chairman – had made it necessary for him to leave his home in Scotland and pay frequent visits to London over the past few years. However, it was his election in 1879 as Liberal Member of Parliament for the Glasgow constituency of Partick that finally convinced him that he needed to buy a London house. The other factor that persuaded him to move was that his two youngest daughters, Laura and Margot, were ready to be launched into society.

The five Tennant sisters were no strangers to London. Charlotte (whom everyone called Charty) had met her husband at a ball in London in 1876, when she was eighteen. After the two of them had waltzed together for the first time, a friend asked young Thomas Lister if the tall, graceful girl who had partnered him so well was his sister: to which the twenty-one-year-old Thomas answered fervently, 'No, thank God!' Less than a year later, his father's death having meanwhile made Thomas the 4th Baron Ribblesdale, the pair were married. They were a rich and fashionable young couple, installed in Mayfair at 57 Green Street. Two other Tennant sisters were also married: Pauline (always called Posie) to Thomas Gordon Duff, whom she had met during the 1874 season; and Lucy, married to yet another Thomas. Hers was not a happy marriage, however: Thomas Graham Smith, who had seemed at first to be a hearty, horsey country squire, and had swept young Lucy straight from the schoolroom to the altar, turned out to be 'an odd fish'. They had no children, and Lucy spent much of her time back at home caring for her mother.

All the five Tennant daughters had their various talents, but the most remarkable and unusual were the two youngest: Laura, who was nineteen when the move to London took place, and Margot, who was seventeen. Neither was conventionally beautiful. Laura was tiny and fragile, with lips that curled in a curious and fascinating way, and slanting eyes like a kitten's; while Margot, though also small and slight, had too bony, strong-featured a face to suit the Victorian notion of feminine beauty. Yet their personalities were such that they not only conquered London society – they changed it.

Their father's immense fortune – by the 1880s he was a millionaire many times over – cannot have impeded their entry into the glittering aristocratic world, but it does not account for their impact upon its manners and *mores*. Barely five years after arriving in London the Tennants had become the nucleus of a new and spectacular galaxy which burst upon the dull and philistine drawing-rooms and country houses of their contemporaries. The old order, far from insisting on being amused, would have found the idea positively immoral. Evan Charteris wrote a filial account of his parents which cannot conceal the excruciating boredom of the home life of the 10th Earl of Wemyss and March:

> Their circle was limited and, more probably by chance than design, included no elements of disrepute. There was a sense of formality and observance at their dinners – people arrived with punctuality, and left about eleven – having conversed in contiguous groups after dinner with apparent decorum and liveliness; there were no cards or diversions; tea was spread out in the drawing-room at about ten-thirty on a table at which my mother presided, and after that the guests drifted away. . . . I think there was less laughter and certainly less freedom, whether of speech or suggestion – taboos were in the air – and restraint guided conversation into safe channels.[1]

In order to appreciate how the young Tennants revolutionized the social world, it is necessary to remember what it must have been like when they first encountered it. 'Limited' – 'no elements of disrepute' – 'sense of formality' – 'punctuality' – 'decorum' – 'taboos' – 'restraint' . . . these were the rules which governed behaviour in an aristocratic drawing-room in the third quarter of the nineteenth century. Into this sepia-tinted, static world there burst the glittering, multi-coloured personalities of Laura and Margot Tennant.

Charles Tennant was fifty-eight when he bought his imposing London house. Although he was a businessman of boldness, energy and prescience, who had been willing to invest in a number of Victorian inventions well before they were universally accepted, he was not a self-made man. His family had amassed its huge fortune over three generations spanning nearly a century. By 1881 his money, and the way he spent it on property and works of art and rare books, had made him one of the new, socially acceptable entrepreneurs who were invading the world of the landed aristocracy.

His father, John Tennant, had shown similar energy and skill in building upon the business foundation he had inherited. Like many a Victorian paterfamilias, he was both deeply kind and formidably severe. It comes as a surprise to learn that he never married the mother of his children; but this may not have bothered either of them, for common law wives (or what was called, in Scottish law, 'a marriage by habit and repute') were accepted in Scotland, and John Tennant was plainly no churchgoer. A close friend once bet him £100 that he could not recite the Lord's Prayer. John began confidently, 'The Lord's my shepherd, I'll not want . . .', whereat his friend stopped him, saying, 'You've won. I didn't think you knew it!'

In 1844 he sent his twenty-one-year-old son Charles away from the family home in Glasgow and set him up in London with £400 a year plus a capital sum of about £2,000 (worth well over £50,000 at today's value).* Shrewd and ambitious, young Charles lost no time in making another fortune of his own. He speculated daringly on the Stock Exchange, usually with outstanding success. By 1849 he was already a well-known, and well-off, young businessman, and 'a good catch' for the modest granddaughter of a country parson, Emma Winsloe, whom he married when he was twenty-six and she twenty-eight. Their daughter Margot, who was devoted to him and very like him in temperament, wrote a perceptive summary of his character: 'My father was a man whose vitality, irritability, energy and impressionability amounted to genius. . . . He had great character, minute observation, a fine memory, and all his instincts charged with almost superhuman vitality; but no-one could argue with him.'[2] Superhuman vitality he certainly had: he fathered sixteen children over a span of fifty-four years! ('Is Papa really Papa, or only a kind of visitor?' his twelfth child, Jack, once asked.)

Emma, his first wife and the mother of twelve of his children, was the direct opposite of her husband. Abandoned by her father, and brought up in France in dire poverty by her mother, she remained throughout her life reserved to the point of timidity; wary of expressing her thoughts and feelings; passive where he was active; absent-minded where he was a master of detail. She never stopped making small, wholly unnecessary domestic economies; yet she was endlessly considerate. When she heard that Lord Napier's coachman had never seen a comet, she wrote to him to inform him when the next sighting was due. She had no close friends, hated society and lived for her family. In answer to those who had claimed she was common and dull, her son Jack wrote: 'She was a most gentle, lovable and beautiful woman, and although she had nothing in her of governing capacity, she had sure sense and shrewdness, and her advice, which was given with such delicacy as to appear almost timorous, was generally full of reason and wisdom.'[3]

With such parents, the Tennant children had a good start in life. It was made better by the nature of the place in which they spent their formative years: a vast pseudo-Gothic mansion in Scotland called the Glen, or sometimes just Glen. In 1853, when he was just thirty, Charles Tennant had bought an estate of nearly 4,000 acres near Innerleithen, in Peeblesshire. He immediately set about demolishing the existing house, and had a new, much larger one built in the Scottish baronial style made fashionable by Balmoral (begun in the same year). It was crenellated, turreted and towered, a product of the Victorian passion for the medieval. Built in grey stone, it had twenty-nine bedrooms, landscaped gardens, and on all sides the wild, rolling hills and heather of the Scottish Borders. By 1858 the building work was finished and the family moved in; and it is hard to imagine a more perfect setting in which to bring up a large and high-spirited family.

*See Appendix I.

Their arrival, however, was not universally welcomed by their dour Scots neighbours. Who were these Glasgow *arrivistes*, with their romping brood, their unconventional manners and their misguided politics? (For Charles was known to be a Liberal, invading the heart of Conservative territory.) None of this bothered the Tennant children in the least: they never cared what other people thought. They grew up roaming the moors, learning to ride and fish and stalk and shoot. Life in the nursery was strenuous, too, especially since the Tennant girls appeared to have inherited their father's energy rather than their mother's gentleness. Little Jack, the youngest, once complained bitterly to his big sisters when they were teasing him, 'You are more like lions than sisters!' Yet the very fact that this little remark was recorded shows that they must have stopped, and laughed, and cheered him up. Margot wrote about her childhood: 'We raged and ragged till the small hours of the morning, which kept us thin and the household awake!'[4]

As the boys grew up they were all sent to Eton, but the girls were educated at home by a series of unfortunate governesses. Had it not been for their father's extensive library, their schooling would have been as inadequate as that of most Victorian young ladies. As it was, all five girls read widely and argued passionately about what they read . . . just how passionately is clear from this recollection of Margot's:

> Laura and I shared the night nursery together till she married. We read late in bed, sometimes till three in the morning, and said our prayers out loud to each other every evening. We were discussing imagination one night and were comparing Hawthorne, De Quincey, Poe and others, in consequence of a dispute arising out of one of our pencil games; and we argued till the housemaid came in with the hot water at eight in the morning.[5]

The girls were not only great readers; they were also taught to draw and paint and play musical instruments and act and recite and sing. It was usual for well-brought-up young Victorian girls to acquire the rudiments of some artistic accomplishment, with which they might catch the eye at a party, posed demurely at pianoforte or music stand. It was most unusual for them to be as gifted as the young Tennants apparently were. Laura played the piano wonderfully, Margot would accompany her on the violin, and the combination was said to be more than merely charming. Small wonder that Mary Gladstone wrote in October 1882, after her first visit to the Glen: 'I have had the strange, rather mad experience of the Tennant circle . . . it is the maddest, merriest whirl from morn till night – wonderful quickness, brightness, wit, cleverness.'[6] Another friend wrote with the same breathless delight:

> It was an adventure to go and stay at the Glen. Most of the usual conventions were neglected, and the ordinary barriers placed between young men and women pulled down; yet the atmosphere was pure and bracing. The fun was unflagging – brilliant talk, laughter and repartee, chaff, mimicry, discussion; a splendid outdoor life, too, with fishing and shooting, and games of all kinds, and long tramps over the hills.[7]

Thanks to the boundless hospitality of Charles Tennant and the uninhibited charm of his daughters, the Glen became a mecca for friends of all ages, from leading politicians to Eton schoolboys. The inner sanctum of the big house was the children's former nursery, next to the bedroom that Laura and Margot shared, which had been named 'the Doo'cot' (Dovecote) because there were so many quarrels there. Another friend described it after his first visit, in 1884:

> The Doo'cote was the girls' sitting room, furnished with many books and pictures, a good fire and windows looking on to the garden . . . green lawns and hills beyond. . . . Saw Miss Tennant's room, very pretty, hung round with old sporting prints – between the two beds a box for East London poor, then a small turret with a writing table and little shelves about in odd corners with books, altogether a unique apartment for the extraordinary mixture of sport, literature and vertu, like the wonderful little animals themselves. . . . After lunch tennis in the covered court: pretty to see the two little T. marmosets play.[8]

Their freedom from chaperonage (that Victorian imperative which bedevilled the lives of young women) was the result of their mother's blithe disregard of the convention and her habit of going to bed early. Margot and Laura continued to entertain friends of both sexes while they themselves sat up in bed: 'On these occasions the gas was turned low, a brilliant fire made up and either a guest or one of us would read by the light of a single candle, tell ghost stories or discuss current affairs: politics, people and books. . . . That these midnight meetings should shock anyone appeared fantastic; and as most people in the house agreed with me, they were continued.'[9]

Years of generous hospitality at Glen meant that, by the time their father bought his Grosvenor Square house, the Tennant girls already knew a number of people in London. But their entry into London society, that artificial, glittering spectacle, was gradual. Their provincial background, their own reputation for being original, indeed disquietingly so, and the fact that their father was not an aristocrat, hardly a landed gentleman, but very much an industrialist – all this meant that when Laura was presented at court in 1881, and Margot a year later, social acceptance came slowly.

In the last decades of the nineteenth century the aristocracy in London bloomed in a stiflingly artificial climate very unlike the fresh air and spontaneous ways of the Glen. But Margot and Laura were confident of their own gifts and content to be escorted by their elder brothers during their first one or two seasons. It is in any case hard to imagine them acquiescing to the careful nurturing that was thought essential if the bloom were not to be rubbed off an unmarried girl. If she spent even half an hour in the sole company of a young man she risked 'ruin'; her marriageability would be put in question, no matter how innocently the time had been passed. A far cry from the 'midnight meetings' in the Doo'cot!

It is paradoxical, then, that their entrée into society, when it did come, happened in the most conventional fashion. In May 1882, when she was eighteen, Margot caught the eye of the Prince of Wales . . . and he was charmed. Laura, too, was 'taken up' like her sister; but she, at twenty, was full of self-questioning about the social whirl that suddenly monopolized her time. In her diary for July 1882 she confessed, 'I've wasted quite five months of this year. I don't know if it is right to look at my London season philosophically as a time to be made up for afterwards or practically, as a time that should never exist. I felt Revolution and Rebellion would be out of place this year – but it is a waste.'[10]

Young as they were, Margot and Laura could hardly have set out deliberately to change the society they had newly entered. Yet this is exactly what happened. Lady Frances Balfour recalled, many years later, '. . . where it broke down was among the coming generation, who grew impatient of the many bonds and restrictions which admittedly bound them. The first movement of change undoubtedly came with a family highly gifted, of totally unconventional manners, with no code of behaviour, except their own good hearts, the young women of the Tennant family.'[11]

Society was not immediately set by its heels. That took a few more years. But meanwhile, largely through their brothers, Laura and Margot came to know some of the most attractive and promising young men of their time: men like George Curzon, later Viceroy of India; Arthur Balfour, later Prime Minister, and his somewhat eccentric brother Gerald, an earnest enquirer into life after death. There was 'Doll' Liddell, secretary to the Lord Chancellor; and – momentously for one of the sisters – there was Alfred Lyttelton. None of them could resist the piquant charm of 'the little T. marmosets'. All of them were founding members, in due course, of the Souls.

Gradually, imperceptibly, the special group was being created, drawn by the charm of the Tennant sisters. To begin with they were based on school and undergraduate friendships, cemented by long vacation reading parties and healthy walking tours. Later they were strengthened by more than friendship, and eventually they formed the permanent bonds of romantic as well as platonic love. Margot describes their early days with affection and pride:

> Nearly all the young men in my circle were clever and became famous; and the women, although not more intelligent, were less worldly than their fashionable contemporaries, and many of them were both good to be with and distinguished to look at. . . . The loyalty, devotion and fidelity which we showed to one another and the pleasure we derived from [these] friendships could not have survived a week had they been accompanied by gossip, mocking, or any personal pettiness.[12]

One must beware of taking the Souls at their own estimate. Modesty was never one of their virtues; and they were fond of casting reflected glory upon themselves by the extravagant compliments which they paid to each other. Certainly they were – by the standards of the vast majority of people of their time – spoilt, self-indulgent, frivolous and pleasure-loving. Certainly they were obsessed by the minutiae of their own tangled emotions. Certainly their 'East End poor boxes' and Sunday school classes were woefully inadequate as a means of adjusting the balance between their own great wealth and the poverty that existed all around them. It is tempting – a century later, in an age which makes their pampered, cosseted lives seem vapid and irresponsible – to assume that everything came easily to them. But many others who enjoyed the same privileges remained boring and boorish.

Gaiety, like honesty, is a kind of social courage. It is not easy to be unfailingly charming, lively and original. It requires energy and generosity always to make the effort to be on one's best form. It is usually those who are themselves dull and humourless who condemn light-hearted behaviour. But the Tennants and their circle believed that charm and wit – though only the first of their talents – *were* important, and that they provided the showcase in which to display their intellectual, social and amorous skills.

The Tennants possessed all these gifts in abundance. Mary Gladstone summed them up: 'There was hardly a gift of God that was not possessed by one or other of them.'[13] Laura, as tiny and mercurial as a child, possessed an extraordinary character that left its mark upon everyone she ever met. She combined charm and spirituality in a manner rare enough in anyone, and exceptional in a girl scarcely out of her teens.

Charm, that most elusive and fleeting quality, is hard to pin down on paper a hundred years later. Laura seems to have had in full measure both its passive and its active elements: passively, a tender and exclusive concentration upon whomever she was with at that moment; actively, a fresh and constantly changing originality, composed of humour, insight and the capacity to surprise – even to shock. Underlying this was a keen sympathy for others; a sharp intelligence; and a religious sense that combined devout Christianity and a passionate love of nature. Many Victorian girls, over-protected and under-educated, must have been tedious company. Laura was never boring.

Many who knew her thought that, in Laura, the Tennant talents were crystallized into genius: a genius, above all, for the ephemeral art of living. But her constitution was not strong enough to sustain the demands that she and others made upon it, and she knew it. From an early age she had always believed she would die young: 'I shan't live a long life. I shall wear out quick. I live too fast,' she once said. In November 1879, just after her seventeenth birthday, she wrote that she had 'a sort of serene longing – a longing for Death – the key to this riddle of life – the interpreter of all there is to interpret and God knows how much there is. . . . In 5 years I will be out of this sad girlhood – perhaps out of this sad world. God help me.'[14] Yet this strain of adolescent melancholy was not typical. Laura was not in the least morbid, but she was profound and complex. Few of those who were dazzled by her cared to delve below the surface gaiety. Those who did were amazed to find an almost mystical strain. And those who responded to this, the deepest part of her nature, were always the people whom Laura loved best.

In September 1883 Laura was invited to join a private cruise to Copenhagen aboard the yacht *Pembroke Castle*. Also in the party were W. E. Gladstone (Mary's father) and the Poet Laureate, Lord Tennyson. Both were so enchanted by her that when, halfway through, Laura had decided to leave the ship, Tennyson told her, 'Nonsense, little witch, you must not go, you are the life of the party – Gladstone and I will sign a round robin to prevent you going.'[15] Laura herself attempted to describe her own appearance and character at the Glen, on Christmas Day, 1883. She was just twenty-one.

And me – what am I?
A little woman with grey eyes with corners to them – & *cendre* [ash-coloured] hair & a mouth Charles Hallé told me was very passionate, & a nose with a lump in the middle, & a square jaw and a nameless complexion with small ears almost round & an ordinary neat figure & next to no legs. Is there anything in the outside? Well come in, what is there here?

A quick heart that beats for the children. A longing to understand – a great overwhelming ignorance – a sympathy for all that's bad except cowardice & ungenerosity – a love of sky & hill & flowers – & a friendship with the shadows that sleep on the moors – with the birds & beasts – & the stars – an impatient irritable temper – a wavering erratic Faith & a passionate love for Symbol & the unseen & a fearful humble but Jesus faithful love of Thee – & an aethereal love for Francie† – What is there then? Charlie Lascelles told me I was the wickedest and the best woman he knew. I am neither.

That diary entry, with its touching blend of humility, realism and mysticism, conveys like an antique scent bottle just a breath of the essence of Laura's captivating personality. That word 'wickedest' is important, too. Laura – as her sister Margot used to say – was no plaster saint. Her wit was bold enough to shock many people; her love of flirting came near to being callous; and she could be waspish when the occasion warranted. When Sir Charles Dilke, the Liberal politician, was visiting her father at the Glen he was evidently bowled over by Laura. He waylaid her in a corridor late one night and said, 'If you will kiss me, I will give you a signed photograph of myself.'

'It's awfully good of you, Sir Charles,' Laura replied, 'but I would rather not, for what on earth should I do with the photograph?'

Margot and Laura's social success in London, when it came after a slow start, was spectacular. The small, slender Tennant girls sparkled like the newly introduced electric light among the duller crowd of their contemporaries. Lady Frances Balfour wrote in her memoirs, 'It was unnatural if every man did not propose to them after a few hours' acquaintance,'[16] and Margot adds, 'On several occasions the same man proposed to both of us, and we had to find out from each other what our intentions were. . . . But she felt sad when she refused the men who proposed to her; I pitied no man who loved me. I told Laura that both her lovers and mine had a very good chance of getting over it, as they invariably declared themselves too soon. We were neither of us *au fond* very susceptible.'[17]

Yet Laura, perhaps unconsciously, was ready to fall in love. Much as she needed – and revelled in – the homage of others, she also needed to return it. At the end of 1883 she had recorded in her diary, written on the last day of the old year, 'I had a crisis in my heart yesterday, a great crisis – which has caused me fewer tremblings and doubts than I expected. I have made up my mind that if in 1884 I meet no one I fall in love with I shall marry Tom‡. . . . He loves me madly, calmly, with all his being – and if I married him I could help him and be happy.'[18]

The following year was to put all thoughts of so bloodless a marriage out of her mind. In 1884 three of the most powerfully attractive men she had met, and all remarkable in their way, fell passionately in love with her. The first was Gerald Balfour, brother of the politician Arthur: just as handsome and philosophical as his brother, with a quirky, even eccentric side to his nature that appealed to Laura's love of the unconventional. The second was 'Doll' Liddell. And the third was Alfred Lyttelton.

She must have come across Doll Liddell the previous year, for in his diary he

---

†Frances Horner, formerly Frances Graham, Laura's best friend.
‡Tom Carmichael, a neighbour in Peeblesshire who had loved her devotedly since she was 18 years old and of whom she was platonically fond.

mentions having sat next to her at dinner at 40 Grosvenor Square and been entertained with stories of her trip with Gladstone and Tennyson on the *Pembroke Castle*. The next reference is in May 1884: 'Drew Miss Tennant in the morning, watercolour. Something Leonardesque about some of her lines.' (He must have meant the pouting curve of her small mouth.) Doll, sixteen years older than Laura, was a close friend of Frances Horner, Laura's dearest and most admired woman friend. He was regarded as exceptionally handsome, in the somewhat wistful, aesthetic manner that appealed to late Victorian sensibility: tall, slight, blond, with a look of the 'pale Galilean' of contemporary Bible illustration. He and Laura shared an almost pantheistic love of Nature.

At much the same time, in the summer of 1884, Laura was placed beside Alfred Lyttelton at a dinner party given by Mrs Herbert Jekyll, the older sister of her great friend Frances. Alfred made an immediate impression upon her. In appearance and bearing he was more manly than Doll, and was indeed the greatest all-round amateur athlete of his time; but far from being a hearty sporting type, he was serious and intelligent (nobody who lacked a mind could have appealed to the highly intellectual Laura for very long) and in addition possessed a sharp humour that delighted her.

For several weeks it was 'Doll' Liddell who was regarded as the main suitor. His profound nature appealed to the mystical side of Laura as other, more frivolous young men had not; and the fact that he was sixteen years older gave him a certain advantage in understanding the whims of a girl not yet emotionally mature, let alone sexually, and bewildered by her own responses. In August 1884 Doll was invited to stay at the Glen for the first time. That fortnight's visit was a revelation to them both. Laura's ecstatic diary entry for her twenty-second birthday makes it clear that Doll made the most of the unusual freedom that the Glen offered:

> I have regretted many things I have been unhappy but *never* so happy. I had one fortnight this August that will never never come again one dazzling fortnight. I was deliriously happy, savagely ruthlessly happy & it cannot ever be like that again. Frances was there & a new friend that has stepped into my life & has lifted me often to the hilltops of ecstasy – a man who probably understands me better than anyone I ever met & whom I feel is my own personal property in an alarming way. His name is Liddell . . . he is beautiful.[20]

By the end of that visit Doll was in love, and he believed that Laura was too. They had developed – as only the most trusting lovers do – a private language of baby talk; they had special nicknames – he called her 'Bambina' or 'Bina', she called him Larry. They had made plans for seeing one another often during the coming months; the only obstacle to be overcome was Laura's deep reluctance to commit herself to any thoughts of marriage. Nevertheless, Doll wrote rapturously, 'We sat on a trunk under the hedge in the twilight, while the wind surged above us and the red gold deepened in the sky and the black drew upon it until at last it went out, or nearly so, leaving an ochre flame in one place above the hill. I looked into the strange grey eyes and saw the oval face close to mine with its knot of twisted hair on *the* day of my life.'[21]

Laura knew she was often capricious, but this was not the usual flirting. For the first time she had discovered in herself a physical need that frightened her.

Both she and Margot had always been less inhibited than most Victorian maidens, for whom a handclasp spoke volumes. Their passionate natures and impatience with the rules that governed acceptable behaviour had always meant they took upon themselves a freedom that would have scandalized their contemporaries. This does not mean that either would have contemplated losing her virginity before marriage – besides which, few honourable young men would have risked taking it. Social strictures held good that far, even without the likelihood of pregnancy. But marriage, as she confided in her diary, frightened Laura, as much for its mundane aspects as because she was afraid of the sexual commitment:

> I suppose I am in love – I should like to remain as I am then – I don't want to marry – that's the awful part. It's what men want to do when they love you & women only want to be still & rest if they love. Marriage is changing & fussing & wearing rings. Being as we are we can ascend the hill top of ecstasy together – & wander through the fields of life – & lie on the gold bars at sunset & sleep in each others' arms at dawn.
>   Marriage means descending into the cellar of life & sitting at its breakfast table – standing behind its counter. . . . [22]

One month later, in a charming vignette of domesticity, she wrote: 'In Larry's [i.e. Doll's] rooms – I toasted bread & he boiled eggs – It was all that eggs & intimacy can give you.'[23] A week later, visiting her beloved friend Frances Horner at Mells Park, Laura was writing revealingly in her diary:

> Her child interests me now – she has eyes like the morning & beautiful deep thoughts in her frown. She is outrageously clever & hurrahs for Gladstone & covers her face with her hands for Lord Salisbury & roars derisively at Randolph Churchill. . . . Frances is like a Botticellian madonna with her & inspires in me an enormous desire to have a baby! She is the one woman who hallows domesticity & when she powders her baby's stomach she glorifies an otherwise mindless action.[24]

Yet this apparent softening towards marriage had not come about because of Doll, but because of the rival he didn't even suspect: Alfred Lyttelton. Throughout her eventful autumn of 1884, Laura encountered the two men frequently, both out and about in society and alone at home. During October, although Alfred visited her often in London, she was still sufficiently in awe of his prowess and good looks to have persuaded Margot to issue the invitation to spend a few days at the Glen. Margot, being more than half in love with the dashing Alfred herself, gladly did so. Alfred, five years older than Laura, wrote to his cousin Mary Gladstone bemoaning the fact that his 'leathery heart' seemed to make it impossible for him ever to fall in love: 'More than ever I look for it in a sort of sanguine way to open out new hopes and new possibilities; but it comes in a slow, halting sort of fashion to *"nous autres* Lytteltons", and I seem as impenetrable as the rest of them. But shall I write like this after a week at The Glen?'[25] Both Laura and Alfred seem to have had a premonition that the visit was to be crucial.

Laura may have been flirtatious, but she was not heartless; and her inability to make up her mind about Doll and Alfred had brought her temperament, always highly strung, close to breaking point. Margot recalls, 'She had become profoundly undecided over her own love-affairs; they had worked so much upon her nerves that when Mr Lyttelton came to Glen she was in bed with acute neuralgia and unable to see him.'[26] So Laura spent most of that momentous weekend ill in bed. By Monday she was up and about, and Alfred was persuaded to extend his stay until Wednesday. Laura wrote:

I saw next to nothing of Alfred that visit owing to being ill, but I remember the last day . . . we went for a walk up the Deans. It was the first time I had been out for several days and I was very weak. It was a calm autumn day. The red cliffs were intense in colour & the bracken was wet and high. I was very weak and had to rest on a knoll of heather. I took off my veil and put it in his pocket. He told me in a letter 2 months later – how he had found it one day in the law courts – a reminder of that autumn afternoon. . . . When I got home I was almost dead & he took my hand and said it was feverish & he ordered me with his irresistible strength & calm to lie down. I took off my things & put on my old red tea gown & came here into the Doocot – there he arranged all the cushions on the floor & I lay down like a little tired child. . . . He sat by my side & read. . . . He did not speak – once or twice he touched my hand & sometimes he looked at me. . . . I said goodnight to him here. How well I remember it. He kissed me & I felt so strange & surprised. . . . The moment he had shut the door I burst into tears & threw myself upon the sofa.[27]

The visit was decisive: for Laura at least. After it was over she told Margot that she had made up her mind to marry Alfred Lyttelton. Who was the man who, after an acquaintance of just a few weeks, succeeded where so many others had failed?

Like Laura herself, he came from a large, happy and unconventional family: happy despite the fact that his mother had died six months after his birth (he was the twelfth child). All of them survived into adulthood, and the household at Hagley Hall was, in its way, quite as lively, as energetic, as talented, and perhaps even more eccentric than the home life of the Tennants. Lord Chandos, Alfred's son, recalled his father's stories of their behaviour after dinner: 'As soon as the ladies had left the dining-room, my grandfather [the 3rd Baron Lyttelton] used to take the soft, uneaten part of his roll, knead it into a ball and throw it at his youngest son as hard as he could, whereupon all eight sons rose up and bombarded him with similar missiles. Port and claret were then circulated.'[28]

After the death of their mother, her rôle in the household was taken over by Lavinia, the oldest girl, despite the fact that she herself was then only fifteen. Her burden was shared by their grandmother, Sarah, the Dowager Lady Lyttelton, who had for years run Queen Victoria's nursery; and by their 'Aunt Pussy', Gladstone's wife Mary – both of whom all the children adored. Lavinia wrote in her reminiscences:

I wonder if I could at all convey what those Hagley times were like when we were all so thick on the ground . . . the 8 brothers and the singing and the fun and the endless jokes – the deafening talk at the meals, with Uncle Billy so often there, undergoing the chaff from the Etonians over his Winchester school . . . it is all unforgettable, the noise and merriment suddenly ending perhaps in a return to books or to a lot of part singing, and to Spencer's beautiful voice singing song after song to Albert's, and often May's accompaniments. And Granny in her chair opposite Papa amused and happy if a bit deafened.[29]

Of all the children, Alfred must have been the one to miss his mother least – he had never known any régime but that as the youngest, in a family of four doting sisters and seven boisterous brothers. When their father eventually re-married, his second wife is said to have remarked to the oldest son, 'Charles! This house will some day be yours, but there will be little of it if the boys are allowed to continue playing cricket in the Long Gallery.' All the eight brothers played cricket for Eton, but Alfred was outstandingly good at it, as he was at all games. His son wrote accurately and with justifiable pride, '. . . he was one of the most richly endowed men of his time. No one before or perhaps since has ever excelled at games as he did. At cricket he was the first choice for England after W. G. Grace; he was Keeper of the Field and Fives at Eton; he was the real tennis champion for many years. . . . Unlike some athletes, he did not lack intellectual powers.'[30]

In a letter to Mary Gladstone Laura wrote a detailed description of Alfred:

He has an infinite brightness in his very presence, and a womanlike sympathy which is very unusual in men and women. I think he is a child of Nature . . . has still the same big generous impulses – the same laughter that makes the little hills hop – and the same splendid animal spirits, though a little softened and subdued by the knowledge and the feeling of the infinite pathos of life – the same capability of enjoyment which with him is genius – the same quick affection and quick dislike – as for his faults – you know him better than I do – I suppose he has some.[31]

Alfred, as an ardent Liberal, was more than acceptable to her father; there would be no family opposition to the marriage. Yet two problems still obsessed her. Did Alfred feel as she did? And if so, how could she avoid hurting Doll Liddell?

The answer to the first soon became obvious. The second Laura handled in a fashion that may appear heartless. She said nothing to Doll, allowing him to go on believing that *he* was first in her affections. He probably knew that Laura and Alfred were present at the same weekend house party at Stanway on 22 November, as guests of the Elchos; but already the circle in which the Tennant sisters moved was fairly close-knit and there was nothing significant about encountering the same man – among several others – twice in a week. And so, for some three months after Alfred had come into Laura's life, Doll went on thinking that he had most to fear from Gerald Balfour – or maybe Arthur: he was not even sure which brother was his rival.

Laura's diary shows that she longed to sustain the easy, loving relationship of 'Larry' and 'Bina'; yet she knew that Alfred could be a husband to her in a way that, somehow, Doll could not.

Then I went to Mells & Larry was there. He was still recent in my heart – & no-one even now can take his place. I love him. I have always loved him. I shall love him till I die – unless my heart changes as much as a sky: but I love him differently – I love him as a bit of myself. . . . He is more than a brother to me. He is Larry & I am his little Bina & always always & not Alfred nor another can drive him from my soul. . . . I never could understand why I could not marry

Larry. But I tried to & could not. Something makes us one & something prevents me from tangible one-ness.[32]

Doll's diary, too, records the emotional turmoil of that weekend, the last occasion upon which they were to be close: 'Felt somehow that she would be there, and sure enough I saw her small figure – pretended not to see it and went out to the brougham: delicious drive, the dear little arms once more round my neck.'[33] Yet just a few days later he was writing disconsolately: 'She won't marry me – says I am too near herself: odd things females: that she should like all this caressing and not be able to go beyond.'[34]

The crisis came – as emotional crises so often do – over Christmas and the New Year, 1884–5. ('How curious,' wrote Laura in her diary, 'that last Christmas I knew neither Larry nor Gerald Balfour nor Alfred – & now all three are deep in my life. . . .')[35] For Christmas itself the family were alone at the Glen: just the eight children, their parents, the three sons-in-law, four small children, and a couple of dozen house servants. But on 31 December, both Alfred and Doll arrived for the New Year's house party: and, as Laura must have foreseen, the next few days were dramatic and decisive. Doll had realized by now that Alfred was his real rival; but Alfred outshone him in a way that he – eleven years older – could not match. 'New Year's Day,' writes Laura, 'we played lawn tennis in the morning. Alfred shines everywhere but at any game he positively dazzles one. How I love to watch his great strong figure clad in flannels & his mighty stroke that is meteorlike in its flight. He has perfect ease & perfect grace & is delightful to play with because of his fine generous temper.'[36] That evening she and Alfred had a private talk in the Boudoir. 'He was so unhappy poor darling that I had ever thought it wrong of him to kiss me that I could have eaten up my words again but I didn't I only kissed him & then I knew I loved him & he loved me. Ah! me.'[37]

Next day, Laura and Doll went for one of the long, solitary walks through the beautiful Border scenery around the Glen that had never failed to work its magic in the past. But this time their mood was very different. Doll wrote in his diary for 2 January 1885: 'Going back she said she had kissed AL. I was torn with jealousy and folly – we both made ourselves very wretched and kissed and almost cried.'[38] This is an edited version of what actually happened. Laura's diary shows that, at the last moment, Doll resorted to something very like emotional blackmail:

He asked if I would marry Alfred if he proposed & I said I thought I would & Larry said, 'It would be a mistake you don't love him enough' & I was angry. . . . Well then he said 'I shall never come back here again' & I found myself choking. . . . He could not understand me & I sobbed & could not understand myself – only I knew I loved Alfred & was quite miserable.[39]

The next day Doll had to return to London. Laura took him to the station. There they sat in the waiting-room, 'she occasionally smiling with tears hardly restrained. . . . One long last kiss. For five minutes I sobbed – very nearly missed the train.'[40] (That last Pooterish comment goes a long way to explain why Laura preferred Alfred.)

The house party had all but dispersed. Only Alfred remained: and he too had to return to his law practice in London by the overnight train. In view of Laura's distressed state, he must have wondered if this was the right moment to speak.

He left it almost too late. All day he said nothing. Her diary, however, tells what finally happened:

> Then I went to dress. I shall always remember what I had on. It was a white muslin gown, nothing round my neck and a shot ribbon round my waist. I heard Alfred playing divinely (*ce que je suis sans toi*) whilst I was dressing & I came in here (i.e. the Doo'cot) 10 minutes before the gong sounded. When I described it all to Lucy I told her Alfred proposed to the accompaniment of the gong. It's not strictly true but very nearly. He said a great deal but it's all like a dream & I remember nothing except the sense of wonderful strength & safe keeping I had & the perfect confidence & undoubting with which I let him take me into his arms – the sweet sense of rest at last – at last. It was very short for I had to send him down to dinner & I just stayed here long enough to thank God on my knees & to tidy my hair – ruffled by his kisses. Margot & I had what she called a pagan rite in bed that night. I told her all about Alfred & we laughed & cried & talked till 3 – when I got into my own springy little couch & worn out by tears & yet with a new joy in my heart I sunk to sleep. So ended the best & worst day of my life January 3 1885.[41]

The culmination of Laura Tennant's love story was to be the starting point of the Souls.

At the end of January, 1885, their engagement was formally announced. Laura went away for the month of March, south, to the sun, to Bordighera in Italy, there to build up her frail strength in readiness for the pressures that would inevitably surround the wedding of two of the most popular young people in society. At the beginning of April she was in Paris, being fitted by Worth for a wedding dress and for her trousseau. She told Alfred about it. 'It is rather a break to hear them all say, *"Ah, Madame, il doit vous aimer beaucoup: votre fiancé! Quel petit dos, mon Dieu, ça n'existe presque pas!"* and for once I feel I love a dressmaker! And I tell them how they ought to envy me, and thrill them with stories of your strength and goodness!'[42] Alfred's letter in reply said, 'Don't get matronly gowns, my pretty babe – but girlish ones – plain colours – white generally – unless you are bored with everyone falling in love; no one can help it, you know, when you have white and pale blue.'[43]

On 21 May 1885 they were married in St George's, Hanover Square, and Gladstone proposed the toast to the bride and groom. Wilfrid Scawen Blunt – who was one of the very many who had admired Laura from a distance – wrote in his diary:

> Gloomy morning – Wedding at St George's – Laura v. pale but spoke part in voice so distinct that clearly heard by us . . . a very pretty, emotional voice that thrilled one like that of a great actress in a great tragic part, moved but self-possessed. As she passed by without seeing me she suddenly turned back, and gave me her hand with a little complex smile. Gladstone made a speech afterwards full of the finest moral sentiments about the virtues of the wedded state to last through age into death.[44]

Their life together promised the utmost happiness. Within a few months, Laura was overjoyed to find herself pregnant. She longed for a child. With that expectation, the task of preparing to move into their first home at 4 Upper Brook Street, and the social whirl that, as ever, surrounded her with friends and invitations, parties and country house weekends, it was an idyllic year. Margot, although she tried to occupy herself with riding and hunting, missed her sister painfully. The two had shared bedroom, secrets, parties, suitors for twenty-one years.

At the beginning of April, just a few days before the baby was due, Margot went to call on her sister before leaving to spend some time hunting at her sister Lucy's house in the country. This was not callous; the family believed that Margot would need some distraction from the thought of Laura's suffering in childbirth. 'I found her alone,' Margot writes, 'sitting in Alfred's room on the ground floor in her tea gown. I was sad at the idea of leaving, and sat on the sofa beside her. She put her arms round my neck. . . . "I am sure I shall die with my baby," she said.'[45]

On the night of 16 April 1886 her child was born, after a tremendous struggle, unrelieved by chloroform or painkillers. It was a boy. The effort had exhausted her; she had no reserves of strength to draw upon. She moved gradually from weakness into coma. Relatives and friends came to the house, stunned by the news. Margot dashed back from her hunting. For days the house was filled with people, silently waiting, hoping for news. Laura rallied briefly; then became semi-conscious. Margot was allowed to see her:

> I felt a rushing of my soul and an over-eagerness that half-stopped me as I opened the door and stood at the foot of the wooden bed and gazed at what was left of Laura.
>
> Her face had shrunk to the size of a child's; her lashes lay like a black wall on the whitest of cheeks; her hair was hanging dragged up from her square brow in heavy folds upon the pillow. Her mouth was tightly shut and a dark blood-stain marked her chin. After a long silence she moved and muttered and opened her eyes. She fixed them on me, and my heart stopped. I stretched out my hands towards her, and said, 'Laura!'. . . . But the sound died; she did not know me.
>
> I knew after that she could not live.[46]

Six days after the birth of her son, Laura Lyttelton said, 'I think God has forgotten me' before she died. She was not yet twenty-four years old.

A very great many people were deeply affected by Laura's death, and for the rest of their lives they never forgot her. First and foremost were her family. Margot was inconsolable for months – years, even. She tried to distract herself by becoming absorbed in the conditions of women who worked in a factory in the East End of London. She visited them several days a week – without ever telling them who she was or why she came – got to know them well, and took them on an annual 'treat' until her own marriage, eight years later.

Others who had only encountered Laura a few times still felt her death as a terrible loss. The painter Edward Burne-Jones, who had met her in the home of their mutual friend, Laura's beloved Frances Horner, wrote to Mary Gladstone: 'We shall all feel it, all of us, to the end of our days: it will be a never healing wound. What a brief delight it was. I am as unhappy as an outsider can well be.'[47] Later he used Laura's poignant face again and again in his paintings, and he designed the memorial tablet to her that is still in Mells parish church, close to the Horners' country home.

Laura was buried at Traquair, near to the Glen and the hills she had so loved.

The immediate effect of Laura's death was to plunge her family and friends into deep mourning. This meant wearing unrelieved black for at least six months; withdrawing from society and the London season for the summer of 1886; and visiting only privately, in one another's homes. It cannot have been an unnatural restriction for a group whose grief was deep and genuine. The sense of shock caused by the suddenness of her death, so pitifully young, was widely felt. As Mary Gladstone wrote in her diary: 'It is impossible to exaggerate the tragedy and pathos of this event: I should imagine that not the death of any single person in the whole world could so deeply cut into the hearts and lives of so many people.'[48] Of all those who missed her, Alfred suffered most. Charty Ribblesdale, Laura's elder sister, moved into his house at 4 Upper Brook Street with her husband, to look after the baby and to try and nurse Alfred through the first, most frantic months of grief. 'You can't think how the sun ceases to shine in my life when I am away from you,' he had written to Laura only a year before. In due course he began to find some comfort in the sweet ways of their little son, Alfred Christopher; but that, too, was brutally ended when the child died of meningitis in May 1888, aged just two.

Those who mourned Laura drew more closely together, sharing their memories of her mercurial personality, her generosity and her profundity. Those who had loved her best – George Curzon, the two Balfour brothers, Frances Horner, and of course her sisters – spent much time together, and even when the first period of formal mourning was over, they found they preferred one another's company, and were not anxious to encounter others. It was during this muted period that the Tennants and their circle began to cohere into the group that gradually became identified as 'The Souls' – although from the first it was a name they disliked, choosing to be known among themselves simply as 'The Gang'. The story of how the name first came into being was told in *The Times* many years later, in the letter from Ettie Desborough that was published on 21 January 1929:

> They were nicknamed the Souls by Lord Charles Beresford, amid laughter, at a dinner party at Lord & Lady Brownlow's house in the early summer of 1888. 'You all sit and talk about each other's souls – I shall call you The Souls!' It was a moderate joke enough, but it persisted – on ever-declining levels of wit – for many years, and out of it there gradually grew, I think, an erroneous and rather heavy and pretentious impression of the little group concerned; and they were both attacked and defended by those who did not know very much about them.

It seems unlikely that a single, unfunny remark could really have fixed the name so firmly in place; and an entry in Wilfrid Scawen Blunt's diary suggests an alternative possible source:

> I made great friends with old Lady Tennant, a quiet little old lady, very well dressed, active and alert, whom I found exceedingly pleasant and conversable, with a heart overflowing with kindness. She showed me a book about Souls, which gives diagrams of the various kinds of souls, the surface soul, the

deep soul, and the mixed soul, half-clever, half-childish (the book had
something to do, I think, with the name given to the set of which her
daughters were such notable members).[49]

The fact that the Tennant sisters formed the original nucleus of the Souls lends
credence to the theory that they may have been responsible for its name as well.
George Curzon also claimed to have invented it. Evidently he had once pointed
out that, in order to become one of the coterie, it was necessary to possess a soul
above the ordinary: and there, he said, the name had originated. Be that as it
may, there is an irony in the fact that the most extraordinary soul of all belonged
undoubtedly to Laura, who died before the Souls came into being.

    The rest of society disliked and distrusted the Souls. They were too clever, or
too conceited, or too exclusive. People were envious because the group was hard
to enter, and so they mocked, because their reaction to being excluded was to
pretend it was not worth belonging. Lady Frances Balfour summed up the early
impact of the Souls:

> We were, in this period, on the brink of Society enlarging its borders, and
> entertaining new personalities and new ideas. Something of the effect of the
> Restoration on Puritan England, though that is only a rough analogy. In every
> movement, social, political or religious, it is not the mass that moves, it is
> always led by some individuals. It may be a small change . . . or it may be a
> profound change in the world's attitude towards a class, or a state of social
> existence.[50]

Lady Frances does not specify which change she has in mind; but undoubtedly
she believed, as did many Souls at the time, that they were changing the future
course of society. They believed that they were moving it away from philistinism
towards patronage of the arts; away from political divisions that meant
neighbours barely spoke to one another, towards a greater tolerance on political
matters; away from the belief that women were childish, pampered chattels,
towards treating them as people with tastes and opinions worth cultivating.
Above all, they believed that they were restoring to the English upper classes an
art they had almost lost, the art of intelligent conversation. These were large
ambitions, and, if fulfilled, would have profound implications for society.

    The Tennant family – long regarded as dangerously unconventional – had
always held such views. It was above all the achievement of the Tennant *sisters*
that they made the ideas and attitudes of the Glen seem natural and desirable to a
circle of people far beyond their own family. And it was the tragic accident of
Laura's death at the age of twenty-four which crystallized that circle into the
Souls.

– 3 –

The Marlborough House Set

1871–1891

The group which society called the Souls was stamped with the personality and tastes of the *women* who brought it into being. The Marlborough House Set was, just as distinctively, a group that revolved around *men*: and one man in particular, the Prince of Wales. 'Bertie' to his family, 'Tum-Tum' to his friends (though not to his face), 'Teddy' to the public, he had dominated society ever since his marriage in 1863. Beside him, his beautiful, unintelligent, rather deaf wife, Alexandra, was a cipher. Her clothes were widely copied – the wide, jewelled chokers that she wore to hide the scar at her throat, and the lavishly trimmed pale-coloured dresses that set off her slender figure so well – but her personality and preferences were irrelevant to the courtiers who clustered around the portly figure of her husband.

Indeed, having remarked – as everyone did – upon the sweetness and grace of the Princess of Wales, her kindness and thoughtfulness and unpunctuality, there was little else to say. That she tyrannized her daughters and mollycoddled her sons must have been obvious; that she refused the sexual advances of her husband after less than a decade of marriage was also much whispered. But the old Queen loved dear Alix; and dear Alix would retreat to her romping, bourgeois Danish family whenever Bertie's amorous exploits went too far, until he, chastened, would realize how much he loved and needed her, and beg her to come back.

Who could have said what Alix's tastes were; and what difference would it have made? She loved waltzing, and she was kind to children and animals and the poor, and she spent more money than her husband liked upon her magnificent dresses (though her three plain daughters were plainly dressed and lived sensible, humdrum lives) but she had neither the panache, nor the intellect, to be a Margot Tennant or an Ettie Grenfell.

The Marlborough House Set was considered 'fast', and much disapproved of by the glum courtiers immured at Windsor or Balmoral in attendance upon the perpetually mourning Queen. Unfortunately, prostrated though she was by the death of her helpmeet, the Prince Consort, in 1861, the Queen had no intention of sharing her rôle with her son. The Prince of Wales was willing and conscientious; he longed to be given something serious to occupy his time. It was in his nature to crave activity, yet his mother − jealously guarding her position as monarch − allowed him no part in the affairs of state. Not until the heir to the throne was over fifty did she even let him see inside the red cabinet boxes.

Unhappily compelled to remain a figurehead whose frequent public appearances would compensate for his mother's long withdrawal into widowhood, the Prince of Wales decided to stave off boredom by making the outward show as overblown, extravagant and spectacular as a Victorian pantomime. He peopled his life with pert, pretty women and with rollicking, boisterous, pleasure-loving men who could make him laugh, and who would come racing with him, and knew a thing or two about bloodstock and form. He invited himself and his retinue to stay with bluff, philistine country gentry with miles and miles of moors to shoot, and spent the evenings gourmandizing and smoking cigars and enjoying risqué stories over the port when the ladies had retired. His nights were a matter of much excited speculation; as were his afternoons. For the Prince had an eye for a good-looking woman that would have scandalized his prim and proper father, Albert the Good . . . but there were those who intimated that poor old Bertie's prowess was all desire and no performance.

The Marlborough House Set was more flamboyant than the Souls, much less esoteric and cultured in its amusements, and even richer. For the first time, money could provide a passport into the innermost circles of royalty. The Prince of Wales's set was cosmopolitan as well as aristocratic. He included among his closest friends Jews and foreigners, bankers and industrialists, Germans, Hungarians, and Portuguese. The sole criterion for membership of his set was the ability to entertain him, and the money to afford it. He had an insatiable appetite, not only for food and wine, but just as much for gossip, novelty and excitement. The people he liked best were hostesses lovely and generous enough to provide all of these: especially if they also had tolerant husbands.

And so the Prince of Wales waited through forty years of adult life to become King, underestimated by the mother whom he loved and feared; and for forty years society feared and loved him, and tried to compensate for her neglect. Many years later Margot Tennant recalled the popularity which had surrounded the Prince when she was young:

> In spite of criticisms made upon betting, baccarat, law courts, loves and ladies, the Prince of Wales had a popularity only equalled by our present Prince.* He was adored in private circles and public places, and mobbed and cheered on every race-course and theatre in England and France; it was the ambition of all the hostesses in London to entertain him. . . . His early training was of a kind to make him long for a little latitude in pleasure. Men did not interest him, and, like Disraeli, he delighted in the society of women. He was stimulated by their company, intrigued by their entanglements, flattered by their confidence, and valued their counsel, and though the most loyal of friends he was a professional love-maker.[1]

Bertie's childhood had been one of spartan discipline, denied the fun and affection that his responsive nature needed. The Prince Consort had set himself a chilling ambition. He was determined to mould his son into the perfect human

*Later Edward VIII.

being. And so the poor lad, intelligent enough by most royal standards but lamentably idle and stupid by those of his father, was subjected to a rigorous timetable of lessons, taken with carefully selected tutors whose expertise in their subject was as lofty as their moral probity. He had no schoolfellows, and seldom saw any children outside the royal nursery. One of the few compensations in this austere régime was the woman whom the Queen had chosen to run her nursery at Windsor: the Dowager Lady Lyttelton, the warm-hearted and sensible grandmother of Alfred Lyttelton. The Queen herself – perhaps because of her emotional absorption in her husband, or perhaps because she had been an only child – found it difficult to know how to treat her children, especially when they were small. So she followed Prince Albert's example, which was to criticize them sternly and often, ensure that they had no dangerous leisure moments when the devil might find work for idle hands, and treat them with a formality which, in Bertie's case, was heightened by his accident of birth. He was the future King of England; and nobody ever forgot it. Greville, the court gossip, observed very early that 'the hereditary and unfailing antipathy of our sovereigns to their heirs apparent seems thus early to be taking root, and the Queen does not much like the child'.[2] Victoria herself once wrote, with a rare flash of insight: 'Bertie is my caricature. That is the misfortune, and in a man, so much more.'[3] It is a revealing comment. It shows that the Queen was well aware of her own strong sensual appetites, her love for pleasure (rigidly suppressed since her more carefree, happy days as a young married woman) and for attractive men and women.

Small wonder that, the moment he was able to make his escape from this emotional and domestic tyranny, the young Prince did so. At the Curragh army camp in Ireland, in 1861, shortly before his twentieth birthday, he had a brief and overdue fling. She was an actress, pretty and witty and discreet, called Nellie Clifden, and she had been smuggled in for his benefit by his brother officers. Unfortunately for the Prince, his associates at the Curragh were not discreet enough. The news leaked out, and reached as far as the ears of his outraged parents. To the end of her life, Queen Victoria believed that the shock of learning of this escapade had been one of the factors leading to her husband's early death. She worshipped, idolized the Prince Consort, and she never forgave Bertie.

Some months before this, however, his parents had realized that it was becoming a matter of urgency to find a bride for the Prince of Wales. Europe was scoured and the *Almanach de Gotha* scanned for beautiful and acceptable princesses. In 1861 the Prince's elder sister, Princess Victoria, tracked down the sixteen-year-old Princess Alexandra of Schleswig-Holstein-Sonderburg-Glucksburg. She was the daughter of the poor but honest Prince Christian, heir to the King of Denmark. The practised mechanism for arranging royal marriages moved smoothly into action. A meeting was engineered between the young couple at which, most gratifyingly, Bertie fell in love at first sight.

This was in July; but by December 1861 the Prince Consort was dead. The Queen was virtually inconsolable for the next forty years. After a period of full court mourning, muted preparations for Bertie's wedding went ahead. Alexandra, evidently schooled by her fiancé, put on her best black dress, met the deeply grieving Queen and tactfully talked of little else except her admiration for the late Prince Consort. The Queen reported to Princess Victoria, in a torrent of approving adjectives, that 'Alix was kind, loving, sweet, sensible, gentle, good, simple, honest, unspoilt, affectionate, intelligent, cheerful, merry.'[4]

On 10 March 1863 the Prince of Wales and Princess Alexandra were married. To one of his sisters, who must have been spiteful about her motives, Alix said on the morning of her wedding, 'You perhaps think I am marrying your brother for his position. But if he was a cowboy I should love him just the same and would marry no-one else.'[5] It is revealing to note that the humblest and poorest man the young bride's imagination could encompass was a cowboy. Yet her brave words seem to have been truthful, for despite all his philandering Alexandra loved her husband until he died. And he, in his way, loved her. She did her best to be a good wife, but once Bertie was no longer dazzled by the novelty of marriage, he discovered that his young wife had little to offer except her beauty – though that was exceptional. Margot Tennant described her:

> I do not think I am exaggerating when I say that [she] was the most beautiful woman in Europe. The perfect oval of her face, the fine brow, clean-cut nose, and dazzling complexion, were enhanced by the colour of her eyes and the radiance of a smile easily provoked. . . . The carriage of her little head set upon a firm white throat, and the outline of her marble shoulders, could not have failed to move the least impressionable.[6]

Margot attended the sort of occasion at which the Princess of Wales shone – a court ball:

> There was a sudden silence, and we all stood up for the National Anthem. Gentlemen in waiting, holding white rods and walking backwards, came in, followed by the Prince and Princess of Wales and all the royal family. Stepping onto the dais, the Prince took his wife's hand and with infinite grace she turned and curtsied first to the row of Ambassadors on her left, then to the Duchesses on her right, and after acknowledging the closely packed company in the centre of the ballroom, sat down beside her Prince. For grandeur, grace and dignity, on these occasions no Monarchs in Europe could rival our Prince and Princess of Wales.
>
> The Palace ballroom was divided by red tape to facilitate the Court officials who were directing the dancing; but those who arrived early enough were in as good a position as anyone else to observe what was going on, and thrilled with admiration I watched our lovely Princess in the opening quadrille moving across the long polished boards like a beautiful ship setting out to sea.[7]

Alexandra's appearance hardly changed, and she never seemed to get any older. The same was true of her character. At a time when women were often expected to behave in a childlike fashion (it was the sort of proof of their innocence and unworldliness that made a man feel strong and protective), Alexandra excelled at this. The fact that she was often unable to hear what was being said around her added to the impression of sweet foolishness that she created. She would nod and smile and make wholly inappropriate remarks, and then summon a lady-in-waiting or a daughter to fetch something, so that the speaker's attention was distracted.

The Princess of Wales failed her husband in two ways. She failed to bear him strong, healthy, even averagely intelligent sons; and she failed to satisfy his sexual demands.

Their first son – who had to be called Albert Victor, at the insistence of the Queen, although his family always called him Eddy – was born prematurely. All his life he was physically puny and mentally so feeble as to be almost subnormal. One of his tutors said of him that 'the abnormally dormant condition of his mind deprives him of the power to fix his attention on any given subject for more than a few minutes'.[8] Had he been speaking of anyone other than the heir to the throne he would surely have called him a halfwit.

It must have come as a secret relief to everyone when, after some dangerous flirtations with highly unsuitable young women, and even a rumoured marriage with a Roman Catholic, young Eddy acquiesced with reasonably good grace in an engagement with Princess May of Teck. She came from good Hanoverian stock, which was thought to outweigh the disadvantage of her being several inches taller than her betrothed. It may have come as even more of a relief to everyone except his doting 'Motherdear' when, shortly before the date of the wedding, young Prince Eddy died of influenza in January 1892, a few days after his twenty-eighth birthday. After a decent interval for court mourning the submissive May inherited her fiancé's brother, the slightly less vacuous Prince George. On 6 July 1893, fifteen months after poor Eddy's death, George and May were married.

After the birth of her last child, Prince Alexander John, who was too weak to live for more than a day, the Princess of Wales appears to have decided not to risk any further pregnancies. She took a separate bedroom, and from 1871 – less than ten years after their marriage – Bertie had to seek consolation elsewhere. He was thirty; his wife only twenty-six. The indications are that she could come to terms with what was, in effect, almost a lifetime of celibacy. She needed admiration, praise and platonic devotion far more than she needed sexual fulfilment. However, the sentimental domesticity so precious to Queen Victoria did not suit her son, though he was a kinder and more indulgent parent to his five children. He sought stimulus elsewhere: and it was this search for amusement that the Marlborough House Set existed to gratify.

As Margot Tennant pointed out, he revelled in the company of women. He prized female beauty and understood about fashions in dress and adored spicy gossip. His liaisons with the young married women who could provide all these delights made adultery acceptable. It cannot have been unknown before 1871; but from now on it was less clandestine – provided certain unwritten rules were kept. The first and greatest of these was, as ever: thou shalt not be found out. Bertie created a society to fulfil his needs, and the double standard suited him perfectly. He never flirted with young girls and he never seduced an unmarried woman; indeed, he preferred comfortably established women in their late twenties. The three great extra-marital loves of his life were Mrs Edward Langtry – Lillie – who was twenty-four when he met her; Daisy, Countess of Warwick – who was twenty-eight; and Mrs Keppel, who was twenty-nine. All three of their husbands appeared content to share their wives' favours with the heir to the throne.

The lead which the Prince of Wales gave in condoning adultery, providing it was handled in a civilized and discreet fashion, was followed and not initiated by the Souls. With very few exceptions, their marriages, too, allowed forays in the direction of newer partners, more gratifying to the mind and the feelings, perhaps; undoubtedly more interesting in bed; but these forays were always followed by a return to the deep peace of the marital bed. No Souls' marriage was ever ended by divorce. Its harmony may, from time to time, have been a little troubled by amorous excursions; but the erring wife or husband was always welcomed back, and any children of these outside liaisons were always accepted and reared as the husband's child.

In the late Victorian era there were overriding practical reasons why this should be so. An affair which became an open scandal led to social ostracism, and, as usual, the woman bore the main burden. After a divorce, her husband was entitled to keep not only the children – whom his wife might be prevented from seeing on account of her moral turpitude – but also any money and property that she had brought to the marriage. Thus a divorced woman was not only disgraced, but penniless, too. Even if a man went mad or became a hopeless alcoholic or beat his wife with a riding crop, that was not a good enough reason for divorce. Marriage was for life. Margot Tennant's elder sister Lucy, who had married at seventeen, lived with her husband until she died, although they were hopelessly incompatible. True, she spent much time at home at the Glen, looking after her elderly mother; and she consoled herself with drawing and painting, until she took to a wheelchair and her hands were crippled by arthritis. But she was Mrs Graham Smith until the day she died. In much the same way, the marriage that was hastily arranged between Margot's eldest brother Edward, later Lord Glenconner, and Pamela Wyndham (when the latter was cruelly disappointed in love) turned out within a very short time to have been an obvious mistake. It made no difference. Pamela found the love of her life in another Edward, later Lord Grey of Fallodon, and the three of them lived in a discreet *ménage à trois*, which lasted until Lord Glenconner's death. Only then did Pamela marry Lord Grey of Fallodon. Between 1876 and 1880 there were just 460 divorces in England; in the next four years there were 462. Between 1886 and 1890 the figure rose slightly, to 556; and a decade later, between 1896 and 1900, it was higher again at 675. A decade after that it was 809. Although the trend rose steadily, the numbers involved are still minuscule.[9]

The permanence of marriage, in a society where women's main function was to look beautiful, entertain brilliantly and bear children, was therefore the secure background against which adultery took place, both among the Souls and in the Marlborough House Set. The difference between the two groups was that the Souls placed a greater romantic and cerebral value on their love affairs, and would regard it as a matter of honour to be faithful to the current lover. The Marlborough House Set cared little for cerebral affairs, and Bertie, at least, had no scruples about multiple adulteries. Besides his three 'official' mistresses he welcomed other encounters whenever the opportunity arose. (An officer on the royal yacht once overheard, issuing from the Prince's private cabin, the peremptory command, 'Stop calling me Sir and put another cushion under your back!') The difference between the two sets of attitudes was that the Marlborough House Set existed chiefly to satisfy masculine needs, while the Souls were equally concerned with women's. Within the narrow circle of London society the Prince of Wales often met women from the Souls – the two sets were by no means mutually exclusive – and was amused by Margot, charmed by Ettie Grenfell, and entertained at the homes of many of them. It would be hard to say whether Millicent, Duchess of Sutherland, was more a Soul or a member of the Marlborough House Set; though her husband would undoubtedly have preferred the latter. But clever women had no influence there, and the Prince himself did not care for strong-minded, well-read women. Thinking women were dangerous. Their rôle was to be the pampered appendages of men.

The Princess of Wales acquiesced in all this with reasonably good grace. She had her own consolations, of a different kind. Apart from her love for her two sons, and especially the elder, Prince Eddy, she also basked in the platonic devotion of one of her husband's equerries. He was the Hon. Oliver Montagu, a younger son of the Earl of Sandwich. He began as an officer in the 'Blues' – the Royal Horse Guards – and rose to become their Colonel. Tall and handsome and highly eligible, he was the very image of dashing and chivalrous Victorian manhood, but having fallen deeply in love with the Princess of Wales when they were both twenty-four, in 1868, he never looked at another woman. Lady Antrim recalled:

It is surprising that, young and lovely as she was, the Princess never gave any real occasion for scandal. I think it must have been due to Oliver Montagu's care for her. He shielded her in every way, not least from his own great love, and managed to defeat gossip. He was looked upon with awe by the young as he sauntered into a ballroom, regardless of anything but his beautiful Princess, who as a matter of course always danced the first after-supper waltz with him. But she remained marvellously circumspect.[10]

She was heartbroken by his early death in 1893. She said – and the words could have been applied to any medieval knight and courtly lover, languishing for the unconsummated love of his great lady – 'He was the best and truest of men . . . faithful, discreet and trustworthy, gentle, kind, just and brave, and noble both in his life and death.'[11]

No one ever quite took his place, and in any case, by 1893 Alexandra was almost fifty. She never lacked devoted admirers, however: such as the Marquis de Soveral, the Portuguese Minister in London and one of the most sought-after guests in England, whose charm and good nature endeared him to both members of the royal couple. His wicked black eyes and wide smile beneath an even wider black moustache beam out from many country house weekend group photographs. He was a notorious lady-killer, but, like all the others, he kept his distance with Alexandra. She was above criticism. She understood perfectly that her rôle demanded, not only an exquisite façade, but that she should behave as the epitome of all that was best in womanhood. She had faults: graver ones than congenital unpunctuality. She was extremely prejudiced against Germany and the Germans, despite her husband's ancestry; because she said the Prussians had 'annexed' Schleswig-Holstein in 1866, when it belonged by right to *her* country, Denmark. Because of this she could scarcely bring herself to be civil to Bertie's innumerable German relations. But there was never a breath of scandal against her name: and this went some way, in the eyes of both the Queen and the British public, towards atoning for Bertie's lapses. By her forgiveness and goodness she saved him from seeming merely gross, self-indulgent and vulgar.

The members of the Marlborough House Set still wanted to appear outwardly respectable, for the benefit of their children, their servants, and other social inferiors. Hence they perfected the hypocrisy of the double standard – a form of behaviour which it is unfair to call 'Victorian' since it would have been anathema to the Queen. It mattered little what went on in private as long as the public façade was maintained. The only other absolute social imperative was that property should be seen to be handed down through a direct bloodline from father to son. In the Prince of Wales's set, this was the only obligation that was considered more important than the pursuit of pleasure. Exactly the same set of priorities would have been recognized by the Souls. In this respect, at least, the two groups were alike.

It had long been accepted by all upper-class families that young men had 'adventures' before they were married; and almost all men, from every class, visited prostitutes. In 1857 *The Lancet* had estimated that one house in sixty in London was a brothel, and one woman in sixteen a prostitute. In 1861, Mayhew reckoned there were at least 80,000 prostitutes in London: probably a good many more. Their price ranged from a few pence to a hundred pounds or more. (An innocent and lovely virgin, gently reared, aged about thirteen or fourteen, would command the latter price.) There were few if any *demi-mondaines* in London, of the kind who were to be found in fashionable Parisian society at the same period: women distinguished not only by their beauty and sexual accessibility, but also by being intelligent, witty and *au courant* with the literary and cultural life of the city. Perhaps the reason was that few Englishmen cared to patronize a woman who could talk to them; perhaps it was the dearth of an intellectual élite in British society before the advent of the Souls. One woman who was, however, well above the status of an ordinary prostitute was the famous 'Skittles'.

Her real name was Catherine Walters, and she had been born in Liverpool in 1839, where, she claimed, her father was a customs official. However, it was widely believed that she had worked in a bowling alley as a young girl; hence the nickname 'Skittles'. She had a passion for riding, and at the age of sixteen her beauty and her excellent seat on a horse were such that she was noticed by a young blood called George Fitzwilliam, who persuaded her to run away from home and come and live with him. Through him she met other young men from society, one of whom was the eldest son of the 7th Duke of Devonshire. He fell deeply in love with the beautiful Skittles, persuaded her to leave her former protector (who, with truly amazing generosity, settled £300 a year on her, as well as depositing £2,000 at a bank in case she should need it), and set her up in a house in Bennett Street, close to Devonshire House, his family's London mansion. The story is complicated by the fact that Skittles claimed, later in life, that his father, the then Duke, was also enamoured of her; at any rate, when the young Marquess of Hartington expressed a desire to marry the ravishing Skittles, she was promptly packed off to Paris out of harm's way. The Devonshires paid her off with £500 a year; and in Paris she quickly found her *métier* as a *demi-mondaine*. There she met the young poet and traveller, Wilfrid Scawen Blunt, in 1863; and he too fell passionately in love with her.

She must have been a bewitching creature, though the few remaining photographs of her scarcely do her justice. She had thick dark hair, a slender pliable figure which she clothed in skin-tight riding habits, and lively dark eyes. Her importance to this story is that when, in due course, she returned to London to resume her affair (more discreetly) with Hartington, she also became the bedfellow of half the men in London society, not excepting the Prince of Wales. He visited her regularly; and when she was quite an old woman, and was taken ill, the Prince paid all her doctor's bills. In her final years she remained friendly with Wilfrid Scawen Blunt, who in turn showed unusual loyalty to his first love; and in long sessions of reminiscences over the tea-table in South Street, Mayfair, where she ended her life, she told Blunt the inside story of her relationship with the Prince of Wales, and a good deal of other gossip about the royal family. All this scurrilous information Blunt entrusted to his secret diary: a document so confidential that he left instructions that it should not be opened until fifty years after his death, by which time he could safely assume that all those mentioned in it would be dead as well.

His credibility as a witness, in this secret diary, can be safely presumed, since no credit or otherwise would accrue to him until long after his death. Skittles's reliability, like her memory, is less certain. She was nearly seventy when she told Blunt the story of her life, and in poor health. However, she cannot have known (for he certainly did not tell her) that all she confided to him he, in turn, confided to his diary. It must have been, at any rate, an astonishing set of revelations. Blunt prefaced his account with the words, 'The story is so important historically that I cross-questioned her pretty closely so as to test its accuracy and found that in all essentials it held well together.'[12]

The common factor in the story, besides Skittles herself, is the German sculptor Boehm; a handsome and impressive man and a fashionable sculptor who – on account of his nationality – was soon taken up by the court. The Prince of Wales commissioned Boehm to sculpt a portrait head of Skittles (and Blunt remembers her, at this time, bringing the sculptor down to his country house at Crabbet, to visit him and see his Arab stud). He had also done a number of busts and statues of the Prince Consort, which greatly pleased the Queen. The story then continues,

> The Queen wanting to have a statue made of her ghillie John Brown he was commanded to Balmoral where he spent three months (that must have been in the summer of 1869 or 1870). While engaged in this work he [Boehm] saw a great deal both of John Brown, his model, and of the Queen. Brown was a rude unmannerly fellow, and he had much ado to keep him in order during the sittings but he had unbounded influence with the Queen whom he treated with little respect, presuming in every way upon his position with her. It was the talk of all the household that he was 'the Queen's Stallion'. He was a fine man physically, though coarsely made, and had fine eyes (like the late Prince Consort's, it was said) and the Queen, who had been passionately in love with her husband got it into her head that somehow the Prince's spirit had passed into Brown and 4 years after her widowhood being very unhappy allowed him all privileges. It was to be with him, where she could do more as she liked, that she spent so much of her time at Balmoral, though he was also with her at Osborne and elsewhere. . . . She used to go away with him to a little house in the hills where, on the pretence that it was for protection and 'to look after her dogs' he had a bedroom next to hers, the ladies-in-waiting being put at the other end of the building. . . . Boehm saw enough of his

familiarities with her to leave no doubt of his being allowed 'every conjugal privilege'.[13]

The story is complicated by the fact that Princess Louise, one of Queen Victoria's younger daughters, herself fell in love with Boehm, and

> used to come to him in his studio on the pretence of modelling and they became intimate, though not to the extent of actual love-making, and one day the Queen coming to see how the statue was getting on found her there and a violent scene occurred between them. . . . They were obliged to get the Prince of Wales, who was very fond of his sister and had most influence over her, to appease the quarrel; and they then set about finding a husband for her . . . finally Princess Louise married Lord Lorne. The marriage however was not a success, as Lorne was unsatisfactory as a husband. . . . 'The King' she [i.e. Skittles] said, 'knows all about it. He was fond of his sister and says he and she were of the same temperament.' So all has been hushed up and Boehm lies sepulchred in the Abbey; and a memorial is being built for 'Victoria the Good' in front of Buckingham Palace, and the Queen's life is held up as a model for us all and for future generations.[14]

And above all, for the Prince of Wales! Her Majesty followed Brown on foot to his grave and remained for a long time half-crazy at the loss of him.

The only confirmation of the truth, or otherwise, of this tale that Blunt offers came from Lord Rowton who, as Montagu Corry, had for many years been Disraeli's private secretary, and thus must have been a frequent visitor at the various royal establishments:

> Of the Queen he has talked much and I was surprised to find him attaching a sexual importance to her affection for John Brown. He mentioned in that connection the statue she had had made of Brown by Boehm, which is precisely what XX [Blunt's usual code in his diary for Skittles] told me as having been related to her by Boehm himself. So I fancy it must be true.[†15]

The final irony to this tale comes from Skittles's other revelation, this time about the Prince of Wales. She claimed that he was impotent, and had been for some years. This evidence is confirmed from another source: Margot Tennant (by then Mrs Asquith) was told by Daisy, Countess of Warwick (who was certainly one of those in a position to know!) that the King was 'quite impotent'. As the physical aspect of their relationship ended well before the Prince of Wales took Mrs Keppel as his favourite, in 1898, the assumption must be that – if Skittles and Daisy were telling the truth – poor Bertie had been unable to consummate his passion since his fifties. Thus the widowed Queen Victoria was universally believed to be faithful to her husband's memory: which she was not; while the pleasure-loving Prince of Wales was equally widely assumed to be unfaithful to dear long-suffering Alix: which, much as he might have wished it, he was for many years unable to be!

It is comforting to know that the omniscient Skittles believed the Princess of Wales to be all that she seemed. Blunt asked her if Alexandra had ever had a

---

†It is in the nature of these speculations that evidence is very hard to obtain. The only other independent corroboration I have been able to acquire is from a university professor who, working in the Windsor Castle archives, was by error brought a pile of letters between Queen Victoria and her ghillie. From them he deduced that the affair was far from platonic.

lover. 'She said, "Oh no. She is not made in that way. She disliked even having her hand kissed. She submitted to her conjugal duties but never liked it. She was v. fond of Oliver Montagu but it was only as a friend. She went to bed & cried for three days when he died. The Prince of Wales said he knew there was nothing in it." '[16] One cannot help wondering how Skittles obtained this information, since it seems unlikely that the Prince of Wales would have discussed his wife's frigidity with a woman who was, after all, mistress to a good many other men in London besides himself.

Whatever the Prince's amorous exploits may have been, the chances were always that – given the sort of company he kept, and the rumours that proliferated about him – he would be involved from time to time in scandal. In the event, it is not surprising that such scandals existed; what is surprising is that, in forty years of waiting to be King, only three of them ever became public property. Each one horrified the Queen and distressed Alexandra, but in the end the consensus of opinion was always that Bertie might have been unwise in his choice of associates, but he himself had behaved honourably; and so he was forgiven. If it came to a crisis, he always stood by his friends; but behind the scenes he did everything in his power to prevent a crisis becoming public, and more often than not he succeeded.

The Souls had almost as great a fear of public scandal and – partly because the spotlight of publicity beat slightly less fiercely upon them than on the heir to the throne – they, too, almost always succeeded in hushing matters up. There might be speculation, rumour, gossip; but as long as the outward proprieties were maintained, all in the end would be well. On two occasions, certainly, the private lives of the Souls came dangerously close to the cliff edge of exposure; but in both cases the erring partner either made amends, or the wronged partner made the best of it. In very many other cases the outer show of a marriage belied a long-standing arrangement whereby one spouse – or even both – took a lover whose presence enabled the show to be kept going.

The Prince of Wales, however, was under fiercer scrutiny. The first scandal which involved him publicly was the Mordaunt case. In itself it was unimportant, except that, for the first time since the days of Henry IV, it led to the appearance in court of the Prince of Wales. For in February 1870 he was subpoenaed as a witness in the case of Lady Mordaunt, whose husband was bringing a suit against her for divorce. (The real reason was that she had gone mad, but he needed evidence of her infidelity to bring a case.)

Lady Mordaunt, beautiful and dashing, had given birth in 1869 to a premature girl. The child, who was probably not her husband's, was apparently stricken with blindness. Her guilt at this catastrophe unhinged her mind. She summoned her husband and in a hysterical confession told him she had been unfaithful on numerous occasions with several different men. Among them she named the Prince of Wales. The following day, after breaking the lock on his wife's desk and removing a number of incriminating letters – and some notes from the Prince – Lord Mordaunt left his country home for his house in London and never saw his wife again.

When he served the writ for divorce, however, her parents claimed that she had been insane at the time of her confession, that she did not know what she had been saying and that in any case the confession was not true. Lord Mordaunt took the case to court. Poor, fragile, raving Harriet, still only twenty-one, was described by witnesses for both sides in sordid and intimate detail. She herself was quite unfit to give evidence. But the case attracted immense public interest, and an enterprising newspaper managed to get hold of the Prince's letters to her . . . letters which, as it turned out, any well-mannered guest might have sent to his hostess, and which in themselves proved nothing – and this added to the sensation. The Prince had warned his mother and his wife that he would have to appear in court. The Queen, although she told Bertie she had complete confidence in him, wrote to the Lord Chancellor:

> The fact of the Prince of Wales's intimate acquaintance with a young married woman being publicly proclaimed will show an amount of imprudence which cannot but damage him in the eyes of the middle and lower classes, which is most deeply to be lamented in these days when the higher classes, in their frivolous, selfish and pleasure-seeking lives, do more to increase the spirit of democracy than anything else.[17]

Bertie was in the witness box for seven minutes, and behaved impeccably. When asked on oath whether there had been any impropriety, he answered firmly, 'There has not.' In all probability this was true: at any rate, it could hardly be questioned. The Queen certainly believed it, and wrote staunchly to her eldest daughter, 'Bertie's appearance did great good but the whole remains a painful, lowering thing, not because he is innocent, for I never doubted that, but because his name ought never to have been dragged in the dirt, or mixed up with such people.'[18] Sir Charles Mordaunt's petition failed. His wife, due to her insanity, could not be party to a divorce suit.

The Prince of Wales's popularity in the country was at a low ebb. He was booed at the theatre and at the races. Not until his recovery from a serious illness the following year (in 1872 he caught typhoid fever and for several days he was close to death) was the royal couple restored to public favour.

The second scandal to involve the Prince concerned two members of the inner circle of the Marlborough House Set, Lord Blandford and Lord Aylesford – the hearty, hard-riding man known as 'Sporting Joe'. It coincided with the Prince of Wales's tour of India in 1876. With him on that trip he took a number of his best friends for company and amusement, among them Lord Aylesford. During the months of their absence, the Marquess of Blandford – heir to the Duke of Marlborough, to Blenheim, to a great name and great riches, but a careless womanizer nevertheless – rented a house in the neighbourhood of the Aylesfords'. He was several times seen leaving Packington Hall, where Lady Aylesford was spending the winter, in the small hours of the morning. On 20 February 1876 Lord Aylesford received a letter in India from his wife, informing him that she planned to elope with Blandford. Her brother, Colonel Owen Williams, was also with the Prince, and he was despatched to England to try and dissuade his sister. A few days later Lord Aylesford followed – but the journey home took six weeks, and by the time they arrived society was agog with rumours of the scandal. Aylesford decided to divorce his wife – who had given him two daughters but not, so far, a son.

But now an astonishing thing happened. Blandford's younger brother, Lord Randolph Churchill, had managed to convince himself that the Prince of Wales was to blame for what had occurred. By taking Lord Aylesford from his wife and home for so long, he must be responsible for the liaison. Feeling that the family name was at stake, Lord Randolph bombarded the Prince of Wales with a series of telegrams urging him to intervene and prevent Aylesford from carrying out his threat of bringing divorce proceedings. The heated exchange of telegrams and letters rose to a crescendo, until finally even the Prime Minister, Disraeli, was involved. In the end Randolph apologized, but so gracelessly that he was boycotted by the Prince of Wales, and hence by the Marlborough House Set. It took all the blandishments of his lovely leonine wife, Jennie, before the pair were restored to favour eight years later. Between 1876 and 1884 they were social exiles. Even his father, the Duke of Marlborough, found it prudent to accept the post of Lord-Lieutenant of Ireland and retire with his family from the English scene for some years.

Lord Aylesford in the end decided against a divorce. Nevertheless, life in English society had become impossible. In 1882 he emigrated to America where he bought a huge ranch in Texas and died of alcoholism three years later. Blandford lived abroad with Edith Aylesford until 1888, when he inherited the dukedom from his father. Then he left Edith to her fate in Paris, and married an American widow.

Such were the penalties for transgressing the unwritten rules.

The third and most serious scandal that touched the Prince of Wales was called the Tranby Croft affair. It made 1891 the unhappiest year of his life – certainly of his adult life – a year in which the loyalty even of his wife seemed to waver. (Alexandra deliberately stayed with her parents in Denmark during Bertie's fiftieth birthday celebrations.) The incident involved not just playing cards – bad enough, in the eyes of many Victorians – but cheating, too, which was almost unthinkable. Once again, there was no question of the Prince himself being guilty; one of his friends was at the centre of the storm. But Bertie's real fear must have been that – as he and a very few close friends knew – behind the open scandal of the Tranby Croft business there was another, clandestine affair in which he was personally, deeply involved. This was the quarrel between Bertie and his old friend Lord Charles Beresford over the bewitching Daisy, Lady Brooke.

In September 1890 the Prince and a group of friends attended Doncaster Races, as they did each year. In the past they had stayed with Christopher Sykes, a great though in some ways unfortunate friend of the Prince of Wales. By 1890, however, Sykes was almost bankrupt, largely as a result of the high cost of entertaining Bertie and his cronies, and was not in a position to offer hospitality. Instead, the shipowner Arthur Wilson, who also lived close to the racecourse, acted as host at his house, Tranby Croft. And there, on 8 September, the first evening of the three-day visit, Wilson's son Arthur saw one of the Prince's party, Sir William Gordon-Cumming, a lieutenant-colonel in the Scots Guards, cheating at baccarat.

By the following evening young Arthur had alerted four others to observe what happened at the gaming table. Once again, all five witnesses decided there could be no doubt about it: Sir William was indeed cheating at cards by adding to his stake after he had placed a winning bet. In the course of the two evenings' play Sir William won £225, most of it from the Prince of Wales who was banker.

His accusers felt they had no choice but to confront Sir William, who denied the accusation from first to last. He was an experienced baccarat player, at a table with comparative novices, and his defence was always that he had merely followed the common practice of letting a winning stake lie on the table, and adding to the bet for the next round: a system known as the *coup de trois*. But it could have been that he was playing the sleight-of-hand trick called *la poussette*, in which a player looks at his hand and, if he holds winning cards, manipulates his stake so as to increase it. Whatever the truth, Sir William was as anxious as everyone else around the table to avoid publicity and keep the accusation secret. That evening, he signed a promise to give up cards for the rest of his life.

It was too late. The news leaked out – partly by way of Lady Brooke (who earned the nickname of 'Babbling Brook' for her indiscretion) – and within days too many people were in the know for the affair to be hushed up. There was a half-hearted attempt to have Sir William's conduct investigated either by the Guards' Club – of which he was a member – or by a military court of enquiry. But both failed, and finally all concerned faced the inevitability of a trial. It was instigated by Gordon-Cumming, who accused the five witnesses of libel.

The trial opened before the Lord Chief Justice on 1 June 1891, with Sir William represented by the Solicitor-General, Sir Edward Clarke. He took the case on, not for its notoriety, but because he fully believed his client's protestations of innocence. He made no attempt to shorten the trial – known as the Baccarat Case – out of consideration for the heir to the throne. On the contrary: he hinted in court that Sir William 'had been victimised to save the honour of a Prince who encouraged habitually an illegal game; who had jumped recklessly to a wrong conclusion on bad evidence. . . . The eye sees,' said Sir Edward, 'what it brings the expectation of seeing'[19] – and the Prince of Wales had been too ready to accept the evidence of witnesses already predisposed to see Sir William cheat.

It was no use. In ten minutes the jury found Sir William had not been libelled – meaning, in effect, that he *was* guilty of cheating at cards. His career was over; his reputation ruined; his social life at an end. He was dismissed from the army and forced to resign from all his clubs, and retired in ignominy to his 40,000 acres in Scotland and his mansion there called Gordonstoun. His one consolation was that the day after the verdict he married a young American heiress and took her into exile with him. There he lived on for forty years, consoled by his devoted wife and his collection of postmarks.

But the trial had made the Prince of Wales more unpopular than ever before – and it cannot have consoled him much to be told by his former enemy, Lord Randolph Churchill, 'My own experience is that praise from the Press is far less conducive to popularity than its abuse!' He also had to tolerate a flood of pious resolutions condemning his behaviour in indulging in wicked card games with dishonourable friends and leading the virtuous middle classes (meaning the Wilsons, his hosts) astray. These came from such august bodies as the Annual Conference of the Primitive Methodist Connexion and the Leicestershire Sunday School Union. The Prince took notice of these complaints. He gave up baccarat and turned to bridge instead.

Furthermore, a deputation of ladies went to Lambeth Palace and tackled the Archbishop of Canterbury about the scandalous behaviour of the heir to the throne. The Archbishop's son, E.F. Benson (who later published a satirical novel,

Dodo, allegedly based on Margot Tennant's life and style) described what lay behind the high-minded ladies' visit:

> With the best and highest motives they had come to ask my father if he could do nothing to stop the moral rot which, they affirmed, was ruining London. Girls newly 'come out', they said, of high tone and upright intentions, were speedily corrupted by it, and what they had been brought up to regard as evil they soon regarded as natural and inevitable; young married women had no standard of morality at all, and the centre of the mischief was the Marlborough House Set.[20]

Another view of society came from the poet and traveller Wilfrid Scawen Blunt, who had just returned to London and wrote in his diary:

> I turned with redoubled zest to my social pleasures of the year before, and at this time saw much of that interesting group of clever men and pretty women known as the 'Souls', than whom no section of London Society was better worth frequenting, including as it did all that there was most intellectually amusing and least conventional. It was a group of men and women bent on pleasure, but pleasure of a superior kind, eschewing the vulgarities of racing and card-playing indulged in by the majority of the rich and noble, and looking for their excitement in romance and sentiment.[21]

In the end the 'romance and sentiment' of the Souls came to much the same thing as what was 'natural and inevitable' to the Marlborough House Set. Both groups were subject to very similar constraints (the lack of reliable contraceptives is only one of the most obvious) and to much the same social conditioning. Stratified by church and class, reared in great houses, largely by servants, educated by schoolmasters or governesses, the differences between the Souls and the Marlborough House Set were not in the end very great. Souls women were more intelligent and less docile than Marlborough House women; Souls men were not quite as wealthy nor quite as hearty as Marlborough House men. The latter, due to their close proximity to the Prince of Wales, tended to play little part in politics (though Lord Randolph Churchill was an exception); and none of them had any links with the academic world. Other than these differences – which would have seemed highly significant, at least to the Souls – they had everything in common.

They both followed the social year through its invariable course. June was the prime month for racing, at Epsom and Ascot; July was for the Eton and Harrow match, Goodwood and the Cowes Regatta; August would see the start of the grouse season in Scotland. The Prince of Wales, towards the latter part of his life, invariably spent a fortnight in August or September taking a 'cure' to expiate the over-indulgence of the three months of the London season. This was usually spent at the Hotel Weimar, in Marienbad; occasionally in Homburg or Baden-Baden. The Souls, who indulged less, were not in the habit of taking cures. In September, the Prince of Wales would return to London, and the late autumn and winter would be spent by everyone in a round of country house visits.

The faces of husbands and wives, and their secret lovers, gaze blandly back from photographs taken to record some house party or day's shooting, and it is hard to believe that such complicated relationships and intense emotions seethed behind their composed expressions. Yesterday's scandal and gossip remain interesting because it is at the point where private passion challenges society that the conventions and taboos shaping people's behaviour are exposed. Today, when a discreet abortion or a quick divorce would tidy it all up, the explosive potential of those clandestine affairs is hard to imagine. But a century ago, passion was an alternative to divorce; hardly ever a prelude to it.

The Prince of Wales himself was more conscious than anyone of the social pyramid, and the rules of behaviour which it decreed: he, after all, lived at its very apex. But the combination of limitless leisure with immense (though not limitless) wealth does not make people acute social observers; and heirs to the throne have an especially blinkered view of life. The courtiers who surrounded the Prince – fortunately, perhaps, for them – had no inkling of the social fuse that was before long to detonate beneath the structure they topped. As for the Prince himself, it can never have crossed his mind that the foundations might one day become unsafe. The world of the Marlborough House Set was impregnable.

The Souls never doubted its permanence, either; but they nevertheless saw reality through fewer layers of luxury than the Prince of Wales. Margot, yet again, summed up his view of the world with scathing accuracy: 'Royal persons are necessarily divorced from the true opinion of people that count, and are almost always obliged to take safe and commonplace views. To them, clever men are "prigs"; clever women "too advanced"; Liberals are "Socialists"; the un-interesting "pleasant"; the interesting "intriguers"; and the dreamer "mad".'[22]

– 4 –

'King Arthur' or 'The Adored Gazelle'

1870–1905

The Prince of Wales was the leader of the Marlborough House Set. Arthur Balfour was the leader of the Souls. It is hard to imagine two men more different: the one stout, forceful, energetic and revelling with immense gusto in all the carnal pleasures; and the other tall and slender, languid, aloof, whose pleasures all seemed to be those of the mind.

Yet between them they headed the two most influential sets in upper-class society for three or four decades, and in both cases the style and personality of each man set the tone for his circle. The Marlborough House Set, with its passion for shooting and racing and evenings devoted to gargantuan meals and pretty women, embodied the preferences of the Prince of Wales. The Souls: aesthetic, intellectual, with their disdain for vulgar displays of butchery and gross self-indulgence, reflected the tastes of Arthur Balfour. Small wonder that the two men disliked each other. In later life, when one was King and the other his Prime Minister, they found it difficult to work together. Had they been more perceptive and less egoistic, they might have discovered that the impression each had of the other was a caricature. The King was more intelligent and much more conscientious than he seemed, and Balfour's indolence was a studied pose, while his languor concealed deep feeling.

So powerful was the spell that these two men cast that, in opposite but complementary ways, they completely changed upper-class English society. Between them they – and the circle over which they presided – were responsible for the differences between the aristocracy of the 1870s, into which they both came as young men, and that of the Edwardian era. During the decades in between – the eighties and nineties – the Prince of Wales, by his fondness for the company of the very rich regardless of whether they were Jewish, or self-made, or foreign (or indeed, as in the case of the South African gold and diamond millionaires, all three), brought about an expansion of the upper classes beyond the tight little circle of the landed aristocracy, who had up till now successfully excluded all 'outsiders'. So it was due to the Prince that the granddaughter of a man who had started life as a penniless German-Jewish bank clerk could marry a great-grandson of Queen Victoria. She was the Hon. Edwina Ashley, and he was Lord Louis Mountbatten.

Of equal importance was the civilizing influence upon what had been an overwhelmingly philistine society that came from Balfour and the Souls. In their homes and at their country house parties writers, artists and poets conversed with aristocrats and politicians. Henry James and Oscar Wilde and H. G. Wells and Burne-Jones and William Morris were, for the first time, guests. English society had until then been extraordinarily clannish. Whereas in the courts and salons of Europe men of genius had always been sought after and lionized, in England the social gap between the fashionable painter and his aristocratic subjects was, in the nineteenth century at least, thought too wide for society to risk. But the Souls bridged it.

In about 1905, when she was eighteen, Lady Violet Bonham-Carter, then Violet Asquith, was placed next to Mr Balfour – 'the Soul of Souls' – at dinner one evening. 'I felt then,' she wrote, 'and have felt ever since, that to talk to him was the greatest luxury, and almost the most exciting sensation I had ever experienced. I shall never forget the intellectual courtesy of his approach, the intense quality of interest he managed to convey.'[1] Yet Rudyard Kipling, describing Balfour, called him 'arid, aloof, incurious, unthinking, unthanking, gelt'.[2] What sort of man arouses such contradictory responses?

He was born in July 1848 at Whittingehame, the ancestral home inherited by his father which he, as eldest son, would in time inherit too. His mother, Lady Blanche Balfour, was the sister of the Marquess of Salisbury, to whom in later life Balfour owed so many of his political opportunities. Thus on both sides of the family he was born with a silver spoon in his mouth. His father, a hunting, shooting landowner and for six years the local Tory MP, died of tuberculosis when Arthur was only eight, leaving his young widow to bring up their eight children alone. This she did with a firm and Christian hand, softened by a brilliant wit and a passion for Jane Austen. Arthur, as the clever and good-looking eldest son, was lucky in her favour. Those children of whom she was less fond she 'alternately scorched and froze', thus blighting their later lives. (Two sons drank themselves prematurely to death; two daughters were eccentric misogynists.) But her eldest son adored her and was grief-stricken when she died, soon after his twenty-first birthday. (Something of her formidable personality can be deduced from the chilling instructions she left for her funeral: 'I wish that my body should not be consigned to the coffin till unequivocal marks of corruption have shown themselves; I wish to have no leaden coffin or leaden wrapping about the body, and nothing more expensive than a plain oak coffin. I wish to have no stone on my grave.'[3])

Young Arthur was delicate as a child. In this too he was lucky: it meant he was spared the worst excesses of Victorian public schools. He was never bullied, never beaten, and never experienced the sadism of nannies or schoolmasters which overshadowed the boyhood of so many of his contemporaries. On the contrary, he was treated with unusual kindness. His prep. school headmaster singled him out for special attention, while at Eton every allowance was made for him. His housemaster wrote to Lady Blanche, 'I have seen instances of men throwing themselves away at College by giving way to languor, and I am therefore very anxious that your son should do something worthy of his undoubtedly fine powers.'[4] (That languor was a lifelong characteristic, though behind its mask Balfour was always capable of intense hard work, once his attention was captured.) By the time he left school, the same housemaster was writing sycophantically, 'His tastes are so refined and his conversation so much more intellectual than that of most lads of his age, that I shall miss him as a companion.'[5] It would be wrong to detect a hint of homosexuality from this. Balfour's contemporaries often wrote disparagingly of his sexuality – Kipling calling him 'gelt' while Beaverbrook went further still and called him 'hermaphrodite', and Margot Tennant, who admired him, said characteristically, 'Shall I tell you what's wrong with Arthur? He's got no womb!' – yet there was never any suggestion that his sexual preference was for men. The problem rather was to find evidence of any sexual inclination at all. When his sister once urged him to marry he said, 'What have I got to offer anyone? Nothing but dust and ashes!'[6]

In 1866 the eighteen-year-old Arthur Balfour went up to Trinity College, Cambridge, to read the new school of Moral Sciences. At university he widened his circle of friends, and got to know two of the younger tutors well: both were eventually to become brothers-in-law. At Cambridge he discovered two things, philosophy and games, and both remained lifelong passions. The games he liked best were tennis – 'court' tennis, as it was then called; 'real' or 'royal' tennis we call it now – and golf. In philosophy he shared the obsession that troubled many Victorian thinkers: the attempt to reconcile religion and science. He was tempted, in spite of his disappointment at only getting a Second in Tripos, to make philosophy his career; but he was dissuaded. Financially, it hardly mattered what he did, for in 1869, just after leaving Cambridge, he came into his inheritance. It included two Scottish estates, at Whittingehame and Strathconan, and a fortune of roughly a million pounds.* Arthur Balfour was never likely to need to work to earn his living. But he was mildly concerned about what to do next:

I have little of interest to relate about my doings in these years which immediately succeeded the attainment of my majority. I saw something of London society; I heard a great deal of music; I played [court] tennis at Lord's with much enjoyment and some improvement; I invited friends to Whittingehame; I visited them in country houses; I travelled; in short, I did the sort of things that other young men do whose energies are not absorbed in learning or practising their chosen profession . . . schemes involving other forms of activity floated lazily through my mind. History? Essay writing? Politics? All had their attractions. Which should I select? . . . If a political career was to be seriously entered upon, a seat in the House of Commons was a necessity, and this required a constituency willing to elect me. Where was this constituency to be found? . . . Moreover, my political ambitions were cool, so that, all things considered, I was well content to let things slide.[7]

In 1870 the young graduate, by now a wealthy bachelor and much in demand, bought himself a London house at 4 Carlton Gardens. It happened to be a few doors away from the home of W. E. Gladstone, the Liberal Prime Minister and uncle to his great friends, the Lytteltons. It was not long before Balfour was visiting the Gladstones regularly for musical and social evenings, at which Gladstone's good-looking daughter Mary fell in love with Arthur; a love that was entirely unrequited. In the early 1870s Mary's diary records evening after

*The money alone would be worth roughly £24.5 million at today's value.

evening spent at concerts. Not the two of them alone, of course: they were invariably accompanied by a Lyttelton or a Balfour brother, or even two, and, towards the end of 1870, by a Lyttelton sister – May. Next, Arthur began to be invited to the Lytteltons' great country house at Hagley, and to the Gladstones' home, Hawarden. Here, and in London, he encountered May Lyttelton often. She was two years younger than he, not beautiful but pretty and interesting to look at, with an oval face, high cheekbones and dark, heavy-lidded eyes. Her expression was demure, but she had a strong intelligence and a forceful nature, like most of the unconventional, high-spirited Lytteltons. Balfour fell in love.

At this stage his closest friends formed the other group – apart from the Tennant sisters and their Oxford friends – that was, a decade later, to become the nucleus of the Souls. Already he had acquired the nickname 'King Arthur' – Mary Gladstone calls him that in her diary as early as 1871 – and already he was a little apart from his contemporaries. May Lyttelton was to provide the first real setback he had encountered. She and Balfour were beginning to meet more often, and she perhaps just beginning to return his interest, when in June 1872 she met a young Cambridge undergraduate of raffish good looks and reputation: Rutherford Graham, the brother of Frances. Arthur Balfour was supplanted and May, to the despair of her family, fell in love with this much less suitable young man. Victorian families could exert a good deal of pressure, especially upon a girl aged just twenty, and May was persuaded to turn down his first two proposals of marriage. But she was not prepared to stop seeing him altogether. In the end a compromise was reached: the family insisted that young Rutherford should accept a year's separation before proposing again. He planned a voyage to America, but in October 1872, at Liverpool, he died of diphtheria.

May was distraught, and disinclined to be consoled by the still attentive Balfour. For a year she remained listless and depressed. But gradually the activities of her large and happy family distracted her, and by the autumn of 1873 she and Balfour were once again seeing each other regularly. A year later, in December 1874, he proposed to her secretly, and she, also secretly, accepted. Balfour's autobiography makes no mention of this; but her family and his friends believed it to be so. What *is* certain is that, just three months later, May herself died of typhoid fever.

Coming less than three years after the death of his beloved mother, this second bereavement plunged Balfour into anguish and gloom. He was too distressed to enter the church for May's funeral – or perhaps afraid that he would give way publicly to his emotion – though he gave her brother, Edward, a sapphire ring that had belonged to his mother and asked him to put it in May's coffin. After the funeral he said to Edward, 'in greatest agitation, "I was to have made her my wife." '[8]

Instead of love, Balfour began to find emotional security in a number of warm and supportive friendships; and his friends seem to have been honoured to fulfil this need. None ever questioned that he stood supreme in their group. Only he had the intellectual depth and originality to have written two books of philosophy; his charm – though we have to take their word for it – was unrivalled; his appearance and bearing were exquisitely refined, as many portraits and photographs show; while his wit, in a circle of famously witty people, stood out for its adroitness and originality. Mary Gladstone, who mentions him constantly in her diary during the 1870s, recalls over and over again how, when he was there, the company 'laughed immoderately', was 'uproarious', or 'overpowered by laughter, as usual'.

Wit is often dependent for its effect on a lightning response, a tone of voice, or the facial expression that accompanies it. Such of Balfour's remarks that were recorded often sound merely waspish or arrogant: as when he said of a colleague, 'If he had a little more brains he would be a half-wit';[9] though one can still enjoy his exchange with Frank Harris, who turned to him at dinner one evening and said, 'The fact is, Mr Balfour, all the faults of the age come from Christianity and journalism,' to which Balfour replied with rapier quickness, 'Christianity of course: but why journalism?'[10] His autobiography, written just before his eightieth birthday and never completed beyond the first few chapters, is dry, occasionally wordy, but still humorous. Perhaps the closest one can get to recapturing the wit that enchanted his friends is in a letter he wrote to the young Winston Churchill, rebuking him gently for a certain lack of party loyalty. Some eighty years after it was written, this letter can still make one laugh out loud. It was prompted by a query from Winston Churchill to his leader, whether, as a report in the *Daily Telegraph* seemed to indicate, he was about to have the whip withdrawn. No, said Balfour, the report had been in error. He went on:

> However the mistake was not without some plausible justification. A hasty reading, for example, of such a phrase as 'Thank God, we have an Opposition', which occurs, I think, in one of your speeches, is apt to lead to misunderstanding. It was rashly interpreted by some as meaning that the policy of the country would be safer in the hands of the Opposition rather than in the Government's, a meaning clearly inconsistent with Party loyalty. Obviously, it is equally capable of a quite innocent construction. It might, for example, be a pious recognition of the fact that our heaviest trials are sometimes for our good. Or, again, it might mean that a world in which everybody was agreed would be an exceedingly tedious one; or, that an effective Opposition made the Party loyalty burn more brightly.
>
> There are, in short, countless interpretations, quite consistent with the position I understand to be yours, namely that of a loyal though independent supporter of the present administration.[11]

Thirty years before this letter was written, Arthur Balfour's political career began: though so inconspicuously that few people, except perhaps the uncle who engineered it, could have taken any notice. In January 1874 he was elected unopposed as Tory MP for Hertford. Bordering on the estates of Hatfield – his uncle's – and Panshanger, where the hospitable Lord Cowper entertained, it was convenient for a young man not disposed to take politics too seriously. He hated canvassing and public speaking, and when, over two years later, Lord Salisbury intimated that it was, perhaps, time that he broke his parliamentary silence, Balfour bent his energies towards finding the subject least likely to attract attention to a maiden speaker. He wrote in his autobiography:

> The surest and most dignified expedient was to select as my theme a question undeniably important, but intrinsically dull; perhaps with a technical side, and in any case recalcitrant to rhetorical treatment. . . . Even these precautions did not content me. In order to complete the story, let me add that my chosen theme was Indian silver currency, and my chosen hour was about

eight o'clock. The reader least experienced in House of Commons habits will
realize that in these conditions I enjoyed to the fullest extent the advantages
of speaking in a silent and friendly solitude.[12]

Even this modest step into the limelight was enough for Lord Salisbury, who
in 1878 took his nephew, by now aged thirty and still almost totally unknown
outside the drawing-rooms of London and the better country houses, with him
to act as his private secretary at the Congress of Berlin. There, he met Bismarck,
to whom he had to confess that he was not, alas, a descendant of the Balfour of
Burleigh who featured in Sir Walter Scott's *Old Mortality*: and this is almost the
only incident he sees fit to record from that historic occasion.

Yet suddenly, two years later, everything changed. After a leisurely, not to say
lackadaisical, start in politics, Balfour's ambition was fired. From 1880 he
determined to reach high political office. The event that caused this *volte-face* was
the illness and political eclipse of Disraeli. Balfour looked around the Conservative party and saw that there was a vacuum at the top – and one that he himself
had every chance of filling.

By 1880 he had played a lot of tennis, listened to a lot of music, published (to
small acclaim) his first book, *A Defence of Philosophic Doubt*, and commissioned a
group of paintings from Burne-Jones on the theme of the Perseus legend, with
which to decorate the walls of his London drawing-room. Then, in April 1880,
Disraeli's government fell, and a year later the great statesman and favourite of
Queen Victoria was dead. Gladstone was back in power, and although Balfour
held on to his seat at Hertford, it was with a greatly reduced majority. Parliament
entered upon a decade dominated by the Irish question and by the personality of
Mr Gladstone: in the House of Commons, a whale among minnows. For Balfour,
the situation was ideal. In Opposition he could develop his powers as a
parliamentary debater and lay the foundation for his claims to advancement. He
was thirty-two; and from now on his apparent detachment was only a pose –
though one which still deceived many, even among his friends. He became
ruthlessly ambitious, discovering the lure of power with the same inner hunger
with which Laura Tennant, at the same time, was discovering the force of sexual
passion. And just as a well-brought-up young lady, a century ago, would have
thought it most improper to reveal her enjoyment of erotic pleasure, so too
Balfour thought it ungentlemanly to display a lust for power. W. E. Gladstone
was one of the few to discern it. He had always liked Balfour, although they
belonged to different political parties, and in 1882 described him as 'a young man
of great ability and character, a high and the best type of English gentleman, in
my opinion the future leader of the Tory party'.[13]

The other candidate for the leadership – and much less reticent about it – was
the brilliant but unreliable demagogue, Randolph Churchill; and in the summer
of 1880 he and Balfour joined together with two older MPs to form the Fourth
Party. Its aim was to harass and discredit an ageing Opposition leader in a
Parliament dominated by a strong Prime Minister with a large majority. In the
1880s, that Opposition leader was Sir Stafford Northcote. The real weight of the
Conservative party sat in the House of Lords, leaving only a feeble Opposition in
the Commons, with a dispirited front bench led by the weak and deferential
Northcote: no match for Gladstone at the height of his powers.

Into this one-sided contest came Balfour and his associates in the Fourth Party. They were everywhere at once. They spoke constantly; asked questions; raised objections; pricked and stung and refused to behave like docile backbenchers. But malicious relish turned into something more after the death of Disraeli in April 1881, when the struggle for position was out in the open. The two contestants were Balfour and Churchill, and Balfour's elegant fencing could no longer disguise the seriousness of the duel. He wrote in his autobiography:

> Before Dizzy's death we were four men who had no personal ambitions beyond the ordinary ones of wanting to get on and make our mark in Parliament. It was quite easy to work together. . . . But as soon as the question of Party leadership became a practical one, a second phase set in. Randolph himself realized what my attitude would be, and never expected me to act differently from the way I did.[14]

The two men were almost exactly the same age, contemporaries at Eton, born into great political families, and leaders of society. Randolph and his smoulderingly lovely wife Jennie had been prominent in the Marlborough House Set until Randolph fell from favour over the Aylesford divorce. In the country he was already well known and popular; in Parliament he was – at least to begin with – a far more compelling speaker than Balfour. At the start it must have looked as though all the odds were stacked in Randolph's favour. Balfour was handicapped politically by having to be at least outwardly loyal to his uncle, Lord Salisbury – which meant to his party, and thus to the ineffectual Northcote. This blunted his foils: though on one occasion he managed nevertheless to deliver an attack which, without ever mentioning the leader by name, left no one in any doubt as to his target.

Even as early as 1881 Balfour was probably shrewd enough to realize that, given enough rope, the reckless Churchill would eventually hang himself. 'We should avoid', he wrote confidentially to his uncle, 'as far as possible all rows until Randolph puts himself entirely and flagrantly in the wrong by some act of party disloyalty which everybody can understand and nobody can deny.'[15] Even Balfour could scarcely have guessed that Randolph's meteoric rise to power would be ended by a progressive deterioration of mind and judgment caused by tertiary syphilis. That was not until 1894, however; though as early as 1886 Randolph himself, by resigning once too often, had effectively put an end to his hopes of the highest office.

In June 1885 Gladstone was defeated by 12 votes over the budget, and the Queen asked Salisbury – not Northcote – to form an administration. The members of the Fourth Party who had been so prominent in securing the fall of the Grand Old Man were all offered ministerial jobs. Balfour was given the relatively lowly post of President of the Local Government Board. But his real value was to act as Salisbury's eyes and ears.

Ireland was fast becoming the storm centre of British politics, though the spectre of Home Rule had not yet begun to haunt party allegiances; but by late 1885 Gladstone had secretly been converted to the belief that it was the one hope for peace in Ireland. In order to pass the necessary measures through Parliament, there would have to be a coalition. Gladstone needed to make a clandestine approach to Salisbury; and he chose to do so at a country house weekend, through the medium of Arthur Balfour. Salisbury himself had been placed in an invidious position by the election of November 1885 which returned 335 Liberals under Gladstone, exactly balanced by Salisbury's 249 Conservatives *and* the 86 followers of Parnell. Gladstone was correct in assuming that Salisbury wanted a solution to the Irish question, but wrong in believing that he would risk splitting his own party to bring in Home Rule. But in that weekend conversation, Gladstone warned Balfour that unofficial soundings had convinced him that the fanatical Home Rulers would bring violence over from Ireland to England if their demands were not conceded. Balfour's record of the conversation goes on, ' "In other words", I said to Mr Gladstone, "we are to be blown up and stabbed if we do not grant Home Rule by the end of next session." "I understand," answered Mr Gladstone, "that the time is shorter than that." '[16] In fact events moved too quickly. In January 1886 Salisbury was defeated by 79 votes (on a quite different issue) and resigned. His nephew's brief taste of power was over: for a time.

In the meantime Balfour had not been neglecting his social life. In 1879, in the studio of Sir Frederick Leighton, he met the famously bohemian Mrs Percy Wyndham. With her was her daughter Mary, then aged eighteen. In 1881, probably through their mutual friend Mary Gladstone, Balfour met the seventeen-year-old Margot Tennant, newly arrived in London. Those meetings, and those two young women, were to shape his private life for the next forty years. With Mary Wyndham he came closer to love than with any woman since May; while through the Tennant sisters he met the rest of that charmed circle who came together after Laura's death, and called themselves 'The Gang', but whom the rest of society knew as the Souls.

Almost half a century later Balfour wrote in his autobiography:

> To me the name of 'Souls' seemed always meaningless and slightly ludicrous. It seems to imply some kind of organisation and purpose, where no organisation and purpose was dreamed of. It seems to suggest a process of selection, possibly even of rejection, by a group which, in so far as it had any separate existence, was a spontaneous and natural growth, born of casual friendship and unpremeditated sympathy. . . . I spent most of my time in country houses visiting my friends, and it was the society of these country houses which in no small degree gave colour to my life.[17]

Colour indeed! The Souls provided something which had up till now been lacking in Victorian society – a *jeunesse dorée*; a gilded, golden, gay young set, sparkling with intelligence, energy and enjoyment of life. Until the Souls coalesced around the Tennants, Arthur Balfour and the Lytteltons, young people in Victorian society were expected to be docile, coy and sweetly accomplished (if women); or arrogant, extravagant libertines (if men); and hence they were often insipid and dull in company. Somehow they got married, usually due to the machinations of their parents, after which they were more than ever subject to rigid social conventions. The Souls, on the other hand, lit up the sombre draperies of Victorian drawing-rooms much as the Impressionists were pouring sunlight through the Paris art world. They were gifted with a lightness of touch that made everyone else seem heavy by comparison. Something of their self-mocking frivolity can be gathered from their nickname for Balfour.

He had been known as King Arthur for years. But they called him 'The Adored Gazelle'!

Balfour mentions by name several of the Souls' country houses, beginning the list dutifully with his uncle's ancestral home of Hatfield. He goes on with an evocative litany of some of the loveliest English country houses, old red brick or golden Cotswold stone, resplendent among long green lawns and avenues of trees, a perfect setting for the clever antics of a privileged circle: 'Panshanger and Wrest, Latimer, Taplow, Cliveden, Wilton and Ashridge'. The longest description is given to Stanway, ancestral home of Lord Wemyss: 'In every characteristic, an English manor-house of the best period. The house, with its Inigo Jones gate-house and facade, and beautiful hall with windows filled with original glass, is unspoilt by modern changes. Behind it the gardens slope upwards towards the Cotswolds, from which are seen the valleys of the Severn and the Avon, the Malvern Hills, and beyond them all, the hills of Wales.'[18] The present Lord Wemyss, he notes, 'married Miss Wyndham, who was our hostess during many memorable visits. In my memory Stanway was associated through many years with a group of friends who have perhaps found a place in English social history.'[19] This, with characteristic reticence, is all the mention Balfour gives in his autobiography to the woman who loved him with passion for half a century.

Yet when he first met Mary Wyndham at the beginning of the 1880s they were both single; their relationship was looked on with approval by their families and friends; there was no apparent reason why they should not have married. Certainly Mary hoped for it very much. She was then not quite twenty and already a beauty, with large dark eyes, very wide open, and high curved brows, her mother's full, sweet-tempered mouth, and a sumptuous figure. She was famous all her life for her vagueness, which people found charming rather than annoying; for her inconsequential way of talking; and for her unselfconscious-ness – rare indeed in an age when women dressed and moved as stiffly as dolls. Her daughter, Lady Mary, recalls travelling with her: 'We were on a train from Stanway to Paddington and she was writing a letter – she was a great letter-writer. At the end of the journey she hadn't quite finished it, so she got out of the carriage, knelt down on the station platform, and finished the letter like that! She was completely unselfconscious.'

Mary inherited her looks from her mother, and from Madeline Wyndham too came an unconventional manner of dressing – they both loved soft, loosely draped clothes in rich Renaissance colours – and a wide circle of artist friends.

Mary was very greatly loved and admired within her circle, and yet for most of her adult life she maintained what must have been a frustrating, because almost certainly unconsummated, love affair with Arthur Balfour. Why did he not marry her when they were both free? In 1896 she said in a miserable letter, 'If only you had married me in '81'[20] – suggesting that marriage was at least discussed. Long afterwards, remembering that time, Mary wrote: 'Mama wanted you to marry me . . . you got some silly notion in your head because circumstances threw Hugo and me together and accidentally kept us apart – you were the only man I wanted for my husband and it's a great compliment to you! (for many wanted me to wife!) but you wouldn't give me a chance of showing you nicely and you never came to Wilbury and you were afraid, afraid, afraid!'[21] In the same letter (which she sent him on St Valentine's Day, 1905) Mary wrote that she was 'too proud and shy and wanted as much luring as Beatrice and [you were] too busy and capricious.'

Meanwhile Hugo – Lord Elcho, heir to the Earl of Wemyss – was a more assiduous suitor, and no less eligible. In 1883, urged by her mother, Mary finally consented to marry him. He was her exact opposite. He hated big house parties and company; suffered from deep depressions and black silences; and was a gambler and a philanderer who created a series of financial crises for the family. Lord Chandos, the only son of Alfred Lyttelton, told the whole story in 1968: 'Lord Elcho had early in life got into some financial scrape by speculating on the Stock Exchange. After the account had been settled he had been disinherited, though not cut off with the proverbial shilling. A trust fund of £100,000 had been formed for his benefit, and the income from it was intended to keep him from positive destitution.'[22] Arthur Balfour was one of the three trustees appointed to administer this fund – which must, at moments, have been galling for Lord Elcho – and the money it brought in would, at today's prices, have produced an income of between £27,000 and £40,000 a year. Since Lord Elcho's love of gambling was lifelong, as was his wife's generous hospitality, this income may have seemed inadequate until the Earl of Wemyss finally died in 1914, aged ninety-six, and his heir no longer had to live on the edge of 'positive destitution'.

Mary Elcho makes it clear that she didn't marry for love, and her husband's gambling and his frequent infidelities soon drove her to seek out the company of her earlier admirer. Laura Lyttelton wrote to Frances Balfour about it:

> She likes him – he fascinates her – her attitude is that of looking up in wonder – not of standing on the same ground with him and piercing him with her understanding. Her weapons are weaponless worship . . . she feels she *must* not disappoint him – she is at the top of her bent with him: she tries to look her best with him. She listens to him and he is not strong enough to withstand the easy delights of constantly pleasing and never annoying, jarring or disappointing her.
>
> What Arthur should do is very easy to see. He should deny himself the gratification of the luxury – but few men make extra commandments for themselves.[23]

Mary Elcho was then twenty-four. She had been married for two years, had already given birth to one son, Hugo, and was expecting a second child. Yet there is little doubt, judging from Laura's letter, that she was once again in love with Balfour – if indeed she had ever stopped – and that he tolerated, and more than tolerated, her love.

When Laura died in childbirth Balfour was heartbroken. He seems to have looked to Mary for comfort; somehow she seems to have been unable to give it. She wrote to him a fortnight later:

> I would do anything for you. I long to be able to do anything that would in a little way lessen the awful blank that the loss of such a friend as Laura leaves: I feel and know I am dumb and awkward – not a friend though with all the will, but a miserable makeshift of a friend but if you could really know my thoughts 'hard' would be the very last word you could apply . . . you must forgive me.[24]

As well as the deep grief he felt himself, Balfour, as a close friend, must have seen much of the tragically bereaved Alfred, Laura's husband. Once again he learnt the bitter lesson, that love brings pain. He was no doubt flattered by Mary Elcho's devotion. He was genuinely fond of her. She probably also acted as a shield against the attentions of other, unmarried, women, not averse to marrying a rising young politician with a large fortune. But he would not commit himself, either emotionally or sexually, to Mary Elcho or anyone else.

In July 1886 Salisbury's government was returned to power again, this time with a huge majority over the Liberals; and Balfour spent his thirty-eighth birthday alone in a hotel room in Great Malvern, where he had gone to play golf after the rigours of the election campaign. He was now the MP for East Manchester – a safer, as well as more prestigious, power base than Hertford – yet was evidently still not entirely confident about his political future. He would not be seen as a vulgar place hunter; his pride, as well as consideration for his uncle, Lord Salisbury, the new Prime Minister, made sure of that. And for all his dazzling social success, he was still uncertain whether he was destined for high political office.

Then, on 5 March 1887, Balfour was appointed Chief Secretary for Ireland: the greatest minefield, then as now, in British politics. The public reaction was outrage and disbelief. First the Irish: 'We have killed Forster, we have blinded Beach,' they said, referring to his immediate predecessors. 'What shall we do with Balfour?'[25] Hardly anyone – perhaps not even Salisbury; certainly not Balfour himself – suspected that the job would be the making of him. 'The history of Irish Secretaries since 1880', Balfour had remarked mildly, 'is not wholly encouraging.'[26]

Yet for the next four years his policies in Ireland proved outstandingly effective, while his performances in the House of Commons were the high point of that Parliament, as with ineffable logic he baited and maddened the Irish MPs without ever once losing his composure, even when they crossed the floor to shake their fists in his face. Sleepily, sarcastically, mercilessly, he destroyed their rhetoric and exposed their weaknesses.

Balfour was fortunate that Salisbury's declared policy for Ireland agreed perfectly with his own opinion. Balfour's temperament and his political philosophy were governed by the fear that if the vigilance of the law was relaxed, or the grip of morality and ethics loosened, the result would quickly be anarchy. Take away the structure, and the individuals will collapse into chaos. That structure Balfour called authority, and it was central to his political creed that authority had to be maintained at all costs. He ridiculed Randolph Churchill's ideal of Tory democracy, for in his view, since people were fundamentally selfish and seeking only their own advantage, the notion of democracy must be a chimera; a fallacy; a contradiction in terms. Perhaps Balfour was aware that his own class embodied more perfectly than any other the evidence for his belief in the selfishness of man. Perhaps he saw that the maintenance of the social order was in fact directed at maintaining their own privileged position within it. He never gave any sign that his own great estates and wealth were not his by any moral or natural *right*, though he did understand that certain obligations went with them: the duty to be a just landlord, for example.

These beliefs governed the policies he intended to carry out in Ireland. While the Irish Nationalists who broke the law would receive no mercy, he would at the same time bring in legislation to try and put an end to the system of exploitation whereby absentee English landlords demanded higher and higher rents from their hapless Irish tenants, and carried out ruthless evictions when the peasants were unable to pay: 'I shall be as relentless as Cromwell in enforcing obedience to the law, but at the same time I shall be as radical as any reformer in redressing grievances and especially in removing every cause of complaint in regard to the land.'[27]

When Balfour was appointed to the Irish post in 1887 he had entrusted his sister-in-law, Lady Frances Balfour, with a letter and a small leather pouch. The letter said:

> My dear Frances,
> Accidents have occurred to a Chief Secretary for Ireland and (although I think it improbable) they may occur again. If the worst (as people euphemistically say!) should happen, cut open with your penknife the accompanying pouch and read the scrawl inside. It relates to a matter with which only you can deal – but leaves unsaid through want of time all the things I would have said to you and all the other dear ones whom (in the highly improbable event above alluded to) I should leave behind.[28]

Although of course he did return safely from Ireland, Lady Frances kept both the letter and the small leather pouch, and in April 1930, after Balfour's death, she and Mary Elcho opened the pouch together. Inside they found a letter, which they read, over forty years after it had been written, and a small diamond brooch. Mary kept them both. It was possibly the closest Balfour ever came to expressing his love for her, and the central position she occupied in his life:

> My dear Frances,
> I write this in a great hurry: but as you will only have to read it in the event of my death you will forgive my handwriting. I think you and all whom I love will be sorry that I am not any longer with you. But you will be able to talk it freely over with each other and all whom such an event may concern. There is however one who will not be in this position. I want you to give her as from yourself this little brooch which you will find herewith: and to tell her that, at the end, if I was able to think at all, I thought of her. If I was the means of introducing any unhappiness into her life I hope God will forgive me. I know she will.[29]

'At the end, if I was able to think at all, I thought of her.' Even when uttering words to be read beyond the grave, Arthur Balfour could not relax the control that held his emotions in check. Even then, he cannot mention her name, or declare that he loved her. She is not even supposed to know that the brooch was his last gift.

The new Irish Secretary's nerve was first tested at Mitchelstown in September 1887, when two Radical Irish MPs harangued the local people and urged them not to tolerate evictions. A riot ensued, and the police fired on the crowd. Three rioters were killed. A measure of the fury this unleashed can be deduced from the fact that fifty-four policemen were injured. (There is no figure for injuries among the crowd.) The police were not proceeded against, for as Balfour said in the House: 'When an attack of that kind is made, are the police, who are men, to be said to have exceeded their duty when they resort to what should be resorted to only in the last necessity, but which, when the last necessity occurs, no officer should shrink from using?'[30] It was the appeal to authority, one of his highest principles; and – though perhaps few people understood the depth of philosophic conviction underlying it – Balfour's actions were the making of him.

From now on the Irish called him Bloody Balfour and chanted 'Remember Mitchelstown!' The agitation moved to London and at a mass protest meeting in Trafalgar Square two people died and a hundred more were injured. That was on 13 November: the first 'Bloody Sunday'. Yet in Ireland police and officials were profoundly impressed by the Secretary of State's evident determination to support them on matters of law and order. Edward Carson, then an unknown junior barrister, said, 'After that there wasn't an official in Ireland who didn't worship the ground he walked on. . . . It was Mitchelstown that made us certain we had a man at last.'[31] The Irish, on the other hand, hated him with passion. Balfour was slow to realize this, and asked a priest one day if it really were true. 'My dear sir,' answered Father Healey, 'if they only hated the Devil half as much as they hate you my occupation would be gone entirely.'[32]

Even in such turbulent times Balfour's life was not all politics. In September 1887, just a week before Mitchelstown, he was one of the guests at a country house party at Clouds, near Salisbury in Wiltshire, given by Mrs Percy Wyndham – Mary's mother. Clouds, large, light and airy, had been completed just two years before. Philip Webb was the architect, and much of the interior plaster-work and decoration had been carried out by Madeline Wyndham's two great friends and protégés, Edward Burne-Jones and William Morris. The result was a spacious, beautiful house, a haven of comfort and relaxation for Balfour.

This particular occasion was a typical Souls weekend, a literary as well as a family gathering. Mary Elcho was there, heavily pregnant with her third child, along with her younger sister Pamela, then aged sixteen, and her brother George, who was Balfour's private secretary in Ireland. He was a poet, a romantic and soulfully good-looking man who had just married the most desirable young widow in London, Sibell, Lady Grosvenor. Also in the party were Sybil, Marchioness of Queensberry – another relative – with her young son, Lord Alfred Douglas, and Wilfrid Scawen Blunt, cousin to his host, with his wife and daughter. Some twenty-seven years earlier, in Paris, Blunt had first fallen in love with Madeline Wyndham, and thirteen years later they had had a short-lived love affair, but remained platonically good friends afterwards. Balfour arrived a day or two later than the others, bringing with him the novelist Henry James to complete the party.

Wilfrid Scawen Blunt was a poet, a traveller, and a connoisseur of women and Arab horses. As well as that he was an ardent Irish Nationalist. During the previous year he had toured Ireland, wanting to get to know the situation at first hand (having first taken the precaution of asking Morley, secretary to the then Prime Minister Gladstone, not to have him imprisoned!) He travelled all over the country; witnessed with horror a number of forcible evictions; and by the end had found a new cause and made several enemies among wealthy landowners. On his return he prudently covered his own Achilles heel by reducing a number of rents for his own tenants on his large estate at Crabbet. ('It will not do to neglect the mote in my own eye while plucking the beam out of Lord Kingston's.')[33]

Clouds was a place of refuge for Blunt too, after his journeys in Arabia and his disturbing visit to Ireland. Set amid 2,000 rolling Wiltshire acres, it must have seemed like a haven of peace, a chance to catch up on news of the family – and to buttonhole Balfour, the current mainspring of the Irish troubles. The hot-headed partisan in him was shocked by Balfour's apparent detachment. Blunt wrote in his diary: 'Balfour is clever and light in hand, but with a certain hardness and cynicism which are not altogether pleasant . . . he is a man of considerable capacity and more backbone than what his "lackadaisical" appearance would suggest.'[34] But he admired Mary Elcho, calling her 'the cleverest, best and most beautiful woman in the world, with just that touch of human sympathy which brings her to the level of our sins'.[35] He could not help observing the relationship between the two, which was virtually common knowledge by then. Balfour had, Blunt thought, a *grande passion* for Mary – 'that is quite clear' – and she in turn had a *tendresse* for him. But not even the sexually omniscient Blunt could work out whether their love was physical as well: 'What their exact relations may be I cannot determine. Perhaps it is better not to be too wise, and as all the house accepts the position as the most natural in the world, there let us leave it.'[36]

The following afternoon the two men were opponents in a tennis doubles match (Wilfrid and his partner won) and that evening the encounter they must both have been waiting for finally took place. Blunt was sure of the inevitability of Home Rule; Balfour – to his opponent's surprise – agreed with him, differing only on how soon it would be. But Balfour declared, 'When it comes I shall not be sorry. Only let us have separation as well as Home Rule; England cannot afford to go on with Irishmen in her Parliament. She must govern herself, too.'[37] But Blunt was looking for trouble, and would not be placated. Later he convinced himself that Balfour had said harsh and repressive things about his intentions for Ireland, and he even came to believe that Balfour was determined to 'take the life out of' – literally or metaphorically – the Irish Nationalist MP John Dillon. 'I am sorry for Dillon,' Balfour had said, 'as if he gets into prison it is likely to kill him. He will have hard labour. . . . He is afraid of prison, and he is right, as it will probably kill him.'[38]

The following day, Monday, Balfour and George Wyndham left, and two weeks later Blunt was back on his rabble-rousing tour of the Irish countryside, inciting the Irish tenants to revolt against the undoubted injustices of their masters. He did not appeal to Balfour not to put him in prison; perhaps he thought there was an unwritten code between gentlemen who had been guests at the same country house party. If so, he was wrong. For on 23 October 1887, Blunt finally went too far.

A meeting had been summoned at Woodford, in Galway – a 'proclaimed' area, that is, one in which public meetings were banned. Blunt decided to challenge the authorities head-on, although he must have known that, by openly defying them, he gave them no choice but to imprison him. Taking his wife with him (Lady Anne, the granddaughter of Byron) he ignored the notice of proclamation, signed by both the Lord-Lieutenant of Ireland and by Arthur Balfour, as well as the ominous presence of 150 police. He attended mass, and then in front of an audience of about 200 he mounted a makeshift platform and began: 'Men of Galway!' He was pulled off by seven or eight men, despite his wife's attempts to impede them; arrested; and sentenced to two months in prison.

If Blunt had chosen this ostentatious martyrdom to discredit Balfour, he was misguided. If he hoped to make Balfour feel guilty he was wrong about that, too. Only his cousin, Balfour's private secretary, young George Wyndham, found himself in an embarrassing position. Balfour wrote to Mary Elcho, in the interval during which Blunt was out on bail, pending his appeal:

> We are trying to put your cousin in gaol. I have not heard whether we have succeeded. I hope so, for I am sure Blunt himself would be disappointed at any other consummation, though I should be sorry for Lady Anne who may not hold the same views about political martyrdom as her husband. He is a goodish poet and a goodish lawn tennis player and a goodish fellow. . . . George asked my advice as to whether he should write a sympathetic letter to Lady Anne. I advised him not. There are some condolences to which it is difficult not to give an air of sarcasm! But it must be admitted that there is a certain awkwardness in George's position.[39]

Two months later, at the beginning of 1888, the sentence was confirmed, and Lord Salisbury wrote approvingly, 'I was delighted to see you had run Wilfrid Blunt in. . . . The great heart of the people always chuckles when a gentleman gets into the law.'[40] Wilfrid hated prison, particularly the numbing boredom of it, and the equally numbing cold. He tried to cheer himself up by claiming to be afraid of being victimized by Balfour. The Secretary of State responded tersely, 'Ridiculous lie.' Afterwards, Blunt claimed that his spell of imprisonment had forced Balfour to mitigate the severity of his treatment of Irish political prisoners. But this was only an attempt to boost his own morale. The truth was that Blunt came out of the episode badly and Balfour did not. Even his cousin George thought 'Wilfrid is temporarily out of his senses';[41] while Balfour was seen to be impartial in his punishment of those who broke the law. It was several years before Blunt found the opportunity to take a peculiarly vicious revenge.

By August 1888 some twenty-one MPs from Parnell's Nationalist party had served prison sentences. The decline and fall of Parnell himself – the man who only a few years earlier had been the hero of Ireland and the scourge of Gladstone – was hastened by Balfour. Unlike Gladstone, he refused to have any dealings with Parnell, secret or otherwise. In October 1891, Parnell died, and with the Irish Nationalists now fragmented and leaderless, Balfour had virtually a free hand in introducing legislation to restore order and help the Irish, especially in the poorest districts. His last few months as Secretary of State were of almost uninterrupted triumph. But the four years had left their mark on him. Arthur Balfour was now forty-three, but he had aged suddenly, his face looked harder and older, his hair was beginning to turn grey, and instead of his former pince-nez he now wore spectacles. The hero of Parliament, 'The Adored Gazelle' of the Souls, had moved irrevocably into middle age.

In October 1891 Salisbury made his nephew Leader of the House – a job he held for the next twelve years. He had said when he became Secretary of State for Ireland that he would lose either his life or his reputation. He kept his head and made his reputation. Now his skills as a parliamentary tactician were to be tested. But in 1892 the Conservatives were defeated, and Gladstone took office for the last time.

By this time Balfour was in his mid-forties and Mary was thirty-one. In the first years of her marriage she gave birth to a child almost every year. Hugo (always known as 'Ego' because that was what, as a toddler, he called himself) was born in 1884; Guy in 1886; Cynthia in 1887; Colin (who died three years later) in 1889. Judging by their appearance, only one of these children could be said remotely to resemble Arthur Balfour, and that is Hugo; and although one can persuade oneself of a striking similarity, he – being the first – is of them all the child whom Balfour was least likely to have fathered. One cannot know about little Colin, who died too young for a likeness to emerge or have been rumoured. Slight as it is, however, the balance of the evidence does seem to suggest that the relationship between Balfour and Mary was platonic, despite being intense and long-lasting; in which case there must be a strong probability that Arthur Balfour lived and died a virgin. The only other woman, apart from May Lyttelton, for whom he felt more than a fleeting affection was Ettie Grenfell. This was known to Mary, and caused her much anguish. Her letters often refer, with painful jealousy, to 'Delilah', as she called the emotionally rapacious Ettie. On the other hand Ettie's own letters to Balfour never take on that note of sated complacency with which she addresses her hapless lovers, batting them about with an idle paw like so many half-dead mice. Past-mistress as she was in the art of emotional blackmail, Ettie never felt herself sufficiently in the ascendancy to try it with Balfour: which suggests that he kept her at arm's length, and that their relationship too was platonic.

Mary Elcho and Arthur seem to have made a pact to be true to one another, and he was probably so used to being the object of her adoration that it never occurred to him that she could be 'unfaithful'. Yet in August 1894, at a Stanway house party, she found herself alone for a moment with Wilfrid Scawen Blunt. In his diary that night Blunt wrote: 'By a sudden inspiration in the evening when we were once more alone I kissed Mary's hand. She turned pale, said nothing and went away to Arthur.'[42]

Blunt's relationship with Margot Tennant had shown – just two years previously – that he had no time for the long-drawn-out platonic minuets that sufficed some of the Souls women. Now the temptation to steal a march on his old enemy, Balfour, was irresistible. Blunt was fifty-four and, although he looked older, he was still reputed one of the handsomest men of his time. He was also certainly one of the most practised and unscrupulous of lovers. And he would have been intrigued, rather than deterred, by the thought of seducing the daughter of one of his earlier mistresses. Perhaps what made Blunt so successful with women was that his heart was easily captured; he was always ready to believe himself on the verge of the grand passion of his life. A year before Mary had told him casually how she envied his adventurous life in Egypt. Now, Blunt committed her to a firm promise to visit him there in the new year. Mary was thirty-two, her husband was blatantly unfaithful, and the man she loved refused her anything more than adolescent caresses.

She took with her to Egypt her three eldest children and their governess. Lord Elcho was detained at his mistress's bedside in Menton. (She, Hermione, Duchess of Leinster, was dying of tuberculosis, aged only thirty. Hugo was known to have fathered her son, and Mary convinced him that it was his duty to remain at her side in France.) Wilfrid laid siege to Mary, confident of his powers and willing to wait.

> She reminds me so much of her mother, whom I also loved thirty years ago. She has the same large-minded view of things and, when at last reserve is broken, the same sincerity. But her nature is a finer one, being without the worldly touch. She is an ideal woman for a lifelong passion and has the subtle charm for me, besides, of blood relationship. I was happy here before she came, but this is more than heaven.[43]

Her surrender took less than ten days. On 14 January 1895, a letter addressed to Balfour lying on the table beside her bed, Mary 'fulfilled his extremest hopes'.[44] Afterwards she felt mild remorse, though not – at this stage – extreme guilt, and the next few days were idyllic, as he read his poetry to her, and to please him she dressed in the flowing Arab garments he had given her and (in the manner of Hedda Gabler) wore vine leaves in her hair. They set off on Arab horses together to explore the desert, followed by the children (on donkeys) and the governess (on a camel). Mary at last divulged the precise nature of her relationship with Balfour. She may have been temporarily besotted with Wilfrid, and it may thus be a little less than the whole truth, but it is the clearest explanation we have.

> Though she and Hugo live affectionately together, it is not conjugally, this for the last six years. He goes his way; she had her friend. To him, her friend, Arthur Balfour, she is pledged far more than to Hugo. She loves, and honours and respects him, and he is constant to her, and she has always been constant to him, and she is bound to him by a thousand promises never to give herself to another. On this understanding he has been content that their love should be within certain limits – a little more than friendship a little less than love. She cannot desert him – and yet – and yet? I must be content with this.[45]

Mary said that her relationship with Balfour was only one of many such among the Souls: 'Nearly all of the group were married women with husbands whom they loved and by whom they had children, but each had her "friend", who was a friend only.'[46] In this she was perhaps not quite as typical as she imagined!

In February, accompanied by Blunt's wife Lady Anne and their daughter Judith, and by Mary's children and their governess, they all made an expedition far into the desert. At night, the women had tents in one part of the encampment; Blunt his own shelter a discreet distance away. There Mary came to him again: 'I think the Arabs with us knew that we were lovers – indeed they must have known it, for there were Mary's naked tell-tale footsteps each morning in the sand . . . Mary is now my true Bedouin wife.'[47] Evidently neither the thought of his true English wife, nor the risk that she, or any of their children, might also spot the 'tell-tale footsteps in the sand', disturbed Blunt's complacency. But already their idyll was being threatened. Mary had written to Arthur Balfour confessing something of what had happened, and by return of post received a letter back from him, bitterly accusing. Mary's guilt on behalf of her friend was now compounded by the arrival of her husband, tired of waiting for his mistress to die. A few days before Lord Elcho's arrival, Mary had told Blunt that she was almost certainly pregnant.

Wilfrid – who hoped for a son – was overjoyed. The presence of Lord Elcho was less pleasing. 'When I came out this morning before sunrise to the tent I found his Christian hat in it where he had left it yesterday, and it moved me to anger. I feel that she has brought a stranger into my tent, she who was my Bedouin wife, and that when I get her once more into the desert I shall cut off her head.'[48] Blunt's emotions could be impelled easily into melodrama; but for Mary the consequences were real. There was a second trip into the desert, this time with the usual retinue of wife, children and servants supplemented by Lord Elcho. Blunt noted proprietorially, 'I would not allow Mary to share her tent with Hugo, as that would not have been proper, Suleyman and all the Arabs know that she is my Bedouin wife and I would not hear of it. So . . . I slept under a bush a little apart, where Mary could come to me as in the night of the honeymoon.'[49]

Nothing else is quite so unattractive as this, Blunt's insistence on not losing face in front of his Arab servants. The feelings of his wife and child – of Mary's husband and her children – are of less importance than the risk that his Arab servants might think he had been supplanted. Mary had begged him to allow her to return to Hugo's bed, to give the semblance of legitimacy to the coming child. 'She will not', expostulated Wilfrid in his diary, 'give up her husband or her children or her friend.'[50]

For Blunt worse was to come. At the end of February Hugo returned to the bedside of his dying mistress, and after seeing him once more the Duchess did finally pass away. During this interval Mary and Wilfrid spent another passionate 'honeymoon' in the wild and uninhabited desert. Blunt had noted callously on a previous occasion five years earlier, when seducing another happily married woman, also a relative of his, 'Danger in love always acts with me as a physical stimulus, and passion is never so strong as when I am conscious of a tragedy approaching and hear its footsteps already in the next room.'[51] The time he spent with Mary must have fulfilled all his criteria: no wonder he was so pleased with himself! He had thoroughly smashed what he called 'the prurient platonism of the little sentimental clique [the Souls] she has lived in'.[52] But their time was almost up. When they returned from the desert, it was to find a telegram for Mary from Hugo: 'I am unhappy shall await you at home.' Mary had to explain to Wilfrid that she and her husband had long ago planned that once he was 'free' again they would have a conjugal reconciliation, with another child to seal their renewed relationship. Now, she had been summoned. The true English husband had asserted his rights and the Bedouin one was left 'sad, sad, sad these last four days past, sick and sorry of my life',[53] as his diary recorded after she had gone.

For Mary, the return to her former life brought deeper unhappiness. She confessed everything to Hugo, who wrote to Blunt (back in England, waiting impatiently for a love letter from Mary): 'You have wrecked the life and destroyed the happiness of a woman whom a spark of chivalry would have made you protect. She was thirty years younger than yourself. You had known her from childhood. She was your cousin and your guest. She was a happy woman when she went to Egypt, and her misery now would touch a heart of stone.'[54] Hugo could not have guessed that all the factors he listed were precisely those which made the seduction irresistible! Mary herself wrote, 'You did try and wreck my life and the only thing that prevents me being utterly angry with you is that I believe you *did care* for me in a way.'[55] And she told Blunt later, in a secret meeting a few weeks before the baby was born, that Hugo had said to her, 'If it had been Arthur I could have understood it, but I cannot understand it now. I forgive you but I shall be nasty to you.'[56] Balfour, on the other hand, had taken the news – though she did not tell him the whole story – with surprising calm. 'He was a little jealous about me at first but he does not suspect.'[57] And on another occasion she said, 'You know he is not like other men.'[58]

On 24 October 1895 the baby was born. 'For the moment I had an Arab pang of disappointment that it was not a boy,'[59] noted the incorrigible Blunt in his diary. He had hoped to name his son Zobeydeh, which would no doubt have pleased his Arab servants. As it was, the little girl was christened Mary, and she grew up to be the most beautiful of all the Elcho children, with lustrous dark eyes, black hair, and the same wide mouth and full lips that Blunt had kissed on her mother and her grandmother. Luckily for her, perhaps, she seldom saw her real father. The truth of her conception was ultimately unimportant, as in so many large families of the time. What mattered was that she grew up happy and loved. A year later the promised child of Mary and Hugo's reconciliation was born: Yvo, a blond son; and in 1902 the last child, this time a daughter, Irene. In between we catch a glimpse only – from one of her letters to Balfour – of Mary's harrowing efforts in 1898 to bring about a self-induced miscarriage. It was evidently successful.

Her love for Balfour never changed, and even after twenty years he had not lost any of his power to hurt her: though he did not do so intentionally but only by being unable to imagine how much she loved him, and therefore, how vulnerable she was. Mary wrote to him once, 'You are more patient – more reasonable (which very word I kick at!) in all things than I am (*of course* it is because you care less! *feel* less).'[60] But another time she was able to write more calmly:

> The thing I am most grateful for is that you do not humbug me or tell sham things to flatter me. We do treat each other more sensibly than that. . . . You know, I never want to know anything for the sake of knowing or to gratify a shallow vanity – but it is different and it's the most exquisite pleasure that I can have – that if you are worried about money, politics, enemies, friends or loves! I never want you to say anything you are not in the mood to say and I always respect you! Above all I should deplore anything that might spoil our relations which have worn for more than a dozen years.[61]

This was what Balfour preferred to hear. As his closest friend she fulfilled an important rôle in his life, and the one he perhaps missed most through not having a wife to whom he could confide the small details of everyday events. The emotional merry-go-round on which the rest of the Souls dipped and swung was not necessary to him.

Nevertheless, even 'The Adored Gazelle' was not immune to the occasional brief infatuation. One such occurred in 1901 with the lovely Mary Curzon, whose husband George was in India as Viceroy. Mary came to England for six months, partly to strengthen her husband's links with the administration, partly to report back to him. He had been away for three years, and he needed government support for his proposed reforms in India. Mary Curzon was much entertained at Souls house parties that summer, but as an outsider and an American who had come late to their circle, she was cool and objective in her appraisal of them. She once told George Curzon, 'I must say no more critical set exists in the world than the friends, as they are merciless to anyone who can't keep up in the race for pleasure. In my cynical moments I know in my heart that the great fuss they make of me is because I am a novelty, unjaded, and the last edition of Georgian news.'[62] Perhaps the women among the Souls, skilled at the elaborate steps whereby they changed partners according to what sometimes looked like pre-ordained formal patterns, feared the intrusion of this observer. Perhaps they sensed her detachment from the emotional cotillion they all trod, for Mary Curzon was genuinely singleminded in her love for her husband. But she gathered intelligence and gossip assiduously for him, and met Balfour a number of times.

Although on her arrival in England she had described him as 'wizened, worried and exhausted',[63] as time went on and she saw him more often, some kind of mutual fascination grew up. At the end of May they were both guests at one of Ettie Grenfell's weekends at Taplow. 'Oh dear,' wrote Curzon to his wife, 'it seems to me that you have fairly bowled over Master Arthur. However he is a tepid though delightful lover. So Pappy does not feel seriously afraid.'[64]

A month later Mary Curzon and Balfour found themselves guests at Wilton, the Pembrokes' home in Wiltshire. It too was one of the main Souls meeting places, and thirty years earlier had boasted an exclusive club, called the 'Wagger', which had been the origin of Blunt's Crabbet Club. Lady Pembroke, the hostess, was a genuine English eccentric. Daughter of the 20th Earl of Shrewsbury, she had red hair (which in middle age she supplemented with hair taken from one of her footmen), a loud voice and a formidable personality, and wore three strings of pearls around her neck at all times, even when fishing in Scotland in a heavy jersey! Known among the Souls as one of the Aunts (the nickname given to the slightly older generation of Souls hostesses) she was overpowering but much loved and immensely hospitable. Her husband, the 13th Earl of Pembroke, was described by the susceptible Margot as being – along with Blunt – one of the handsomest of the Souls. He had also been – like Alfred Lyttelton – a man who combined outstanding intellect with great sporting abilities. But he was cursed, as were so many of his contemporaries, with the then incurable tuberculosis, and he had died in 1895, aged only forty-five.

During that Wilton weekend Mary Elcho invited Mary Curzon – who was seven years younger – to come to her room for a private talk. Mary recounted the conversation in a letter to George in India: ' "I suppose you know Arthur is very fond of you," she said. I said, "I don't think he is at all. I am only in the *galère* with his other friends, and after all, you Mary, are the only one that matters with AJB in the least." "No," says she, "I know when he is interested, and he loves being with you." '[65] This was probably true. Mary Curzon described Balfour a month later: 'When the sun shines and women smile, he is a picturesque, rare, enchanting creature',[66] and he in turn called her 'intoxicating, delicious and clever'.[67] Mary Elcho had not failed to observe their mutual attraction: and it caused her agony. Mary Curzon described to her husband an incident which reveals the depth of Lady Elcho's passion.

Balfour had asked both Marys to lunch with him. She wrote to George:

Well, at 2 I went to Willis's. There was Arthur – no Mary – so we sat on a sofa to wait for her . . . 2.10 came, and no Mary. So he said, 'Let's begin', and we did, and got all through lunch and forgot Mary, Arthur saying from time to time, 'I love this *tête-à-tête*, but it was unexpected.'

After coffee, I said, 'I am worried about Mary, and I shall go to Cadogan Square to see what has happened to her.' So he said, 'Very well, we shall go together', so off we went to 62 Cadogan Square. Once there, we asked for her, and the footman went off to fetch her, while we waited in the library. Suddenly Mary appeared, wild-haired in a *filthy* dressing-gown, and for two seconds we all stood quite still. Then Arthur said, 'Well, why didn't you come?' 'Come where?' said Mary. 'To lunch,' said A. 'You never asked me,' cried Mary, and hurled herself on the sofa. Arthur said, 'You must be mad.' Then Mary said, 'Don't you think I would have come if I had thought you wanted me? Would I miss an hour when I could be with you? I have suffered agonies to think you didn't want me, and you had promised to lunch alone with me.' A. said, 'I am dazed. All was arranged, and time settled, and as you didn't come, Lady Curzon and I came to see if you were ill.' I said, seeing her on the verge of tears, 'It was all a mistake. I must fly away. I will take your hansom, Mr Balfour, and you can get another.' Arthur was quite stern and cold with his poor trembling wild Mary, and he said, 'Yes, I will go back to the House directly, but let me understand clearly [with a smile] that you and I meet for dinner tonight at the House of Commons.' I hope for Mary's sake that she flew into his arms and repented. . . .[68]

It seems far from obvious that it was Mary Elcho who should have repented. The episode, told in such revealing detail, seems to show a wilfully cruel side to Balfour's nature – at least, where Mary Elcho was concerned – especially that final smile.

The decade of the 1890s may have seen little change in Arthur Balfour's emotional life (such as it was), but for his political career these were the crucial years. He was in his mid-forties and rising fast towards the very pinnacle of power. As he had predicted in 1880, there was no heir-apparent for the leadership of the Conservative party. A decade later, with his uncle Lord Salisbury well into his sixties, it had become automatic to assume that Balfour would be his successor. Although he would not stoop to endearing himself to his fellow MPs in his new rôle as Leader of the House, he did at least try not to alienate them. This was all that was needed to smooth his path to the premiership.

He managed also to make himself popular with Queen Victoria, now more than ever obsessed with minutiae of European dynastic succession. When Balfour was at Balmoral, in his capacity as a Privy Councillor, she turned to him for advice on the vexed question of the marriage of the Duke of Clarence, elder son of the Prince of Wales, and thus second in line to the throne. Clarence was feeble in body, mind and morals. Finding a docile and acceptable bride for him was not easy. The young man himself was set upon marrying the Princesse Hélène d'Orléans, daughter of the Comte de Paris, the pretender to the French throne and a Roman Catholic. The former attribute made her unacceptable on grounds of politics; the latter on grounds of religion. Young Clarence would have to be persuaded to change his mind. What, asked Queen Victoria, were Balfour's views, since he had been so 'kind and sympathetic'? Balfour expressed them to her Majesty in several memoranda of consummate tact and firmness; but to his uncle the Prime Minister he was more succinct. His letter shows that age had done nothing to dim his acerbic wit. The Queen, he said, told him:

> that there was no one else whom he should be asked to marry or whom he would consent to marry, if asked. According to her there are but three marriageable princesses at the moment in Europe, besides the Teck girl and the Hesse girl. The Teck girl they won't have because they hate Teck and because the vision of Princess Mary haunting Marlborough House makes the Prince of Wales ill. The Hesse girl won't have him. There remain a Mecklenburgh and two Anhalt princesses. According to Her Majesty they are all three ugly, unhealthy and idiotic – and if that be not enough they are also penniless and narow-minded! . . . they might do perhaps (as she said) for a younger son.[69]

However, it was not to be Queen Victoria whom Balfour would serve as Prime Minister, but her son. Edward VII was crowned King on 9 August 1902. A month earlier, on 10 July, Balfour had become Prime Minister.

Now that he had reached the highest office, Balfour was quixotic in his distribution of favours. The Souls looked to him for advancement and support . . . their hour had dawned at last, just as had that of the Marlborough House Set. But whereas the new King rewarded his patient courtiers for their long wait in the wings, Balfour seemed sometimes deliberately to disappoint and even humiliate his old friends.

When he reconstructed his cabinet in September 1903, he chose to appoint St John Brodrick – admittedly Mary Elcho's brother-in-law – as Secretary of State for India. Brodrick was a dear, dull man, stolid in bearing, long-faced and unimaginative. He had, despite this, been one of Curzon's closest friends for thirty years. The two men could not have been more different. Yet the political battles that now ensued between them, exacerbated by Balfour's inability to speak openly to either of them, destroyed their old friendship in three years. By August 1905, humiliated and bitter, Curzon was forced to resign. He never forgave either Balfour or Brodrick.

The new Prime Minister also came close to destroying his former private secretary in Ireland, George Wyndham: Mary's brother. When Balfour became Prime Minister, one of his first acts was to promote Wyndham into the cabinet. Unfortunately political recognition had come too late for George. His character was undermined by self-indulgence and drink. His marriage was little more than a façade. He lacked the powers of application needed to take on Balfour's former job as Secretary of State for Ireland. He began to skimp his paperwork; to rely overmuch on officials. He became increasingly depressed. Balfour wrote to Sibell, in January 1905: 'I am seriously alarmed about George's state. His nerves seem to be – nay are – (for the moment) utterly ruined. He is really hardly sane. . . .'[70] A few weeks later, Balfour was forced to announce in the House of Commons that Wyndham had resigned.

In December of the same year he was unable to save his party, either, and the Conservatives suffered one of the greatest defeats in British electoral history. In the same year fifty-three Labour MPs entered the House of Commons. The age of government by a small and privileged élite drawn from the landed aristocracy was almost at an end. Balfour's long years of brilliant promise as the figurehead of the Souls were finally unfulfilled. For all his legendary personal charm and intellectual adroitness, he was – as he had been to Mary Elcho – a man of straw, a dilettante, a games player. Or perhaps it was just that the tide of historical change was flowing too strongly now to be resisted. In November 1908 Percy Wyndham – Mary's father – wrote prophetically: 'The truth probably is that the reign of the upper and middle class is over.'[71]

– 5 –

But Not as Equal Souls

1887–1901

'He likes their society for entirely leisure moments – they are of no real importance in his scheme of things. He likes them rather in the spirit in which other men like fine horses or good wine, or beautiful things to embellish a man's leisure, but not as equal souls. . . . '[1] Elinor Glyn was describing George Curzon when she made this comment about his attitude to women; but it applied in a more general sense, not only to the Souls, but to all of society. Women were valued for being beautiful, aristocratic, gifted or amusing, and highly sought after if they were rich, but they were never regarded as the equals of men. Few of them would have wished to be. They were content in supporting rôles, providing a comfortable background against which the men they loved or were married to could relax from the demands of their lives as members of one or other of the Houses of Parliament; less often of the professions; or simply as landowners and sportsmen. Besides, this was an age that valued women for making a contribution that was distinctively different from anything that men could offer. The Victorians, and in particular the Souls, did not take the view that the only worthwhile activities were those of public achievement. Lord David Cecil has commented:

> In that society private life, the life of family and personal relations – quite rightly I think – was looked upon as being just as valuable and important as public life, and those responsible for it just as important. It was the women who were responsible for it. They ruled in family and social life as much as the men did in public life and they were eminent for the qualities that made private life and personal relations precious; sensibility, imaginative sympathy, social ease, and often instinctive wisdom. They shone in these qualities.[2]

The Souls women prided themselves on their originality and their unusual freedom from many of the inhibitions surrounding the rest of society. Those who have perfect confidence in themselves are seldom anxious about the impression they may be making upon others. The Souls felt confident enough to set their own standards of taste and behaviour, and never doubted that these were superior to everyone else's. In the case of some Souls women, their very clothes

Margot Tennant at nineteen: the youngest of four remarkable sisters whose talent and wit acted as a magnet to the other Souls.

Above: *Laura Tennant aged about twenty, though no photograph can do justice to the impression of pathos and charm which captivated everyone she met.*

Lucy Graham Smith, who had considerable gifts as an artist, bore a striking resemblance to her sister Margot.

Charlotte or 'Charty' Ribblesdale, tall and ethereally blonde, was the only Tennant sister who was beautiful as well as clever.

*Sir Charles Tennant, in a watercolour
portrait by his daughter Lucy. He fathered
sixteen children over a span of fifty-four
years, and at the time of this picture had just
married his second wife.*

The young George Wyndham, often called the handsomest man in England, triumphed over eighty rivals to win the hand of the widowed Countess of Grosvenor.

Sibell, Lady Grosvenor, in her late twenties: the archetypal rich and lovely young widow. Although she married George Wyndham for love she continued to be known by her first husband's title.

Charty Ribblesdale was a central figure among the Souls for thirty years, admired just as much for her intelligence as for her gifts as a hostess.

Charty's husband, Lord Ribblesdale, was regarded as the very picture of a sporting English aristocrat.

Godfrey Webb was the oldest and one of the best-loved founder members of the Souls, and a frequent guest of the Tennants (this one is Margot) at their Scottish home, Glen, in Peebleshire.

Two young Etonians in the 1870s – E.O.P. Bouverie and (right)
*Alfred Lyttelton, the most famous amateur athlete of his generation, a
devotee of 'real' tennis and a brilliant cricketer.*

Adolphus ('Doll') Liddell in a watercolour painted by Lucy Graham Smith some fifteen years after he had failed in his courtship of her sister Laura.

Alfred Lyttelton, whose good looks helped to make him the successful rival for the hand of Laura Tennant. Their happy marriage was cut short by her tragically early death in childbirth.

Daisy, Countess of Warwick, with her son, the Hon. Maynard Greville. (His father was almost certainly not her husband.) Ravishingly pretty and a great heiress, she became the Prince of Wales's favourite in the 1890s.

Queen Alexandra and King Edward VII at Balmoral shortly after he came to the throne, still in deep mourning for Queen Victoria.

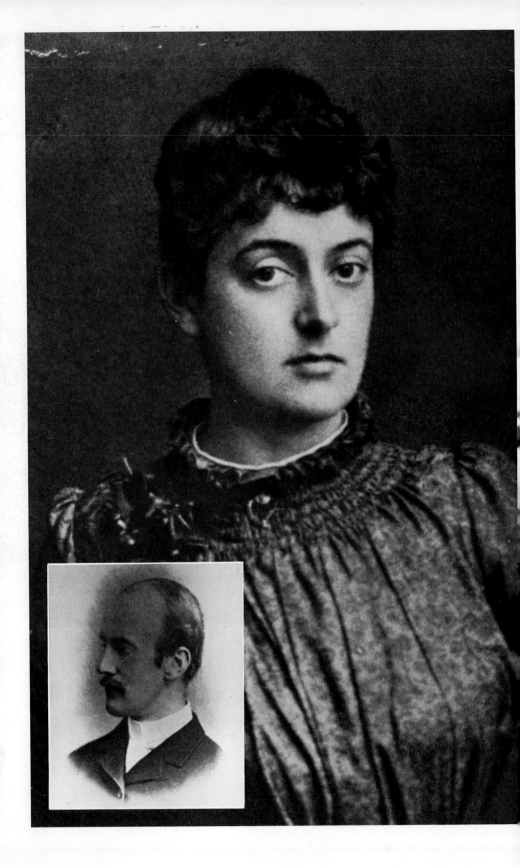

Opposite: *Lady Elcho, a favourite
Souls' hostess whose husband, Lord
Elcho* (inset), *was apparently content
to share her in a lifelong* ménage à
trois *with Arthur Balfour.*

*The extraordinary family likeness
between three generations is evident
from these pictures. Madeline
Wyndham* (above) *was the mother
of Lady Elcho* (opposite) *and
grandmother of Lady Mary Charteris*
(left), *seen here as a schoolgirl. All
three share the same intense dark
eyes and curved lips that epitomized
Wilfrid Scawen Blunt's ideal of
beauty.*

Arthur Balfour, philosopher and Prime Minister but not, evidently, a man of sensual passions. This photograph shows him at about the time he fell in love with Alfred Lyttelton's sister May (inset), but she died before their engagement was formally announced and he remained a lifelong bachelor, consoled by his platonic love for Lady Elcho.

distinguished them from their more restricted contemporaries. Mrs Madeline Wyndham and her daughter Mary Elcho wore 'aesthetic' clothes: flowing, loosely pleated dresses in strong colours, untrammelled by elaborate lace or jewelled trimmings. Lady Horner, too, was much influenced by the Pre-Raphaelite imagination of painters like Burne-Jones, Rossetti and William Morris. Souls houses – Clouds, Stanway and Mells – were decorated with Pre-Raphaelite drawings and designs, including fabrics and wallpapers. Their homes and their clothes would have looked almost bohemian beside the rigidly whaleboned ladies of the Marlborough House Set, fixed in their heavy, over-crowded drawing-rooms that denied all light and colour.

Yet the Souls' independence from the prevailing orthodoxy was purely aesthetic or social. Not one single member of the intelligent, independent, strong-minded women who made up the inner circle of the Souls ever spoke out in favour of any reforms that might have eased the lives of their less well endowed contemporaries. On the contrary: they were passionately opposed to votes for women – or higher education for women – or birth control or easier divorce or the Married Women's Property Act – or anything that could have registered seismic changes in a world that might have been designed expressly for their benefit.

It was not impossible to be a great aristocrat and a political thinker. The most iconoclastic woman in society was an heiress in her own right as well as being so great a beauty that Queen Victoria considered her a suitable bride for her son Prince Leopold. Frances Maynard Brooke, later the Countess of Warwick, but always known as Daisy, had been a convinced socialist since 1895. She was proof that even the most privileged woman could take an interest in politics and perceive the shape of things to come. She alone among her class welcomed rather than deplored greater freedom for women. 'Society in my youth,' she said, 'walked like sheep. Women, and even some men, who were ahead of their time experienced ostracism.'[3] If Daisy could be so critical of her own generation, what had she to say about the Souls?

> There was a coterie that shot up in London in the 80's which for want of a better designation was called 'the Souls'. Although far too cosmopolitan myself to belong to any clique, I was intimate with several of these young people. . . . They loved literature and art and were perhaps more pagan than soulful. They were decidedly ambitious, clever and well-read, and exercised great influence on London society for five or six years.[4]

Influential they were, and for decades rather than years; but the Souls never defied society as the Devonshire House Set had done nearly a century earlier. Wilfrid Scawen Blunt, a frequent guest in their houses and a perceptive and detached observer, described their unwritten rules:

> The restraints they acknowledged were of their own imposing only. They read the Bible and they read the *Morte d'Arthur* in the same spirit and with the same reverence, and they have founded on both a code of superior morals suited, as they considered it, to women of their own superior kind. It allowed them almost every latitude of feeling, including passion between the sexes, for they held it that without passion life would be colourless and the higher emotions could not be enjoyed. Only . . . there was a line drawn short of complete

indulgence, and it respected the full connubial rights of procreation. It was a maxim of their set that 'Every woman shall have her man; but no man shall have his woman.'[5]

The most interesting thing about Blunt's analysis is that it makes clear that the philosophy of the Souls was laid down by its *women* members, chiefly to suit themselves. However, the rules were very often flouted, as Blunt was able to prove with Mary Elcho in Egypt.

Both Daisy Warwick and Wilfrid Blunt agree in ascribing certain qualities to the Souls. They call them clever, well read and intellectual; poetic, fond of literature and art; refined and superior. But they are also described (most surprisingly, for these were not words lightly attached to Victorian women) as pagan, ambitious and passionate. It would be rare in any age to find a group of women who embodied these attributes drawn from so narrow a section of society. But in an era when girls were sheltered and over-protected, scarcely educated and not expected to have serious thoughts at all, it was extraordinary. The women among the Souls were, in most cases, more cultivated, more original, and better conversationalists than their husbands. It is curious that no married couple were both equally brilliant. Quite the contrary: it seemed that a Soul always had to have a more stolidly corporeal partner, to act as foil and anchor.

The main reason why women could not be 'equal souls' a century ago was that they had no status in their own right. Not until they had acquired a husband did they earn respect and a place in society. A single woman was a schoolgirl; a daughter; perhaps an heiress; then she became a wife and mother; then a widow. Otherwise she was a spinster, a maiden aunt, an old maid. There was no word of approval for an unmarried woman. If she could not persuade some man to marry her she was a sexual innocent at best; at worst, a social embarrassment and an object of veiled contempt. Any husband was better than no husband at all. Many girls had been so thoroughly inculcated with this belief that they married straight from the schoolroom, little more than children. Many must have lived to regret it.

One who married young, but without living to regret it, was Ettie Fane. She was the heiress to the immense Cowper fortune, including its priceless art collection, and was greatly in demand during her first London season. Had she been plain and penniless she would still have attracted men to her irresistibly; for the quality of her conversation, or, more precisely, her power of stimulating conversation in others and then listening with flattering concentration, was remarked upon all her life.

As a child she had been orphaned by the time she was three years old; she lost her beloved only brother when she was eight; and the grandmother who had brought her up died three years later, when Ettie was eleven. For the rest of her life Ettie tried to protect herself against a recurrence of this pain and loss by being emotionally involved with several people at once. From her earliest girlhood she had lived in a household peopled by men – apart of course from her governess and later her ladies' maid – and headed by her aunt and uncle, the childless Earl and Countess Cowper. She understood men, at an age when most Victorian young ladies were terrified of them, and she enjoyed their company. Of all the

Souls, Ettie was most skilled in the emotional and sometimes sexual games they played. Her grandson, who was very fond of her and remembers her vividly, says she had always been unconscious of her power; yet she needed to dominate everybody around her . . . which, being a woman of her age, she did in the only way open to her: by charming them. It might have made her unattractive, in a more analytical society, but as it was, people sought her out for her gaiety and humour, and above all for her surpassing gift of friendship.

Such a one as Ettie Fane was a rare matrimonial prize. She must have been expected to make a brilliant marriage; to attract a title, great estates, several ancestral homes. She did not. In 1887, when Ettie was twenty and in the middle of her second season, she met Willy Grenfell, who was thirty-one. He was by no means a great catch; but he must have been a dashing and attractive figure. After reading classics at Balliol College, Oxford, he took his finals in 1876 (he got a Second, contrary to the commonly held belief)[6] and then went off as special correspondent for the *Daily Telegraph* to Suakin, a port in the Sudan overlooking the Red Sea. It must have given him some more intriguing topics of conversation than many of the etiolated fortune hunters she was being pursued by; but more important than this even, Willy Grenfell was spectacularly good-looking. He was six feet five inches tall, and muscular and athletic in build. One of the most famous all-round athletes of his time, he had been both a running and a rowing blue at Oxford.

Ettie married Willy – say all those who remember her – because, quite simply, she fell madly in love with him. Their sexual attraction was obvious enough; Willy adored her, and all his life could never quite believe his luck. They remained devoted to one another throughout over fifty years of marriage, in spite of Ettie's compulsion to exact devotion (to the point of real suffering) from the other men who surrounded her. In the early days of their married life Willy could be jealous, but as time went on he realized that no other man would ever seriously challenge him in his wife's affections. She was capable of feeling strong emotions, and she evoked passion, even obsession, from those who became entangled with her powerful personality; but she was not a woman of strong sexual responses. Her needs in that respect were almost wholly satisfied by her handsome, kindly, simple and devoted husband. All her children looked exactly like him – their two elder sons almost comically so – and while she may have permitted a good deal of hand-holding and caressing, perhaps on occasion even a little more than that, there was never any possibility that Willy would be supplanted.

Intellectually he was a simple man and, as he grew older, a man of ever fewer words; but he and Ettie had an unusually close and happy family life. Ettie Grenfell was one of the 'good young mothers', as they were known. Evidently, being a good mother was rare enough to be commented upon. She kept a minutely detailed account of her children's early years, filled with remembered scraps of their childhood conversation, and almost every letter they wrote to her. (However, she was not above doctoring this account, when she later prepared it for publication, so as to include scraps of other people's children's quaint little remarks, as well. Mary Elcho records one of her sons murmuring confidingly, 'I aren't as sweet as that lady thinks, are I?':[7] a titbit which Ettie later included in an essay called 'Play' in her privately published *Flotsam and Jetsam*.

She need not have bothered: their own remarks are good enough. Billy, her second son, at the age of five said memorably, 'If my wife ever lays an egg I shall blow it.'[8] The same infant misogynist said stoutly, 'I never 'it a woman, if I can 'elp it.'[9])

Ettie's *Pages from a Family Journal*, which was privately printed and circulated to her friends, gives a fascinating insight into the home life of a rich young couple in the last twenty years of Victoria's reign. It records a succession of children's parties, pantomimes and outings; family holidays in Scotland and Brittany; visits to relatives and friends, to the zoo, and once to a biscuit factory. It does sound idyllic. If ever there were a justification for the myth of the golden age, it lies between these pages. All is leisure, and closeness, and making entertainments together, as a family. One envies the five children the security and calm of their blissful childhood.

Any twentieth-century family photograph album, though, or home movies, would appear to tell much the same story . . . long, sunny days, happy, laughing children on the beach, big warm groups of relatives with their arms round one another. In newspaper photographs of small battered children, they are usually smiling. Certainly the Grenfell children had a privileged life, buttressed by twenty-seven servants, at Taplow Court, an enormous house with 3,000 acres of land. Nevertheless, one of Ettie's sons was permanently scarred by his inability to come to terms with her emotional demands. Another grew up a rough, tough, overbearing bully. At least one of her daughters was positively intimidated by her ruthlessly successful mother. Perhaps that, too, is a normal family record: but it does suggest that the golden age of childhood may not have been quite as perfect as it appeared.

The five Grenfell children always had to compete with their mother's popularity as a hostess. ('Like him to go away,' said one of her small sons about a visitor; and then, imperatively, 'Like to see him *start!*')[10] Her attention was dispensed to an unending stream of friends and admirers and would-be lovers. She accompanied her husband on a number of trips abroad. But above all, it was in her capacity as one of the most celebrated hostesses of her period that Ettie Grenfell was in demand.

From the moment that marriage had given her status as an independent adult, Ettie became the most magnetic hostess among the tirelessly hospitable Souls. She was a virtuoso in conversation, a genius at personal relationships, and – it is a word that occurs over and over again when people talk about her – a source of the most tremendous *fun*. Everyone hoped to be invited to Taplow by Ettie. She made people enjoy themselves, not least because they felt they were being brilliant and amusing and of the most absorbing interest to her: whether she was listening to the Prime Minister, or Lord David Cecil's shy young maths tutor. It is the very essence of charm.

In the massive, leather-bound visitors' books from Taplow, the first Grenfell family home, certain names recur constantly: chiefly, of course, those of the inner circle of Souls. Arthur Balfour is there so often that he was given the rare accolade of having his own bedroom – 'Mr Balfour's Room', between 'Buttercup' and 'Tulip'! George Curzon is there, when not away on his foreign travels; and the Tennant sisters; and Violet Granby (slightly less often, though: Ettie did not like Violet); and the Elchos (in spite of the fact that Mary didn't care for Ettie); and Mrs Grenfell's constant adorers, John Baring — later Lord Revelstoke, senior partner in Baring's Bank — and Evan Charteris, who both loved her faithfully for over forty years. John Baring never married, and Evan Charteris did not until 1930. There was George Wyndham, whom she captivated soon after his marriage to Lady Grosvenor (for the sweet and lovely Sibell had little to offer beyond her sweetness and loveliness) and who wrote her several dozen anguished letters, turning on the rack of her alternate encouragement and neglect. Eventually he reached emotional sanctuary in the arms of Lady Plymouth.

Their dashing, black-inked signatures appear almost every weekend during the 1890s, often alongside their brooding, moustachioed faces: for it was the custom to leave one's photograph for the conscientious hostess to stick into the book next to one's signature. Many of these photographs have, over the span of the last century, left a faint shadow, like the imprint of a miraculous handkerchief, on the opposite page; so that lovers and their mistresses are superimposed, as they must often have been in real life. . . .

Ettie Grenfell, for all the rapturous accounts of her genius for hospitality, remains a puzzling and enigmatic character. In a circle and an age whose women were celebrated for their beauty, her looks were nothing out of the ordinary, though she had a more than conventionally wasp waist and a graceful figure. But she was not well dressed — nor was her house well decorated; she had no sense of visual style — and she was not even particularly pretty. She had a trick, say all those who remember her, of lowering her eyes in conversation, sweeping them downwards or aside. She did the same for almost every photograph, to such an extent that when she was once caught unawares looking straight into the camera, she later tried to black out her face in the picture.

Ettie's voice was her most distinctive feature. It was very mannered, even artificial, yet men loved it. It was deep and yet soft: the perfect instrument for her emphatic and gushing speech. 'She never used a comparative', said her dearest friend, Lady Salisbury, 'where a superlative would do.'[11] Furthermore, Ettie — due to her upbringing with her uncle Harry and aunt Katie Cowper — was probably the very last person to speak with the celebrated 'Devonshire House drawl', passed down to her through the great Whig family, and transmitted unchanged from their Lamb ancestors of a hundred years earlier. Ettie Grenfell spoke in the accents and manner of Georgiana, Duchess of Devonshire, and Lady Caroline Lamb. Small wonder that she dominated those around her. At times she seemed almost to hold them in thrall.

Those who loved Ettie adored her, and speak of her still with protective devotion, as though to shield her from the world's posthumous criticism. She had intense friendships with men, but these were never allowed to interfere with her marriage. She had an extraordinary power of sympathy; yet she exaggerated and even lied whenever it suited her. She was worldly, and more than worldly, earthy; and more than earthy, *pagan*. All these adjectives have been applied to her by people who loved her. In the next sentence they may say, 'She was the most *agreeable* person I ever knew.'[12] One concludes that, despite her very great faults, she was the richest and most complex character of all the Souls, with the exception perhaps of George Curzon.

Ettie Grenfell, like most of the Souls, confined her amorous encounters to members of her own immediate 'Gang'. But nearly all the Souls women enjoyed an *amitié amoureuse* with one, or several, men. Mary Elcho and Arthur Balfour were unusual in that their love for each other lasted so long and so constantly, yet without consummation. But the other leading ladies of the Souls – Ettie herself, Violet Granby (later the Duchess of Rutland), Sibell Grosvenor, Pamela Wyndham, Lady Windsor (later Lady Plymouth) – all these had physical affairs with a man, often the same man. George Wyndham and Harry Cust cut a swathe through their ranks. They looked like medieval knights, the one dark, with great soulful brown eyes; the other fair, with great soulful blue eyes; both were described as 'the handsomest man in England'; both were adept at turning out lovesick verses and expert at the art of country house flirtation . . . one can only marvel that the husbands of the Souls whom they so regularly seduced continued to welcome them as guests. But then, most of them were equally busily engaged upon deceiving their wives.

Mary Elcho was another of the 'good young mothers', although her husband, Hugo, Lord Elcho, was a less supportive husband and father than Willy Grenfell. His children often bored him; indeed, most people bored him. His was a vigorous and impatient character and he liked strong pastimes. Gambling was his downfall, causing his wife and children financial hardship which lasted until his father, Lord Wemyss, finally died, aged ninety-six. Lord Elcho had a prolonged love affair with the handsome beauty, Hermione, Duchess of Leinster, whose bold, sculptured profile adorns many pages in the Taplow visitors' books. Their relationship was unusual in that the Duchess and her husband had been estranged for some years after having produced two little boys, in 1887 and 1888, which was thought to ensure an heir; so that when a son was born in 1892, it was widely rumoured that Lord Elcho was the boy's father. At any rate a reconciliation was effected between the Duke and Duchess, just in time to give sufficient semblance of legitimacy to their newborn son, before the Duke died in 1893. In the event, of the three sons of the Duchess, the one who succeeded to the dukedom was fathered by Lord Elcho. But they must have had a sad childhood. Two years after her husband's death the Duchess died too, leaving the three little boys to be brought up by relatives.

The most genuinely unconventional among the Souls women, and the one who really shattered social taboos, was Violet Lindsay, who married Henry Manners in 1882, just before he became the Marquess of Granby. Later, in 1906, he himself inherited the title of 8th Duke of Rutland. Had he not been directly in line for a dukedom it seems hardly likely that Violet would have married him; for even in the highest echelons of the aristocracy, where men were often dull and philistine and intolerably proud, Henry Manners seems to have been unusually stupid. But he *was* a strikingly handsome man, tall and well-made and an apt foil for the pale, moonlike beauty of his young wife.

Violet herself, although no intellectual, was an active and creative young woman. As both painter and sculptor she was very gifted, and her pencil drawings of her children and her friends are far better than the standard 'accomplished' sketches that any Victorian young lady could turn her hand to. (She signed them, after 1906, with the small initials 'VR', which has led to a disappointed stream of people bearing them to auction houses or museums for verification as the work of Queen Victoria!) She had a delicate line and a real ability to capture a likeness, as well as the intangible atmosphere of the time. Her portraits were greatly prized among her friends.

Yet she was more than just unconventional; despite her wistful and poetic looks, Violet Granby had a dashing and even bohemian streak. She was secretly disapproved of even among the supposedly open-minded Souls, who thought that hobnobbing with actors was going too far. Her greatest friends were the actor-manager Sir Herbert Beerbohm Tree and his wife, and their three daughters. She adored the theatre, and the company of theatrical people, and always felt perfectly at home backstage and in costume. She would encourage her daughters to take walk-on parts in the Tree productions, where they would stand on stage muttering crossly, 'Yes, Antony, we lend you our ears.'

One who did not find Violet too unconventional was the palely handsome, intensely romantic Harry Cust. In 1888 Violet's dull-witted husband Henry had become Lord Granby. She had borne him three children, including two sons, thus safely perpetuating the lineage of the House of Rutland. Duty done, she turned her large, soft eyes in search of more stimulating company. Her first lover, Montagu Corry, was a former secretary to Disraeli and an old friend of the Manners family. In 1888 their daughter Violet, always called 'Letty', was born. But Corry, already more than fifty, was too old for the ardent Violet, and she soon craved stronger diversions. She was tall and slender, white-skinned, with a cloud of soft upswept hair. The effect she had upon men was understandable and even Mrs Patrick Campbell once described her as 'the most beautiful thing I ever saw'.[13] Violet could pick and choose among the men of the Souls, most of whom would have been intrigued by her bohemian reputation. It seemed inevitable that she and the equally ardent Harry Cust should find one another. In his mid-twenties when their relationship began, he responded to the artistic streak in Violet Granby, while the other side of her nature – a dreamy romanticism – found its ideal in him. He was to be her most intense and long-lasting love. She had just embarked on her thirties when she fell in love with him, and in her late fifties she loved him still.

Their relationship quickly became 'established' and was tacitly condoned by the Souls (and indeed by Lord Granby, himself preoccupied by a series of jolly little actresses) until in the end, after more than five years of devotion if not fidelity, Cust began to tire of her. In August 1892 their daughter, Lady Diana, was born. Contraception was less easy in those days, but neither it nor self-induced miscarriages were unknown. Perhaps Lady Granby hoped to hold on to her lover by bearing his child. In the event, she failed; for although he continued to be a family friend for years, he had fallen in love with Pamela Wyndham, the sister of Mary Elcho and George Wyndham, and who in 1892 was twenty-one – fifteen years younger than Violet. Pamela returned his love.

Harry Cust's affairs were never simple. It was not just a matter of disengaging himself from Lady Granby and marrying the beautiful, high-spirited young Pamela (who even had hopes of a fortune eventually, from the will of her uncle, Lord Leconfield). For another young woman had entered upon the scene; Cust had been unable to resist fascinating her, too; but she turned out to love him with the strength of an obsession. Her name was Nina Welby-Gregory, and she was twenty-six.

When all these tangled webs were most intertwined, Cust went to confide in his old friend and mentor from the Crabbett Club, Wilfrid Scawen Blunt. Blunt was himself a man of the world, and well known to the Wyndham family. He must have seemed a likely person to offer consolation. Poor Harry cannot have known of Blunt's secret diary, to which the whole story was gleefully confided:

Cust had become attached to his cousin Nina Welby, a quiet, dark-eyed girl, only daughter and heiress, after his many adventures. Cust was 'on the footing of the most favoured nation, for he had long been Lady Granby's lover' in her house. She encouraged him with Nina, thinking, as indeed proved the case, that it would not interfere with her own affair. Therefore he half engaged himself to Nina and she was entirely in love with him. A little later he met Pamela & fell in love with her but at Ashridge slept with Nina several times before parting & she became or thought she was with child.

He was now in love with Pamela more than his cousin Nina & owing to threat of scandal in family and his whole set pressure was put on him to play the honourable part. Appeal was made to George [Wyndham?] & through him to Arthur Balfour as head of the 'Souls' society & intimate with them all & he decided in Miss Welby's favour, & added his political to their social insistence, & under a threat of a double ostracism thus applied Harry was over-powered and yielded. His half engagement to Pamela was broken off to her sorrow & followed by marriage to Nina in a London registry office. George had taken Pamela his sister to Saighton after her last tragic interview with Harry who really loved her & whose sins she would have forgiven. (Nina became ill abroad & it was thought to be a miscarriage.)

She – Pamela – puts a brave face on it however & writes that while it is a sad ruin to her own hopes of happiness she considers that Harry has acted heroically.[14]

Pamela Wyndham was sent out to India, to 'get over' Cust: and evidently succeeded, for within two years she had married Edward Tennant, Margot's elder brother, who later became the first Baron Glenconner. However, her real love was elsewhere: for Sir Edward Grey; although the person she loved best of all in her life was her sweet-natured, doting son, Edward Wyndham Tennant, or 'Bim'.

Harry Cust also recovered in due course, though his passion for the impetuous twenty-one-year-old Pamela had certainly been real enough at the time. Reading a letter he wrote to Sibell, the wife of George Wyndham, it is impossible not to despise his docility in the face of prevailing morality. He was prepared to abandon the woman he loved and – just as bad – to enter upon a totally sham marriage with a woman who adored him, but for whom he felt little or nothing – all in order to conform to a set of rules that he, of all men, knew to be hypocritical. He punished poor Nina cruelly, first by refusing to sleep with her after their marriage (and after that first mishap she never bore him a child) and then by neglecting and ignoring her to such an extent that many of his newer acquaintances did not even know he was married. His letter to Sibell brims with self-pity:

At least for a while the punishment is greater than I can bear. Do not say a world to my darling little Pamela, but help me first for a little while. . . . Do you understand, do you feel what it is, every dragging miserable minute of the twenty-four hours, with the one pure perfect love of my life, always always with me, filling all my heart and all my mind and all the room of all my love. . . . But first if I ask your help and, for her sake, your love and patience, I must make one thing very clear; which I could not tell to her and yet which I want her in some way to know. Except by English law I am not one bit married save to Pamela only. Not before God and still less before my legal wife in the ways of married men and women, of merest touch of hand or glance of eye there is not the faintest possible remotest question.[15]

It is an unattractive letter of infantile emotional blackmail, and one is not surprised that Pamela's family thought it safest to keep her well out of Harry Cust's way for a while.

In the end, nobody came well out of the episode: except perhaps poor Nina, for those in the grip of a grand passion will always choose to be with its object, on whatever terms. After setting her up in a house in Carlton House Terrace Cust, having paid his debt to society, then virtually abandoned her, and continued his philandering. But his life was never quite the same again. Not long afterwards – in 1896 – he was dismissed from the editorship of the *Pall Mall Gazette* and, still handsome, but increasingly bitter and weak-willed, he began to drink. He had resigned his seat in Parliament, as the Conservative-Unionist MP for the Stamford division of Lincolnshire. It is hard to know how he can have spent his time, other than in the continuing round of country house parties, most of which he attended without his wife.

The Duchess of Rutland always loved him, although she too had endured some social opprobrium around the time of his marriage, with some of the primmer ladies in society refusing to speak to her. But her life, too, was blighted after the glorious fling with Harry. 'Lady Granby older much than last year. The Cust scandal must have caused her trouble,'[16] Blunt noted brutally in his diary when he saw her at Margot Tennant's wedding in 1894. That year her beloved elder son, Haddon, died aged nine. Heir to the dukedom, he had all his mother's pale beauty, and much of her love. She sculpted a monument for his tomb which is heartbreaking in the intensity of thwarted emotion it embodies.

Cust, for all his brilliant early promise, achieved very little. The main reason was, as a wit said, 'Cust was throughout his life consistently run after by women, and such was his temperament that they seldom had to run very far or very fast!' Although he was to sit in the House of Commons again, it was as a dilettante MP; a far cry from the Eton master's prediction of the premiership for him! Violet was never again entirely accepted as 'one of them' by the Souls . . . for, as Blunt had observed, they had their rules, and it was dangerous to ignore them.

By now, even the daring and defiant Margot Tennant was becoming oppressed by her unmarried state. She was twenty-six by 1890, which by the standards of her age and class was auguring badly for her chances of marriage. She had been in love ever since the time of Laura's marriage with a hunting man called Peter Flower: handsome, brave and a wonderful rider, but in no way her intellectual match. He was Lord Battersea's brother, and Margot had met him while indulging her passion for hunting in Leicestershire. His life was complicated by a long-standing relationship with another woman, who begged Margot so piteously not to entice Peter away that Margot's heart was touched. In addition he was not to be trusted with money: he was a great gambler; and

Margot's parents both disapproved of him. She decided finally in 1891 to make a break:

> I felt a revulsion of feeling towards Peter. His lack of moral indignation and purpose and his incapacity to improve had been cutting a deep though unconscious division between us; and I determined at whatever cost, after this, that I would say goodbye to him.
>
> A few days later, Lord Dufferin came to see me in Grosvenor Square. 'Margot,' he said, 'Why don't you marry? You are twenty-seven, and life won't go on treating you so well if you go on treating it like this. As an old friend who loves you, let me give you one word of advice. You should marry in spite of being in love, but never because of it.'[18]

In that same year she first met her future husband, then a rising young Liberal politician and barrister named Henry Asquith. At this time Asquith was still married to his gentle, retiring first wife, Helen, and they had five children. But Helen disliked the hurly-burly of political and social life; while Asquith knew that, if he were to make a success of it, he must attend the clubs, the parties and the dinners that were essential for advancement. It was at such a dinner, given by Lord Battersea, that he found himself placed beside Margot Tennant, and was immediately fascinated by her. Within a short time he was greatly in love with her, and when his first wife died of typhoid, in September 1891, he began a serious courtship of Margot.

Asquith was not her only suitor, however. By 1892 she was also being pursued (if a little half-heartedly, for his worship of Ettie was well known) by Evan Charteris, Lord Elcho's brother.

In September 1891, Wilfrid Scawen Blunt had been invited for a brief visit to the Glen. He had been a friend and admirer of Laura's before her death, and he knew and flirted mildly with sad little Lucy Graham Smith (another who pined for the love of Harry Cust), but he had never come to know Margot very well. However, his good looks and his worldliness appealed to Margot, and in July 1892 she invited Blunt and his daughter Judith to lunch with the Tennants at their house in Grosvenor Square. Here, if Blunt the compulsive womanizer can be believed, it was Margot who for once made the first move: by inviting him upstairs to her room at the top of the house. 'I sat down and she came close to me and said, "Why don't I know you better? All my friends know you better than I do, you were so fond of Laura; why not of me?" So I kissed her, and she kissed me, and we came to an understanding of love, & she agreed to come to me tomorrow in Mount Street. [Where Blunt had his London flat.]'[19] A few days later they went riding together in the Park, and Margot told him:

> 'I made up my mind to enjoy my girlhood and I have done so. But you must not suppose that I ever give myself quite away. The men who are charming with women disappoint you in other ways, & the intellectual ones are rather dry & awkward. I never met one who combined both things.' . . . I said, 'You must promise me one thing before we go any further, whatever happens you will not quarrel with me.' And she promised. She is to come and spend a day next week at Crabbet, & I am to stay with her at the Glen after the 15th till the end of the month.[20]

Blunt may have flattered himself that he was about to seduce Margot; but reading the diary it seems quite clear that she, on the contrary, had tired of her virginity and decided that Blunt (whom she once described as one of the four handsomest men in England) was the man who should relieve her of it. In August 1892 he was fifty-two, and Margot just past her twenty-eighth birthday. After two or three days, Blunt wrote:

We had many sweet little moments together, & it was arranged that I was to come to her late when all were in bed 'to wish her goodnight'. Her father is away & her brother & . . . we all went to bed rather early. At about midnight I found her there, very sweet & gentle in her little virginal bed, & stayed with her a great part of the night, she talking of a 100 delicious things in her wonderful way hour after hour which hardly even love could stop. Of all the nights of my life I remember not one more perfect, soul & body. Not that Margot is a *great* beauty, but she has a sweet little body, & I found her a virgin still, in spite of her great love for Peter & her little loves for the rest. Of her soul who can tell except that it is unique in all the world. People may say what they will but a night like this is the purest & most exquisite delight our lives can give. To be ashamed of it is to be unworthy of all that is noblest & best & tenderest in our possibilities of feeling. 'I am so ashamed,' she said, but she did not mean it, & there was not a word of reproach or tears. She is 28 & she has seen how much of life, how much of men! But she was there like a little child in my arms. . . . Then we agreed to take the oath together, & I left her in the early morning. What a treasure to have won from Time!

August 25: Margot a little pale when came down to breakfast & a little silent but spirits soon rose & all day inspired them with wit & merriment. Idle tennis after lunch & then showed me more of her journals & Laura's. Wonderfully brilliant at dinner. . . . After dinner we read out stories from Kipling and played games. . . . It was however a convention between us that our one night was to be our last, & I fear that we shall not have another.[21]

The inference is once again unmistakable: Margot had decided to be deflowered, and had laid down the terms upon which it was to happen. Blunt, who preferred to think of himself as the all-conquering pursuer, cannot have cared for this!

However, a year later he was back at the Glen for another visit, and this time Margot took him into her confidence about the problem of which of her suitors to marry. Evan Charteris and Henry Asquith were both still importuning her. Of the two men, Asquith seems to have been more in love with Margot. She showed Blunt a long and passionate letter which he had written to her on 26 August, and which she was evidently undecided how to answer. She told Blunt she did not love Asquith, though he satisfied her intellectually:

'But,' she says, 'he has no outdoor life. I want to do the best for myself, not in the sense of worldly advantage but all round mind & body. I want somebody who will be a companion & sympathetic in all the things I love: intellectual things & artistic things & sport too. Asquith has no artistic sense & cares nothing for the open air. Evan is at home in this last, he has an artistic mind too and is not unintellectual though nothing to compare with Asquith. I am not in love with either of them but I like Evan as a companion & feel the want of him when he is not there; he is just my own age, 29.'

I said, 'Do you mean to take marriage seriously or not?'

She said, 'Oh yes, I am tired of love-making & want a quiet domestic life.'

'In my view,' I said, 'unless you are very much in love which you are not, I consider for happiness in a domestic way it is best to choose the husband for the sake of his relations & the family you will be connected with. For this reason I advise Evan rather than Asquith. You know & like his people [i.e. the Wemyss family and the Elchos] you & he are of the same world & I should think you would find your life more comfortable & pleasant with him than with the unknown relations Asquith might bring you. I would choose him rather than the other.' And so I fancy she will decide. Evan has adored her for years.[22]

By March 1894, however, Margot had ignored Blunt's advice and made up her mind to marry Asquith. He was a fast-rising politician, and her entry into his life as wife and hostess could only advance his career. It was true that she would take on five children; but she came from a large family and did not anticipate any problems. In any case, she hoped very soon to have children of her own. Evan Charteris, on the other hand, was more of a dilettante, and his long devotion to Ettie – whatever he may have assured Margot of his love for *her* – must have made her wonder if he were not simply marrying her for convenience – and for her father's money, which was known to be a considerable fortune.

Poor Margot could not defy the laws of her time by choosing to be single. Even she, unconventional and independent as she was, felt that she had to marry: although marriage was, for her, an unnatural and ultimately an unhappy state. But she felt sure that Asquith would one day be Prime Minister, and she thought she would make a good politician's wife.

In December 1891, Margot had written in her diary: 'When I read of Parnell or Lassalle or smaller men who have arrested attention, I feel full of envy, and wish I had been born a man. In a woman all this internal urging is a mistake; it leads to nothing, and breaks loose in sharp utterances and passionate overthrows of conventionality.'[23] In her case, this was exactly what happened . . . and increasingly so, as she grew older. Her choice between Evan and Asquith was, in effect, the choice between being a Soul and a non-Soul; and at a time – 1894 – when the Souls were at their peak of brilliance, she chose to be a non-Soul. Her friends tried to like Asquith: not very successfully. Blunt said disparagingly, 'Truly he is a dull fellow, though he tries his best to be amiable and sprightly.'[24] Margot's marriage set her just outside the charmed circle she had adorned for so long. By the time she realized how essential they had all been to her, it was too late. Of course, the Souls continued to see her, and she was invited to their houses, with Henry; but the most glittering period of her life was over.

In trying to understand the pressures upon women to marry, which compelled Mary Elcho, at her mother's insistence, to accept the man she did not love because the man she did love could not bring himself to the point of a proposal; or Pamela Tennant to acquiesce in a suitable marriage because the man she loved had been frogmarched into an unsuitable one; or Margot, finally, to feel that she had no future status except as some man's wife – in understanding why these clever, confident and talented women should all have bowed to social pressures, one needs to hear those pressures enunciated in the accents of their own time. A diary entry survives from a conversation that took place ten years earlier, in April 1884, between the young Laura Tennant and her best friend, Frances Horner. Lady Horner, four years older than Laura (but fifteen years younger than her husband, Sir John) lived at Mells, the beautiful old house in Somerset that had been in the Horner family for generations. The two young women were sitting on Frances's bed at midnight, and Laura, in her innocent curiosity, sounds more like a little girl than one adult talking to another. The conversation must have been important to her, since she went back to her own room afterwards and wrote it down almost word for word:

Laura: Do you think that as a rule a woman knows at first glance the man she will eventually marry?
Frances: Well you know I think one talks to him and likes him and one says to oneself, 'If he worried me very much to marry him I might . . . perhaps.' . . . and then if he does – one marries him. It is so rarely that perfect ideal affinities meet . . . and then you know it is doing things for people every minute of one's life that makes one love them.
Laura: Yes. I often think the very sacrifice of marrying a man must make one love him, unless of course one hates him.
Frances: Oh yes, it's often like that. It is horrid – one does it for him – and not for oneself – and then love covers the sacrifice, and ideal love is the ideal sacrifice.
Laura: Do you never regret your marriage, darling?
Frances: No, never . . . at least . . . I can hardly explain myself . . . but of course moments come when . . . when I think it may be . . . well, maybe I have refused the Highest . . . but . . . it is very very difficult to be unselfish. . . .
Laura: Yes!
Frances: I must go, darling. Jack will be up.
Laura: How wifely!
Frances: Do you think I am?
Laura: It must be so boresome when you want to read or talk – Jack comes up to bed. I should hate it.
Frances: Oh no! Jack's always awfully late. He has never yet gone to bed before me. I am always asleep first – and then he wakes me . . .!
Laura: Of course! It would be more [illegible] than being an Oxford undergraduate: to go to bed after your husband.[25]

And there, tantalizingly, with the crucial word illegible, the conversation ends. It is surely a conversation about women's uncomfortable duty to marry, despite the drawbacks that marriage entails, and, in particular, sex. Frances, already the mother of one child and shortly to bear another, describes it in terms of 'sacrifice'; 'it is horrid', and other regrets that she is too loyal and too sensitive to articulate.

Fortunately, Laura's marriage, brief though it was (only eleven months, and then she died in childbirth) did not turn out to be like her friend's. Her diary is filled with rapturous descriptions of Alfred's love-making: 'Oh! the bliss of his arms around me and the touch of his curls and the seal of his kisses on my hair and eyes and throat and the strong swift pulses beating everywhere and filling the air with fast music and filling my brain with deep draughts of thought-annihilation and my whole being with a sense I never knew before. . . .'[26] Clearly, not every marriage bed was a place of stern duty in obedience to the need for procreation! But of the fifteen married couples who made up the core of the Souls (there were a number of bachelors floating around the nimbus) only three could be said to have been really happy: the Curzons; Alfred Lyttelton, with both his wives; and the Grenfells. But all the others lasted until death.

By the last decade of the nineteenth century, although the Queen lived on, the Victorian era was over. Society was affected by the undertow of a tide that was on the turn. On the surface, it was revealed in greater self-indulgence, greater-than-ever luxury, and yet more decadent froth to amuse the jaded Marlborough House Set. More profoundly, the first stirrings of great political upheavals could be discerned . . . though not by the Souls. Seemingly unrelated events were all moving in the same direction, although the distant trumpets of democracy were still largely unheard.

Not that the Souls would have registered the election of Keir Hardie, first Independent Labour party MP, in 1892; and if they had, they would have dismissed it as an aberration. They might have paused to congratulate themselves when the 1891 Factory Act finally forbade children under eleven to work in factories . . . but by now child labour was hardly needed: from the mid-1890s wages fell steadily, so that cheap labour was always plentiful. In 1899 the General Federation of Trade Unions was formed in England, followed in 1900 by the founding of the Labour party. In 1901, Queen Victoria died at last. The world of the Souls was within sight of its end.

The myth of the golden age dies hard. Were these not the last but greatest years of that British Empire over which the sun never set? How exquisite, surely, the reign of Edward VII must have been . . . those years of long afternoons, when the sun slanted across smooth green lawns and ladies in trailing lace dresses strolled beneath their parasols to take tea beneath the spreading cedars? Surely, even for the working classes, life in the employment of a benevolent master or a kindly landowner was good? Surely, women were never lovelier, men never manlier, children never so innocent again?

Like all over-simplifications, blurred by nostalgia and wishful thinking, this too is a myth. Certainly the upper-class denizens of that era enjoyed the kind of agreeable (that oh so Edwardian word) leisure that has now vanished forever. Those who can still recall it speak wistfully of the pre-1914 world of the sheltered few, when agreeability was enormously important. People did not work as hard then as now; especially not politicians. There was no parliamentary session in the autumn – far too many members would have been away shooting – and the pressure of newspapers and telexes and telegrams and press conferences did not then exist.

Instead, it was a world in which women cultivated social gifts and personal relationships to a high degree: and, in particular, the women of the Souls. It was not quite like the fabled *douceur de la vie* before the French Revolution, but the arts and pleasures of civilized life were practised regardless of time or money. Being pleasant was essential. The great families were not effete, or decadent – quite the reverse: they could be almost primitive in their belief in the mystical bonds of land and blood. They still retained to a remarkable degree the manners and assumptions of the eighteenth century, although these had been varnished over, by the beginning of the twentieth, with the very earliest of the trappings of the modern world. But most of the things that mattered to the aristocracy were the things you could only be born to. Even for them, it could be a ruthless world as well as a pleasant one.

Wilfrid Scawen Blunt called it 'pagan', for many of the Souls were people of strong passions and intense emotions. Mary Elcho was described as a 'savage' woman; Ettie Grenfell as a 'primitive' one. This must be why the veneer of agreeability was so important. It should not, however, be mistaken for the reality. What lay behind its smooth façade could be heartbreaking, especially for the women who had no means of escape. What did Mary Elcho really feel about Balfour's lifelong detachment? What was Violet Granby's reaction to the life sentence that meant she could never leave her dull, simple husband? What did Margot Asquith reflect, as she found her dragonfly brilliance pinned down on the green baize board of her husband's political ambition?

A letter has survived, in curious circumstances, which goes some way towards answering these speculations. It was copied by Wilfrid Scawen Blunt into his secret diary in 1912. He received it from a woman whose identity he goes to great lengths to disguise. She could have been one of the women of the Souls; in any case, she was presumably someone important and well known, or he would not have bothered to cover her tracks so thoroughly when he is so indiscreet about everyone else. We can only guess at her identity; but perhaps her anonymous voice speaks all the more directly and poignantly about the real stresses and hypocrisies of her life in that golden age:

> I have been the most miserable and lonely of creatures, all the more so on account of the 'good cheer' and kindness shown to village boys and gardeners and myself *alike*, & whenever in the early years of my marriage I made an attempt to get a little closer & wanted just a little more besides the 'good cheer' I was rebuffed with courteous contempt as if to say, 'What more do you want? I am always polite to you.'
>
> It would have been easier to be treated badly than treated with polite distance by one I loved (though only in my own way) & to feel I occupied the place of an upper servant. I have sometimes felt frantic when keeping all this to myself, laughing and surrounded by the good cheer. I felt the loneliest creature in the world.
>
> I looked for a reason, thought it must be another woman and lamented that if his reason for not caring for me was a former attachment. . . . He practically owned it, then, seeing I had no proof, denied it. From there began a series of brutalities and cold-blooded torture. Then I spent six weeks in bed at home, moaning night and day and fighting with my reason against my heart. . . . By that time I was afraid of him and of what he might do. I thought if I went back I would one day get into some awful corner and separated from my children.[27]

This wife is most to be pitied because she is locked by social custom and economic dependence into a misery that she cannot escape and cannot even share. All she feels able to do is maintain the glittering façade. The effort drives her into a nervous breakdown. Before very long the same sort of thing was to happen to society itself.

– 6 –
Souls at Play

1890–1910

'Games are a good thing,' wrote Ettie Grenfell, 'but Play is better – and quite different. Play . . . does not mingle with struggle and competition, and needs a holiday spirit of detachment and defiant idleness before it will even peep out.'[1] This distinction between sport (or Games, as Ettie calls them) and play was one of the things that the Souls understood better than most of their contemporaries. One of the reasons why many Victorians were such philistines was that at their public schools they were indoctrinated with the belief that team games were infinitely more important than scholastic success. A *Punch* cartoon of 5 October 1889 has a Headmaster of the 'muscular Christian' variety saying to a boy, 'Of course you needn't *work*, Fitzmilksoppe, but play you *must*!'

Yet the worship of games was not always part of the public school ethos; it developed from about the 1860s. Before that, the great English boys' public schools (there were none for girls, whose education, insofar as it happened at all, was carried out at home, by governesses) were centres of anarchy, sadism and élitism. New boys, unless they were either titled or unusually big and strong for their age, were tortured into conformity with the school's elaborate private rules, language and ideology, while masters turned a blind eye. Gradually, around the middle of the nineteenth century, this began to change, although it took nearly a century before the most extreme forms of cruelty were finally extinct. One of the great reforming influences was the new passion for team games, and the moral ethic which glorified sport and those who excelled at it.

In the last decades of Queen Victoria's reign, the public schools built up a games-playing machine that far outweighed in its status and prestige anything on the academic side. The athlete – manly, modest and decent – was worshipped by masters and boys alike. The scholar was despised as a 'swot'. Little credit was given for intellectual distinction, while the captain of football or cricket experienced a degree of hero worship and power that he probably never enjoyed at any other time in his life. Boys who were physically delicate – or short-sighted, or small, or unco-ordinated – found the twenty hours a week of compulsory games a source of misery and humiliation for which no amount of cleverness could compensate.

Not surprisingly, this attitude led to low academic standards in most public schools. The curriculum consisted very largely of teaching by rote or from the driest of textbooks great swatches of Latin and Greek, without in most cases encouraging boys to progress to mastery of the classical literature, history and philosophy for which this drudgery was only the preparation. Edward Lyttelton, brother of Alfred and Headmaster of Eton in the 1880s, called the teaching there 'tragic'. Only boys who were blessed both with high intelligence and with parents who possessed good libraries and some reverence for culture had any chance of rising above the prevailing boorishness which this school régime produced in the sons of the Victorian upper classes. The wonder is not that they *were* boorish, but that many of them achieved intellectual distinction when, as Harold Nicolson wrote in a study of his uncle, Sir Arthur Nicolson, 'It was taught on all sides that manliness and self-control were the highest aims of English boyhood. He was taught that all but the most material forms of intelligence were slightly effeminate. He learnt to rely on action rather than ideas.'[2] Cotterill, in his *Suggested Reforms in the Public Schools*, wrote: 'Cleverness! What an aim! For a while it may succeed, but only for a while. But self-sacrifice – this is what makes and preserves men and nations – yes, and fills them with joy – only this. Big brains and big biceps – yes, both are well enough. But courage and kindliness, gentle manliness and sacrifice – this is what we want.'[3] The underlying assumption is quite clear: these virtues are unlikely to be found allied to cleverness.

So it was the games field, and not the classroom, that prepared the upper-class youth of Britain for its future, valuing team spirit above individuality and physical courage above intellectual agility. For young men whose destiny was to go out and rule a far-flung Empire, the former qualities were often appropriate in practical terms; while when it came to supplying a generation prepared to die on the battlefield they were tragically apt.

The natural product of the public school games-playing ethic was a young man biddable but aggressive, 'decent' in thought, word and deed, chivalrous and xenophobic, and intellectually incurious if not positively undistinguished. And he was big: physically broad, solid, muscular. In 1905 the young Rupert Brooke, then an eighteen-year-old schoolboy at Rugby, wrote an essay called 'The School Novel', in which he analyzed the hero in such fiction: 'He is called "a type of that healthy and clean-limbed boy who has made England what she is"; in plainer language he is an unspeakable prig in whom a painfully dull intellect is counter-balanced by a "pure and lofty" soul (not however very prominent) and a remarkable propensity for games.'[4] This character is also typified in the following poem from a school magazine – written, almost unbelievably, after the First World War. It is perhaps more naïve and ingenuous than most, but representative of thousands. It was written by W. E. Remisol and printed in *The Lorettonian* in 1922 under the title 'The Man to Look For':

> He mayn't be good at Latin, he mayn't be good at Greek
> But he's every bit a sportsman and not a bit a sneak,
> For he's the man of Scotland, of England, Ireland, Wales;
> He's the man who weighs the weight in the Empire's mighty scales.
> He'll play a game of rugger in the spirit all should have;
> He'll make a duck at cricket, and come smiling to the pav.,
> Now he's the man to look for, he's sturdy through and through;
> He'll come to call of country and he'll come the first man too.

Encouraged from boyhood to think of leisure and relaxation in terms of strenuous physical exercise, and success in terms of athletic prowess, it was natural for Englishmen who had the means and the moors to regard play as an opportunity to chase or hunt or kill – and the greater the numbers of animals, or 'game', thus disposed of the better. The dead were carefully recorded in a game book. The English aristocracy excelled at organized slaughter outdoors, but indoors they were often at a loss for entertainment. Conversation centred largely on details of their hunting adventures, or their sons' athletic triumphs. The interest aroused by the Boat Race, the Derby, or the Eton and Harrow match at Lords, can hardly be overestimated. In 1871 the latter event was attended by exactly ten times as many spectators – 24,626 – as a century later, in 1972!

The Souls were more cerebral than most, but even they were not immune to the Victorian passion for games. Two of them were classic examples of the public school ideal of athletic manliness. Alfred Lyttelton, youngest of the famous Lyttelton family cricket XI, grew up to become the most brilliant player of them all. At Eton he was the last of eight Lyttelton sons, all of them members of the school cricket team (a remarkable achievement in itself) – but Alfred's legendary prowess made him an object of awe and hero worship to his contemporaries at school. He used to say that 'no position in after life, however great, could be as complete as that of a swell at Eton'.[5] By the time he reached his final year at school he was captain of the eleven, president of Pop and editor of the *Eton College Chronicle*! In 1875 he went on to further triumphs at Cambridge – where he first met Arthur Balfour – and divided his time between work (history), athletics and talk. The wonder is that, after winning so many glittering prizes at such an early age, he retained a genuine modesty. And, as well as his record as an athlete, he evidently had a good enough mind to appeal to the cultivated and original intellect of Laura Tennant. Much as she was attracted by his splendid physique, he could never have captivated her without a good brain as well.

Alfred's sporting career was almost exactly paralleled by that of Willy Grenfell, except that Willy's triumphs were scored at Harrow (where he twice played for the Harrow XI) and Balliol, where he first met George Curzon. Willy rowed in the 1877 dead heat Boat Race, and again in 1878, when Oxford beat Cambridge by ten lengths. In due course he became president of the Oxford University Athletics Club and the Oxford University Boat Club. Rowing was always Willy's preferred sport, but he also excelled at shooting, climbing and fencing. He once stroked an eight across the Channel, he swam the basin of Niagara Falls not just once but twice, and he climbed the Matterhorn three times. Yet he, too, presumably had some intellectual substance or he would not have been able to attract Ettie Fane, an heiress whose conversational gifts were almost as dazzling as her fortune.

George Curzon and Arthur Balfour had been among the few for whom games at school were not regular and compulsory. Debarred by ill health – for Curzon was in his teens when he developed the back trouble that plagued him throughout his life; while Balfour was considered delicate by his mother, who therefore persuaded the school that he should not play games – they focused all their energies on study in the extra twenty hours a week thus gained. Yet even the fastidious and cerebral Balfour became something of a sportsman later in life. In a letter to Curzon in 1896 he wrote, '. . . time presses, as I find it difficult to squeeze in the claims of both golf and politics into the 24 hours.'[6] He was also a devotee of the craze for bicycling which swept the country in the 1880s, bowling many of the Souls along with it; and that for tennis, which sprang up about the same time. Only Curzon, among all the Souls, handicapped by the rigid iron brace which he always wore, seems never to have taken part in any sport. But even he walked and trekked and rode for miles on his expeditions, and his stamina during those gruelling trips was prodigious.

The Souls rebelled against the bucolic and tweedy conservatism of the huntin'-shootin'-fishin' upper classes, just as they were bored by the Marlborough House Set's penchant for card games and practical jokes. They disapproved of gambling, which they thought vulgar. They preferred sports that required skill and elegance rather than boisterousness; indeed, they disliked anything coarse or brutish, and would always choose sports or pastimes that called for tactics, subtlety and expertise.

The Souls women liked activities in which they too could join – like tennis and bicycling – which gave them the opportunity to twirl a neat waist and a slender ankle, rather than staid activities like croquet, or battledore and shuttlecock – hitherto the only exercise that men and women had been allowed to indulge in together. The women of the 1890s were becoming perceptibly freer than those of twenty or thirty years earlier, and one of the signs of this relaxation of the absurd restrictions that had hemmed in their mothers was a new acceptance of women – aristocratic women – on the En Tout Cas tennis courts, the skating rink, and even occasionally the golf course.

Ettie's arch remarks at the beginning of this chapter make it clear that the Souls sought in play for distraction from the pressures and responsibilities and sometimes the tedium of their public lives. That is to say, the men sought it and the women provided it. But while the rest of society looked to be entertained, the Souls devised their own entertainments, not as spectators but as players. Play was central to their leisure: as Lord Ronaldshay said of Curzon, 'It was at play and in his intercourse with his many friends when the restraints which always seemed to hamper him in public were cast aside, that his individuality found more ample scope for its expression. Much may be learned, consequently, by watching him at play.'[7] Curzon's febrile energy, his competitiveness, his interest in the dramas of human relations, particularly under the spur of rivalry, made him and many other Souls virtuosos in the art of play.

The pattern of the Souls' activities had been established very early – almost before they had acquired their name – because it derived from the home life of the Tennant family, and their passion for games. Margot wrote to Curzon in September 1887, when he was travelling through America, and this letter (which was addressed to him in Salt Lake City) shows that most of the features of the Souls were already present.

> At this moment I am writing in the drawing room. Doll is drawing the Sir Joshua Reynolds & Alfred is playing hymns; Rennell Rodd, Spencer, Eddy [Lyttelton brothers], Godfrey [Webb] are in the library with Susy Lister & Charty is up in Posie's room with the children. . . . The Pembrokes & Francie Horner & Bungo came which was perfect only Lady P. will not fit any household quite, she had lurid proposals to make at all times & if fine reads out loud indoors & if wet enough tramped the hills till my heels ached. . . .

Harry Cust came . . . [and] . . . wrote first rate poems, epitaphs & all our
ridiculous games – but we miss you. . . . [8]

The Souls played as dolphins play: not indolently, casually, half-heartedly, but
with the supreme grace and confidence of creatures in their element, revelling in
their mastery of it. They sparkled and shimmered, tossing aside crystalline drops
of laughter, playing according to obscure rules of their own devising; rules that
changed and were broken and were anyway never quite what they seemed and
always baffling to outsiders. Gazing a century later at photographs of costumed
Souls at their fancy dress balls, or tea parties, or Saturdays-to-Mondays, their
frivolity looks enchanting. It concealed a terror of stillness, boredom or banality.
Not a moment of the day could be solitary or unplanned. Whatever Ettie may
have believed, Play for the Souls was a serious business.

Besides their own esoteric entertainments, they enjoyed at least some of the
same pleasures as the rest of society. Maurice Baring was thinking specifically of
the Souls when he described the summer of 1896 in rapturous, wistful vignettes
such as this one:

> I went to the Derby that year and backed Persimmon; to the first performance
> of Mrs Campbell's *Magda* the same night; I saw Duse at Drury Lane and Sarah
> Bernhardt at Daly's; I went to Ascot; I went to balls; I stayed at Panshanger;
> and at Wrest, at the end of the summer, where a constellation of beauty
> moved in muslin and straw hats and yellow roses on the lawns of gardens
> designed by Le Nôtre, delicious with ripe peaches on old brick walls, with the
> smell of verbena, and sweet geranium; and stately with large avenues,
> artificial lakes and white temples; and we bicycled in the warm night past
> ghostly cornfields by the light of a large full moon.[9]

The magic comes down to earth in Doll Liddell's account of a weekend party at
Panshanger three years previously. (Doll was Laura's disappointed suitor; older,
and perhaps more prosaic than other Souls.) He wrote to Constance Wenlock on
2 July 1893:

> This is a regular Panshanger Sunday party – Etty, Brodricks, Margot, Lady A.
> Portal, Harry Whites, Evan [Charteris], Lord and Lady Roberts, Milner etc.
> There were quite the elements for a drawing room drama – Margot would
> play off Milner against Evan – Evan would play off Etty against Margot, and
> Etty would play off any man she pleased against Evan. . . . Alas, I must
> confess it, I am getting a bit bored with the ladies of our lot – even with Margot
> in her conventional form. The interminable conversations about conversa-
> tion pall upon me. . . . [10]

One of the Souls' favourite diversions was creating elaborate and fiendishly
difficult word games, involving literary or historical guesswork. These games
took charades – a popular Victorian pastime – as their starting point, but built
upon it an edifice of dramatic ability and literary expertise, to such an extent that
the 'games' sound virtually impossible. However, with constant practice, Souls
like Etty, Margot, Curzon and Harry Cust became astonishingly good at them.
With almost intuitive speed they would discover the personality or word they
had to guess. The prime mover in both inventing and playing these games was
Margot Tennant, always an adroit conjuror with words. But all the Tennants
were enthusiastic games players, with a family knack of thought reading which

enabled them to leapfrog over clues. Margot wrote in her diary for 20 October 1893: 'I invented a very good new game: everyone telling the story of a novel as shortly and graphically as possible, reading it out and letting the others guess. Lucy took *Rob Roy*, I did *David Grieve*, Jack *Tess* and Eddy the Old Testament, which was quite excellent and took us all a long time to guess.'[11] A more literal-minded family might have demurred at classifying the Old Testament as a novel!

New games were constantly being invented, and old ones refined to make them yet more difficult. There was Styles: the players had to write parodies of well-known authors in prose or verse (this was presumably the origin of Curzon's poem 'The Belles'); there was Epigrams: which meant inventing new ones; and Clumps: a development of Twenty Questions but with subjects like 'the last straw' or 'the eleventh hour'; or – 'most dangerous of all', said Margot, with satisfaction – Character Sketches, in which somebody present was described in terms of something else – a vegetable, perhaps, or a building or a colour. This game was still being played with gusto half a century later. Lord Longford recalls his first weekend at Taplow when, as Frank Pakenham, he was a young man in the early 1930s:

> I was asked to these parties because I was the younger son of an Earl – I was kind of a reserve suitor for Imogen. It was very frightening going to Taplow. I didn't know a soul there except Moggie, and after dinner we played games. 'What vegetable does this person remind you of?' one would have to ask, and the answer might be 'a turnip'. . . . You had to think up very erudite questions, to which they might say, 'A peach melba with a little sprig of mistletoe – oh, that's *giving* it away! You *must* see who it is now!' And I had no idea.[12]

There were more diabolical games still. One, called Breaking the News, involved impersonating yourself announcing the death of someone to their wife or dearest friend, while those present tried to guess the identity of the deceased. But Margot says robustly, 'These games were good for our tempers and a fine training; any loose vanity, jealousy or over-competitiveness were certain to be shown up; and those who took the buttons off the foils in the duel of argument – of which I have seen a good deal in my life – were instantly found out.'[13] It is hard to imagine Breaking the News being played without foils dripping with blood; but Margot could be surprisingly insensitive. Her husband, H. H. Asquith, when he was Prime Minister, managed a further refinement of this game. In cabinet, he would play it all by himself. The Secretary of State for Ireland, Augustine Birrell, wrote: 'When the PM is bored . . . at a Cabinet meeting he distracts himself by composing tributes to his colleagues. He looks round the table, selects a victim, and we know upon which exercise his mind is engaged.'[14]

These games were played in all the Souls' houses, but particularly at Glen, with the Tennants; at Taplow or Panshanger, with the Cowper and Grenfell families; and at Stanway, with the Elchos. Lady Angela Forbes – the hard-riding, hard-swearing virago who became the mistress of Hugo Elcho after the death of the Duchess of Leinster – describes her first experience of playing these games:

> Having selected your victim, you describe him or her by the scent, the flower, the architecture, even a good dish of which he or she may remind you. It is a game calculated to add to your enemies – to be described as resembling a

cauliflower, a toad, macaroni and sage green is not likely to make you feel friendly towards the author of such an uncompromising word picture.[15]

Evidently, on this occasion at least, the foils were unbuttoned!

Another after-dinner game popular at Stanway consisted in inventing the most surprising titles for books which those present might have written. This was the outcome one evening: Lord Elcho, *Tina's Bible Stories for Tiny Tots*; Arthur Balfour, *Three Girls and a Horse*; Mary Elcho, *Talks About Chaps*; and Lady Angela, *Ragged Homes and How to Mend Them*. One longs to know who was responsible for the latter – which apparently hurt Lady Angela's feelings a good deal, *not* for its implication that she was a marriage-breaker, but for implying that her home was shabby!

At Taplow on one occasion the game was to invent riddles. This one, thought up by Norah Lindsay (the sister of the Duchess of Rutland), is interesting because it unwittingly reveals an attitude that all present took for granted. The question was: Why is Mrs Pankhurst like a she-bear? To which the answer – thought worthy of record in Ettie's *Family Journal* – was: Because one is barely a woman and the other is a womanly bear.

The language of any society, especially the language of élite circles within that society, deliberately expresses the attitudes of its members – but it also unconsciously reveals them. The words themselves are clues. They have echoes and resonances below their surface meanings: echoes of which the users are usually unaware, and which can sometimes only be heard years later. Thus, the clean-cut, square-jawed public school hero is now an obsolete figure, and so the words which were once used about him, with no suspicion of parody, have also become dated; the stuff of caricature. Merely to list a succession of words like 'upright', 'clean', 'square', 'staunch', 'candid', 'open', 'trusty', 'loyal' and even 'white' (all of which appear in *Roget's Thesaurus* under the sub-heading 'Probity') is to conjure up an image in white flannels, the boyish idol of nineteenth-century playing fields. Today, the words themselves evoke a world of nostalgia. They have become as remote and old-fashioned as the youths they celebrate. Their surface meaning may no longer be relevant, but their echoes still ring in the ears.

The British upper classes have always understood the value of language and the necessity to decode it. They staked out their territory with a vocabulary that could only be acquired after years of inside knowledge. Items of tribal folklore like the names of classrooms or the nicknames of masters at Eton or Harrow, known only by those who attended these schools, signalled membership of an élite as clearly as the wearing of an old school tie, and less blatantly. They were used as passwords; as were the surnames, estates, marital history, family motto and heraldic quarterings of the aristocracy. But even these details could be – and were – mastered by diligent *arrivistes* prepared to pore over *Debrett's* for long enough.

The Souls used their private language to set themselves still further apart. Their love of verbal games, their use of nicknames and of words that didn't mean what they seemed to mean and were therefore incomprehensible to outsiders – all these manipulations of language reflected their attitudes, but also fossilized them. Fifty years after the intellectually snobbish young Tennants had invented games like Clumps, Lady Desborough was still using them to test and discomfit the young Frank Pakenham. His place in the charmed circle could only be won after a trial by ordeal. 'I was, after all,' he said, 'only the *younger* son of an *Irish Earl*. . . .'[16]

Like all Victorians, the Souls could be unselfconsciously and mawkishly sentimental. They used infantile nicknames freely, a practice which still survives among the upper classes. There is no evidence that even the detached Arthur Balfour felt any embarrassment at his adulatory nicknames; not merely 'King Arthur' or 'The Adored Gazelle' but also 'Pretty Fanny' and – by Mary Elcho's children – 'Mr Rabbit'. Names like these were used in affection, not sarcasm. The older generation of Souls hostesses – Lady Brownlow, Lady Pembroke and Lady Cowper – were called 'the Aunts'. Balfour's niece and biographer, Blanche Dugdale, was called 'Baffy'. Alfred Lyttelton's second wife was always 'D.D.'; her suitor, and Laura's (the poor fellow lost them both to the same man!), was 'Doll' Liddell. Mary Elcho, for some reason, was called 'Napoleon': she, the least commanding of women! Maurice Baring called Ettie 'Madame Sottise', though silliness was the last characteristic one would associate with her, and Mary Elcho called her 'Delilah'. Lord Hugh Cecil was always known as 'Linky' and his brother, Lord Cranborne, was called 'Bobbety'. . . . By such disguises, impenetrable to an outsider, they defined membership within their circle of initiates.

They also used a jargon, whose origins are a guide to the origins of the Souls. The ancestry of the words traces the family trees of the people who used them. This jargon derived from two main sources. The first was the family language of the Gladstones and Lytteltons: an extensive and remarkably complete language which they called 'Glynnese'. The second source was the special voice, intonation and vocabulary passed down from the eighteenth-century Whigs, through the Holland House and Devonshire House Sets that reigned within society at the turn of the nineteenth century. Glynnese probably began as a children's language, such as is found in many close-knit families, between Mary Glynne, her brother Stephen and sister Catherine. Mary grew up to marry the 4th Baron Lyttelton and it was he who – years later, in 1851 – compiled a glossary of Glynnese. It passed into wider currency when Catherine Glynne married W. E. Gladstone, and was used both among their children, and the great tribe of Lytteltons. Between them the Glynne sisters had nineteen children. Those children spread Glynnese far and wide among the families they married into: which included the Tennants, Cavendishes, Custs and Talbots – all of them founder members of the Souls.

The comprehensiveness of Glynnese was due to the fact that scores of people, all drawn from the same narrow stratum of society, kept it alive and flexible; and to their special skill with words. Some Glynnese expressions, like 'sitting tight' and 'over the moon', or 'killing!' and 'I died!' (to register amusement) passed into upper-class slang and survive today. Many more words and phrases were common parlance among the Souls, though rare outside them. Glynnese thus became part of a private language used from the nursery onwards by a significant section of the aristocracy to identify – or to exclude – those who were its peers.

W. E. Gladstone (himself a practised exponent of Glynnese) had a whole speech in the language composed for him by his brother-in-law, Lord Lyttelton. Had he ever delivered it in the House of Commons, a surprising number of

Members would have been able to understand some, at least, of it. The rest would have found it pure gobbledygook: 'Sir, I am sorry to see you looking so grubous and taken out of by the moral sag of this long debate. I fear that it is one of ours. This House is in the chair for rotgut and offal and false flash; and some of the debates are beyond.'*[17] And so it could go on and on and on – infinitely reassuring to those who knew the secret code; infinitely intimidating to those who did not, but wished they did.

Recurrent Glynnese words used among the Souls were 'phantod' (pronounced not 'fantod', but with the p and the h separated) which meant imbecile (so useful to be able to use an insult that the victim couldn't understand); 'false flash', a sporting metaphor like flash in the pan, taken from shooting. It meant a misleading spark, and so something sham. The *nouveau riche* would be called 'false flash', and damned not only by the words but also by their failure to understand them. 'Unearthly' meant from below the earth and thus fiendish or diabolical. A 'maukin' was someone unknown and so of small account. (It is remarkable how many Glynnese words were disparaging.) Others were more elegant, derived from Latin or from classical mythology: such as 'niobe', which meant dissolved in tears.

Another family, too, contributed its special language to that of the Souls. The Barings, like the Lytteltons, were a large and happy brood; and like many large and happy broods they too, as children, had made up or distorted many words. These were passed on chiefly by Lord Revelstoke, the oldest of the Baring brothers and one of the men in thrall to Ettie Grenfell, and by Maurice Baring, his younger brother, a brilliant conjuror with words and an assiduous letter writer. Godfrey Webb, doyen of the Souls, a close friend of the Barings, and a regular visitor both at their house and at Ettie's, was another through whom they were spread far and wide. Baring words included 'heygate' (dull or banal – more disparaging adjectives, defining the Souls' general view of non-Souls); 'culte' or 'spangle' (both meaning a lover, or at any rate someone aspiring to be); 'relevage' for gossip, 'dewdrops' for compliments – and many more. Apart from the covert insults, it is noticeable how many Baring words were about speech itself: the one attribute the Souls prized above money and birth. A 'floater' was a gaffe; 'having a dentist' was a heart-to-heart talk; to 'block' someone meant to talk about them, and to 'wash the block' was to change the subject; a 'rebound' was a compliment relayed through a third person.

The English upper class often prided itself upon its taciturnity. The truth was that many of them were too dim-witted, ill-read and narrow-minded to be anything else. The brusque or the banal passed as conversation among men, while women were not expected to be other than vapid or feather-headed. Anything else was ostentatious, and therefore suspect. Against this background of empty small talk, the emphasis laid by the Souls upon being articulate, and their high-wire skills of conversation and flirtation, were distinguishing features. In addition, their talk was often genuinely intellectual, and men like George Wyndham, Harry Cust and George Curzon were said to have scaled heights of verbal brilliance.

*Translated as 'Sir, I am sorry to see you looking so dirty and sickened by the strain of this long debate. I fear that it is characteristic. This House is pre-eminent for badness and rubbish and sham; and some of the debates are indescribable.'

Lord Charles Beresford identified another salient characteristic in his famous remark, 'You are always talking about your souls – I shall call you the Souls', which Ettie Grenfell later claimed was the origin of the name by which society knew them. They were endlessly absorbed in dissecting the precise nature of one another's feelings. This fulsome and elaborate enquiry into emotion would have been anathema to most outsiders, which was partly why the Souls needed a 'safe' language in which to indulge their curiosity about one another. Daisy Warwick gives us a glimpse of how they must have seemed to their contemporaries: 'all of them wrote poetry and explained their emotions to each other. A shamelessly inquisitive world eavesdropped when it could – especially during the explanations. It was inclined to let the poetry alone.'[18]

The Devonshire House manner of speech came into the Souls almost entirely by way of Ettie Grenfell. The Cowpers, who brought her up, were familiar with it as inheritors of the Melbourne–Lamb tradition. It was a way of speaking, an intonation, a pronunciation, that has now vanished. It was impossible to describe, yet everyone who knew Ettie refers to her distinctive speech. Lord David Cecil, whose mother was her greatest friend, knew her from his earliest childhood:

> My mother's older sister Mabell, Countess of Airlie, could just remember Lady Palmerston, Melbourne's sister. I asked her what her voice was like. My aunt answered, 'It was rather like Ettie's.' This was a very distinctive voice, rather deep, slow and laying great emphasis on certain words. I suppose a stranger might have thought it mannered, though it was natural to her. I take it, and my aunt agreed, to be a survival of 'the Devonshire House drawl' characteristic of Georgiana, Duchess of Devonshire, and her sister, Lady Bessborough, and, possibly, Lady Caroline Lamb. My cousin Ettie Desborough also had an odd impediment that led her to pronounce l's almost like n's; but I never heard anything of this kind in descriptions of 'the Devonshire House drawl'. I think it was peculiar to her.[19]

Lord Longford describes that lingering over syllables – 'Tttappp', she would say, meaning Taplow Court, or 'PPannns', for the lovely house, Panshanger, now lost, that she inherited from the Cowpers. Ettie's artifice, her elaborate speech and effusive letters, were élitist yet sincere. Her integrity may have been peculiar to herself, yet it was utterly consistent.

If Ettie was the impresario of the Souls, Margot was their magician, pulling out of the hat flashes of speech that could be brilliant, wounding or ridiculous. 'Ettie is as strong as an ox,' said Margot. 'She will be made into Bovril when she dies.' Her comments were as thoughtless as a child's. 'That hat makes your face look just like a ham!' she once said to a friend, untroubled by the hurtfulness of the comment because it was obviously true. Yet she could pin down in a phrase an impression that would have taken others a paragraph to convey. 'The salad was decorated with the Lord's Prayer in beetroot!' she said of a hostess's over-elaborate food; or, of someone's delicate watercolours, 'Like a mouse's sneeze!'

The Souls' tendency to verbal flamboyance was matched by their passion for fancy dress parties: a passion shared, in this case, by most of their contemporaries. With time and money to spare, what could be more delightful than the hours whiled away planning an elaborate pageant in which both sexes could indulge in fantasy and disguise. A woman might dress up as the Queen of Sheba, her limbs more ostentatiously bared than was permissible in ordinary evening dress, if she were tiring of an established lover and wished to catch the eye of a new one. A man who felt that a fencing bicep or muscular thigh was seldom displayed to its best advantage could attend in the costume of Samson, or a Roman gladiator. The last years of the nineteenth century were marked by a series of such fancy dress balls, famous for the lavish preparations that preceded them and for the hundreds of pounds spent on costumes hand-made to be worn for a single evening. From 1905 until the First World War, Ettie Grenfell gave one at Taplow every year at the beginning of January.

The first was a children's party for 180. Julian was nearly fifteen, Billy exactly two years younger, and their sister Monica was eleven. Little Ivo was six and a half. It was attended by the children from all the leading Souls families, who were given live kittens as presents at the end of the party. 'Beb' Asquith was dressed as a monkey; his sister Elizabeth came in gold brocade as an Infanta; while the young Billy Grenfell was already hinting at his later obsession with violence by dressing as a bullfighter, in a miniature suit of scarlet and gold. The party was such a success that by 1907 it had graduated into being a more grown-up occasion, while remaining ostensibly a treat for the children. Ettie wrote in her *Pages from a Family Journal*:

> Cynthia Charteris will always be remembered as Ophelia, with her wonderful hair hanging down. . . . Monica [Grenfell] was a Bacchante with wreaths of grapes. . . . Hugh Godley an Arab, Rex a Dervish. . . . little Imogen was Cupid. . . . Julian looked beautiful as Lohengrin in silver armour and swan helmet and long white cloak and Billy was a Viking, all in white and a gold helmet with wings. George Brodrick had a beautiful (old) Hussar uniform.[20]

Dressing their children up as heroes of Nordic mythology and battles long past, the Souls unconsciously prepared them for their future rôle as willing sacrifices. On the sports field and the ballroom floor they had played at war for so long that, when the real thing came, they were well schooled in its formalities. Nothing ever prepared them for its chaos.

The season of 1911 was a particularly good one for fancy dress balls. George V's accession had put everyone in the mood for pomp and pageantry, and on the eve of his coronation, 20 June 1911, a great Shakespearian fancy dress ball was held. It had to be accommodated in the Albert Hall, since nowhere else was big enough. The culminating, if not quite the last, of Taplow's fancy dress balls was held a few months later, on 8 January 1912. We have an exceptionally vivid and detailed record of it because a photographer was hired for the whole night, 'who did quantities of photographs of the people by electric light. The dresses were most lovely, of both men and women. It went on till $\frac{1}{4}$ to 5! The ghosts of Monica and her mother and many of the party travelled on to Knowsley the next day, for a shooting-party, and then to Hatfield, for their Ball, and to Gisburne for the Ball there.'[21] The winter season of 1912 must have been particularly gruelling. Had they but known it, there were only two more to come and then social life would suddenly become much less exhausting.

The Souls and in particular the women among them lavished fortunes on their ordinary clothes as well as on fancy dress. Female fashion reached heights of extravagance in the Edwardian era, after freeing itself from the absurdities of the bustle in the 1880s. In addition, country house parties required women to change their clothes as often as five or six times a day so that they were always dressed to suit their activities and the formality of the occasion. Armies of ladies' maids would arrive with trunks (called 'Noah's Arks') full of dresses, to be unpacked, laboriously ironed and laid out ready to be worn for an hour or two, along with half a dozen layers of exquisite underclothing, before the clothes, the coiffure and the jewels were changed once more, in keeping with the minutiae of social etiquette.

Although the Souls believed themselves less in thrall to the vagaries of fashion than most of their contemporaries, their wardrobes would nevertheless have cost their husbands several thousand pounds every year. Daisy, Countess of Warwick, though purporting to despise the extravagance of her dresses, quotes in great detail descriptions of herself taken from the social pages of newspapers and magazines. Even allowing for the fact that she was a famous beauty and an heiress, the expenditure such clothes must have entailed is stupendous. 'Lady Brooke defied all competition in a soft, green, gauzy gown, held to her waist by a band fastened with an emerald and diamond buckle, and finished at the neck by a deep falling collar of chinchilla. . . . '[22] Or again, 'In violet velvet with two splendid turquoise and diamond brooches in her bodice, and a turquoise pin fastening on her purple velvet bonnet. She had purple and white orchids tucked into her gown, and carried a bunch of lilies-of-the-valley. . . . '[23] This particular outfit beggars the imagination.

Violet Granby, later the Duchess of Rutland, was the person whom the drifting, softly draped dresses of the time suited best. With her slender waist and long, drooping neck, she was a touchingly romantic figure, and one whose palpitating emotions fully matched the vulnerability of her appearance. Yet her love affair with Harry Cust was in the end *too* blatant to be acceptable, while her passion for the London theatre and her friendships with many leading actors and managers made her slightly more raffish and bohemian than was quite *de rigueur*. Ettie could write whimsically of Play as 'an escape to the great white fields, to serenity and ecstasy',[24] but even ecstasy had its rules.

The men of the Souls might toy with nude tennis, ribaldry and iconoclasm at the Crabbet Club, and the women pride themselves on their reputations as 'the good young mothers' (unusual in the days of nannies and nurseries and children banished to both for all except an hour a day), but the game that most of the Souls played with most skill and absorption was the game of love. It was a game played only by the married. Single girls approached their wedding night in a state of unblemished chastity and profound ignorance; though one newly married husband said briskly to his terrified young wife, 'Now you know what has to be done, so don't make a fuss.'[25] Daisy Warwick summed up the tacitly understood conventions that governed the behaviour of young women:

Society girls, if not as innocent as they were pure, were often unbelievably ignorant of the physical facts of marriage. Marriage – their goal, their destiny, their desire – was all in a rosy haze. Afterwards, as wives, they accepted the code of their day as unchanging and unchangeable. Nearly all the young men had mistresses, so most bridegrooms had a second establishment to pension off or maintain. . . . If a society woman met a man – even her own brother – in the park or a restaurant when he was accompanied by his mistress or an actress, he would not raise his hat to her. He cut her, and she understood.[26]

That was the rule if a man were inadvertently seen with a woman of a different class from his own. He would not have allowed himself to be seen with a woman from *his* class in such compromising circumstances, since she could only have been married, and the gesture would have been tantamount to openly flaunting their relationship. Such relationships were conducted circumspectly; which did not mean that they remained secret for long, but that, providing the unwritten rules of love were kept, the relationship would be ignored. Few long-standing liaisons in so tightly knit a circle as the Souls could remain secret. There were no casual affairs. Too much strategy was required for an unpremeditated fling.

After the initial flirtation, the advances of the would-be suitor would progress towards a definite courtship, fanned by ardent letters and facilitated by country house weekends. Then, if the suit were accepted, the lover would become 'established'. This would lead to his discreet appearances at her London house in the afternoons, at an hour when her husband could be counted upon either to be at work, the House, or his club – if not paying some visit of his own. Later still, certain bedrooms would be placed in tactful proximity when the pair found themselves – as by now they invariably would – invited to the same country house parties.

These arrangements were formalized into a ritual understood by all concerned. Vita Sackville-West, whose sharp dark eyes missed nothing when, as a teenage girl, she was invited to Taplow by Ettie Desborough, described the conventions. Her novel, *The Edwardians*, is the most perfect evocation of the period:

> The name of each guest would be neatly written on a card slipped into a tiny brass frame on the bedroom door. This question of the disposition of bedrooms always gave the duchess and her fellow-hostesses cause for anxious thought. It was so necessary to be tactful, and at the same time discreet. The professional Lothario would be furious if he found himself in a room surrounded by ladies who were all accompanied by their husbands. . . . There were the recognised lovers to be considered; the duchess herself would have been greatly annoyed had she gone to stay at the same party as Harry Tremaine, only to find that he had been put at the other end of the house. . . . It was part of a good hostess's duty to see to such things; they must be made easy, though not too obvious.[27]

Such relationships flourished in an atmosphere of opulence and leisure, intensified by the regularity with which the players could count on meeting. The predictability, even boredom, of the social round was greatly alleviated for those engaged in becking and advancing, glancing and retreating, signalling and denying, nodding and surrendering. The game was thought more acceptable the more skilfully it was played.

The crudities of slaps and guffaws, *double-entendres* and fumbles in the pantry would have horrified the sensibilities of the Souls. Their advances had the same goal and the same consummation, but the steps between were infinitely more subtle and mannered. It was the difference between a courtly minuet and a peasant dance. And so every hostess would have sacked the housemaid without a moment's hesitation had the girl been found to be pregnant by the footman. Servants were allowed no 'followers'. The cook and housekeeper were given the courtesy title of 'Mrs' and that sufficed. There was more than a grain of truth in the old joke about sex being much too good for the lower orders.

Even among the upper classes, however, sex had its pitfalls. Society punished those who were found out. Harry Cust was effectively dismissed for breaking that rule, and the other which said, thou shalt not trifle with unmarried girls. For all his poetic brilliance, sense of humour, social gaiety and profound erudition, the overriding quality that distinguished Harry Cust was his sexual attraction. Photographs show his large pale eyes, blond hair and self-consciously patrician profile; but they cannot convey that physical aura which made him irresistible to women. As early as 1884, Mary Gladstone wrote in her diary, 'Protracted and ardent flirtation with Harry Cust, a nice boy in the cynical stage.'[28] Cust was then twenty-three. It was probably the last time anyone called him 'a nice boy'.

His power over women was rapidly established; but unlike most notorious womanizers, his company was also in demand on masculine occasions. Once, when Evan Charteris was a struggling young barrister trying to impress an eminent solicitor, he invited Cust, together with the solicitor, to dinner. Harry Cust began the evening by being highly entertaining, but later became uproariously drunk. Next day Evan Charteris sent him a telegram, saying, 'You have ruined my life but it was worth it', to which Cust replied, 'That is a sentiment I am more used to hearing from women.'

Other men regarded him less tolerantly. Sir Charles Petrie called him 'the most notorious lecher of his day'.[29] Yet he was a founder member of the Souls, and with good reason. Margot Asquith wrote of him:

> Harry Cust was the most brilliant young man I have ever known. He had a more unusual mind than George Curzon and a finer sense of humour than George Wyndham, and if he had not had a fatal fascination for every woman that he met, he might have gone far in life. But he was self-indulgent, and in spite of a charming nature and a perfect temper, he had not got a strong character. . . . He was a brilliantly suggestive talker, more faithful in friendship than in love, and by his intellect a stimulus to the Souls.[30]

The truest assessments came, not from the women who loved him, but from those who resisted his advances. Frances Horner was another: 'Harry Cust was a very gay companion, and present at most of our feasts. He always called me Attila, the Scourge of God, when I refused, generally on ethical grounds, to do anything he wanted.'[31] Plainly, the glamorous and godlike Harry was not accustomed to having his wishes flouted!

Harry Cust was not by any means the leader of the Souls – that pedestal was always reserved for Balfour – yet he was in many ways the most typical of them all. The Souls excelled at all the skills that do not last. Talking, improvising, punning, playing, flirting, dancing and making love: these were the arts that Harry Cust had mastered, and the irresistible enthusiasm with which he practised them all was the reason he was so much loved. Yet, apart from a talented host of illegitimate children whom he was rumoured to have fathered, he left almost nothing permanent behind him. There was a poem, 'Non Nobis Domine', which he wrote to Pamela Wyndham, and which was published anonymously in Quiller-Couch's *Oxford Book of English Verse*. However, Helen Gardener's 1972 edition no longer includes it, so even that slender claim to fame is now denied him. The ephemeral artifice of the Souls had its apotheosis in Harry; and the ultimate failure of his life, in terms of any solid achievement, reveals why their fame, too, was short-lived. They built glittering castles in the air that none of their contemporaries could begin to match. Their glamour and wit and charm were constantly remarked on – spitefully by outsiders, admiringly, by themselves of one another. Yet in the end nothing tangible remains . . . it is all atmosphere, and fantasy, and myth, and the froth of vanished talk. . . .

PART II

DECADENCE

1900–1914

− 7 −

Iron in the Souls

1889−1905

One man proved the exception to the rule that the Souls were insubstantial and their qualities of the most ephemeral kind. One man possessed all their wit and charm and gaiety but added to them real achievements, too. One man widened his sphere far beyond the confines of London drawing-rooms and country house dinner tables, and left behind a monument to his prodigious energy and ambition. It cannot be coincidence that, finally, the Souls felt ill at ease with him and came close to rejecting him, or that in the end their leader, Arthur Balfour, betrayed him. The lone figure of real weight was George Curzon.

After Curzon's successful dinner of 10 July 1889 he went to Switzerland for the 'cure' that his doctors had recommended, and then set off for Persia. He spent six months there, alone. His journey covered much of the ground traced by Alexander the Great: nearly 2,000 miles, mostly on horseback. For a man with Curzon's history of spinal trouble it was foolhardy: which means absurdly courageous. He must often have been in agony. Throughout his life, he would set himself physical and mental ordeals, pitting his imperfect body against his implacable will until he was exhausted. At the same time he managed to write not only a series of articles for *The Times* about his journey (for which he was paid £12 10s each:* enough to cover his travel expenses) but also frequent letters back to his friends in England. 'This is my thirty-third letter today,' he comments in one to his friend St John Brodrick.

He covered about sixty miles a day, suffering extremes of climate and constant hardship from primitive lodgings and barbarous food. In one of his despatches to *The Times*, published at the end of December, 1889, Curzon wrote:

> '*Chuppar*' riding, which is variously described by travellers, according to their tastes, endurance and fortune, as a pleasure, a tedium, or a torture, is the recognised method of speedy journeying in Persia.... *Chuppar* riding I should describe as a melancholy and sometimes miserable operation. The horses are frequently ill-fed, broken down and dilapidated animals, with sore backs and ill-regulated paces ... the best *chuppar* horse would elsewhere need to be classified at a low level of equine mediocrity.[1]

*In today's terms, over £350.

He is trying to complain, but unquenchable good humour breaks through. He was happy. This was no pampered aristocrat's Grand Tour, with all the paraphernalia of servants to look after mounds of named and numbered trunks, leather dressing cases and picnic baskets with monogrammed silver cutlery. Curzon was a real explorer, now and for the next six years: inquisitive, open-minded, fearless. Already he was gaining sufficient insight into the Arab mind to know that an imposing first appearance was essential. Modesty had no place in Persian manners – or, indeed, in Curzon's. He adapted himself to the ritual of arrival, announcement, exchange of gifts, hospitality; the guarded pleasantries, the cautious barter of information before anything like friendship and trust could be assumed. He met the Shah – who had himself only recently visited England – and found him wealthy beyond the dreams even of the English aristocracy; corrupt, uncouth, sadistic and proud. Despite Curzon's relative youth (he was just thirty in 1889) and lack of great wealth and status, it is clear that what Margot Tennant had called his 'enamelled self-assurance'[2] stood him in good stead. He wrote to her on 18 November 1889: 'Had a parade of troops in my honour. Commend me to that for a droll situation! George, the incorrigible and unmitigated civilian, seated on horseback at saluting point by the side of General, evolving discreet comments out of the deep resources of his ignorance and praising the worst army in the world.'[3] And he remained enough of a tourist to scratch on one of the stones of the palace at Persepolis, 'G. N. CURZON, 1889'.

By the spring of 1890 he was back in England. A brief trip to the Mediterranean, on the advice of his doctors, restored his health. On 9 July 1890 – a year to the day after his first Bachelors' Club dinner – he gave a second. Once again, the inner circle of the Souls was there, with a few extra names added to the guest list. They included the nineteen-year-old Lady Sybil Erskine, sister of the beautiful Millicent, Duchess of Sutherland; Curzon had flirted briefly with the debutante Lady Sybil that summer. Then there was Princess Wagram, widowed a couple of years previously when she was only twenty-six, in whose villa at Cannes he had stayed in the spring. Julia Peel, the black-eyed and white-skinned daughter of the Speaker of the House of Commons, was included as well. There were in all forty-eight guests at the second Bachelors' Club dinner. The summer of 1890 was the heyday of the Souls, and all their loveliest women were present, full-blown and splendid like summer roses. But the woman Curzon was to marry was not yet among their number.

He met her just eight days later, on 17 July, at a ball given by the Duchess of Westminster. She was twenty, American, and had been in England with her mother for only a month. Yet already the beauty and grace that had made her the belle of Washington had created such an effect in London society that Mary Leiter opened that ball, dancing the first quadrille with the Prince of Wales himself. In such an exclusive set, deeply wary of *arrivistes*, it was an extraordinary tribute to her charm and social skills. American heiresses were a familiar enough phenomenon as they trawled the poorer aristocracy, willing to exchange a transatlantic fortune for an old English title, but Mary Leiter, though her father was indeed a multi-millionaire, was not offering her person in search of a coronet in exchange for his dollars. George Curzon was immediately struck by her air of distinction, her evident intelligence, and her adroitness in a critical group of people who were still largely strangers to her. He later told his friend and rival, Cecil Spring-Rice, that he 'never loved Mary Leiter more than at that moment when he first saw her walk into that great assembly'.[4]

A few days later they met again, at a Saturday-to-Monday at Ashridge, the country home of Lord and Lady Brownlow. Adelaide Brownlow was – or at any rate had been – a famous beauty; one of the 'Aunts', as the Souls irreverently nicknamed the older hostesses in their circle. She and her husband had been invited to both Curzon's dinners. It was therefore not surprising that he, too, should have been among the party at Ashridge that weekend: though whether by chance or design we cannot know. Plenty of other Souls were there, including Harry Cust, who was Lord Brownlow's cousin and heir, but Mary Leiter would have been immune to *his* charm. Less than two weeks after meeting George Curzon, their second encounter had confirmed her first impression. She was in love, and she remained so, singlemindedly, through one of the strangest courtships of its time, and one of the most demanding marriages, until she died.

More worldly, more experienced, Curzon can hardly have failed to realize that she was deeply attracted by him. Within hours, she was writing him subtle reminders of the time they had spent together at Ashridge and the subjects their conversation had ranged over. Curzon replied, on 31 July 1890:

> I got your letter this morning. Thank you for it, dear, and for the words. It is a pleasure for me to have met and known you here. I shall think of you while you are away; and beg you both to come back and not wholly expel me from your memory in the interval. I wish you a happy season in Washington, and American males whose charm will just fall short of making you forget that Englishmen can also be charming. God bless you, Mary Victoria.   G.[5]

It is a clever letter, giving her freedom – but not quite; acknowledging interest – but not too much. He may have thought it prudent to be non-committal, since Mary was about to return to America. She, on the other hand, wanted to impress upon him the memory of their brief time together. The next day – in a gesture that she must have known was 'forward', even by American standards – she sent him a pearl from her necklace, set into a gold tiepin. The symbolism was not lost on the deeply romantic Curzon. It also reminded him that she was exceedingly rich.

George Curzon appears contradictory only to those who do not believe that a man may have two personalities – one public, and one private. Brought up in a magnificent, vast, neglected mansion, the eldest son in a noble but impoverished family of ten, he had felt the responsibilities of his position from his earliest childhood. They were drummed into him still further by a governess, Miss Paraman, whose methods with small children were of such mental and physical brutality that she must have verged on the insane. But she had the melancholy effect of creating in her young charge a driving and excessive conscientiousness which remained with him all his life. Just as, on his travels, he would compel his body to perform feats of endurance, so equally he worked on his official duties for twelve or sixteen hours a day as a matter of course. He stayed up far into the night, overseeing the most trivial detail, and never learnt to delegate. Mentally as well as physically he taxed himself to the outer limits. As a result he was plagued by headaches, insomnia, and a number of near breakdowns.

Yet behind the public face of this rigid, arrogant, brilliant, obsessional man there was a private personality of such sweetness, such craving for affection, such capacity for laughter and play, that it entranced those who were allowed to see it. All four of the discerning Tennant sisters adored him. Women always responded to the combination of the sentimental and the passionate in his nature. Men, too – especially if they shared the sentimental streak – men like George Wyndham and Harry Cust, and adventurers like Blunt, prized the friendship of George Curzon all their lives. The public Curzon, with his love of display and grandeur, his orotund eloquence, was born to administer and rule in the Empire. The private Curzon, albeit heir to the 4th Baron Scarsdale and Kedleston Hall, was a comparatively poor man. His father managed to give him an allowance of £1,000 a year, while he himself earned about the same again from various sources including his writing. In modern terms, it amounted to a more than comfortable if not extravagantly generous income for an eligible bachelor moving in the highest levels of society.

Mary Leiter, eleven years younger, was in her own way no less remarkable a character. She possessed, even at twenty, a calm dignity of bearing and an underlying seriousness which must have appealed to the public side of Curzon. She had an uncommon awareness of political matters. She was intimate with White House circles in Washington, sometimes even acting as co-hostess there for President Cleveland. She spoke excellent French; was widely read and cultivated; and expressed herself with grace and fluency. Curzon's private side cannot yet have known that she also had depths of sympathy and under-standing and a heart as warmly loving as his own. But he would certainly have noticed that she was beautiful; and with just the kind of beauty which most appealed to him: tall, slender, with a classically oval face and thick, wavy auburn hair.

Ever since 1887, when he had failed to secure the hand of the poignantly pretty, temptingly rich young widow, Sibell Grosvenor, George Curzon had indulged in a series of light-hearted flirtations – usually several at once. However, from that July day in 1890 when he first met Mary Leiter, he felt a growing certainty that she was the woman he would marry. Mary herself never doubted it. The love of these two, simple, fulfilling, and unchanging, stands almost alone among the turbulent emotional dramas and sexual infidelities that most of the Souls enjoyed. Yet it was to be nearly five years from the day they met until they day they married. During this interval, Curzon set about making himself an unchallenged expert in Asian and Oriental politics. He embarked upon a programme of arduous travelling.

Over the next five years he and Mary Leiter met only occasionally. She, after all, lived in America, while he was travelling almost continuously, mostly in India, Afghanistan and the Far East. She kept his interest alive with constant letters; thoughtful, warm letters that displayed her concern with world affairs, the arts, and – in particular – him. Curzon wrote much less frequently, hardly more than half a dozen times and in tones of studied frivolity; never committing himself in case he came back to find her changed; or – since his pride could not endure the blow of another successful rival – engaged to someone else. It was an unconventional wooing. Meanwhile, in the eyes of everyone else Mary Leiter was the belle not only of Washington, but London and Paris too; courted for her beauty and her fortune, urged by her puzzled parents to marry one of the eligible young men who were so plentifully available.

After a separation of nearly two years they were reunited, in Paris, on 3 March 1893, for a single evening. He dined with Mary and her mother at the Hôtel Vendôme. By now her parents must have suspected that there was more than just pen-friendship between the two of them. Tactfully, they were left alone at the end of the evening. Many years later, Curzon described what had happened:

> I had entered the hotel without the slightest anticipation that this would be the issue. She told me her story. How she had waited for nearly three years since the time when we first met, rejecting countless suitors and always waiting for me. I told her that while I felt from the beginning that we were destined for each other, I had not dared to speak, and had even run the risk of losing her because there was certain work in my scheme of Asiatic travel which I had resolved to do, and which I could not ask any married woman to allow her husband to carry out. Some of it, notably the journey to the Pamirs and Afghanistan, still remained undone: and even now when we became secretly engaged, it was on the understanding that I should be at liberty to complete my task before we took the final step.[6]

It is a romantic tale that Curzon tells; and if it was somewhat airbrushed by nostalgia, the facts remain. They did wait for each other for another two years, in total secrecy, and they did live happily together from their marriage until the day of her death.

It was to be another year before they met again, although Mary continued to visit London for the summer season. She came to know many of the Souls, and to admire, without ever quite sharing, their glittering repartee, their supreme self-confidence, and their social bravado. It was the decade for opulent, creamy women, their throats encircled with jewelled collars above delicately frothing lace. Their sexual freedom never appealed to Mary, quite apart from her pledge of fidelity to George. She could flirt, like every American girl, with a sparkle that never shaded into vulgarity, but now she did not choose to, and so, perhaps, the Souls were a little nervous of her, and mistook her secret devotion to Curzon for primness. All the same, she was seen everywhere. Her intelligence and independence of mind appealed greatly to Margot Tennant, who invited Mary and her parents to stay at Glen; while her distinction and beautiful manners appealed to the Salisburys, who invited her to Hatfield; as an American, she appealed to the raffish Jennie Churchill; and as a thinker and a lover of music she appealed to Arthur Balfour.

In June 1894 she and George met again, for two days, and Mary persuaded him to allow her to confide the news of their secret engagement to her parents. Doubtless she could no longer bear the pressure they must have been putting upon her to select one from the crowd of suitors who laid siege to her. It was honourable of Mary not to ask him to release her from her promise of secrecy in a letter, or to present him with a *fait accompli* by saying she'd been forced to admit the truth; but to wait until she could discuss it with him face to face. It was his last chance to back down from the marriage: instead, he, equally characteristically albeit with a touch of condescension, offered her the opportunity to withdraw. 'You are a young child, though a stately woman, and you are on the threshold of life.'[7] Plainly, the image of Mary, pursued by all, as Curzon's child bride, appealed to him. Neither of them had changed, and indeed Mary wrote: 'You know I shall not marry if you do not come back. Do not smile incredulously for I am not likely to change my mind. You know I have not in four years (which are probably the most impressionable of a girl's life) in spite of immense pressure to do so. The worldly marriages have not the slightest attraction for me.'[8]

In August they had a few hours together, before Curzon embarked on his long-planned, fearfully risky journey to the Pamirs and Afghanistan. Mary must have been terrified for him. She wrote begging him to alter his itinerary: perhaps the one time in her life when she tried to make him abandon a project on which he had set his heart. It made no difference. He told her in jocular terms about the hardships, knowing that she could picture the dangers for herself: 'Melting as I now am, on this day a month hence I should probably give half of what I possess in the world to feel even moderately warm. Why travellers do these things no-one knows; least of all the travellers themselves.'[9] At the same time he was writing to Wilfrid Scawen Blunt: 'I have been in countries whose practices would render the people admirable candidates for the Crabbet Club. At Chitral I fraternised with fratricides, parricides, murderers, adulterers and sodomites. I start tomorrow for Kabul, where the female donkey is the object of favourite solicitude.'[10] A few months later, when the strain of the journey was over for him, and the ordeal of waiting for news had ended for her, she timed a letter so that it should be waiting for him in Paris on his way home:

> Think of your being in Paris! It will be almost two years since our memorable meeting at the Hôtel Vendôme – and the two years of waiting will be nearly up ... The waiting years have been fruitful ones for you, and they've not been lost to me, for love and devotion and trust count for a great deal and my feminine philosophy believes in tests and patience greatly improving and developing a woman. I believe we shall be eternally happy.[11]

With Curzon safely back in England, Mary still the queen of Washington, and all their friends blissfully unaware of the relationship, only one obstacle remained. Curzon had to do what he had for so long put off, and break the news to his father. Lord Scarsdale – irascible, eccentric, high-handed and parsimonious, and vicar in the Church of England to boot, might not take kindly to hearing that his son and heir planned to mary the daughter of a first-generation American millionaire named Levi Z. Leiter. In the event, he took it very well: 'So long as you love her and she loves you, that is all that matters. You are not likely at your age to make a mistake, and she is old enough to know her mind.'[12]

And so, on 4 March 1895, in Washington and London simultaneously, the engagement was announced. People always hate to feel they have been kept in the dark, and as it gradually dawned on their friends on both sides of the Atlantic how unobservant they must have been, their reaction to the news was sometimes less than gracious. The Americans were furious that one of their most brilliant daughters was deserting her own country to marry an Englishman: and a mere *Mr* Curzon at that! The English – even the Souls, Curzon's dearest friends for fifteen years or more – felt that he, in turn, might have married a girl from the charmed circle of the English aristocracy, not this rather too clever, too formidable outsider.

Mary knew little of this – and would not have cared – and Curzon took no notice. He left for America on 10 April; arrived in Washington on the eighteenth, and spent two days cloistered with the lawyers and his prospective father-in-law while they drew up the marriage settlement. Finally, he would have enough money to live in some style: though at £6,000 a year it was less than he had hoped, it was still five times more than he had had so far. On 22 April 1895, Mary Leiter and George Curzon were married at last. The list of their wedding presents filled a whole book. Among hundreds of greetings on their marriage came one from one of Curzon's newest friends, the Amir of Afghanistan, who wrote to him after seeing Mary's photograph:

> I congratulate you, my honest friend, that though you have only married one wife, she is competent. . . . Faithfulness, wisdom and honesty, all these I gather from her photo and according to Phrenology. . . . If she should at any time thrash you I am certain you will have done something to deserve it. I am your sincere friend and well-wisher
>
> Abdur Rahman, Amir of Afghanistan[13]

Back in London a few weeks after their wedding, George and Mary Curzon began married life in the house in Carlton Gardens which Mary's father had rented for them. They should have embarked upon a season of triumphant social success and private happiness. In the event, it was very nearly a disaster. Not that they were disappointed in each other. Curzon wrote to his friend Cecil Spring-Rice: 'Matrimony is a success so overwhelming that celibacy, once a delight, has now become a puzzle.'[14] (This was perhaps tactless, for as George well knew, his friend in the British Embassy in Washington had long been in love with Mary himself.) Marriage proved all that they could have hoped for during their five years of waiting. Mary was delighted to find, within weeks, that she was expecting a child. Yet still there were problems. She was homesick for her family and her country. She was lonely in England, although at first the Souls gave the impression that they had forgiven her for marrying their George. How difficult she found them – especially after the adulation she had been used to at home – can be seen from this letter to her husband: 'I must say no more critical set exists in the world than the friends, as they are merciless to anyone who can't keep up in the race for pleasure. In my heart I know that the great fuss they make of me is because I am a novelty, unjaded, and the latest edition of Georgian news.'[15] While to her parents she wrote ambiguously, 'My path is strewn with roses, and the only thorns are the unforgiving women.'[16]

By 1895 the Souls themselves were becoming jaded. Their group had now been in existence for a decade. Grief over the early death of Laura Lyttelton, which had originally drawn them close in a spontaneous expression of sorrow at the shared loss of one whom many of them felt to have been the rarest of them all, had now, inevitably, receded. Alfred himself had married again, after six lonely years. Margot had written to Curzon in February 1892: 'You will have heard that Alfred is going to marry DD [Balfour]. You know us *so* intimately that you will know in a kind of a way how much we mind – DD is a very dear nice good intelligent wife and we shall like her ever so much but still it's no use pretending Alfred will be the same to us.'[17]

The first carefree impulses which had led the group to nickname themselves 'The Gang' – youthful impulses, defying the rigid stratification of society and its deference to rank and age – were gradually being forgotten, as the Souls came more and more to resemble the very society they had set out to challenge. The impulse to look for entertainment among like-minded people who required more than crude practical jokes to make them laugh, and found competition and excitement in more stimulating forms than gambling, was in turn being formalized into ritual jokes and a predictable round of Saturdays-to-Mondays. These house parties meant that – inevitably – the Souls began to play the same emotional roulette that they had initially deplored in the Marlborough House Set. In the space of a decade, most of the young people who had mourned Laura's early death had grown up to become, still ravishing, witty and games-loving, but also clandestine, self-seeking, increasingly disposed to compromise principles for pleasure and friendship for politics. The velvety glory of the summer roses was curled fully open now, and just beginning to brown here and there at the edges.

Mary, with her clear-sightedness and idealism, knew that his friends the Souls were not quite all that George had led her to expect. He, perhaps, did not yet perceive that their days of innocence were over. Shared memories and lifelong friendships bound him too closely to them for that. But Mary began to feel the breath of disillusionment. Then, too, she was an American; and even the wealthiest American girls were brought up to notions of democracy and equality which had never troubled the pretty heads of young Englishwomen. She was not disloyal enough to let her true feelings show, either to George or his friends; but her homesick letters to her family revealed much of what she was secretly thinking: 'London life is a continuous striving, striving, striving to keep going, the little people praying to be noticed by the great, and the great seldom lowering their eyelids to look at the small.'[18] Nevertheless she tried to do her duty as a hostess, and to entertain George's friends, now that at last he had a wife and an income that allowed him to repay the years of lavish hospitality. She gave weekend parties at the Georgian house near Reigate which they had taken as a retreat from Carlton Gardens. Already her guest list betrayed a more catholic taste than was usual among the increasingly inward-looking Souls. Henry Adams, the American historian, and the novelists Thomas Hardy and Pearl Craigie all figure alongside more predictable names like Grenfell . . . Asquith . . . Granby . . . and Charteris.

George had no idea how homesick she was. In fact, it was making her ill. There was a scare around Christmas, when it seemed as though her baby might be born prematurely. She was carried up to London from Reigate in a litter hung with white roses. On 20 January 1896 their first child, a girl – Irene – was born.

They spent the year of 1896 quietly: George immersed in his Foreign Office boxes, Mary in the baby, and both of them in each other. The following year was still subdued, with Curzon working away painstakingly till the small hours of every morning on the ceaseless flow of official papers that he had to study in his position as Parliamentary Under-Secretary of State at the Foreign Office. In 1895, well over ninety thousand telegrams and despatches were received by the Foreign Office, and Curzon would have read almost all of them . . . and drafted replies to a fair proportion, as well. In addition he had speeches to write and deliver, and he answered some five hundred parliamentary questions every year on foreign affairs in the House of Commons. Meanwhile, Mary's activities were curtailed by her continuing weakness. She wrote a melancholy letter home:

> I do very little. There are things I cannot help doing, married as I am, but I do nothing that is not absolutely necessary. I never rush about London seeing people and exhibitions and concerts and theatres and charities and the hundred things the world expects you to do. I wish I had the strength, for no one would enjoy more than I do the vast amount of interest and amusement that London affords. I do nothing outside my own house, and only see people on a visit like this or if they come to the house. I quite realise that I shall never be able to take my place and be a help to George unless I am strong, for an ailing wife is no help to a politician. She must always be ready to be a kind of smiling, hand-shaking machine.[19]

It was to be the last quiet year of her life.

George Curzon acquitted himself brilliantly at the Foreign Office under Lord Salisbury. Since his chief combined the posts of Prime Minister and Foreign Secretary, he was more than usually dependent on Curzon, who was his deputy in the House of Commons. Curzon had been hard-working – of course; loyal, invariably; and had steered an impeccable course through the Scylla and Charybdis of the Concert of Europe and the question of Turkey and Eastern Europe. His fame in the country was now matched by his reputation in the House of Commons. Both in public and in Parliament his oratory – always the mode of speech that came most naturally to him – commanded attention and was widely reported.

It was often said of him that he was the very model of an eighteenth-century aristocrat. Curzon was proud and autocratic; bowing the head to no-one except his Sovereign, yet obsessively self-critical. Driven by an unforgiving, stern conscience (the legacy of his sadistic governess, Miss Paraman), he was already an anachronism in his own time. His peculiar combination of *noblesse oblige* and patrician arrogance in public life, with a craving for love and warmth in his private life, gave him a dedication to duty and an inner vulnerability unthinkable in any other of the Souls. Few people, except his wife, ever saw more than one side of him. The received view would have been that expressed by a parliamentary opponent, T. P. O'Connor: 'His triumph will be as much of temperament as of sheer intelligence. He has a great deal of intelligence, it is true; but he has more temperament. Self-confident, ambitious, masterful, hard – he is determined to be a master of men and he will be.'[20]

By 1898 his grasp of foreign affairs was supreme. When Lord Salisbury was absent in the South of France because of illness, and his nephew Arthur Balfour had to deputize for him, Curzon had to be invited to attend all cabinet meetings, for no one else could understand the ins and outs of the China problem. As well as his expertise as Under-Secretary, his travel in the Far East had made him an unrivalled authority on the political and territorial situation there. He was still only thirty-nine, yet already the triumph for which he had been in training all these years was almost within reach. 'The Viceroyalty,' he once said, 'was the dream of my childhood, the fulfilled ambition of my manhood, and my highest conception of duty to the State.'[21] He genuinely believed that the British Empire was 'under Providence, the greatest instrument for good that the world has seen . . . there has never been anything so great in the world's history.'[22] Only his precarious health – exacerbated by the compulsion to overwork – stood between him and the prize.

In June 1898 his life's ambition was realized. The Prime Minister informed him that his name had been submitted to Queen Victoria as the next Viceroy of India.

Curzon had never made any secret of the fact that he believed himself to be uniquely suited to the post. In 1897 he was alarmed by a rumour that the next Viceroy might be the ineffectual Marquess of Lorne, whose main claim to esteem was that he had married the Queen's fourth daughter, Princess Louise. (The marriage had been undermined by the Princess's continuing dalliance with the sculptor, Boehm, commissioned by her mother to make innumerable busts of the late Prince Albert and, in due course, of her ghillie, John Brown.) Curzon was not prepared to sit back passively and allow another man to succeed Lord Elgin as Viceroy without pressing his own claims to the job. He wrote his political chief and patron, Lord Salisbury, a letter of several thousand words, setting out in detail his own qualifications. He knew that no other contender could truthfully list among his attributes:

I have for at least ten years made a careful and earnest study of Indian problems, have been to the country four times, and am acquainted with and have the confidence of most of its leading men. . . . I have been fortunate too in making the acquaintance of the rulers of the neighbouring states, Persia, Afghanistan, Siam, friendly relations with whom are a help to any Viceroy. . . . At the India Office in 1891–2, thanks to the appointment with which you honoured me, I learned something of the official working of the great machine. . . .

And he ended his plea, with a sincerity which was to be borne out by events:

But my strongest impulse is, I can honestly say, not a personal one at all: it is the desire, while one is still in the heyday of life, to do some strenuous work in a position of responsibility and a cause for which previous study and training may have rendered one in some measure less unfit for the effort.[23]

For the time being nothing happened. Salisbury wrote a bland, non-committal reply; but Lord Lorne faded from the scene. A year later, in April 1898, knowing that the next Viceroy must be chosen within months, Curzon wrote again, pressing his candidacy more strongly:

For 12 years I have worked and studied and thought – with a view should the chance ever arise – to fitting myself to the position. But I have also said to myself that I would not care to take it unless it were offered to me before I was 40: the reasons being in my opinion the work is such as demands the energies of a young man in the prime of life. . . .[24]

As Salisbury well knew, Curzon was now thirty-nine. The implication was unmistakable: he was not prepared to wait another five years. It was a dangerous threat to have risked holding over his political patron. What he could not know was that his chief had already written in January to sound out the Queen for her reaction to the appointment of Curzon as Viceroy. In June, the Queen gave her guarded approval. She knew Curzon personally, and approved of his industry and high moral principles. In addition, she had met Mary once, and been charmed by her grave sweetness and obvious devotion to her husband. Although American, and very young (Mary was now twenty-eight), she would not be an unworthy Vicereine. In a letter to Lord Salisbury, the Queen wrote her own assessment of how a Viceroy should govern his (meaning her) Indian subjects. If only all her imperial administrators had shared such wise and liberal views!

> The future Viceroy must really shake himself more and more free from his red-tapist narrow-minded Council and Entourage. He must be *more independent, must hear for himself* what the *feelings* of the Natives really are, and do what he thinks right and not be guided by the *snobbish* and vulgar, over-bearing and offensive behaviour of our Civil and Political Agents, if we are to go on peaceably and happily in India. . . . [25]

How, one cannot help wondering, had the octogenarian Queen obtained this remarkably accurate picture of the behaviour of her servants of Empire? As it happened, Curzon's own views were in perfect agreement with those of his Sovereign, as he hastened to assure Salisbury:

> I shall not fail to bear in mind her wise injunctions. They might furnish a Rule of Conduct to anyone about to occupy a position of authority over Asiatic races. In travelling I have seen something of these and have been thrown so much in their society that I hope I have lost – if indeed I ever had – the insular arrogance of the Englishman. [26]

On 11 August 1898 the appointment was made public, giving the Curzons just over four months in which to make their preparations before leaving for India. Mary's first reaction to the news was expressed in a letter to her parents, filled with pride, modesty – and apprehension:

> It takes my breath away, for it is the greatest position in the English world next to the Queen and the Prime Minister, and it will be a satisfaction, I know, to you and Mama that your daughter Maria will fill the greatest place ever held by an American abroad. Heaven only knows how I shall do it, but I shall do my best to be a help to George and an honour to you and Mama, and I shall put my trust in Providence and hope to learn how to be a ready-made Queen. [27]

The very lightest of her responsibilities now was to choose a sumptuous wardrobe; but that had to wait for the birth of their second child. Mary knew that – for George – a son would set the seal upon his glory; but on 28 August another daughter was born. They called her Cynthia.

In September, the Curzons embarked upon a round of congratulatory parties, dinners, receptions and speeches. Suddenly – Mary must have reflected – they found they had friends everywhere. Three years of comparative social neglect ended overnight, and they became the most sought-after guests in London. Once again, the Souls clamoured for their company, and heaped praise upon Mary. The Grenfells had them to stay; and the Cowpers; and all Curzon's old Etonian friends gave a sumptuous dinner to herald his new rôle. Finally, since the Viceroy of India could not be a mere 'Mr' Curzon, a title was found for him. He was created Baron Curzon of Kedleston, in the Peerage of Ireland (the latter a formula that would enable him to return to the House of Commons eventually, if he so wished: although in practice an earldom was almost automatically conferred upon a returning Viceroy). Mary was now Lady Curzon, and wrote endearingly to her parents: 'I feel like a ship in full sail upon the high seas of dignity!'²⁸

Finally, the very night before Mary set sail with the two children and their nanny (Curzon was to catch up with them a few days later in Marseilles) the assembled hosts of the Souls gave a final, farewell dinner for them at the Hotel Cecil, then newly built and affording the most luxurious dining-room in London. In its warmth of feeling, good humour and sense of shared and long-standing friendship, it mirrored his two earlier dinners at the Bachelors' Club. It was possibly the last occasion on which the Souls were all together for a common purpose.

A photographer was present on that evening of 9 December 1898 to record the scene. There is no 'top table' and surprisingly little formality. Curzon and his closest friends sit – including A.J.B. – at a round table in the foreground, leaning over the backs of their chairs to gaze into the lens of the camera. The other guests, under the great gas-lit chandeliers, have turned out in their finery to celebrate with the new Viceroy; every man in white tie, every woman resplendent in jewels and bare shoulders. Several of them are laughing into the camera; yet Balfour – at Curzon's table – looks grave.

Just as Curzon had saluted each of his guests at those earlier dinners in verse, so now they did the same for him. George Wyndham was the poet, and the verses were of rather higher quality than Curzon's amiable doggerel of nearly ten years ago. Wyndham's lines have something of the rolling gusto of Gilbert and Sullivan, then at the height of their fame. They have, too, given the benefit of hindsight, a bitter irony . . .

> So 'Go in and win!' what's five years but a lustre
>   To shine round a name that already shines bright?
> Then come back, and we'll greet you and go such a 'buster'
>   As never was seen; no, not even tonight!
>   Come back in five years with your sheaves of new Fame:
>   You'll find your old Friends; and you'll find them the same
>   As now when you gladden their sight.

Even Curzon himself, in a sobering flash of prescience, reflected that he seemed to be riding the caparisoned elephant without having yet proved his right to do so: 'There is something to me incongruous in the whole thing. It is all very generous and very encouraging. But surely the entertainment and congratulations ought to come after, not before, performance. One goes out amid the glare of magnesium. How shall I return?'²⁹ How indeed?

But for the present all was ebullience, and optimism, and a warmth of friendship to which Curzon paid tribute in his speech to the assembled Souls:

> Tonight is a night that I can never forget. Surfeited as I have been with the public demonstrations of the past few weeks, squeezed dry as I am of the last platitude about India, it is with positive relief that I find myself in the wholly frivolous and utterly irresponsible society that is collected round these tables. For here I see about me the friends, and sometimes the critics, of a tumultuous

but absolutely unrepentant youth – the comrades of a more sober and orderly middle age – and when I return five years hence, what I hope may be the props and the solace of dull and declining years. Lacking, as I am popularly supposed to be, in most of the adornments and in many of the requisites, of a gentle and diffident personality, and of a modest and alluring career – there is one commodity in which I have never been wanting – and that is in the possession of whole-hearted and loyal friends.[†]

And thus, with perfect trust, George Curzon saluted his friends. That evening, perhaps that moment, was the apotheosis of the Souls.

India was the *raison d'être* of Curzon's whole life. He described it to George Wyndham as 'a vast mystery, a prodigious experiment, a genuine glory'. By birth, temperament and training he was ideally suited for it. His energy and application were equal to its demands. He had the breadth of vision to conceive of what might be done; and the grasp of detail to ensure that it *was* done. He had a wife and young family who fulfilled him emotionally, so that he was never dehumanized by the pomp and power that as Viceroy inevitably awaited him. He had a deep and genuine respect for the Indian people: their ancient culture, their achievements and their character. And yet – India almost destroyed him.

The government of the British Empire was carried out by three kinds of people. There were those who were genuinely inspired by a vision of Empire and the desire to serve, though perhaps their main desire was to serve Great Britain and the Queen, rather than those people over whom they governed. Then there were the inadequate, the incompetent, those in disgrace; the younger sons who had always been a bit of a problem, those who were mentally or physically slightly feeble, about whom their families would feel more comfortable if they were a few thousand miles away, or the aristocratic scoundrels, whose gambling debts or sexual misadventures forced them to seek anonymity abroad – the upper-class equivalent of sending convicts to Van Diemens Land. Such people, once they found themselves under some tropical sun, either deteriorated altogether or – just as often – they buckled down and did a surprisingly good job. Finally, there were the venal, the corrupt, the sadistic, the authoritarian. They were simply out to exploit 'the Natives' whom they despised and regarded as 'lesser breeds without the law'.[30] Although the smallest group of all, they did untold damage.

Curzon, it goes without saying, fell into the first category, and added to his high ideals the advantages of a brilliant brain and, initially, the admiration and support of the British government. He was horrified to find, when he arrived in India, how many of the civil servants working under him fell into the second category. And he soon came across army officers who undoubtedly belonged in the third: which discovery led to his own eventual undoing. Isolated by his lofty position, cut off from social and intellectual stimulus and virtually debarred from friendship with anyone else, Mary became almost his sole support and confidante. For the first time, perhaps, he realized what an exceptional woman he had married.

Curzon as Viceroy personified the highest ideals and achievements of the

[†]From Lord Curzon's handwritten speech in I.O.L., Mss Eur F 111/24–25. For the rest of this impromptu speech see Appendix 2 where it is printed in full and for the first time.

imperial ethic: given its inherent shortcoming, namely the assumption that the British had any moral right to rule India in the first place. This assumption is not one that Curzon ever seriously questioned, although his attitude towards the Indian people showed more humility than many a petty official or clerk. In the speech he made on arrival in Bombay on 31 December 1898, the new Viceroy had declared: 'You do me no more than justice in saying that I desire to respect the traditions and customs of your country. Such respect is, I think, the foundation on which British rule in India must rest as well as the natural impulse of any man who feels that the natives of India are indeed his fellow-subjects, and share with him in the common heritage of the great Empire of which we are proud, and which it is our ambition to conserve.' His respect for the country was genuine. Curzon devoted a great deal of time to restoring the glories of Indian architecture. The preservation of the Taj Mahal was largely due to him: he ordered it to be cleared of algae, fungi, weeds and grass, and thus restored its gleaming Rajasthani marble. He wanted to learn as much as possible about the continent he had dreamed all his life of governing. It became a crusade, pursued with almost moral fervour, to leave that government better – meaning faster, more efficient, and more incorruptible – than it had been when he arrived. Although he was handicapped by at best the inertia, at worst the outright opposition, of his subordinates, he set about the giant task of reforming the entire bureaucratic structure. Slow and cumbersome as an elephant, and much less intelligent, it ruled the lives of India's 280 million people. Curzon often despaired of being able to complete his reforms. All the same, he described the obstacles he encountered to his friend – the writer Pearl Craigie – with all his old wit: 'Nothing has been done hitherto under six months. When I suggest six weeks, the attitude is one of pained surprise; if six days, one of pathetic protest; if six hours, one of stupefied resignation.'[31]

Curzon's grandiose plan was impossible – then as now – for a reason he could never have accepted. The overloaded and bribable Indian civil service, down to its smallest ramifications in its furthest-flung states, was derived from and compatible with the Indian character and climate. A country where labour is cheap and where one relative in a clerical job confers status on the entire family may not wish to streamline its administrative system. Patronage and bureaucracy may be seen, not as contemptible or inefficient, let alone corrupt, but as a reasonable way of exchanging favours and securing one's ends. What looks like apathy may be stoical acceptance. What looks like resignation may be faith. The Indian and the British temperament were fundamentally different. Most of what Curzon tried to introduce was based on the conviction that the Indian could and should become more like the Briton – and *would*, if only he, and the echelons of officialdom below him, tried hard enough. Certainly no one could have tried harder than Curzon.

The Indians recognized his industry for what it was: a devotion to their well being. They respected his impartial application of the law, to high and low, brown and white, regardless. Many of his own officials did not thank him for either. Furthermore, the Indians shared the Viceroy's love of magnificence and display, rather than censuring and even ridiculing him for it, as some of his colleagues did behind his back. His British subordinates grew restive under Curzon's stream of urgent and well-informed questions, his insistence on being apprised of the smallest detail. Soon, mutters of discontent began to filter back to England.

Mary, while unswerving in her loyalty to her husband and her belief in the rightness of all he did, also helped with her tact and sweetness to mitigate the effects of his sometimes impossibly high standards. She was universally loved, despite being so young and an American by birth. Her early experience in White House circles now stood her in good stead. She knew how to charm strangers, how to be diplomatic and at the same time natural and spontaneous. She could sit down when she observed that Curzon's back was troubling him, thus enabling him to sit down as well. She could laugh or yawn when those around her were intimidated by the formality of a state occasion, and thus break the ice. She could stretch a friendly hand towards women and children where her husband could only converse formally with their menfolk. Yet she must often have been bored, and already the merciless Indian climate was beginning to have an effect upon her health. As a girl she had had a strong constitution; now, she began to suffer agonizing headaches. Whenever possible, she concealed these from her husband, knowing how much he relied upon her. Her iron self-control could match his, as she drove herself to perform her official duties at his side, knowing how much it mattered that she should always be there. An account from a letter written to her parents shows how great her discipline was, even in the throes of a severe migraine:

> Yesterday I had one of my headaches, but in spite of it I went to a party on board the Admiral's ship. George also, and I smiled when I could have sobbed with pain. When I came back I had to be carried upstairs, and the doctor thought I was mad to go out to the Lt. Governor's to dine, but a dinner of 70 had been arranged for us and I could not give out. I nearly fainted twice dressing, and nothing but my will carried me through. I was carried to the carriage and had to drive $3\frac{1}{2}$ miles to the house. I thought at times I should die, as when I arrived I had to shake hands with 70 people and talk all through dinner, and afterwards I had to talk with each lady. The only thing I ate was a water-biscuit and a teaspoonful of brandy. I collapsed in a heap in the carriage on our way home. Our doctor met me at the door and I was carried up to bed.[32]

On this occasion he could not have failed to notice her suffering, but whenever she could, Mary concealed from Curzon the full extent of the demands he made upon her, knowing that if he knew, he would ask less: and she wanted to give him everything. Their love for each other was so great that even a few hours spent apart were an ordeal and days were misery. Yet in the spring of 1901 she travelled home to England. She had now spent over two years in India. It was time to renew contacts with family and friends. It was time, above all, to bring first-hand news of the Viceroy into the heart of a cabinet which seemed to be losing some of its confidence in him. No one could do this better than Mary. In this way, the Souls learned for the first time, perhaps, that she was indeed worthy of their George.

No woman among them could have made a better job of the rôle of Vicereine. Mary Elcho would have radiated as much sweetness, and evoked as much love and warmth in response, but she lacked Mary Curzon's discipline and tact. Ettie Grenfell would have been unrivalled in scenting intrigue and detecting who were the allies of the Viceroy and who was not to be trusted, but her mannered tones and fey expressions would have puzzled the Indians, and after the first six months no one would have told her the truth. Margot would have loved every moment – and been a disaster from the day she arrived.

And so Mary Curzon found herself, for the first time, an object of some respect and admiration in the critical eyes of the Souls. She had acquired new maturity from the awesome experience of being Vicereine, and she certainly brought the savour of fresh experience to enliven the London social scene.

Queen Victoria had died on 22 January 1901. The Prince of Wales, king-in-waiting for forty years, succeeded to the throne at last. Among the English aristocracy, grief at the death of the old Queen was largely a matter of form. She had been in retreat for so long, in the fastnesses of Windsor or Osborne or Balmoral, that few people other than her ministers and her household had felt close to her as a human being. Now, the Marlborough House Set rejoiced at the accession of their favourite. Nevertheless, when Mary Curzon and her two daughters arrived in England on 4 May, society was still wearing deep mourning. The contrast between what she had left behind and what she found must have been startling: like a colour photograph replaced by a black and white one. Indian women's skin could be any colour from pale gold to deepest bronze, and they wore saris of shimmering fabrics in jewel colours, often iridescent with embroidery. In England, complexions were white after the long winter, clothes black and heavy with the full panoply of court mourning.

She wasted little time. Only the conviction that she could serve George better by being in England could have persuaded Mary to leave him for several months. Less than three weeks after her arrival, Clinton Dawkins – an old friend – was writing to Curzon:

> I had the pleasure of seeing Lady Curzon last week (and hope to see her again this week). She was looking remarkably well, and, if I may be permitted to say so, more radiantly beautiful than ever. . . . We had a good talk about Indian matters. But I am afraid that Lady Curzon finds that society is little interested in India, or in anything serious. Bridge is its one interest. And, if I may say so without treason, the advent of the new Ruler has not done much to promote interest in serious things.[33]

Nothing was allowed to interfere with the summer calendar of house parties. Mary, a novelty after her two-and-a-half-year absence, was invited everywhere. After staying with the new King and Queen at Windsor – where she found the one prejudiced and the other ignorant – she moved on for a Saturday-to-Monday at Taplow Court with the Grenfells, among her husband's oldest friends. Loyally, she hastened to tell him about it: 'Such a heavenly party! AJB, Milner, Asquiths, Vincent, Cranbornes, Winston, Wyndham, Elchos. At dinner AJB sat by me again.'[34] Curzon knew her too well to suffer a moment's jealousy, even at 4,000 miles' distance. The person who did feel threatened was Mary Elcho, of course. She instantly noticed that Mary had become the focus of everyone's attention, not least Balfour's.

Finding herself in society without George for the first time since their marriage six years before, Mary realized she was at last being invited for herself, and not merely as an appendage to her husband. She blossomed. As Vicereine, she need fear condescension from no one. But her visit to England had a serious purpose, and to Curzon she deplored the frivolity of the season: 'Everyone is doing the same old thing – just flirting, and dining, and dawdling.'[35] And she was no more complimentary about some of the Souls: 'Henry Asquith [is] obese and hopeful about his political future, and Margot revelling in a garrulous, selfish grief which gets on everyone's nerves.'[36] One man did seem to recognize the skill with which Curzon was handling his responsibilities: the Prime Minister. Mary reported back: 'Lord Salisbury said to me, "George is having a very great career in India. His frontier policy will keep us in India 50 years longer." '[37]

The message behind her letters was quite clear. Mary believed that the highest political offices in the country – perhaps even the premiership, if he chose – were now her husband's for the taking. Beside him all the others looked etiolated, world-weary, disillusioned, frivolous. And so, more than ever, she moved with limpid grace and assurance through the summer, universally welcomed, but making certain that everyone knew how great was Curzon's task in India; how immense the effort and talents he brought to it; how triumphantly he was rising to the challenge. To George himself she wrote at the end of her stay, in September 1901:

If you keep your health, as I pray you will, you have the whole future of the Party in your hands. Arthur will not take the trouble to lead. St John isn't inspiring enough. George Wyndham is a sentimentalist, and hasn't the hard sense to do strong things. So who is there but my Pappy? No-one has anything like your vigour, and there is apathy in London about everything and everybody. It was illustrated by Arthur saying of bridge, which he now plays the whole time, 'I like it because it saves the effort of conversation.' Inertia seems to have attacked them all. They will need you to come back and wake them up. Great as your work is in India, it will be even greater in England, where the Party is slipping down the well of indifference and incapacity.[38]

Mary knew that the surest appeal to her husband was through his sense of duty. Had she spoken to him of the political ambitions he might fulfil by hurrying back the moment his five-year term as Viceroy was up; or of the effect India was having upon his health – or, even more persuasively, hers; or of the pleasure of being among friends again, and in a temperate climate . . . all these appeals she knew he could resist. The suggestion that the Conservative party and the country needed him was the only one that might tempt him back. Mary must have known by now that her husband, having grasped the immensity of the task that confronted him, realized it would take a second term as Viceroy to complete. She had seen how his health – mental as well as physical – was suffering under the demands he made upon it. And she must have begun to appreciate that her own constitution, too, was becoming frail.

On 26 September 1901, after nearly five months in England, Mary gathered up the two little girls and set sail back to India. Her task had been twofold: to inform herself, and tell George, about what was happening back home; and to tell his friends and colleagues what was happening to George. Her success at the latter can be judged from the words of Lord Esher – friend and adviser of the new King, and the ubiquitous *éminence grise* of court and politics:

I have just finished a huge bag of papers, and long letters to George Curzon in

India about one or two things. He is one of the greatest of Viceroys, if not altogether *the* greatest. Certainly, except Cromer,[39] no other Englishman possesses his qualities as an administrator, and possibly none as a statesman. He has enormous capacity for work, and a brilliant imagination, with supreme gift of expression.[40]

George Curzon seemed poised to top his achievement as Viceroy with even greater glory at the pinnacle of government at home. Yet, somehow, the tide of his life turned and began to run the other way. He was to endure, in the course of the next two decades, neglect, unpopularity, and occupations that were trivial beside those he felt himself to be capable of. His ill-health and natural arrogance were exacerbated by overwork. He seemed to know that he was making impossible demands upon himself, for he wrote in a letter to his old friend and rival, George Wyndham (who was also under great strain at the Northern Ireland Office at this time): 'I shall imperatively need some rest. No-one can do the work that I am doing here, with no interlude or holiday for five years – following upon three years as Under-Secretary for Foreign Affairs at home – with two very bad physical breakdowns in the course of it (and I am always trembling on the verge of a third) without feeling the effects.'[41] He became grossly intolerant of any breath of criticism or interference from those in the India Council, whose job it was to oversee his rule. Always brusque to subordinates, he was now openly rude. He alienated colleagues and supporters, both in India and England, and all Mary Curzon's charm could not protect him from the consequences of his own hubris.

Initially, however, many people tried to save him from himself. In 1902 his old friend and fellow leader among the Souls, Arthur Balfour – who was by now Prime Minister – wrote to Curzon in what were intended to be tactful and conciliatory terms:

> You seem to think that you are injured whenever you do not get exactly your own way! But which of us gets exactly his own way? Certainly not the Prime Minister. Certainly not any of his Cabinet colleagues. We all suffer the common lot of those who, having to work with others, are sometimes overruled by them. I doubt whether any of your predecessors have ever received so large a measure of confidence from either the Secretary of State or the Home Government. I am ready to add that probably none has ever deserved that confidence more.[42]

Another old friend, Sir Arthur Godley, put the matter more succinctly: 'The responsibility for every one of your acts, great and small, lies with the Secretary of State, the Prime Minister, and the Cabinet; and where the responsibility is absolute and unshared, there must be a corresponding right of control, absolute and unshared.'[43]

Curzon was never able to accept that the seeds of his undoing germinated deep in his own character. He attributed his problems to the fact that, during the latter half of his first term of office, two men came to share with him the government of India. They were St John Brodrick and Lord Kitchener. The irony was that the former was one of his oldest friends – a man whom he had known both as a schoolboy at Eton and an undergraduate at Balliol, who had been one of his most trusted confidants ever since; while the latter came to India at Curzon's own insistence, and against the advice of many of his friends. The sagacious Esher warned him that the hero of Khartoum was 'uncouth and ruthless'. When Lord George Hamilton wrote to Curzon confirming that his own choice of Lord Kitchener for Commander-in-Chief of the Army out in India had been carried, he added: 'I look with some apprehension upon this appointment, as I fear the effect of his rough and unsympathetic manner and strong economic hand upon the native army. You will have carefully to watch him.'[44]

But Curzon would not listen to the warnings. He wanted the best for India; he believed that Kitchener was the best military man alive; therefore India had to have him. Curzon's probity was such that, even had he known the bitter conflict which lay ahead, he would still have been determined to have Kitchener. Besides, after four years as Viceroy, Curzon was showing symptoms of a hubris that could not imagine any man in India, under *his* rule, would not ultimately have to defer to him. He also overlooked the fact that Kitchener had powerful friends at home, and had been more recently in touch with them. His intimacy with Lady Salisbury, and his avuncular devotion to Ettie Grenfell's handsome sons, had made Kitchener into an 'honorary Soul'. He had influence at the very highest level of politics – that so-called 'Hatfield connection' – and would not hesitate to use it. Mary, more up-to-date with the Souls and their liaisons, may have tried to warn Curzon.

The omens were there. Curzon chose to ignore them. In October 1902, then, Kitchener became C-in-C. In September 1903, Brodrick took over as Secretary of State for India, thereby becoming Curzon's main channel of communication with the British cabinet. Between them, they were to make Curzon's last three years in India among the most troubled of his entire life. Kitchener's unscrupulous ambitions, and his scheming and secret enlisting of support behind the Viceroy's back, undermined Curzon's credibility with his friends and colleagues at home. St John Brodrick – a much lesser man than Curzon and consequently, perhaps, jealous and ultimately vindictive – completed the process of discrediting the one-time golden youth acclaimed by the Souls. It has to be added that Curzon did not help himself to avoid disaster, and Mary could not.

By the time Kitchener arrived in India Curzon had managed to alienate the Army. It happened as a result of his behaviour over two incidents; and while in both cases the Viceroy was right in principle, in practice he was so high-handed as to carry moral rectitude almost to the point of self-destruction. Once again, characteristically, the risk he personally ran would only have increased Curzon's conviction that he must do what he believed to be right.

The first incident took place in Rangoon in 1899, soon after Curzon had taken over as Viceroy. A group of drunken soldiers from a British regiment stationed there were accused of raping a Burmese woman. At the subsequent trial matters were hushed up, native witnesses bribed to withhold their evidence, and the men concerned were acquitted. Curzon got to hear about it, and was outraged. He not only sent the accused men back to England in disgrace, he also demanded fierce reprisals against the entire regiment, which was accordingly sent to Aden for a year without leave or privileges.

The Army simmered with resentment, but did not learn its lesson. The second incident followed a similar pattern. In April 1902, two troopers from the 9th

Lancers – a famous and fashionable regiment which had just arrived in India after winning new laurels in the South African War – quarrelled with their native cook and beat him up so severely that the man died from his injuries. Once again, the commander of the regiment tried to hush matters up. News of it reached the Viceroy, who, exactly as on the previous occasion, not only punished the men concerned, but determined to humiliate their entire regiment as well. He cancelled all leave for six months. 'I will not,' Curzon wrote unflinchingly, 'be a party to any of the scandalous hushing up of bad cases of which there is too much in this country, or to the theory that a white man may kick or batter a black man to death with impunity because "he is only a d—— nigger." '45 At a time when public opinion was automatically, unthinkingly, racist, and took for granted that a black man's rights were not the same as those of a white man, Curzon's courage was both remarkable and well in advance of his time.

Unfortunately for him, the popularity and fame of the 9th Lancers were then at their height. Curzon found himself vilified in the British press, while at the Coronation Durbar the Lancers were singled out by all the Europeans present for the loudest cheer of the day: a conspicuous, and intentional, snub to the Viceroy. The fact that the far larger crowd of Indians observed this in grim silence may have buttressed Curzon's certainty that he was morally right, but it could not lessen his consciousness of the insult to him. Even his personal guests at the Durbar had been unable to resist greeting the immaculately caparisoned Lancers with wild enthusiasm.

Kitchener, then, would have found when he arrived in India at the end of 1902 that the Army was already ranged sullenly against Curzon. Within three days the new C-in-C took complete charge, and embarked on a course of action which undermined and eventually destroyed Curzon's supremacy in India. He clashed with Curzon, and for that matter with the whole India Council, by demanding that the Commander-in-Chief should be the sole arbiter of military matters in India. Kitchener – the hero of Khartoum, darling of the British public, boundlessly confident – refused to be subject to any of the normal administrative checks and balances. He demanded the abolition of the Military Member in Council, whose duty was to share responsibility for the Army (much as the Ministry of Defence at home was there to oversee the conduct of military men in the field, and plan strategy with them), and he claimed that all power over the Army should be vested in him alone. On grounds of constitutional propriety as well as plain common sense, Curzon and the Council refused to agree. For over a year, correspondence and memoranda ricocheted between Viceroy and Commander-in-Chief and the India Council and the cabinet back home. Curzon and Kitchener grew more and more intransigent. Both staked their personal prestige and thus their careers in India upon the outcome.

Early in 1903, when his five-year tenure as Viceroy was entering its final year, Curzon had decided that he would – if the government allowed him – stay on for a second term, probably of two years. It was a decision no Viceroy had made for nearly a century, for the job was so gruelling, the climate so enervating, and the personal sacrifices required so enormous, that most men felt that one period in office was more than enough display of public spirit. At the time when he made up his mind, Curzon's troubles with Kitchener had not yet come out into the open, and he was still able to convince himself that the new C-in-C was an ally. In June the Prime Minister – Arthur Balfour – agreed to allow Curzon to stay on; a decision he later said he regretted more than almost any other of his premiership. In August the announcement was made public.

The Indians were jubilant. Not so Curzon's friends back home. Sir Schomberg MacDonnell – his old friend 'Pom' – wrote: 'I speak with the brutality of friendship, you are a street ahead of all your contemporaries in ability. You suffer from the instincts of the great ruler and the great gentleman, and you are going to sacrifice the certainty of being Prime Minister to the splendid ambition of being India's greatest Viceroy.'[46] Like Mary before him, 'Pom' found that an appeal to ambition cut no ice. In any case, Curzon believed that a second term could only strengthen his claim to the premiership. He had as yet no inkling of how powerfully Kitchener was intriguing behind his back. But he requested six months' home leave first; and he did accept the offer of the ancient title of Warden of the Cinque Ports, an office that was held for life, and included an official residence at Walmer Castle in Kent.

Mary had sailed for England in January 1904. On 20 March their third child was born: another daughter. They christened her Alexandra, at the request of the Queen; but all her life she was known as 'Baba'. On 30 April Curzon left India for his first journey home in over five years, to rejoin his wife and children. He hoped for a warm welcome – and, from the public who had heard of and admired his achievements as Viceroy, he got it – but he still did not realize how far he had fallen from favour in the eyes of the government. Kitchener maintained his close intimacy with the new Lady Salisbury, writing her regular letters which put his own, highly partisan, version of the events between him and Curzon. Thus it was he, rather than the Viceroy, who had the ear of the Prime Minister: Lady Salisbury's cousin by marriage, Arthur Balfour.

For the time being, however, the Souls welcomed him to a brilliant Edwardian summer, fêting him and Mary as much as his obsessional devotion to work and her worsening health would allow. They stayed in their house in Carlton Gardens to begin with, enjoying great social success. Curzon was touchingly proud of her. 'What other woman in London,' he wrote, 'combines great beauty with exceptional intelligence as well as a tact which is an inspiration? There is no limit to the influence which you can exercise at home, as you have done in India, smoothing down those whom I ignore and offend, and creating our own atmosphere of refinement and devotion.'[47]

It was indeed a perfect marriage. Mary was now in her mid-thirties; Curzon eleven years older; and their joy and absorption in one another had been deepened by their isolation in India, and the veiled hostility or empty sycophancy of those around them, until they could scarcely bear to be apart. England caught a glimpse of the nobility of their partnership when George was installed as Warden of the Cinque Ports in a historic ceremony at Dover, attended by several of the Souls. His old friend George Wyndham – MP for Dover – made the speech of welcome, in the presence of Curzon's one-time love, Sibell, Lady Grosvenor (as she still called herself after nearly twenty years of marriage). That evening the new Warden and his wife gave a ceremonial dinner for many of their old friends. It was noticed that, though Curzon was in the best of humours, Mary looked ill, and had lost the bloom with which she had dazzled the Souls on her previous visit. Curzon attributed it to the latest pregnancy, news of which she had broken to him just that day. 'The poor chick is too delicate and we must take special care,' he told his guests solicitously. On 9 June her father's death proved a heavy blow to her, and throughout that summer she was – as far as she would allow people to realize – listless, weary and depressed.

She cheered up briefly in August when they moved into Walmer Castle, where certain repairs and modernization work had been carried out. But on 20 September disaster struck with dreadful suddenness. A month earlier, Mary had miscarried (the child would have been their longed-for son, Curzon's heir) and, although she seemed to recover swiftly, her constitution was no longer strong enough to sustain another shock. After a drive along the coast on a damp afternoon she came back to the Castle feeling chilly and feverish, and was put to bed. Within hours she was dangerously ill. She fell into a coma, and for several days, with intervals of lucidity, she lay on the point of death.

Curzon was distraught. He scarcely left her bedside, watching in anguish, expecting her to die every hour. During the worst of the crisis he wrote down faithfully, word for word, everything she said and many of his replies. This document – which he preserved – is so poignant in what it reveals of their utter devotion that much of it seems almost too personal to quote . . .

> *Thursday Sept. 22. 2.20 p.m.*
> Try to keep up. Make a good struggle. Keep your strength.
> I haven't got any.
> My darling, my beau. Don't make me cry.
> *Sept. 25*
> She was now perfectly tranquil and began to talk to me about our love and our life.
> Oh how happy we have been. You have been my only love. I have loved you intensely and you have made me utterly happy for ten years. We have done a great deal together, George. We have succeeded. It has been a wonderful time.
> When I said that we had loved each other long and been all in all to each other, she asked that that might be inscribed on her tomb. After a while she grew more composed and presently asked to see the doctors again. Her wound was again dressed without pain. This cheered her a good deal: and she asked the doctors if it was worth while making another fight. They encouraged her, and with set lips she said, 'Well then, I will.'[48]

She did. She fought and, little by little, she recovered. By the end of September she was well enough to sit up; by mid-October she was out of danger. But she had been told she would never be able to bear another child.

At this point, had Curzon changed his mind about a second term, and resigned as Viceroy, no one would have been surprised and no one would have blamed him. Instead, almost incredibly, he prepared to go back, on his own, not knowing when – or whether – she could rejoin him. He was prepared to face the possibility of two or more years without her, rather than fail in what he saw as his duty. From Bombay he wrote in a letter to Lord Northcote:

> I come back, I assure you, with no pleasure. Six years as Viceroy are enough for any man. I have passed through a terrible six months at home: and I have long ago formed the opinion that few, very few in India want any reforms to

be carried through at all. However there are a few things I positively mean to see through. The rest must depend upon Lady Curzon's health. Whether she will ever come out again is more doubtful. When I left she was not at all in a good way though the major symptoms had almost been vanquished. . . . I earnestly hope that you may never live night and day with death – as I did for many weeks.[49]

Mary's courage and resolution were equal to his. Away from the damp and unhealthy atmosphere of Walmer Castle, in a country house he had rented for her and the children before leaving, she began slowly to get better. On 25 January 1905 she sent him a telegram to say she was on her way back to him. A letter explained, 'I would not come unless I felt I had strength enough. I feel that the Indian heat could do no more harm than the gnawing pain in my heart and my anxiety about you.'[50] They were reunited at Bombay in March 1905; and the Indian people gave Mary a welcome such as no Vicereine can ever have received in her own right. People were incredulous with joy that she had returned. But when a journalist told her she looked as though she had risen from the dead, 'She turned towards me with that direct and level glance which was one of her most attractive characteristics, and answered, "Yes – but one may not do these things twice." '[51]

Mary's return to health seemed like a miracle. But once the euphoria died down, it became clear that nothing else had changed. The political crisis was still acute. Kitchener's attitude had not mellowed – although he loved Mary to the point of idolatry – nor had Brodrick, the Secretary of State for India in the British cabinet, altered his ways or shifted his support. Curzon himself grew even more intractable; convinced, perhaps, that Mary's recovery was some kind of God-given sign that he was right. The year 1905 moved with ever-increasing momentum towards the harrowing climax to his years in India.

When Kitchener first arrived, Curzon's judgment had erred on the side of sentimentality: moved by the great soldier's recent exploits, and touched, perhaps, by Kitchener's devotion to Mary and friendship towards himself. He had not realized that his chosen Commander-in-Chief matched him in daemonic energy and force of will. He had underestimated his formidable character, and been curiously naïve about his ruthless ambition. The effects of their quarrel were worsened by St John Brodrick's mishandling of the affair at home, lacking either the skill or the tact to smooth matters over. More and more, the cabinet began to take sides; more and more, the side they were on was Kitchener's. Finally, on 8 August 1905, Balfour wrote to the King: 'The way in which Lord Curzon has used Lord Kitchener's name, his extreme sensitiveness to even the gentlest comment and the violence of his language towards those who differ from him can only be due, in Mr Balfour's opinion, to the combined effect of overwork, climate and ill health.'[52] The implication was clear enough. Curzon was no longer fit to continue as Viceroy.

Both men had used the threat of resignation as a weapon; but Curzon was thunderstruck when, on 21 August, his latest offer to resign was accepted. Almost immediately, the government announced his successor, Lord Minto: further evidence that Balfour and the cabinet had long anticipated Curzon's move – although its timing caused them some inconvenience, as the new Prince of Wales, later George V, was on the point of paying a royal visit to India. Curzon stayed on for the first week of the royal visit, then handed over to his successor the Viceroyalty that had meant so much to him, and left India – with one final display of pomp and all the ceremonial that was, for the last time, his due – in a state of mental and physical collapse. To the end of his life he never ceased to feel bitter towards the two men whom he believed had engineered his downfall, and made the circumstances of his departure so humiliating.

Balfour wrote to Curzon, a day or two after the resignation had been made public, in terms very different from those he had used in his letter to the King. In it he tried – out of political prudence (for he was certain to need Curzon's support one day), and perhaps real distress at the spectacle of his friend's inglorious defeat – to salve Curzon's wounded feelings: 'I have now no desire but to save from the political wreck all that is possible of private friendship and mutual esteem . . . of one thing only shall I be mindful – that for nearly seven years, in sickness and in health, you have devoted with untiring energy your splendid abilities to the service of India and of the Empire. And this is enough.'[53]

When George and Mary Curzon arrived back in England expecting the habitual welcome to a returning Viceroy, they found themselves ignominiously ignored. Not a single representative from the government or the court was there to greet them. The snub rankles with their daughter, Lady Alexandra Metcalfe, still:

> The Government never sent anybody to meet him when he stepped off the train at Charing Cross: he had a third secretary to meet him. That is unbelievable. The King should have said, 'I insist upon Lord and Lady Curzon being met by a representative.' No Viceroy has come back from India without being met. I mean, considering my mother had organised most of the beautiful dresses that Queen Alexandra wore, by having patterns sent out, getting them all embroidered in India . . . all the letters between them are full of thanks. To think, that having been on those terms the King shouldn't have said, 'Somebody's got to meet them.' It was dreadful.

Not a friend from among the massed ranks of the Souls had turned out to greet them either. Alfred Lyttelton – 'My dear old Alfred', in Curzon's affectionate words? He was not there; nor was George Wyndham, his friendly rival at the Crabbet Club and author of the rousing verse with which the Curzons had been speeded on their way that evening at the Hotel Cecil. Curzon must have remembered:

> Come back in five years with your sheaves of new Fame:
> You'll find your old Friends; and you'll find them the same
> As now when you gladden their sight.

The King *had* apparently foreseen this possibility and, to his credit, had made a special point of asking Balfour, as Prime Minister, and St John Brodrick, as Secretary of State for India, to be at the platform for an official welcome. Both stayed away. The rest of the Souls were spending a week at Stanway with the Elchos, in Gloucestershire, and all considered it too far to come to London. Ettie Desborough has recorded their reaction: 'We were trying all Sunday to concoct a telegram of greeting which all, including A.J.B, could sign. Nothing less jejune seemed to evolve itself than "Glad you're back". Hugo Elcho said, "If we don't look out, it'll turn into "Glad your back's worse".'[54] And so the Curzons' arrival in London was not only ignominious, but friendless, too.

That was 3 December 1905. But Curzon was not the only old friend and founding Soul to have been shabbily treated by Balfour. George Wyndham in Ireland had found himself less and less able to cope with his rôle as Chief Secretary in that tortured province; while Schomberg MacDonnell, who had been Lord Salisbury's private secretary for fourteen years, and was now Under-Secretary for Ireland, was also implicated in his failure. Balfour withheld from both of them the support they might have expected from the man who was their friend as well as their leader, and to whom they owed their appointments; and earlier that year – in March – George Wyndham had also resigned, a broken man. The fiasco of the Boer War; the sharp divisions of opinion in Ireland; the long controversy with Chamberlain over free trade; and, finally, the open breach with Curzon over India, were too much for the shaky Conservative government. On 4 December Balfour resigned, and on the following day Campbell-Bannerman was asked to form a government. The ensuing general election brought the Liberals the greatest electoral victory of the twentieth century.

The fact that the Prime Minister and cabinet by whom he had been so humiliated were now humiliated in their turn was small consolation to Curzon. By now the Souls were generally discredited. Their politics were seen to revolve primarily around the maintenance of their own life of aristocratic wealth and privilege. Even in the first years of the century, it was already clear that deep currents of social change and technological progress were rushing through the broad river of English government. The upper classes could no longer rely solely upon their 'inherited' right to rule, buttressed by a subservient working class and a fawning middle class. The Souls did not discern these movements. They behaved as though nothing would change, or ever could; and they pursued an increasingly hollow round of pleasure. Twenty years had made it less original; more vapid. Outwardly, it was still exquisite. The women seemed ageless; Ettie was still girlishly slender despite having borne five children; Mary Elcho still absent-minded, impulsive, and beautiful; only Margot had lost whatever she once had of good looks – and even she remained formidably chic. But what had made the Souls remarkable in their earliest years was a willingness to question the way of life and the social patterns that they had grown up into. Now in middle age they clung to privilege and convention as tenaciously and selfishly as their parents once had. The Souls, having been talked about and envied – though never emulated – were now seen as passé by society and positively distrusted by everyone else. Lord Winterton recalled many years later, 'The public did not know exactly what the Souls were, but vaguely disapproved of them. Thus one's supporters would say to one, "We want a man like good old Joe Chamberlain as leader, not a 'Soul' like Balfour." '[55] The reign of the middle classes was on its way.

Between Curzon and Balfour the rift was personal and deep. The two young darlings of the Souls had become estranged. Wilfrid Scawen Blunt's diary records what happened when they first met in private:

Mary Elcho lunched with me yesterday & told me of the meeting between George Curzon and Arthur Balfour at dinner at Lady Ribblesdale's. Charty had written to both of them beforehand to ask whether they would mind meeting & both had said 'no'. Nevertheless, when after the ladies had left the dining room Arthur went & sat down by George, George evaded talking to him. He was not quite rude, but distinctly *uncordial*, & would not have any separate conversation with him. This has caused a terrible commotion in the social circle . . . & nobody knows what may happen.[56]

It was probably the intervention of Asquith, however, rather than malice on the part of Balfour, that prevented Curzon from being offered the earldom which was the reward and recognition given almost automatically to a returning Viceroy. It seems likely that Asquith warned the new Liberal premier, Sir Henry Campbell-Bannerman, that Curzon's elevation to an English earldom, and the seat in the House of Lords that went with it, would dangerously strengthen the Tory contingent in the Upper House. Be that as it may, not even the mild disapproval of the King – who felt that precedent, if nothing else, decreed the title – would persuade the government. So Curzon was conspicuously unhonoured: which meant, in his eyes, dishonoured. He wrote to Mary in the spring of 1906: 'One wonders when the hailstorm that rains upon us is to stop; we are nearly beaten to the ground.'[57]

India was Curzon's first and greatest ambition, and in achieving it he learnt the truth behind Oscar Wilde's savage aphorism, 'In this world there are only two tragedies. One is not getting what one wants, and the other is getting it.'[‡][58] But for Mary, the price to be paid for her dedication to her husband, and, therefore, to India, was too high. For seven years she had exerted the uttermost willpower to put on a display of effortless charm in public and unswerving support in private. Her will in overcoming physical suffering was as formidable as the discipline that Curzon himself showed. The tragedy was that because of his own obsession with his work, and her desire to spare him anxiety, he did not know until it was too late that she was sacrificing her life for him. Their daughter, Lady Alexandra Metcalfe, believes it was so:

> I would think that he very likely had no idea of what she was going through until she collapsed. He had this really incredible sense of putting his work and his duty ahead of his private life and this made him unaware of what she was putting up with and doing. And she wouldn't have wished him to know . . . it was the last thing she would have wanted. I think she knew, though, herself, that her health was failing. But everything always had to be done for him, the way he wanted it done, at whatever cost to her. I still think if she hadn't gone back to India she would have lived. But after that she had no reserves.[59]

By the spring of 1906 Mary was visibly frail. Friends commented on the change in her. Mary herself wrote ominously to her brother on 21 June, 'I sometimes fear and feel that I shall never be well again.'[60] But she was only thirty-six, and back in England in a milder climate, freed of the burden of responsibilities she had carried so whole-heartedly. Nobody dreamed that her life was ebbing so fast.

On 18 July, after four days in bed, low in health and spirits, she came to the end of her strength and even of her will. At six o'clock in the evening, with

‡It is interesting that Shaw used almost exactly the same words in *Man and Superman*, Act IV, written twelve years later; and so did Sir John Vanbrugh in 1705!

Curzon's arms around her, she suffered a heart attack and died. She was buried at Kedleston, with no show, no friends, and a single flower from him. Only the immediate family was present, including the three little girls she left behind: Irene, aged ten, Cynthia, aged eight, and little Alexandra, who was not quite two.

– 8 –

Country House Weekend

1905–1906

Autumn was the season for country house weekends. The debutantes had been presented at court and were, for better or worse, 'out'; Ascot, Henley and Cowes were over. Family holidays had been spent in Scotland or Frinton or even abroad, and now adolescent sons were back at public school. The House did not resume until after Christmas. Autumn was the season when the landed gentry indulged themselves and their guests in those pursuits that reassured them all – even in 1905 – that England was what England would always be: rural, sporting, safe.

The country was the place for relaxation after a gruelling London season. Cynthia Asquith, Mary Elcho's eldest daughter, recalled that 'almost mythological existence', the London of Edward VII:

> I see striped awnings, linkmen with flaring torches; powdered, liveried footmen; soaring marble staircases; tiaras, smiling hostesses; azaleas in gilt baskets; white waistcoats, violins, elbows sawing the air, names on pasteboard cards, quails in aspic, macedoine, strawberries and cream, tired faces of cloakroom attendants, washed streets in blue dawns, sparrows pecking the empty pavements, my bedroom curtains being drawn apart to let in the late morning light; a breakfast tray approaching my bedside; bandboxes, tissue paper. . . . [1]

Three months of this five nights a week was enough to send the upper classes flocking thankfully to the less demanding pleasures of country house visiting.

One of the Souls' favourite houses was Stanway, where Mary Elcho held court. It was not as aesthetic as Clouds, the home designed for her parents by Philip Webb, and one of the first Victorian houses to be built with light, airy, pale rooms and every modern comfort. It was not as spacious or as luxurious as Taplow Court, where Ettie dispensed hospitality. But it was more informal than either, which was perhaps why, on the eve of dissolving his government, Arthur Balfour chose to spend the weekend of 3 December 1905 at Stanway: the weekend that coincided with the Curzons' return from India.

Stanway, in Gloucestershire, was more than four centuries old, built of golden Cotswold stone and untouched by the Victorian passion for improving (which often meant remodelling, or even demolishing) their country houses. At one end of the great hall an oriel window, two storeys high, poured a stream of slanting light through lattices of sixteenth-century glass. The gentle old house gave an air of timelessness to the shabby furniture where guests lounged contentedly. The East Room was Mary's own sitting-room – once described in a letter to Arthur Balfour as 'a right paradise for both of us' – and here she would sit planning how to entertain her guests. Although people always thought of her as vague, absent-minded and unpunctual, Mary went to immense pains to ensure that every detail of comfort and every moment of the day was taken care of:

> The plan of the bedrooms would be pored over until some way of packing fourteen guests into ten spare rooms was devised. Perhaps one might be put in the stables, another in the apple room, and so forth. . . . Whilst Mamma organised the transport, sleeping and eating arrangements for those visitors already within her gates, a large fraction of her mind would be simultaneously engaged in planning ahead exactly how next week's party should be occupied during every hour of their stay: 'But Cynthia, if you and your friends go to the dance Saturday evening, who will make a fourth at Bridge with Papa and the This and Thats?. . . Then, there's Sunday evening when I've promised to hear Professor L. read his lecture, and the D's want to listen too, but poor Mrs B. is much too deaf for either reading aloud or for charades. Who is to talk to her? I *believe* she plays Bezique. Can you think of anyone in the neighbourhood who plays Bezique?'[2]

'Poor Mrs B.' was probably a country neighbour, for Mary Elcho as a hostess was unusually scrupulous about including local people. But besides them, and of course Balfour and other Souls, she also liked to have the literary lions of the day among her guests.

The Souls of both sexes were unusually well read (in contrast to, for instance, the Prince of Wales, who kindly brought the ailing Gladstone a copy of the latest Marie Corelli novel for his sick-bed reading!). That they had a grounding in classical literature goes without saying. Latin and Greek made up a large part of the public school curriculum and even girls would have picked up something of the classical texts, if not from governesses, then from their brothers. A knowledge of Shakespeare, Milton, Byron, Wordsworth and the more contemporary poets such as Browning and Tennyson could also be taken for granted. It seems probable that Meredith's *Modern Love* would have appealed to the soul-searching Souls.

The novelists of the day were known to them, both personally and through their works. Curzon, in particular, had a marked penchant for lady novelists, but all the Souls would have read Oscar Wilde (before, if not after, the Queensberry scandal broke), Henry James and H. G. Wells. Ettie Grenfell and Margot Asquith were particularly well read. Margot relates with relish in her *Autobiography* how, as a young woman, she once had the satisfaction of scoring off a supercilious hostess who doubted whether she had actually read *Essays, Suggestive and Speculative*, the latest work by J. A. Symonds, by remarking triumphantly, 'I am afraid, Lady Londonderry, you have not read the preface. The book is dedicated to me.' In 1893, E. F. Benson's *Dodo*, a *roman à clef* said to be modelled upon the personality of Margot, enjoyed immense popular success, though Margot herself dismissed it and could see no resemblance.

Indeed, the Souls inspired many fictional versions of themselves, thinly disguised. Mrs Humphrey Ward's *Robert Elsmere* was dedicated to Laura Tennant. In it, Rose was said to be a portrait of Margot, while Laura herself was depicted as Catherine. (Jowett, a great admirer of both the young Tennants, said, however, that the portraits were quite unlike the originals.) *The Courts of Love*, an unfinished poem begun by Blunt in 1895–6, when he was most involved with the Souls, was an elaborate literary comment upon their chosen way of life. In H. G. Wells's *The New Machiavelli*, the character of Evesham was clearly modelled upon that of Arthur Balfour; while Max Beerbohm's *Maltby and Braxton* contains a satirical portrait of Ettie, as does Maurice Baring's short play, *Ariadne in Naxos*. It is not kind, and Ettie cannot have been pleased. The Souls undoubtedly seized the literary imagination of their time, so rare was it for a group of upper-class men and women to make a conscious effort to read the best that was being written by their own contemporaries.

They too were writers, and not just of family reminiscences, like Ettie and Mary Elcho and Frances Horner. Margot wrote a novel about her own young days, when she was the best huntswoman of her time, called *Octavia*. It is a vivid, dramatic piece of work, and not just for its wistful evocation of her years of freedom:

> Brought up in an atmosphere of Scotch austerity, Octavia had a spiritual side to her nature which, however neglected, tugged at her like a kite at the end of a string. She could not always see it for the clouds; but she never let go of the string. Her love of searching self-examination was almost as great as her love of excitement.[3]

That, and not the mannered pettishness of *Dodo*, captures the young Tennants.

In November 1892 there was evidently a plan to publish a journal of the Souls. It was to have been called *Tomorrow*, with the revealing sub-title *A Woman's Journal for Men*. Charty Ribblesdale seems to have been the prime mover, and she visited Blunt to obtain his professional opinion about the idea and the proposed design. He suggested that the motto of the magazine should be *Solus cum Sola* – but in the end neither motto nor magazine ever came to anything.

Of all the Souls women, Frances Horner was the most profoundly artistic and the only one who could truly be called a patron of the best of her time. Her father, William Graham, had been a notable collector, and had commissioned and bought works from the Pre-Raphaelites long before they became fashionable. His clever, sensitive daughter continued this practice. Margot says of her, 'She was a leader in what was called the high-art, William Morris School and one of the few girls who ever had a salon in London.'[4] But the Horners were not 'in society', probably because they lacked the money to provide the lavish entertaining which society demanded, and so Lady Horner was better known to artists like Burne-Jones than to the wider circle of Souls. Mells Park, although large enough for family entertaining, could not have accommodated the house-parties of one or two dozen that were ordinary weekly events to Ettie or Mary Elcho.

A Stanway gathering might include H. G. Wells, who came often, and continued to be invited even after the publication in 1909 of his 'scandalous' novel, *Ann Veronica*. It described the relationship – part mentor, part lover – of a distinguished older man with a younger, unmarried woman, and reflected the passionate but clandestine love affair between Wells himself and the young Rebecca West. (She, however, would certainly not have been asked to Stanway. The taboos were still not openly defied, and Wells took care to keep their relationship secret.) Sir Walter Raleigh, Professor of English Literature at Oxford, was another regular visitor; an explosive and unpredictable talker who could be relied on to galvanize his audience. Sidney and Beatrice Webb were frequently invited to Stanway, too – even though, as Cynthia recalled without a trace of irony, Beatrice 'gave me the uncomfortable feeling that she couldn't possibly think I was justifying my existence'.[5] Beatrice herself felt guilty about liking 'brilliant little parties and interesting folk versed in great affairs'.[6] She tried to remedy this deplorable enjoyment of society by turning every dinner party into a committee, or else by proselytizing:

> One of her set conversation pieces . . . was dividing humanity into what she called the 'A's' and the 'B's'. The A's comprised Aristocrats, Artists and Anarchists; the B's the Bourgeois, Bureaucrats and Benevolents, the implication being that though, admittedly, she found the company of the A's more enjoyable, the world would have to learn to do without the luxury of their existence.[7]

Balfour said of Beatrice Webb, 'It is sad that enthusiasts should have more influence than anyone else, for few enthusiasts tell the truth.'[8] How she must have smarted under this elegant flick – while he would have been unconcerned by her judgment of him as 'too sceptical to be more than negatively beneficial'.[9] The presence of the two of them at the same dinner table . . . the energy of her fervent socialist convictions languidly opposed by the last Conservative Prime Minister but one to personify the landed aristocracy . . . must have produced some brilliant conversational exchanges to amuse the rest of the party.

It is likely that Mary Elcho enjoyed the company of writers, artists and intellectuals because her childhood home had been filled with them. Her parents, Percy and Madeline Wyndham, were enlightened patrons and cultured people. Madeline was a friend, as well as a distant relative, of both Wilfrid Scawen Blunt and Lord Alfred Douglas, and entertained them both at Clouds – and later Oscar Wilde as well. Both mother and daughter on occasion had Henry James to stay: though he, despite being a friend of Balfour's, cannot have enlivened their dinner tables. Blunt's impression of him recorded: 'James distinctly heavy in conversation and for a man who writes so lightly and well it is amazing how dull-witted he is. This is not only that he had no talk himself but he is slow to take in the talk of others. He tries hard, but he is always a little behindhand, but when he does find anything to say he spoils it in the saying.'[10] By 1905, however, ten years after the episode in Egypt, Blunt himself was no longer *persona grata* at the houses of either Mary or her mother, though he remained in contact with them both and even saw his daughter fairly regularly. The child was growing up to resemble him, with flashing dark eyes and high spirits. Blunt was very proud of her, and never ceased to mourn the shattering of his idyll with her mother.

In more ways than one, the history of Stanway mirrored that of many of the oldest English country houses. Dating back to the sixteenth century, and in parts even earlier, it had been the summer retreat of the Abbots of Tewkesbury. In 1540, at the time of the dissolution of the monasteries, it came into the hands of the Tracy family. It passed into the Wemyss family by marriage, when Susan Tracy, an eighteenth-century heiress, married the eldest son of the 5th Earl of Wemyss. Added to over the centuries, with its beautiful Inigo Jones gatehouse and a garden of lawns and magnolias bounded by yew trees, the village church just beyond, Stanway epitomized all that the English country house stood for.

The country house weekend, which became an established institution in the 1890s, was not of course confined to the Souls. These so-called Saturdays-to-Mondays were at the hub of Edwardian society; the fulcrum on which it turned. First, and simplest, they were an opportunity to see one's friends and exchange news at greater leisure than was possible on formal occasions in London. Second, by extension, they provided the perfect opportunity for sexual encounters. It was far easier for married couples to separate, by night or day, over the course of a weekend, and pursue their romantic interests for a few private hours, than it would have been for two people who were not married to each other to meet illicitly at a hotel or even a restaurant. Restaurants were still largely out of bounds to respectable society women; and hotels even more so. Third, a weekend in the country was an ideal setting for political, social or financial intrigue. Under cover of a group of twenty or thirty people, it would have been easy for three or four of them to repair discreetly to the library or billiard room for a confidential sorting out of important matters, well away from the curious eyes and ears of their political opponents. By means of their London clubs and country seats, the English upper classes held the reins of power in firm and practised hands. There was little that could not be arranged in the course of a long, relaxed weekend: whether it concerned politics, or the law, or the City, the armed forces, or a scandal that was best contained within the charmed circle of those who would know how to deal with it. In the intervals of all this, the guests pursued the most expensive and exclusive of all country pleasures; for most country houses (though not, in fact, Stanway) offered the chance to hunt, or shoot, or fish.

In so doing, the upper classes reaffirmed to themselves and their subordinates the absolute and unchanging rightness of the system by which England and Empire were governed. For who else but the landed aristocracy could have access to the people, the experience and the authority that confer power? Continuity and stability were at the heart of the English country house weekend. The next decade or two were to show that the undermining process which had been happening over the previous thirty years – noticed by few, understood by fewer still – had rendered that continuity and stability an illusion.

If the country weekend was a symbol of power, and proof of its possession, so in a more extended sense was the country house. The ownership of a landed property had been the ambition of the newly rich for centuries, and never more so than in the Victorian age. The 15th Earl of Derby summarized crisply what he and his kind stood for when he wrote, in 1881:

The objects which men aim at when they become possessed of land . . . may I think be enumerated as follows: (1) political influence; (2) social importance, founded on territorial possession, the most visible and unmistakable form of

Hermione, Duchess of Leinster: the lovely, lonely Duchess whose love affair with Lord Elcho brought her some consolation in the final years before her early death.

Wilfrid Scawen Blunt: poet, traveller, patriot, diarist – and lover of several Souls' women. This photograph dating from the 1890s hints at the piercing gaze and sexual energy that made him so attractive to women.

A family group showing two newly married couples at the Tennant home, Glen, in 1895.
Back (left to right): *Henry Asquith, Pamela Tennant, née Wyndham, her husband Edward Tennant, later Lord Glenconner;* front: *Lucy Graham Smith, Margot Asquith and her brother, Jack Tennant.*

This Spy cartoon from Vanity Fair *shows Willy Grenfell in a characteristically sporting pose. As well as hunting and shooting, he also fished, rowed (across the Channel), swam (the Niagara Falls basin – twice) and climbed mountains.*

Willy's wife, Ettie Grenfell, in her late twenties. She was perhaps the most celebrated hostess of her time, but she also prided herself on being one of the 'good young mothers' to her angelically handsome sons Billy (left) *and Julian* (right).

Right: *Lord Granby, later the Duke of Rutland, possessed of good looks and good manners but, alas, few brains.*

Below: *This drawing by Lady Granby shows Harry Cust in 1898, soon after she had borne him a child and then lost him in a loveless marriage to a young woman who had claimed (probably falsely) to be pregnant, thus compelling Cust to marry her.*

Lord Granby's lovely wife Violet did her duty and perpetuated the legitimate Rutland line, but then found in Harry Cust a more stimulating lover who appreciated her bohemian spirit and her original dress sense.

Mary Leiter, painted in Paris in 1887 by Alexandre Cabanel, when she was seventeen and making her first visit from America. Already she possessed the serious grace that entranced George Curzon at their first meeting three years later.

George Curzon in his late thirties, his face lined from the constant pain he suffered in his back and from overwork. He was about to be created the youngest-ever Viceroy of India.

Lady Curzon in the famous peacock dress that she wore for the Coronation Durbar of 1902. As Vicereine of India she occupied the highest post that any American has ever held within the British Empire.

Above: *On 9 December 1898, the eve of the Curzons' departure for India, they were entertained at the Hotel Cecil to a magnificent farewell dinner given by all their friends, including most of the Souls.*

Right: *Lord Curzon (centre) and Mary (centre right) on a viceregal tiger shoot. Although this was a traditional form of recreation for both the Indian and the British aristocracy, neither of the Curzons much enjoyed it.*

*St John Brodrick, later the Earl of Midleton. He had been the stolid
friend of Curzon since their schooldays at Eton, but his lack of sensitivity
and tact contributed to disastrous misunderstandings in Curzon's last two
years as Viceroy.*

April 1905 – and the strains of office and middle age are beginning to show in the faces of Alfred Lyttelton (left) *and Arthur Balfour* (right).

Above: *Henley in the late 1890s – the panoramic scene at the annual regatta, one of the highlights of the London summer season.*

Below: *The drawing room at Clouds, the light and airy house designed for Percy and Madeline Wyndham, which was one of the first to rebel against the stuffy heaviness of Victorian domestic architecture.*

Above: *Always known as the Inigo Jones gateway, this Jacobean entrance to the Elcho family home of Stanway, in Gloucestershire, was in fact designed by a lesser architect: which does not diminish its beauty.*

Below: *Inside, Stanway was more relaxing, and shabbier, than many Souls' houses, but Mary Elcho's warm hospitality made it a favourite retreat for country house weekends.*

The Elcho family pose, around 1908, outside the great oriel window that was a feature of Stanway. Back (left to right): *Guy Charteris, Lord Elcho, Ego Charteris;* front: *Lady Mary Charteris, Lady Elcho with Irene ('Bibs') on her lap, Yvo Charteris, Lady Cynthia Charteris.*

wealth; (3) power exercised over tenantry; the pleasure of managing, directing and improving the estate itself; (4) residential enjoyment, including what is called sport; (5) the money return – the rent.[11]

Although he put the money aspect last, in fact when the return from land began to decline, as it did towards the end of the nineteenth century, all the other reasons for maintaining estates fell in their turn, like dominoes. The agricultural depression which began in the mid-1870s demonstrated the unthinkable: that land was not necessarily the most secure investment, and that the return on it could waver. Once this happened, it put at risk the financial structure which underpinned the whole hierarchy of class.

By the late nineteenth century virtually all land – 95 per cent – was still privately owned, and of that, nearly half was in the hands of a mere fifteen hundred families at the top of the social pyramid. In a beautifully simple equation, they were there because they owned land, and because they were rich; and it had been the ownership of land that had made them rich. As soon as land no longer *guaranteed* wealth, its possession ceased to be the surest way to power and influence. This process had been happening throughout the last quarter of the nineteenth century, but it took many years before its effects were fully grasped by the class which was in the process of being replaced. Behind the lavish façade of Edwardian society there lurked a number of landowners who had already been obliged to adopt a more modest lifestyle. Set against them was a growing contingent of the *nouveaux riches*, whom both the new King and practical necessity had made socially acceptable. Land was no longer an enviable possession, unless it was combined with a good income from other sources. Land – unthinkably, fifty years before – now had to be subsidized.

Throughout the nineteenth century, anyone aspiring to be a gentleman had regarded ownership of a country estate as the first essential for social acceptance. The new men from the City, Rand millionaires, railway kings and industrialists, had acquired, or built, huge country houses. After a generation or so, a local member of the established peerage would graciously condescend to accept a daughter, along with a substantial dowry, from the *arrivistes*. Thus the two groups gradually fused.

In law, a gentleman was still 'a man who has no occupation'. (Hence the vulgarity of the very word 'weekend', because it implied that the weekdays were spent earning a living elsewhere than in the country. It was the 'Monday' in 'Saturday-to-Monday' that was the crucial word.) In practice, however, country gentlemen had always had plenty to occupy them. The older landed aristocracy and gentry had run their estates, practised politics at local and often national level, and conducted the predictable rituals of their social lives. These rituals, organized and dominated by women, were the means whereby dynastic marriages were arranged and the line of succession to land and power was safeguarded.

Between 1874 and 1898 agricultural rents *fell* by over a quarter, and in the worst affected areas of England, the south-east and the north-west, by much more than that. The ownership of land became an increasingly expensive luxury. It now offered poor returns on investment – on average about 2 per cent – whereas a Victorian entrepreneur would expect an annual profit of at least

8 per cent on his capital. Land had always offered status and prestige, and this had not changed. But it no longer offered a good economic return.

To what extent were the Souls affected by the slump in land values? None of them experienced any real hardship – their friends in the House of Commons saw to that, by keeping income tax and death duties down – and nearly all were buttressed by other forms of investment. The Grenfells had 3,000 acres around Taplow (Willy's family had acquired the estate earlier in the nineteenth century from the proceeds of Cornish tin mines) and it never occurred to them to sell off an acre. Ettie came into money from her Cowper fortune in 1905, when her uncle died and the earldom became extinct. She inherited the rest of it, along with Panshanger, in 1913. The Grenfells never felt the pinch. When Ettie wanted to install central heating in 1914, she simply sold a Raphael. It fetched £70,000: the equivalent of nearly £2 million today.

The Elchos had never been really comfortably off by the standards of their circle (by anyone else's standards they were sumptuously comfortable), due to Hugo's early misdemeanours as a gambler and an unsuccessful investor on the Stock Exchange. His eldest daughter, Lady Cynthia, described the apparent paradox between their style of life and the constant need for economies:

> Since we lived in a large house, amply staffed and almost continually full of visitors, there must, according to present-day standards [she was writing in 1950] have been a considerable amount of money, yet I cannot remember a time when finance was not an ever-present worry to my parents. There was always talk of the necessity for 'retrenchment' – sometimes even, desecrating thought, of the letting of Stanway, and in most ways we were brought up most unluxuriously.[12]

Perhaps Lady Cynthia was being discreet, out of respect for her father's memory; but maybe she really didn't know that his gambling had been the reason for their constant money worries. But in any case the family had never had extensive land holdings in England. Their principal estate was at Gosford, in East Lothian, Scotland; so they were relatively unaffected by the agricultural depression.

The Tennant fortune was enough to underpin the family for decades to come, thanks to the baronet's shrewd spread of investments, and the fact that his heirs sold his large collection of Victorian pictures at exactly the moment when they commanded the highest prices. Sir Charles died in 1906, leaving behind him a young wife and four daughters by his second marriage, as well as the six surviving children of his first. His eldest son, Edward, inherited and farmed the Scottish estate but, as happened more and more often, it was the newer sources of wealth – chemicals, in the case of the Tennants, and mining investments abroad – that formed the safety net which ensured the upkeep of the land. Money derived from coal or railways, from cotton mills or beer, no longer automatically relegated a man to the despised category of 'trade': always providing there was enough of it. A coal merchant was trade, the owner of a coalmine was not.

George Curzon's father, Lord Scarsdale, died in 1916, enabling his son – with the help of his American wife's fortune – to carry out the restoration of Kedleston that he had planned for so long. At Hagley Hall the Lytteltons continued undisturbed. The family seat had survived the potshots of eight sons playing cricket in the Long Gallery, and it survived the depression as well.

Ironically, the only member of the circle whose fortunes took a real downward turn was the one who had started out richest of all: Balfour. The vast inheritance that became his when he was twenty-one, the estate at Whittingehame with its 10,000 acres, turned into a financial drain upon him. He was too engrossed with parliamentary and philosophical concerns to concentrate upon the management of his agricultural holdings, and after the turn of the century he was increasingly worried about money. In 1915 he told Mary Elcho, 'The family fortunes are critical.'[13] They were not helped by his ill-fated speculations. He played the Stock Exchange, usually unsuccessfully, and became obsessed with an eccentric company called Wet Carbonising Ltd, into which he poured hundreds of thousands of pounds that he could no longer afford. Alone among the Souls, Balfour's wealth was substantially reduced during his lifetime: though not primarily because of the agricultural depression, and certainly not to an extent that made him a poor man.

Politically, he continued to enjoy the prestige of an aristocratic landowner. Until 1885, landed interests provided a majority of the members of the House of Commons; and they continued to dominate the House of Lords right up until the introduction of life peerages in 1964. More than that, members of the upper echelons of the landed aristocracy supplied a majority in every cabinet until Campbell-Bannerman's, which replaced Balfour in 1906. Asquith was the first Prime Minister – with the exception of Disraeli – who did not come from a landed family. Small wonder that the old English aristocracy thought themselves inviolable. They enjoyed the deference of everyone else in society in return for the privilege of ruling over them; a deference which grew more and more subservient as it passed down the ranks of social class. In 1872 Bagehot had remarked, 'I doubt if there has ever been any country in which all old families and all titled families received more ready observance from those who were their equals, perhaps their superiors, in wealth; their equals in culture; and their inferiors only in descent and rank.'[14]

Yet almost imperceptibly, that traditional deference was being eroded. The halcyon days of Edward VII's reign were troubled by faint, oppressive thunder. Issues that were to loom and break over the next decade gathered pace during these years. In 1903 the Women's Social and Political Union (the WSPU) was formed by the Pankhursts to further the cause of votes for women. The word 'suffragette' was coined in mockery, and still had an unfamiliar ring; but the suffragettes were mustering all the same, drawing attention to their cause by insisting on going to prison rather than pay fines. In 1905 the Sinn Fein party was organizing in Ireland. In Russia, the first dark rumblings that were to grow into the full clamour of revolution could be heard. In 1907 the Hague Peace Conference, a futile attempt to limit the arms build-up, failed. By 1909 the women's suffrage movement had been militant for a number of years . . . there was no one any longer to whom the word 'suffragette' was unfamiliar. Women chained themselves to railings, and endured the torture of force-feeding in prison. In 1910 a mass meeting outside the Houses of Parliament was brutally broken up by the police . . . the notorious Black Friday. That same year, the last of Edward's reign, became known as the Year of Strikes because the miners, railway workers, seamen and dockers all struck for better working conditions. The Indian summer of Victorian England was a myth indeed. Not even the weather was very good. With the exception of 1900, which was a glorious summer, the weather ranged from average to appalling every year until 1911, when it was glorious again.

The Souls' main concern was the servant problem. Good servants were becoming harder and harder to find. Many young women now chose to work in offices, as 'typewriters', rather than enter domestic service. Even those who did no longer displayed the old docility. For women like Mary and Ettie, this was perhaps their only brush with democracy, and it did not disturb their confidence in the aristocratic right to rule. Not even their husbands – not even their good friends among the politicians – perceived how that aristocratic supremacy was being threatened. Political setbacks caused them distress. Military disasters caused them pain, if not yet anguish, since their sons were still too young to have fought in the Boer War. But the only issue that seriously divided the Souls during Edward VII's reign was that of free trade versus protection, and here it was felt that Asquith's impassioned support of free trade was perhaps excessive. Not until the constitutional crisis of 1911 did feelings run high between them about any political issue.

Margot's marriage to Asquith had distanced her from the main spotlight of the Souls. Family life – she had five stepchildren, as well as two of her own – absorbed much of the driving energy that had previously powered her social life. Three miscarriages meant that she was frequently ill. Those who met her during these years spoke of her selfishness and self-pity; in fact, she was probably deeply unhappy and beginning to suffer the 'nervous crises' (probably breakdowns) that were to afflict her for the rest of her life. Marriage never really suited Margot. By now – according to her sister – she hated 'all that', meaning sex; and she found it difficult to cope with five adolescent children who were temperamentally so unlike herself. In addition, her husband was never fully accepted as a Soul. Too heavy-handed for their patrician lightness, his mental agility was never as quick as theirs either. From 1900 it fell increasingly to other Souls women to take the centre of the stage and act as magnet or catalyst to the widening circle.

The social life of the Souls was as crowded as it had ever been, if a little dulled by repetition. But Ettie Grenfell – or Lady Desborough, as she became in 1905, when Balfour ennobled Willy as a special favour – had refined the art of entertaining at Taplow Court to a dazzling confection of mutual admiration. She and her guests vied with each other: she to provide the most exquisite setting, they to sparkle most exquisitely within it. Nearly everyone who speaks of her gifts as a hostess topples into hyperbole. 'Her distinction might have seemed alarming had it not been that her fastidiousness was accompanied by an artistic perfection of courtesy,'[15] said Harold Nicolson, and even John Morley – the dour biographer of Gladstone – conceded that a couple of days spent as a guest at Taplow were 'most blighting to one's democracy'.[16] Ettie was a muse, who inspired nothing more permanent than the conversations that took place around her. She hated music, though was glad of concerts as an opportunity to sit quietly and arrange her future entertainment. Once, when Lord David Cecil asked her what she had been thinking about during a performance, she told him,

'I make my little summer plans.'[17] She was widely read; but her own letters ran the gamut from simper to gush, and her books are so ingenuous that one suspects her of being insincere. In the 655 pages of her *Pages from a Family Journal* she refers to herself winsomely as 'the boys' Mother', and was not above doctoring their letters for publication so as to reflect even greater adoration of herself. This *Family Journal* chronicles in minute detail the life of her family; yet there is only ever one mention of a servant in it. She describes, really quite movingly, how her children's old nanny died at the age of eighty-four:

> The children were going to see her the next day, and their mother was with her until eleven o'clock of the night she died, when the doctor said there was no immediate danger. Her very last words were about Julian and Billy; their mother said something about them, and Nannie said 'Dear boys', very tenderly, with the very happy smile with which she always talked of them. She did not speak again afterwards. . . . Nannie was a great conservative and aristocrat. When Willy was given a peerage she was very much pleased, but could not often remember to call him by his new name, which vexed her very much indeed. She used to say, 'It seems to me such a strange thing, me being so used to the nobility all my life.' She did not like the children to play with the village children, and there was one family she especially disapproved of, and always spoke of as 'That scum.'[18]

Other than this, the people who slaved under her roof to make her fame as a hostess possible might as well have been invisible. They are not referred to.

Rather surprisingly, Ettie *did* print a scathing verse that Julian, her eldest son, wrote in 1905 about social life: 'This was his reply [she recorded] to some invitations to him, of which his mother told him, to ball parties at Christmas:

> Sound, sound the clarion, fill the fife,
> To all the social world say 'Hang it,
> I, who for seventeen years of life
> Have trod this happy hustling planet,
> I won't go woman-hunting yet,
> I won't become a Social Pet.'[19]

The confrontation between mother and son was about to begin. It was a confrontation between her social mask and his angry search for the truth behind it. It was a deadly serious conflict that lasted for a number of years and almost destroyed Julian. Part of his resentment must have been because Ettie embarked, in 1904, on the first of a series of romantic melodramas with men much younger than herself. Archie Gordon was the third son of the Earl of Aberdeen. He was just twenty; Ettie seventeen years older. She used him both as an example and a rival to Julian. He was more malleable than her prickly, depressive son, and had three years' extra confidence and maturity, so his infatuation must have been as galling for Julian as it was flattering to his mother. Like so many of Ettie's involvements, it was expressed mainly in the form of letters – suppliant protestations of ecstasy and devotion from him; fulsome recollections of ardent joy from her; and no suggestion on either side that all this emotion should be sullied by any physical consummation. Such relationships, between an older woman and a younger man, were – and always have been – not infrequent. The Hamlet complex which it triggered in Julian was more serious. He probably could not understand what was happening, and Ettie did not choose to. A few years later, however, when Julian was the younger man and the beautiful Pamela Lytton the older woman to whom he was devoted, his mother used every weapon to ridicule and break up their relationship. Her husband had never been unfaithful to her, and her sons were not permitted to be either.

Other members of the Souls enjoyed more conventional affairs. George Wyndham, a former admirer of Ettie's, had settled into a liaison with Gay, the widowed Countess of Plymouth, which was tacitly condoned by his wife Sibell and was to last until his death. George's sister, Mary Elcho, was absorbed in Arthur Balfour; yet perhaps even she had momentary infatuations with younger men: in 1898 Blunt had remarked jealously on the constant presence of a young American called Spencer Eddy. Hugo Elcho, after the death of the Duchess of Leinster, had established a long-lasting relationship with the robustly unconventional Lady Angela Forbes. She was a half-sister of Millicent, Duchess of Sutherland, and though not nearly as beautiful, Lady Angela appealed to the down-to-earth side of Lord Elcho, and enabled him to view with complaisance his wife's cerebral devotion to Balfour. By 1905 Margot's elder sister Charty Ribblesdale was weakening with tuberculosis, the disease that had already killed another Tennant sister, Posie. Her husband Lord Ribblesdale, whose tall and patrician looks were captured by Sargent, was the epitome of the English hunting gentleman. He, too, had enjoyed the favours of Lady Angela and, as his wife's illness developed, he sought comfort and superb cooking at the Cavendish Hotel, run by the redoubtable Rosa Lewis. After Charty's death in 1911, Lord Ribblesdale moved into the hotel permanently. Another denizen of the Cavendish was Sir William Eden, putative father of Sir Anthony, later Lord Avon: although the gossips claimed that he too was in fact fathered by the indefatigable Harry Cust!

These affairs, and countless more, were made possible by the institution of the country house weekend. How intense, if unspoken, the erotic atmosphere must have been! Picture the formal breakfasts. Married couples would appear together, of course – the six o'clock warning bell would have taken care of that – but what meaningful glances must have flickered across the plates of kedgeree and kippers, between lovers whose warm bodies had only a couple of hours previously been clasped in each other's arms. Tact was needed, above all on the part of the hostess, to ensure that assignations in the gazebo or the copse, or (if wet) the library or one of the smaller drawing-rooms, might be made and enjoyed unobserved. All the dramas of ending an old relationship, or initiating and sealing a new one, were carried out under cover of a perfect social façade. There was a convention for everything, made possible by the seamless web of hypocrisy and double standards that Julian Grenfell found so intolerable in his mother. Beneath this veneer of formality and beautiful manners, the country house weekend must have throbbed with illicit sensuality.

All this the servants observed like deaf mutes. Not for them the hints, the confidences and the betrayals. They *knew* what was going on – after all, they were responsible for changing sheets, laundering clothes (a laundrymaid might spend an entire day ironing a flounced and pleated petticoat to perfection, for it to be worn once) and for the warning bells or knocks that made sure everyone greeted the morning in the correct marital bed. In spite of this, the upper classes felt themselves to be morally superior to their servants. Even a comparatively liberal writer like Bagehot could declare in all seriousness:

> If men differ in anything they differ in the fineness and the delicacy of their moral intuitions. . . . We need not go as far as the savages to learn that lesson; we need only talk to the English poor or to our servants, and we shall be taught it very completely. The lower classes in civilised countries, like all classes in uncivilised countries, are clearly wanting in the nicer part of those feelings which, taken together, we call the sense of morality.[20]

Whatever the upper classes permitted themselves, it was far too dangerous to risk their servants indulging in the same pleasures. Thus the virtues of sobriety, thrift, industry and chastity were much preached by those who did not practise them. One wonders how servants ever contrived to marry, when they had so little free time for courting, and were allowed no 'followers' at the house. In the 1915 edition of Mrs Beeton's *Book of Household Management*, employers were advised:

> A lady should never allow herself to forget the important duty of watching over the moral and physical welfare of those beneath her roof. Without seeming unduly inquisitive, she can always learn something of their acquaintances and holiday occupations and should, when necessary, warn them against the dangers and evils of bad company. . . . The moral responsibility for evil rests largely on the employer. . . .[21]

Once George Curzon discovered that a housemaid at Carlton Gardens had allowed a footman to spend the night with her. 'I put the little slut out into the street at a moment's notice,' he wrote to his wife. Yet a servant girl who had 'lost her character' was lost indeed. Without a good reference no one else would employ her. Many servant girls thus disgraced ended up on the streets. Respectability was all – at any rate, for the servant classes. But Curzon would have been thought insufferably priggish had he tried to prevent the guests under his roof from sharing beds that were not strictly their own.

The elaborate trappings of the Edwardians' life and leisure needed to be maintained by enormous numbers of servants . . . a ratio of three or four to each member of the family was quite normal, and the wealthiest households would have twice that number. At Eaton Hall in Cheshire the Duke of Westminster had fifty indoor servants and forty gardeners. Labour-saving domestic equipment was not only unknown but unnecessary. When domestic servants could be had for £40 a year who would bother? The first such device to be generally accepted was the vacuum cleaner, first known as the 'Puffing Billy', and invented in 1901. A version of it was used to clean the blue carpet beneath the throne at Edward VII's coronation, which must have done a lot to hasten its acceptance. But other than this, all preparation and cooking of food, all cleaning and washing and polishing of utensils, dishes and cutlery; all laundering, starching, pressing, mending and brushing of clothes; as well as the maintenance of huge houses and highly ornamental furniture to standards of the most spotless cleanliness – all of this was done by hand. The servants at the bottom of the hierarchy worked from six o'clock in the morning till ten or eleven at night, and were virtually slaves.

The butler at Cliveden – reigning monarch in the servants' hall – said of the scullery maids:

> Poor little devils, washing up and scrubbing away at the dozens of pots, pans, saucepans and plates, up to their elbows in suds and grease, their hands red raw with the soda which was the only form of detergent in those days. I've seen them crying with exhaustion and pain, the degradation too, I shouldn't wonder. Well, let's hope they get their reward in heaven.[22]

Despite such treatment, it was considered a privilege to serve the nobility and the gentry, albeit for long hours and pitifully low pay. In 1891 there were over one and a half million domestic servants in the United Kingdom. At nearly 16 per cent of the labour force, this meant that domestic service was the largest single occupation in the country. When Lord Derby died in 1893 he left a staff of 727 indoor and outdoor servants: though this was quite exceptional, even in his own time.

Alfred Lyttelton's only son Oliver recalled in his *Memoirs*: 'The servants of my youth had a tradition of service. It was not thought servile to serve, and many a butler and nurse or maid were the trusted and loved friends of the family. They taught the youth the standards that were expected of them.'[23] It sounds idyllic; and no doubt, in the kindly Lyttelton household and indeed many others, servants *were* well treated. But it is significant that in 1898 the average length of stay by a servant in any one household was less than a year and a half. This scarcely reflects a below-stairs world of trusted family retainers contented with their lot. Most servants were taken for granted if they were conscientious, and summarily dismissed if they were not. There were always more where they came from.

Girls went into service between the ages of twelve and fourteen, still hardly more than children. They would earn perhaps 9*d* or 1*s* a day to start with, rising to about 10*s* (50*p*) a week by the time they were sixteen. Those whose spirits were not broken by the years of their adolescence, or who had not been seduced by a guest or son of the house (if they were pretty) or by a visiting manservant or tradesman, would hope to rise to the higher echelons of the below-stairs hierarchy and become a cook or eventually housekeeper.[24] Rosa Lewis, who became cook to royalty and finally had her own establishment at the Cavendish Hotel in Jermyn Street, was unique.

Ettie Grenfell kept a careful note of the cost of housekeeping at Taplow. At the end of 1899, she recorded, her bills had been £2,118. The purchasing power of the pound then was about thirty-five times as much as it is today; so Ettie had spent roughly £74,500 that year on housekeeping, including the wages of staff and the cost of food and entertaining. It is an enormous expenditure; but she was virtually running a small hotel – and one in which the guests never paid! Considering how frequently she had people to stay (almost every week) and the lavishness with which she fed and housed them, she must have been a watchful employer and a careful housekeeper.

The Grenfells' basic household at this time consisted of about twenty-six people (Ettie and Willy, their four children – Imogen was not born until 1905, seventeen years after Julian – and twenty staff) and that number would have been more or less doubled by their visitors during the autumn and winter. In the summer, the London season would have been the main attraction; but Taplow was only some twenty minutes from London by train, and Ettie must have had people staying then, too – particularly around the time of the Fourth of June, and the Eton and Harrow match, for which she always had a big house party. Her housekeeping budget, then, was such as to allow roughly £26 a week for all those living and staying under her roof: very much more, of course, would have been spent on the family and visitors; very much less on the servants. A rough comparison can be gauged from the fact that in 1914 – fifteen years later – an ordinary working-class family was estimated, by the Board of Trade, to spend 25*s* per week on food for the whole family: about £35 at today's prices. If one assumes six members to that family (probably a low guess), then each person's consumption must have cost slightly less than £6 a week. In other words, Ettie Grenfell's budget was at least four times as high, and given that she probably spent more like the £6 per head on her servants, leaving close on £50 a week for family and friends, then the true figure would be closer to eight times as much as that of an average (*not* poor) family. But then, so of course was her wealth.

Many of the Souls women would have spent a further £2,000 a year on their clothes. When staying at a country house, a lady would appear at breakfast in a (relatively) simple morning frock. If there were no formal luncheon, she would change into a dress, slightly more elaborate, at noon. If she were joining the men for a picnic lunch during the shoot, she would change into a tweed coat and skirt, or something appropriately sporty. In the late afternoon she would change once again, for tea. These tea-gowns, in their splendour and intricacy, were closer to what would today be called a 'cocktail dress' – itself all but outdated. Finally, for dinner she would change into the full splendour of an evening gown. Each outfit had to be embellished with suitable jewellery. Pearls were for day wear, diamonds were only correct in the evening and tiaras had to be worn in the presence of royalty. In addition, she needed gloves, belts, shoes or boots, bags, wraps, shawls, furs and other accessories. No lady would be seen wearing the same outfit twice during a Saturday-to-Monday. Thus, each short visit entailed something like fifteen different sets of clothes, which all had to be swathed in tissue paper, along with their accompanying lingerie, by a hard-worked ladies' maid, who packed it all up in leather Saratoga trunks (the so-called Noah's Arks that could be seen piled up at any country railway station), portmanteaux and hat boxes. On arrival, everything had to be unpacked, pressed, hung up and put away. Any lady would have been quite helpless to take care of this herself; so much so that one wonders whether adultery was necessarily accompanied by undressing. Presumably gentlemen had to be skilled at lacing corsets and doing up dozens of tiny buttons at the backs of dresses and blouses. The only alternative was to summon the maid at a suitable moment, to clothe her – and his – mistress again.

These maids, although among the most privileged of the servants, had to submerge their identity in that of their employer. In the servants' hall they were called by *her* name – not their own – and obeyed the same order of precedence at the servants' table: so that a duchess's maid would sit in the place of honour to the right of the butler, a marchioness's maid to his left, and so on.[25] Often these maids were more snobbish than their employers, and they could be merciless to the youngest scullery maids, or any servant below themselves in rank. They purveyed news and gossip from one great house to another, missing nothing, while seemingly accepting that different rules of behaviour applied to the likes of them. They lived vicariously, and in the greatest detail, the intrigues and misdeeds of their employers:

> A friend of mine asked his valet, who had been with him for a number of years, how they amused themselves downstairs of an evening. 'Well, my lord,' he answered, 'one of our favourite amusements is piecing together the letters found in the wastepaper baskets in the morning – better than any jig-saw puzzle, I can assure your lordship, and much more entertaining!'[26]

George Cornwallis-West, whose recollection this is, may not, however, be a reliable witness, since he also recorded his belief that, 'in many cases their wages were, to them, a secondary consideration'.[27]

Male guests, too, required several changes of clothing, presided over in their case by a valet (who would sit to the right or left of the housekeeper, according to rank). Men would bring tweed suits or plus fours for shooting or fishing; a dinner jacket and velvet smoking jacket for the evening; a white tie and tail coat if there were to be a formal dinner or a ball; as well as anything up to half a dozen special outfits in which to hunt or ride or motor or golf or bicycle.

Beneath all these outer layers of clothing the Edwardians were often surprisingly dirty. Men smelled of sweat and tobacco and leather and whisky and possibly some hair preparation from Trumper's or Penhaligon's: but mainly they smelled of sweat. Women perfumed themselves, and washed more frequently, but it is noticeable in their photographs that their elaborately piled-up hair was usually dirty. It had to be carefully back-combed (again, by the ladies' maid, of course) to conceal the hairpieces or 'rats' with which most women had to supplement their own hair to create the fashionably piled effect, and secured with pins and diamond brooches so as to stay in place for several hours under a hat or tiara. Hair that was clean would be too soft to hold its shape.

Besides, daily baths were by no means taken for granted; partly because, although most houses had installed bathrooms by now – one at each end of the guests' corridor rather than one to each bedroom – running hot water was still unusual. So, from about eight o'clock in the morning, or seven in the evening, the corridors would be filled with servants bringing heavy brass or enamel jugs filled with steaming hot water up to the guests from the kitchen, where it had been boiled in great cauldrons; while an hour later, by which time the guests were downstairs eating yet another enormous meal – a five-course breakfast or eight-course dinner – the servants would have to scurry along the corridors once again, emptying hip-baths and jugs, whisking away damp towels, straightening crumpled beds, and restoring stillness and order ready for it all to be disarrayed once again. 'And so the house-party, shut off from the outside world, sang and danced and flirted and shot and hunted and fished in a little self-contained kingdom, of which the host and hostess were the undisputed king and queen and which . . . was immune from unheralded invasion from outside,'[28] wrote Lord Ernest Hamilton.

Or so, at any rate, it must have seemed.

– 9 –
Second-generation Souls: The Corrupt Coterie

1906–1914

> There'll be no war
> As long as there's a King like good King Edward,
> There'll be no war,
> For 'e 'ates that sort of thing!
> Mothers needn't worry
> As long as we've a King like good King Edward.
> Peace with 'Onour
> Is his motter,
> So God save the King.

Thus went an old music-hall song of 1909.

The myth of a golden age, an Indian summer, that has been spun around the country house visiting and the *douceur de la vie* of the Edwardian aristocracy is a fantasy of later generations. Born of guilt and nostalgia after the First World War, it was already prevalent in the twenties and thirties. But the younger generation living at the time, the children of the Souls, who grew up in the decades before and after Queen Victoria's death, were more clear-sighted. They observed the meaningless tyranny of the social round. They knew that it was often boring, shallow and spiteful – a charade played out by people revolving like puppets against a set of gorgeous backdrops.

Very few, however, were bothered about the social inequalities that buttressed their parents' lifestyle . . . extreme luxury at one end of the scale, widespread penury at the other. This most of them took for granted. It was part of the natural order of things. Lady Diana Manners, for example, would have agreed absolutely with George Curzon's views about the morals of maidservants. When the flamboyantly high-spirited extravagant Edward Horner seduced Lady Cunard's beautiful young parlourmaid in 1906 after a drunken lunch, the fourteen-year-old Diana thought it 'eighteenth century and *droit de seigneur* and rather nice'.[1] Had the young woman been one of her sisters or friends, her reaction – and everyone else's – would have been very different.

It is notoriously difficult to be a successful son of a famous father or a brilliant mother. It must have been even more difficult for the children of a whole group, like the Souls. They responded in two ways: first, by being sceptical of their parents' achievements; second, by attempting to outdo them. The children of the Souls were well aware of the sexual hypocrisy and social compromises upon which their parents' lives were based, and yet at the same time were bound to them by love, loyalty and financial dependence. These ties created a conflict which made for a good deal of unspoken resentment and, occasionally, open rebellion. But the Souls had become so used to basking in one anothers' reflected admiration that few of them realized the extent to which their children had found them out. 'My mother was untrammelled by convention',[2] said Lady Diana succinctly, referring to the bohemian tastes of the Duchess of Rutland. But when Edward Horner abruptly told seventeen-year-old Lady Diana that her real father was not – as she had always supposed – the Duke of Rutland, but in fact Harry Cust, she evidently bore no ill-will. She loved the Duke and she loved Harry Cust, an old friend to all the family, and she minded little which of them was her 'real' father as long as she retained the respect and the title given to a Duke's daughter.

Raymond Asquith – son of H. H. Asquith, Liberal Prime Minister – was much more scathing:

> Eighteenth century methods worked well enough when we had a talented aristocracy, but we can't afford nowadays to limit our choice of Ministers to a few stuffy families with ugly faces, bad manners and a belief in the Nicene Creed. The day of the clever cad is at hand . . . I always felt it would come to this if we once let ourselves in for an Empire. If only Englishmen had known their Aeschylus a little better they wouldn't have bustled about the world appropriating things in the way they have. A gentleman may make a large fortune but only a cad can look after it.[3]

He was twenty-three at the time: old enough to have arrived at his own beliefs. Five years later he writes about his friend Bron Herbert's account of a visit to the Grenfells (actually Desboroughs by this time):

> Bron is more black against society & especially women than ever before. He has been living with the Grenfells in the full flow of the social tide these last two months & now he creeps in & out of their house by the back door & is conducted straight to his bedroom by a servant holding a green umbrella before him to prevent his seeing or being seen. I think I am coming round to his view. There are half a dozen women & perhaps a dozen men whose company I enjoy – but not in the way one gets it in London, tempered by a hundred conventions and restrictions & pomposities with bows and grimaces and hurry & clatter & insincerity – women twittering like tired birds and men tinkling like empty glasses.[4]

Who were the second-generation Souls, and how did they come together in the first place?

Twenty years earlier, in the mid-1880s, it would have been difficult to become a Soul; but nobody was *born* one. The children of the Souls, on the other hand, were automatically born into the Coterie . . . the Corrupt Coterie, as it was called . . . and had known one another from the nursery upwards. It was much harder to *become* a member of the group. The children who were dutifully listed by Ettie or Mary Elcho, in their family memoirs, as having attended various childish birthday parties, were still together ten or more years later, attending debutante balls and fancy dress parties. So the Asquiths were in the group – Raymond, Herbert (or 'Beb', as he was called), Arthur ('Oc'), Cyril and Violet; and the Charterises – Mary and Hugo Elcho's family – were in the group: Hugo ('Ego') and Guy and clever, cryptic Cynthia, and Blunt's daughter Mary, and young Yvo. The Grenfell boys wanted to be in the Coterie, though Ettie's deep disapproval of all their girlfriends often made things difficult for them: but Julian and Billy and Monica Grenfell certainly knew all its members. Edward Horner, big and tactless but evidently charming, belonged, as did his beautiful sisters Katharine and Cicely: the children of Laura Tennant's great friend Lady Frances and Sir John Horner. Laura's elder sister Charty had married Lord Ribblesdale, and their children – Charles Lister, and Diana and Barbara and Laura – were Coterie members too. But of them all, the most outrageous and sought-after were the three lovely Manners daughters: Lady Marjorie, Lady Violet ('Letty') and Lady Diana. They were central to the Coterie, as well as being the main reason that it earned the adjective 'Corrupt'. Their friends Viola, Felicity and Iris Tree, daughters of the actor-manager Sir Herbert Beerbohm Tree, were admitted to its inner circle despite the fact that their parents had only really been accepted as 'occasional' Souls, and then mainly because of their close friendship with Violet Rutland. Others drifted in and out of the group, either because they had been at school (generally Eton) or at university (generally Oxford) with someone from the core group of the Coterie; or because they were in love with one. So Duff Cooper was in due course admitted on both counts, in spite of the fact that his father, so far from being a Soul, was a surgeon specializing in venereal diseases. His friendship with John Manners at Eton, and later with a daughter from the other branch of the family, enabled the Coterie – though never their mothers – to overlook his immodest origins.

Many parallels can be drawn between members of the Coterie and the Souls, but the most striking of all is that between Duff Cooper and Harry Cust. Both men were slight, blond and fine-featured; both inordinately attracted to women; both had intellectual promise that was unfulfilled because both were finally burnt out by their fondness for drink, gambling and society. It is easy to see why Harry Cust's daughter was so powerfully drawn to Duff Cooper.

Reared in the nurseries of the great Souls houses, the Coterie grew into a clique determined to challenge the reputation of their too-powerful parents. Where the Souls had been mildly original (in allowing women to make intelligent conversation, to wear unstructured 'arts and crafts' dresses) the Coterie was wildly avant-garde. The Souls were vivacious; the Coterie must be frenetic. If the Souls had sometimes been controversial, the Coterie must frequently be outrageous. If the Souls had flouted some of society's taboos, what was left for the Coterie but to flout the rest? And so the young, in the last peaceful years between the Boer War and 1914, not only drank too much champagne but turned as well to morphia and 'chlorers' (chloroform) for oblivion after dances or death. They did not merely flirt; they kissed, and sometimes more than kissed, though hardly ever more than that. They evaded chaperones, shocked their parents, scandalized society. They drove three times round the Park in darkened hansom cabs. They preferred suggestive new dances like the tango and the turkey-trot to the shimmering waltzes of their parents. In short, the glamour of the Souls had flashed before their children's eyes for so long that – however spurious they knew it to be – the Coterie's only possible response was to outdo them in flamboyance. The irony was that, by 1914, most of them were finally settling into good marriages within their own circle, just as their parents would have wished.

If Duff was the Harry Cust of the Coterie, its Arthur Balfour was Raymond Asquith. He dominated the Coterie and was the focus of admiration and love just as 'King Arthur' twenty years earlier had been the acknowledged leader of the Souls. Raymond too was somewhat older than the rest of his circle. Born in 1878, he was the eldest child of H. H. Asquith, a hard-up young barrister, and his gentle first wife Helen. In 1886 his father became a Liberal MP, and eight years later improved his chances of high office by marrying, after his first wife's death, the influential and wealthy Margot Tennant. Raymond was thirteen when his mother died, and the pain he must have felt probably contributed to an impression of emotional coldness which he – like A. J. Balfour – conveyed to those outside his closest circle of friends. Raymond went to school at Winchester, where his outstanding intellect was nurtured to such good effect that he won the top scholarship in his year to Balliol, and went up to Oxford in 1897.

So far his career had been the exemplary one of a clever and industrious schoolboy. Tall and distinguished to look at, with striking grey eyes and thick reddish-brown hair, he was already seen by some as the paragon of his generation. Beneath the faintly aloof, always perfectly mannered surface, the first sparks of originality could be discerned, along with a sharp wit. He wrote a letter to his old school friend, Harold Baker, in which he dissected the society gathered for Christmas 1897 at Glen:

> It is a strange and mixed household I can assure you: statesmen, financiers, admirals from Cathay, Generals from Spain, Etonians, Wykehamists, women – They quarrel about Trades Unions – the financiers and politicians being at daggers drawn – Their only bond of sympathy is gluttony – in some cases genuine, in some assumed to meet the exigencies of fashionable society: apparently it is good form to discuss the entrée with scientific fervour, to apply the higher criticism to the turtle soup, and to complain of the temperature of one's claret – if too hot, to break the glass, if too cold to fondle and cuddle it in one's hands and bosom till it acquires the desired heat. These things are a continual source of amusement to me. . . .[5]

Raymond's wit was at its keenest when pointing out the foibles of fellow guests. A few months later he was writing again to Baker, from yet another house party:

> . . . a vast and miscellaneous assortment of military sparks, blasé almost to the point of decomposition: I asked one of them what regiment he belonged to: he replied in a plaintive drawl that he really didn't recollect, but he believed they had buff facings. There is also a Colonial Premier whose name I never gathered but last night I had a most trying experience with him . . . I was left tête-à-tête in the smoking room with this awful Australian: after talking for many hours about tinned meats and other colonial subjects, I suggested we should go to bed: accordingly we set off – the premier rather wild in his gait: we reached the door of the Duchess's [of Cleveland] room and my friend opened it and bade me goodnight: I pointed out as respectfully as I could that she was not a suitable victim, and that there were many younger ladies in the

house if he was so disposed: he however indignantly disclaimed any libidin-ous intention. . . . [6]

Gifted and somewhat remote, like Balfour; impatient with the society around him – as Balfour was not – Raymond Asquith became a Fellow of All Souls, and while he was reading for the Bar, met the young Katharine Horner at her parents' beautiful house, Mells Park. Like Stanway, Mells was a former monastic establishment; it too was centuries old, set in that great golden basin of England that stretches from the Cotswolds down through Somerset. Mells was near Frome, made beautiful by the artistic talents of Lady Horner, one of Burne-Jones's earliest models and patrons. On his first visit it was the older sister, Cicely, who appealed to him ('about as perfect a specimen of female beauty as I have ever seen')[7] but he was soon more taken with Katharine, as he wrote to Baker:

> She is quite young – 17* I suppose – and not out yet; not technically beautiful but to my eye much more so than the other – a low broad brow, a delightful nervous voice, and that lively and significant eye which one usually misses in women. She is really very clever both by instinct and knowledge. . . . I really became rather friendly with her for the time, finding in her many of the qualities I admire in boys – especially a combination of purity and vivacity which I am coming to fear is rarer in them than in girls.[8]

Raymond was obliged to wait six years before he could marry Katharine, partly because of her youth, but also because he was making his way only slowly at the Bar. More obedient than some of their contemporaries to the seemingly absurd restrictions imposed by parents on young people in love, Raymond and his Fawn, as he called the reticent, wide-eyed Katharine, conducted their courtship more by letter than in speech. Their meetings were usually public, at London dances or country house parties. His letters are wistful and tender . . .

> The ball was a wretched business and leaves me still humpy and angry . . . you must be almost ashamed to be loved by such a feckless unhandy kind of oaf – my only excuse is that I have never much wanted before to have lonely talk with a woman and so I have no tricks. I ought to have fallen in love with someone like Margot who would find a solitary and peaceful nook in the Black Hole of Calcutta. . . . Still, it is a comfort to me that you were in such a great mood of beauty and I can call up in lonely moments the lovely shape of your head which I deliberately fixed by study in my imagination where it still lasts. . . .[9]

In another he writes, with poignant prescience: 'I am not tired of you yet, Katharine, and I believe I shall not be for a little while still – perhaps till we both are so old that we are tired of everything. Indeed my fear takes a different direction – that I shall not have time to get tired of you – time and opportunity – before I die.'[10]

In July 1907 they were married at last. He wrote to her mother, 'One of the pleasantest features of our new situation is the fact that we are – for the first time in our lives – out of a crowd.'[11] After this, Raymond and Katharine Asquith formed the nucleus of the Coterie, in spite of being two of its least Corrupt

---

*In fact she was only fifteen when they met.

members. Nevertheless there were some among Raymond's contemporaries who found him dangerously clever. Cynthia Charteris, who was in due course to marry his brother 'Beb', wrote of their group:

> . . . through Edward [Horner] I gained some lights on the creed of the Coterie. I'm sure there is an insidiously corruptive poison in their minds – brilliantly distilled by their inspiration, Raymond. I don't care a damn about their morals or manners, but I do think what – for want of a better word – I call their anti-cant is really suicidal to happiness. I am much more in sympathy with the elder generation – what one might call Ettyism – which is an object of ridicule to them.[12]

Her disapproval is confirmed by Lady Diana Cooper's spirited defence of the Coterie, as she recalled it many years later:

> I do not know how it came to be the Coterie – the Corrupt Coterie, to give it its full title. As a name I am a little ashamed of it, as my mother was of the 'Souls'. There was among us a reverberation of the Yellow Book and Aubrey Beardsley, Ernest Dowson, Baudelaire and Max Beerbohm. Swinburne often got recited. Our pride was to be unafraid of words, unshocked by drink, and unashamed of 'decadence' and gambling – Unlike-Other-People, I'm afraid.[13]

The Tennant sisters, who had been central to the early forming of the Souls, had their counterpart in the Coterie. The Manners sisters – supposedly the daughters of the Duke of Rutland, though only Marjorie, the first-born of the marriage, was actually his – the spirited, high-stepping Manners sisters were the inspiration and the electricity that lit up the Coterie.

Lady Diana, the youngest of them all, arrived on the scene late. It was the summer of 1906, and she had been invited to spend some weeks staying with the Trees at Brancaster, on the north Norfolk coast. There she came across a reading party of Oxford undergraduates, gathered together for several weeks – ostensibly to read and study. Staying in a nearby house, she found to her delight, were Edward Horner; Patrick Shaw Stewart – brilliant, aggressive, ambitious, with gingery hair and a pale, freckled skin; Charles Lister, the son and heir of Lord Ribblesdale and, most surprisingly, a true and committed socialist; and Alan Parsons, an Etonian like the other three, an acute critic of literature and drama, and the ballast to the group. There were others too, but these four belonged to the select inner circle of the Coterie. Lady Diana was only fourteen at the time, a precocious child with a well-stocked mind and the promise of beauty. She was dazzled by the brilliant young men, and they in turn were flattered by her and already entranced by her older sisters.

It was about now that the Manners daughters began to be singled out by the mothers of the young eligibles in the Coterie. Ettie called them 'The Hothouse' or sometimes 'The Hotbed': and it was not meant as a compliment. In the wake of their mother, the bohemian Violet Rutland, whose familiarity with the backstage world of the theatre was shocking to her contemporaries, the daughters in their turn were too exotic for their elders. Lady Diana numbered among her passions a young Swedish airman, Gustav Hamel, and the raffish heir to the baronetcy, Denis Anson. The young men themselves found it all dangerously desirable. In the spring of 1909 Julian Grenfell – by then hopelessly in love with the beautiful, dark-eyed Lady Marjorie – was writing to his mother: 'You like the smart set: I like the solitary life – a few people at a time. That is God; and we had better leave him alone. The one set you hate is the Hotbed: *the one set I like is the Hotbed*. That is God: & I cannot see, & I'm sure you cannot either, that there is the least obligation on me to give them up for you.'[14] Although Ettie quoted reams and reams of boring schoolboy letters from Julian and Billy in her *Family Journal*, this letter, because it articulated a difference of opinion between them, she did not quote. It is reasonable to assume that Ettie's demands upon her sons in real life were the same as the image which she perpetuated after their deaths, when they were no longer able to give the lie to it. Their rôle was to be her worshipping acolytes, reflecting credit upon her in the eyes of her friends and society, while remaining blind to her private behaviour.

Towards the end of 1907, when Julian was a sensitive nineteen-year-old and Billy seventeen, their mother was deeply involved in a love affair with the young Archie Gordon, son of the Earl of Aberdeen, seventeen years younger than Ettie, and a shining example of everything she wanted Julian to be. He had been a constant visitor at Taplow for some years; but while he was at Balliol (Willy's old college, as it happened) the relationship developed into something more intense. Young men in their early twenties often have a penchant for sophisticated, hospitable women *d'un certain âge*; but Ettie, emotionally rapacious as ever, seems to have encouraged this infatuation to the point where it almost ran out of control. Under the flimsy pretence that Archie was in fact Monica's admirer (Monica was hardly into her teens) Ettie indulged herself in the flattery of his love, impervious to the pain it might be causing her sons or indeed her husband. 'My beloved E.,' Archie wrote to her from Italy, 'I can't begin to speak of all the joy of seeing you *often* and *much*, I trust, during the next weeks. I have the whole universe waiting to be talked about, and all my life to be submitted to you. And my love precedes me from here, warm from the sun and the joy that is here.'[15]

The injustice and immorality of the situation lay not in the fact that Ettie was encouraging this relationship. It was the fact that she was simultaneously preaching quite different standards of social morality and private behaviour to her sons that made it intolerable. Lady Diana Cooper says:

> She was enormously vital and amusing. She was so involved with young Oxford – her son's group – and I think she had probably very light love affairs with many of them. It wasn't at all discussed . . . having an affair, you know, it sort of went without saying. Probably they hardly knew, and if they did know they couldn't have believed it: somebody of their own generation, sleeping with their mother. There was never any talk, not like that.

The Coterie rebelled against these double standards – which were hardly different, in fact, from those that had been enforced by their parents upon the maidservants. Ettie Desborough might enjoy a passionate intimacy with Archie Gordon; but Raymond Asquith could not be permitted to spend a few moments alone with his beloved fiancée. The younger generation reacted in different ways. Julian, being closest and thus most acutely affected, suffered from a nervous breakdown followed by two years of deep, occasionally catatonic depression. Ettie never connected this with her own behaviour, but blamed it on lack of vital energy and determination on Julian's part. His friends at Balliol reacted to the pressures by being more troublesome than was expected of the studious high-fliers at that college. Although clever, and reasonably hard-working, they were bellicose, drunken and constantly being hauled before the authorities.

The Coterie as a whole loved and respected their parents, and turned tactfully away from illicit relationships that had in many cases lasted so long as to become almost licit. There is no evidence that any of the Charteris children resented their mother's long devotion to Arthur Balfour; or their father's consolation in the arms of Lady Angela Forbes. Both were frequent visitors at Stanway, where the young Charterises still called Balfour 'Mr Rabbit'. The Asquith children appear to have been completely unaware of Margot's continuing friendship with Wilfrid Scawen Blunt (how should they know, when it had shrunk to nothing more improper than taking the occasional cup of tea with him, and pouring out her highly strung heart in return for a reminiscent cuddle). But society's *mores* had changed since the 1880s, and the Souls had been in charge of the forces of change. They themselves had revelled in the freedoms made possible by adroit manipulation of the double standard after the dead hand of mid-Victorian morals. Now, it fell to their children to sweep away the hypocrisy and be more open in the way they conducted their relationships. It happened gradually – by the timescale of the impatient young – if too fast for their parents.

More threatening to their parents was the change in the nature of the political beliefs held by some of the young lions of the Coterie. The Souls had believed what their parents – or, in due course, their husbands – believed, when it came to politics. You were born to a political party, rather than deciding your own views. In the words of W. S. Gilbert:

> I often think it's comical
>   How Nature always does contrive
> That every boy and every gal,
>   That's born into this world alive,
> Is either a little Liberal,
>   Or else a little Conservative![16]

It had been true in 1885; it was noticeably less true in 1905. Many of the Coterie were aware of the ideology of socialism, though only Charles Lister became converted to its doctrines. And yet there was enough injustice to fire anyone's idealism. In the years before the First World War a mere 2.5 per cent of the population still held two-thirds of the country's wealth, while 16 per cent lived in 'primary poverty' in 1913. This did not mean poverty caused by gambling, or drunkenness, or extravagance, but the poverty of people who simply could not earn enough to buy the bare necessities. Malnutrition was common: people – children, even – still starved to death. So marked were the differences in food and health that teenage boys from working-class backgrounds were on average three and a half inches shorter than boys from professional families. They were also likely to weigh at least ten pounds less. At the time of the Boer War, four out of ten would-be recruits had to be rejected on medical grounds, despite a reduction in the minimum height requirement to only five feet; and twenty years later that proportion of rejects had not changed. In 1915, four out of five recruits – even of those accepted – had such bad teeth that they could not eat properly.

Ego Charteris was another Coterie member who showed signs, from time to time, of breaking out of the shell of conventional ideas. As a very little boy – his mother recorded with amusement – he had remarked, 'Nanna says that soldiers think it glorious to be shot in battle. *I* should think it a horrid nasty thing.'[17] But such innocence did not of course persist for long. Despite early flirtations with unorthodox views, not one of the Coterie maintained lifelong political convictions that were radically different from those of their parents. They dutifully opposed women's suffrage; opposed trade unions; opposed strikes; and mourned the death of Edward VII. Billy Grenfell wrote to his mother; 'I am sad about King Edward, aren't you? It seems as if the glory had departed: and there will be lots of war, and mothers will have to worry considerably.' But Billy – pugnacious Billy – didn't worry at all. His letter went on: 'Oxford has really been the greatest fun and caviare, and I find myself drifting rapidly into the riding and cock-fighting set.'[18] Julian's forebodings were slightly more sincere:

> Isn't it funny that the sort of *Daily Mail* things are really true now for once in a way, the things about feeling the tragedy in the atmosphere and seeing it in people's faces. Everybody *is* looking quite different, and one can feel the thundercloud in the air. I am really sorry about him, he must have been a jolly man and a glorious king. Will it complicate things very much?[19]

While the eleven-year-old Ivo wrote from prep school to his parents: 'I expect you will have seen in the newspapers that King Edward is dead.'[20]

People felt it to be the end of an era, and it was, far more than the death of Queen Victoria had been. Edward VII had stamped his personality on society for half a century. He had been the average Englishman writ large – indulging agreeable vices like gluttony and drinking and womanizing, all taken royally to excess. But there was more to him than that. He had truly longed for and worked to keep the peace in Europe. Both by the ties of blood and by astute diplomatic negotiations he had held apart the forces of belligerence and warmongering. His dull, dim son, the new King George V, had not the prestige, nor the skill, nor even much sign of any inclination, to avert war. With Edward the Peacemaker gone, the field was clear for the many who wanted to fight.

The ten years of Edward's reign were followed by four of the most scintillating years English society had ever known, yet all the time the undertow was dragging the country towards war. Everybody knew it could not be long delayed . . . and yet, they did not know. They were holding their breath waiting for it, and yet its outbreak took them by surprise. During those glittering years isolated events – private deaths, public dramas – showed how, by certain attitudes, a mixture of idealism and acquiescence, England was swept towards the maelstrom.

First, two public events of great drama and significance took place; although in retrospect their emphasis is a good deal clearer without the drama, and their significance not quite what it appeared to be at the time. The first was the death of Captain Scott and his two companions on their journey back from the South Pole. They died at the end of March 1912, but their bodies were not found until 12 November, so that it took almost a year before news of their deaths reached the outside world. The second was the sinking of the *Titanic* on her maiden voyage, with the loss of some fifteen hundred lives. That was on the night of 14 April 1912, and the news was relayed to the world within hours. Both events received immense publicity, largely because the men who were involved seemed to exhibit the very qualities of gallantry and cheerfulness in the face of terrible ordeals upon which the upper classes prided themselves, and by which they set great store in their sons. Courage and courtesy were the hallmarks of a gentleman, and the whole nation felt uplifted by tales of Antarctic heroism and Titanic tragedy.

Yet behind the public perception of both events lay very different stories. What is interesting is how they were manipulated by the press, and later by countless books of boys' own heroes, so as to tell the world only the story it wished to hear. The fact was that, although Scott and his team were indeed brave and unimaginably cheerful, they were also under-financed, ill-equipped, stubborn and foolhardy. Likewise, the reality behind the loss of so many lives when the *Titanic* sank was the ignoble scramble by some of the rich passengers to commandeer the few lifeboats, well ahead of steerage-class women and children whose final misfortune was to be poor.

The accuracy of Scott's description, in his diary for 16 or 17 March 1912, of the way in which Captain Oates went out to meet his death cannot be questioned; while Oates's last words ('I am just going outside and may be some time') have passed into legend. What is less sacrosanct is the way in which Scott, himself close to death, invented thoughts for his comrade and gave them too the status of fact. One begins to understand how within a couple of years a whole generation of young men could rise up and go willingly to die in the trenches. Captain Oates was thirty-two when he chose to end his life, which had become a burden upon his companions. 'Oates' last thoughts', wrote Captain Scott, 'were of his mother, but immediately before he took pride in thinking that his regiment[†] would be pleased with the bold way in which he met his death. . . . We knew that poor Oates was walking to his death, but though we tried to dissuade him, we knew it was the act of a brave man and an English gentleman.'[21] Even Apsley Cherry-Garrard, one of the expedition's support team waiting at base camp, was aghast at the enormity of Scott's miscalculation, and the consequent waste of their feats of endurance:

> I now see very plainly that though we achieved a first-rate tragedy which will never be forgotten just because it was a tragedy, tragedy was not our business . . . our expedition, running appalling risks, performing prodigies of super-human endurance, achieving immortal renown, commemorated in august cathedral sermons and by public statues, yet reaching the Pole only to find our terrible journey superfluous, and leaving our best men dead on the ice.[22]

The sinking of the *Titanic* with 1,316 passengers and 891 crew on board was a very different matter. While there were undoubtedly acts of individual heroism, the analysis of the lists of those who drowned tells its own unanswerable tale. Although the statistics were published in the press, the myth of the band playing 'Nearer My God to Thee', and of dinner-jacketed gentlemen standing to attention on deck as the ship went down, still lingers. The myth was so much more palatable than the truth.

†The Inniskilling Dragoons.

There were 2,207 people aboard the ship for her maiden voyage: 703 of them were saved. The loss rate was higher for third-class children than for first-class men: so much for 'women and children first'. All the children in the first class were saved, and 97 per cent of the women, and 44 per cent of the men – among them the White Star Line's chairman, the man ultimately responsible for safety on board, Sir Bruce Ismay. All the children in second class were saved, too, and 84 per cent of the women – but only 6 per cent of the men: just 13 out of 147. In third class, 30 per cent of the children were saved, just over half of the women, and only 12 per cent of the men. Or, to put it another way, the figures for all survivors were: 63 per cent in first class; 42 per cent in second class; and 25 per cent in third class. Class disadvantages were the same in death as in life. Gentlemen might try to put ladies into the lifeboats first – but not women. Two from the third class who had managed to find their way on to the lifeboat deck were told by a ship's officer: 'Madam, your boats are down on your own deck.' But there were no boats on their deck.

There was an enquiry in England: long drawn-out, measured and judicious. It decided that an unfortunate accident had occurred and no one should be blamed. Wilfrid Scawen Blunt, still at the age of seventy-two an indefatigable diarist, recorded: 'One thing is consoling in these great disasters, the proof given that Nature is not quite yet the slave of Man, but is able to rise even now in her wrath and destroy him.' And he couldn't resist adding, 'Also if any large number of human beings could be better spared than another it would be just these American millionaires with their wealth and insolence.'[23]

If the *Titanic* was an omen on a grand scale, it had far less impact upon the Coterie than three individual deaths, of young men whom they knew personally as members of their circle. The first of them to die had been Ettie's young lover, Archie Gordon. At the beginning of December 1909 he had smashed up his car and himself in an accident. The effect it had upon Julian is evident from a letter he wrote at exactly the same time to Marjorie Manners – Diana's sister – for whom he felt hopeless, despairing love:

> I don't know what I am doing now, I feel as if I had been smashed up into little bits and put together again very badly with half the bits missing. All Thursday I felt as if I had something inside my head which was just going to burst; and then it did burst, and I broke up, and didn't know what I was or what was going on, except that I had gone right out of myself and become something quite different; and the agony of it, just the pure physical agony was like being hammered to death without dying. . . . But I *do* think you have been good to me – and please let me love you properly.[24]

What did he mean by 'properly'? Sexually? But he, and Marjorie, both knew that was impossible. Sexual love was only for married people, like his parents, his mother. . . . She was allowed sex, but he was not. And now her lover was dying.

Archie Gordon, in hospital in Winchester, took nearly three weeks to die. Gathered round his bedside were his mother, and Violet, and Ettie. There they sat for days, Ettie still determinedly joyful, so that his deathbed should be a happy place and he should not think that any of them were sad. It was the first demonstration of what was later called 'her stubborn gospel of joy'. On 16 December he died. Julian wrote to her in painful, staccato phrases:

I am miserable about Archie beyond power of speech. It was angelic of you to write; it is so terrible after the recovery a few days ago, and the glorious hope it gave one. I suppose there is no hope now; my heart bleeds as I write these words. I go to Taplow today, and if you aren't there, straight on to Winchester. I am glad you are with him. I never stop thinking of you.[25]

Billy's letter was more in the style she liked:

You will know how wonderful I thought you during our tiny time together, so calm and rest-giving and hopeful, with all your marvellous understanding and tenderness and love. I know how great your love for him was, and God knows he worshipped and adored you. . . . I am sure it is no good dwelling on the tragedy of it; Archie was so brilliant and brave a giver of happiness in his life, that I am sure he would have no-one too unhappy after its end.[26]

The belief held by Ettie and inculcated in her sons that the death of a young man was not a tragedy but a happy thing, a belief which her contemporaries admired, was surely among the attitudes that allowed Britain to drift helplessly towards war. Ettie asked many of her friends, and even her son Billy, to write their recollections of Archie, and these she printed in her *Family Journal*. Her own valediction was entirely characteristic:

Oh Bird of the Morning, O Spirit of Love
Are you near? Is it Joy? It is Joy.[27]

Julian's depression turned into a complete nervous breakdown, and he lay for weeks, motionless and speechless, until he was sent away to his aunt in Italy, and there he began to recover. Ettie wrote:

Julian was very unwell indeed all that Christmas and all the Winter. He was taken to Dr Maurice Craig, who said he would get perfectly right, but that it would take three months; and so it did. It was just the same sort of illness as in the previous Spring, only worse, and they said it came in the same way from complete overdoing in every way, after his rapid growth.[28]

Ah yes, of course – growing pains! Julian came back, took a pass degree at Oxford, and then joined a cavalry regiment, the Royal Dragoons, and went with them to India in November 1910. Ettie launched into a new relationship with Patrick Shaw Stewart who, aged twenty-two, was exactly the same age as Julian and four years younger than Archie had been.

Archie's death had been a solitary ill omen. Five years later in rapid succession came two more. The first was that of the young Swedish airman Gustav Hamel, one of the very few complete outsiders to penetrate the inner circle of the Coterie. Diana Manners had a crush on him; more serious, perhaps, was Monica Grenfell's love for him. By 1914 Monica was twenty, launched in society, and, though plumply pretty, an object of disappointment to her mother, who thought she wanted a daughter as brilliant and successful as she herself had been. Ettie had been married by the time she was twenty; while Monica was in love with someone quite unsuitable, and apparently disinclined to marry any of the rich and titled young men whom her mother so assiduously invited to Taplow and Panshanger (the Cowper family home which she had inherited in 1913).

Hamel was the idol of the Coterie for a year or so. He was handsome, debonair and brave; he danced wonderfully and performed absurd acrobatic feats in flimsy aircraft. When he was not flying his frail machine low over England he was racing along its lanes in fast cars. He allowed Sybil Hart-Davis (Duff's sister) to come up in his plane with a piglet under each arm . . . to prove, of course, that pigs might fly. Blond and carefree and reckless as Icarus, he took off from Hardelot in France on 23 May 1914 and was never seen again. The crowd waiting at Hendon Aerodrome to welcome him waited in vain for news. It was hard to believe that aeroplanes could simply fall out of the sky; harder still to imagine *that* pilot dead. Another lesson; another omen. A scarf, said to belong to him, was picked up in the North Sea. Diana Manners was, she recalled, 'hysterically upset, more really than my affection for him warranted. . . . It was the first violent death of a young man in my life.'[29] What Monica Grenfell felt is not recorded.

Less than six weeks later there was another death. This time the young man concerned was a long-standing member of the Coterie. Rich, sporting Denis Anson, in his mid-twenties, had just inherited a baronetcy. The previous year, he had been one of the crowd who went to Venice in September 1913, and there his antics were funnier and sillier than anyone else's. They were the sort of escapades that are infuriating to outsiders; hysterically funny to the show-offs involved. Lady Diana was staying, with her mother and Harry Cust, in a house party given by Lady Cunard in the Palazzo Catecumini. In another palazzo nearby, the wealthy young George Vernon – also a Coterie member – had installed himself and half his friends. The Prime Minister, H. H. Asquith, was there too with his family, revelling in the company of the gay and giddy young. 'In Venice on his birthday,' wrote Lady Diana Cooper later, 'we dressed him up as a Doge and hung the *sala* with Mantegna swags of fruit and green leaves and loaded him with presents, tenderness and admiration. I think he was ecstatically happy that day.'[30]

The follies of the Coterie were at their height that summer of 1913. It was the Carne-Vale, the farewell to feasting and mirth. Lady Diana Cooper recalled:

There were the young, and no authority or sobriety. There was dancing and extravagance and lashings of wine, and charades and moonlit balconies and kisses, and some amateur prize-fighting with a mattress ring and seconds, and a girls' sparring match and, best of all, bets on who would swim the canal first, Duff or Denis Anson, and in their evening clothes. . . . And it was done for love of one of us, or so exploits were always said to be done in those romantic days.

All of us, pretty and unconventionally dressed, were naturally followed and stared at by the perambulating Venetians on the Piazza at night. . . . One evening our knot of gaping citizens seemed smaller and less interested than usual. 'What shall we do to people the Piazza?' I said thoughtlessly. It was enough for Denis Anson, with the help of a piece of soap, to throw an epileptic fit in a space at one end of San Marco's. In a moment a crowd had coagulated, plus a posse of *carabinieri*. The sad case of Denis's infirmity was explained to these alarming men of the law by Charles Lister, who was an attaché at the Embassy in Rome. The epileptic would be taken home by his friends, he said, and he offered apologies for causing a scene in a public place. The officers moved off, the crowd solicitously followed the poor Englishman, who within three minutes had sprung like a mad ape away from his keepers and flung a far worse epileptic fit in another part of the Piazza. Repetition was too much for the police, who this time frog-marched him off in the direction of the Bridge of Sighs and clapped him into a cell. . . . [31]

They all vowed to go back to Venice the next year, for more and wilder follies; but the next year was 1914, and by the time the war had finished, there was hardly anyone left for the reunion.

But there was still the summer of 1914 to enjoy, and the giddying spiral of play went rocketing on, with many twirls to go before its collapse. At the beginning of July, the Coterie were gathered after a party late on a humid evening (1914 was the hottest summer since 1911) on a boat moored on the Thames. They had had supper, and then the boat took off, with a live orchestra playing on board, and drifted gently down the river towards Battersea Park. Someone suggested bathing, and instantly Denis Anson dived in: without even shouting for help he was carried away out of sight. The boat was stopped, and turned round, and went back to the spot. Two men dived in to search for him, and one of them, a bandsman, was drowned too.

The party were stunned, unable to comprehend a death so sudden and unexpected. But the tide was strong, and the water cold. In the dark, in the moments it took to turn the boat around, young Denny – just twenty-five and the darling of the Coterie – had drowned. A dashing escapade had gone hideously wrong and he was dead. Some of the party made their way back to his flat, in case, somehow, he might have gone back there. He had not. Later Lady Diana Cooper wrote: 'The Great War was upon us and Denis would surely have been the first to be killed, but with all my resilience, this was a gruesome soul-shattering end to the carefree life I knew.'[32] In retrospect it was a small tragedy, set against all the others, and perhaps a better way to die than in the mud of Flanders. At the time, the sudden death of a young man was still shocking, however, and it plunged the Coterie into mourning. 'Sir Denis Anson's death at the age of twenty-five caused a sensation,' wrote Osbert Sitwell. 'His death was a symbol of his generation, kind and coterie, as similarly on a grand scale, the sinking of the *Titanic* had been a symbol of the approaching fate of Western Civilisation.'[33]

To the older generation, the Souls, this death was a symbol too. The disapproval that Margot Asquith felt for the Coterie and their doings was exaggerated, like all her reactions, but she probably said aloud what many others only dared to think when she described the last months before the War as 'our Frightfulness':

We observed tepid, passionless young people exercising fine intellects in a manner more impoverishing than enriching to their natures: artists indulging in meaningless portraiture of confused limbs; women qualifying for political responsibility by blowing up gardens, burning down churches, and threatening the lives of innocent women and children in low letters – not only threatening – but attacking them with sticks, stones, axes and dog-whips. We saw old friends insulting and cutting each other over politics; great soldiers intriguing to put the Army against the Government; great lawyers defying the law; and finally, pleasure people watching a man they loved drown, while incapable of either feeling or showing mourning for him. When we curse 'the Frightfulness' of the Germans we had better remember our own.[34]

Most of the Souls, however, despite their close links with politicians and the stolid new court, failed to discern more than a vague uneasiness; a disquieting notion that maybe all was not quite as it should be, despite the glorious weather, the elegant parasols, the unending round of parties – a feeling so remote and intangible that it was easily dismissed. The summer round of gaiety eddied on, weeks – almost days – from catastrophe. Ettie's *Family Journal* sounds more and more like a gossip column, as she tries to cram in all the social details of those last thrilling times: 'The Eton and Harrow match (with Ivo) took place in lovely weather . . . all went on to Rachel Dudley's ever-remembered "Eton Cotillion" – from which they returned at 3 a.m., nine in the motor, laden with Persian kittens and white mice for Imogen. . . . Monica went to 40 Balls! . . .'[35]

Yet the Souls, too, had suffered changes, and some deaths, during these last years. Charty Ribblesdale, one of the original tribe of Tennants who had been the founders of the Souls, had fought a long battle against tuberculosis. Like her sister Posie, who had died more than twenty years before, Charty had searched in vain for a cure. For three years she moved between Davos, in Switzerland, and her circle of devoted friends in England, often seeming better, only to become yet worse. In May 1911 she died; and Alfred Lyttelton, her beloved brother-in-law, was poignantly reminded of the death of his young wife Laura, a quarter of a century earlier. He wrote in the stilted language of shock and grief: 'I can hardly write. I will come across from the House directly. I spent an indescribably sad evening. I went alone down into the night and saw her in the empty house with the nurse. I cannot describe the pathos of the dear beautiful face, scarcely altered except by the deep sleep.'[36]

Two years later Alfred himself was dead. Although he had never ceased to be the most warmly loved of the Souls, Laura's early death had subdued his natural ebullience. A spell as Colonial Secretary between 1903 and 1905 broke his spirit. Arthur Balfour had chosen his old friend to perform a task that was beyond his powers, that of administering South Africa in the aftermath of the Boer War. Although he wrestled conscientiously with the problem of Chinese labour, Alfred was too thin-skinned to bear the slings and arrows of Parliament when things went against him. He did his best, and his best wasn't good enough, and it shattered him. In the election of January 1906 a volley of abuse was directed against him personally, as the instigator of the detested 'slavery' of imported Chinese labourers. Alfred lost his seat – as did Arthur Balfour – and the Conservatives suffered a humiliating and total defeat. Alfred was not yet fifty; but his useful professional life was over. His second wife wrote later of 'a certain detachment from the world which was latent in him always. He constantly spoke of his own death, of the end drawing near, not with any morbidity but as a fact. He seemed forewarned that he was not to know old age.'[37]

Later in 1906 he was offered a parliamentary seat made available to him by the convenient resignation of the sitting member; but although he took it, he was a dilettante MP rather than an active politician. In one respect only he was remarkable: alone among his circle he was a fervent supporter of votes for women. In a speech in the House of Commons in 1913, when demonstrations by and against the suffragettes were at their height, Alfred Lyttelton courageously spoke in their defence: '. . . women of hitherto blameless lives and high aspirations have faced in this cause the greatest ignominy and the greatest suffering.' Less than six months later an accident while playing cricket apparently caused an internal rupture or haemorrhage, and although it did not at first seem serious, he was operated on, and died five days later. He had not been the most spectacular of the Souls, nor the cleverest, and his domestic life was a model of fidelity and quiet contentment. But Alfred Lyttelton was the most cherished of them all, and his friends mourned him with unusual depth of feeling.

George Wyndham was another founding Soul who was spared the anguish of seeing the world he had known collapse in chaos. His triumph in marrying Lady Sibell Grosvenor had not been rewarded by a perfectly happy marriage. Form was preserved, however, and they were united in their devotion to their only child, Percy Wyndham. George pursued a number of liaisons until he finally settled down to many years of extra-marital bliss with Lady Windsor. She possessed both great beauty and great tact, so that his wife and social peers condoned their relationship as a civilized and painless arrangement. Meanwhile his political career seemed to be moving on to great things. At the end of 1900 he was made Secretary of State for Ireland, a post that could elevate him – as it had Balfour – into the leading ranks of his party. But when his moment came, Wyndham, like Lyttelton, had not the ability to rise to it. His character was flawed by laziness – everything had come to him too easily – and in addition he was prone to fits of manic depression. To no one's surprise, in March 1905 Wyndham had to resign. He was only forty-two, but already his best years were over. More clearly than most of his generation, he could see that the best years for his class and his kind were over, too. He became increasingly removed from both the political and the social sphere, settling down to belated rural contentment and watching with pride his son's career in the Coldstream Guards.

In 1911 the constitutional crisis was at its height, with the new King unhappily compelled, at the behest of Lloyd George, to agree to create 500 new peers if necessary, to swamp the House of Lords and force through the Parliament Bill. Lloyd George owed no allegiance to the landed aristocracy. If it took 500 new peers to curb the Lords' power of veto, it should be done. George Wyndham was passionately on the side of the 'die-hards': stubborn members of the Upper House who swore to resist rather than accept any limitation of their ancient – and *rightful* – constitutional rôle. They believed in it as firmly as monarchs had once believed in the Divine Right of Kings. George Curzon, who had learnt a little about pragmatism for all his pride in titles, took the opposite view; and so emotional were these differences of opinion that Wyndham wrote to his wife: 'Of course we can never meet George Curzon or St John Brodrick again . . . now we are finished with the cosmopolitan press – and the American duchesses and the Saturday to Mondays at Taplow – and all the degrading shams . . . for the House of Lords today – tho' they did not know it – voted for Revolution.'[38] He spoke in the authentic tones of a descendant of Lord Leconfield married to the daughter of an earl . . . but his day was done, all the same.

The Souls had outlived their loyalty to one another. And George Wyndham, young as he was, had outlived his era, let alone the one that was to come. His last happiness was in seeing his beloved son Percy married to Diana Lister, the Ribblesdales' daughter. The marriage took place in April 1913, and six weeks later George Wyndham died of a heart attack while staying in Paris with his mistress. The beautiful and angelic-faced Lady Sibell, once adored by Curzon and, as her brother had said, at least eighty others before her marriage to George Wyndham, was alone again. But this time she was in her mid-fifties, and now her chief consolation was her only son, Percy, and his young bride.

By 1914 the Souls had become just another group of old friends, diminished in numbers by defections and death, and no longer the envied leaders of society's most brilliant set. Now it was their children who glittered hectically in a more feverish world than they had ever known, enamoured of the strange new rhythms of the Imperial Russian Opera and the Ballets Russes with its visceral designs and barbaric dancers. The new names were those of Bakst and Diaghilev, Nijinsky and Karsavina and Chaliapin, whose very sound evoked their exotic Slav allure. Their influence was immediate and ubiquitous. 'Every chair-cover,' wrote Osbert Sitwell, 'every lampshade, every cushion reflected the Russian Ballet, the Grecian or Oriental visions of Bakst and Benois. . . . This ballet [Petruchka] was, in its scope as a work of art, universal; it presented the European contemporary generation with a prophetic and dramatised version of the fate reserved for it.'[39]

Against such novelty the Souls looked tepid and bygone. Ettie was now forty-seven. Mary Elcho was fifty-three and her still beloved Arthur Balfour sixty-six. Harry Cust, now increasingly often seen in the company of his wife, was fifty-three. Margot Asquith was no longer the phosphorescent dragonfly she had been in her youth, but a spiky, critical, often rather sad woman of fifty. Her husband had been Prime Minister since 1908, but his emotional favours were lavished on what Margot called 'his little harem' of beautiful young women whose admiration and flattery he craved. By 1914, he was concentrating on one in particular: the twenty-seven-year-old Venetia Stanley, a central figure in the Coterie.

H. H. Asquith was sixty-two in 1914. He had been writing regularly to Venetia – and to a number of other young women – since 1912, but early in 1914 a gentle flirtation began to turn, on his side at least, into a grand passion. By that summer he was obsessed. Venetia was one of the Stanleys of Alderley, and by all accounts a woman of remarkable presence and intellect. Asquith was not alone in loving her. In the summer of 1912 Edwin Montagu – an ugly but brilliant and immensely wealthy young Jew – had proposed marriage, and been rejected. He continued to pay court to her, but she was always surrounded by admirers. One of them, Lawrence Jones, wrote of her later:

> Venetia had dark-eyed, aquiline good looks and a masculine intellect. I delighted in her, and we were close friends, but she permitted herself, in the morning of her youth, no recourse to her own femininity. She carried the Anthologies in her head, but rode like an Amazon, and walked the high garden walls of Alderley with the casual stride of a boy. She was a splendid, virginal, comradely creature, reserving herself for we knew not what use of her fine brain and hidden heart.[40]

The person of whom this description most reminds one is, ironically, the young Margot. She herself always maintained that she was not jealous of her husband's relationship with Venetia, for all the fervour that scorches through the letters.

Lady Diana Manners, some years younger than Venetia but also one of Asquith's favourites, commented: 'She didn't object, she thought that you had no right to claim one man. But I didn't either. I mean, jealousy was common; the awful word was common.'[41]

By midsummer 1914, two issues preoccupied Asquith. One was his need for Venetia; the other was the Irish Question. It still dominated British politics far more than any thought of war with Germany, although the portents were now unmistakable. Those young men – like Percy Wyndham – who had chosen to make the Army their career, were fretting like highly strung racehorses under starter's orders. Their wives and girlfriends ached and prayed that it might still somehow be averted. But the cabinet and the government were chiefly concerned to pilot the Home Rule Bill safely through a rebellious House of Commons. It was a skilled and delicate political balancing act whose details occupied the politicians to the exclusion of more distant and peripheral matters . . . such as the assassination of the Archduke Franz Ferdinand on 28 June 1914. His death passed virtually unnoticed; that of young Denny Anson five days later caused a much greater stir.

The month of July was preoccupied with details of the Irish conference, which met on 21–24 July. The Bill was due to come up before the Commons on 28 July, but was first postponed by two days – not because of Austria's declaration of war upon Serbia on that date, but because of an incident in Dublin which led to the deaths of three people. Then, on 30 July, the debate had to be postponed again. The international crisis could no longer be denied.

Throughout these last crucial days of July 1914, the Prime Minister's overwhelming passion for Venetia Stanley grew until it outweighed everything else. He wrote to her daily, sometimes more than once, and schemed and plotted so as to spend a few minutes – an hour – or more in her company. He still managed to persuade himself that his passion for her was unknown to others. ('I hate even the possibility of gossip about us.')[42] In fact his wife had known since March that this relationship was more serious than most, and had written sadly to her confidante, Ettie Desborough: 'She is even teaching Henry to avoid telling me things. . . . I'm far too fond of H. to show him how ill and miserable it makes me. . . . A woman without refinement or any imagination whatever!'[43]

Perhaps Venetia found the Prime Minister's dependence on her excessive; at any rate, on 24 July she went away, to stay at a family home in Penrhos, on the Anglesey coast near Holyhead. Asquith spent the next few days desperately trying to arrange to spend some hours with her there. The situation in Ireland, the deepening crisis as Europe slouched towards war, weighed less heavily in his mind than the need to be with her after a week apart. On 27 July he wrote to her, 'We seem to be on the *very brink*',[44] and then, almost unbelievably, the next day: 'I have just sent you a telegram to say that I seem to see my way clear to come at the end of the week. I hope the prospect gives you half the joy it does me.'[45] (He had an engagement in Chester, nearby, and planned to slip away from there to Penrhos.) The next day, 'I count the hours till Saturday, and picture myself joining you & the dogs & the penguin on the rocks, and telling you all that I have left unsaid since we parted.'[46] That was written on 29 July. On the thirtieth, Russia mobilized. Asquith wrote:

The European situation is at least one degree worse than it was yesterday. . . .
I think the prospect very black today. . . . But unless Fate is very unkind I shall
all the same hope to come to you Saturday, and see you – perhaps in your new
striped dress, not the 'yellow peril' – You say you would be 'really disappointed' if I didn't come. I wish I cd. tell you how *I* should feel![47]

War was five days away.

On Saturday 1 August Asquith finally realized that he could not possibly fulfil
his plan to visit Venetia. Germany declared war on Russia; and the Prime
Minister of Britain – referring, not to that, but to the fact that it had killed his
private hopes, wrote:

I can honestly say that I have never had a more bitter disappointment. All
these days – ever since Thursday in last week – full of incident and for the
most part anxious & worrying – I have been sustained by the thought that
when today came I should once more see your darling face. . . . All that has
been shattered by a truly devastating succession of the blows of fortune.[48]

Right up until the final days, the Coterie, the Souls and society itself pursued
their round of pleasure. Goodwood, it is true, was a little subdued that year: as
well it might be, meeting on 28 July. Ettie's *Journal* conveys the ambivalence of
the time:

On July 25th there was the last Saturday-to-Monday party of the summer at
Taplow . . . the first murmurs about graver causes of anxiety had begun. On
the Monday, Imogen and her mother went to see Ivo at Eton. It was a strange
hot oppressive day. . . . Then the sun came out, and they went to have ices at
Leyton's and the dark chances seemed very far away. The next day, July 28th,
War was declared between Austria and Serbia; Monica's parents met Lord
Lansdowne and Mr Balfour at a small dinner party. . . . On July 29th, Monica
and her mother went to Hatfield, and dined there. . . . The tension was
increasing steadily with the days. The next day they went to luncheon at the
Asquiths'. Sir Edward Grey was there. The news was very bad. . . . July 31st
was a day of very great anxiety and excitement. . . .[49]

The popular mood was one of contradictory swings and roundabouts. They
wanted war. They didn't want war. If there had to be a war, it would be all over
by Christmas. They wanted to put the Kaiser in his place. The young men wanted
their chance to fight. The old men thought it would be the Boer War all over
again, only this time they would get it right. No one dreamed how different this
war would be.

As Bank Holiday Monday approached, there was a run on the banks, and the
interest rate rose from 4 per cent on 30 July to 10 per cent on 1 August. The
government took over the railways for troop movements, and extended the
Bank Holiday right up to 6 August. The golden holiday days moved sluggishly.
People began to stock up with food, and prices in the shops soared.

On 3 August the King of the Belgians telegraphed to George V appealing for
diplomatic intervention to safeguard Belgium's neutrality. It was far too late.
The Schlieffen Plan, which had been outlined ten years earlier, and which the
German High Command had been incubating for months, demanded that the
German Army should roll swiftly through Belgium so as to win a quick victory
over France, thus freeing her to concentrate on war in the east. Once Russia had

mobilised on 30 July, it was imperative that Germany should activate the invasion of Belgium without delay. It took place on 4 August.

Britain immediately served an ultimatum, requiring Germany to withdraw her forces by midnight. There was no reply. The ultimatum expired at 11 p.m., and war began . . . to extraordinary, universal public rejoicing in almost every capital of Europe. The Kaiser told the German Army, 'You will be home before the leaves fall from the trees.' Ettie wrote, 'It was thought that the whole War might be a matter of months, or even weeks.' Julian Grenfell, whose regiment was stationed in South Africa, wrote to his father: 'It is hateful being away in a corner here at this time. I suppose that the whole thing will be over in a very short time? I only hope that they will move us quickly, and that we get somewhere in time for something!'[50] and to his mother: 'It must be wonderful in England now. I suppose the excitement is beyond all words? . . . I wonder how long it will last? (Ie the war.) Isn't it bad luck, that it should come when we are at Potchefstroom? Or do you think that they will fetch us over in time?'[51] They got him back in time. His regiment sailed home from South Africa in September. Rupert Brooke's lines were widely quoted:

> Now God be thanked Who has matched us with His hour,
> And caught our youth, and wakened us from sleeping.[52]

The outbreak of war was intensely welcome. There was a feeling that England had honoured her commitment to Belgium. But it was more than that. People were jingoistic, belligerent, *bored with peace*. On 5 August, Asquith made a speech in which he declared – as politicians always do at such moments – 'Britain is fighting for the principles whose maintenance is vital to the civilised world.' The streets were filled with cheering crowds.

Only Mary Elcho seems to have kept her head while all about her were throwing their caps to the winds. She wrote in slow, elegiac phrases of the last days of peace:

> I have lingered lovingly over these insignificant details, describing the tiny happenings of home life in the country and the London jaunts enjoyed by groups of cousins and friends; because this 'fond and trivial record' belongs to the last days of the Era of Peace. When Yvo came again to London in August 1914 he stood in the crowded streets reading the Declaration of War. How many youths must have gazed with innocent, untroubled eyes, and pleasurable thrills of interest and excitement, at their own death warrant, as they read the fatal Declaration which was to destroy so many millions of lives, shaking all things to their foundations, wasting the treasures of the past and casting its sinister influence far into the future![53]

The day after war had been declared Mary Elcho was up in London, to be close to her beloved Arthur Balfour and to give him what support she could muster. She lunched with him, and then left him at the House of Commons to return to Stanway. On the way home, at Oxford station, she met Sibell Grosvenor, ash-white. 'All she said was, *"Percy is getting ready."* '[54]

Six weeks later Percy Wyndham was dead.

PART III

FIFTY-ONE MONTHS OF HELL

1914–1918

It was the regime of Cant *before* the War which made the Cant *during* the War so damnably possible and easy. On our coming of age the Victorians generously handed us a charming little cheque for fifty guineas – fifty-one months of hell, and the results.

Richard Aldington, *Death of a Hero*, 1929

– 10 –
Dances of Death

August 1914–June 1916

Within a week of the outbreak of war, thirty thousand men a *day* rushed to enlist. The British Army almost broke under the strain. It had not the administration, the uniforms, or the weapons to accommodate such huge numbers of men avid for honour and glory. Few, as yet, thought realistically in terms of sacrifice. All classes were united in the eagerness with which they welcomed the war, and the certainty that they would win it within months. Four days after war was declared, the Poet Laureate, Robert Bridges, had published in *The Times* a poem whose concluding lines summed up the simplistic attitude of many:

> Thou careless, awake! Thou peacemaker, fight!
> Stand, England, for honour, and God guard the right!

The patriotism of this poem; the assumption that God and England and Honour and Right were only different facets of the same thing; these were the beliefs that impelled people to fight. Pacifists were viewed with incomprehension and pity at first; later, with contempt.

Pacifists may have questioned the need to defend England's cause in battle, but nobody doubted the justice of that cause. How *dared* Germany oppose the God-given supremacy of Britain and her Empire? For it was an Empire, of 450 million subjects, that went to war against Germany and her allies. It was inconceivable that this Empire should not be victorious: indeed, people expected victory to be quick and easy.

The British had ruled over vast areas of the globe for so long that the challenge which Germany presented was an affront – to their self-esteem, certainly, but also, they believed, to the natural order of things. A century of peace had allowed people to delude themselves that Britain had finally established the one absolute, right and proper balance of power in the world. A quarter of the globe was coloured pink, for British possessions, and so it should remain in perpetuity. They forgot that Germany, too, had imperial possessions and territorial ambitions; and they probably never knew that the German sense of patriotism and nationhood was at least as strong as their own. The British upper classes had been used to getting their way for so long that they had overlooked the fact that this state of affairs was inherently unstable. Now, it was about to be toppled forever.

Hardly anyone seems to have noticed, or worried about, the disparity between the British and the German armies in August 1914. Britain's pre-war strategic planning had always assumed that naval superiority would be the deciding factor. Germany, where conscription had been in force for a hundred years, could call upon a trained and disciplined army 4 million strong. But Britain, because of her reliance on the Navy, had an Army that, in January 1914, numbered fewer than a quarter of a million. They were scattered all over the world . . . some (like Julian Grenfell) stationed in South Africa; others in India; while Kitchener himself was the British Representative in Egypt.

Yet the British Army opposed the military might of a far larger, better trained and better equipped German Army with such an upsurge of confident pride because it simply did not occur to them that they might be beaten. God would not allow it. They overlooked the fact that the Germans had just the same belief. Every German infantryman had '*Gott mit uns*' (God with us) emblazoned on his belt buckle.

Within hours of war being declared, the British public was demanding that Kitchener, its hero since Omdurman and the Boer War, should be put in charge of the British Army. Kitchener was on the point of embarking to return to Egypt when Asquith acceded to the popular will. On 5 August 1914 he appointed Kitchener, now sixty-four, as Secretary of State for War. (Margot, in one of her best quips, remarked that he might not be a great man, but he made a great poster. It was true. Within weeks Kitchener's pointing finger, above the imperious summons, YOUR COUNTRY NEEDS YOU! was to be seen everywhere.)

And so, within the first twenty-four hours, Asquith had made one of the great mistakes of the war. Eminence had made Kitchener stubborn and blinkered. As he had shown in his dealings with Curzon in India, he would settle for nothing less than autocratic rule. In fact he was so ignorant of politics that when he first took his seat in the House of Lords as the newly created Earl Kitchener of Khartoum, he caused laughter by seating himself on the bench reserved for bishops. But the real disaster lay in the fact that his strategic thinking was more appropriate to the Boer War. To do him justice, he was among the very few who were aware at the outset that this war would not be swift and easy and over within months. But the only war he knew how to fight was a war of movement. Neither he, nor anybody else, anticipated a war of attrition: a war fought at a standstill, in the trenches.

The British public, however, had got what they clamoured for: a figurehead, the man who could secure victory. And they responded to his magnetic appeal. Men of all ages stood in long queues all day in front of recruiting depots. Schoolboys lied about their age (the youngest combatant on the British side to die in the fighting was fourteen years old) and old men made light of theirs. By mid-September, half a million volunteers had signed up. All were ardent for some desperate glory.

Despite this intense jingoism, and the shockingly sudden belligerence that had within a week transformed the mood of the carefree Bank Holiday crowds, the propaganda machine rolled into action. A Central Committee for National Patriotic Organizations was immediately set up, with the Prime Minister, H. H.

Asquith, as its honorary president, and Arthur Balfour as vice-president. Harry Cust, making the only appearance of his life as an establishment figure, was its chairman. The salient characteristic of the Souls in earlier days – their willingness to defy received opinion and follow where their own philosophy and inclinations led – had finally become set in the aspic of increasing age, and succumbed to the rhetoric of jingoistic propaganda.

Not only the Souls abandoned the practice of independent thought. Prominent pacifists like Gilbert Murray – who had signed a plea for British neutrality on the first day of the war – performed a *volte-face* of acrobatic agility and wrote about the 'strange, deep gladness' of war. Even worse, he was responsible for the earliest of those myths about life in the trenches which hoodwinked the British public for the next two years. In a pamphlet called *How Can War Ever Be Right?*, Murray wrote:

> Day after day come streams of letters from the front, odd stories, fragments of diaries, and the like; full of the small intimate facts which reveal character, and almost with one accord they show that these men have not fallen, but risen. . . . 'Never once,' writes one correspondent, 'not once since I came to France have I seen among the soldiers an angry face or heard an angry word. . . . They are always quiet, orderly, and wonderfully cheerful.'[1]

Even Rupert Brooke could write, in November 1914, to the girl he loved, 'The central purpose of my life, the aim and end of it, now, the thing God wants of me, is to get good at beating Germans',[2] and to his friend John Drinkwater, 'Come and die. It'll be great fun.'[3] The *Daily Mail* advised its readers: 'Refuse to be served by an Austrian or German waiter.' As if natural fervour were not enough, the government established a secret War Propaganda Bureau. Within months even Julian Grenfell, whom war had confirmed as the most patriotic and bloodthirsty of men, was writing home to his father (he could never have said it to Ettie): 'They are dashed good, these Huns. I wish that we didn't lie so much in all our reports.'[4] Lord Northcliffe, proprietor of the *Daily Mail*, was put in charge of propaganda. In an essay called 'What to Send Your Soldier', full of helpful tips for those back home, he suggested sending peppermint bulls' eyes:

> The bulls' eyes ought to have plenty of peppermint in them, for it is the peppermint which keeps those who suck them warm on a cold night. It also has a digestive effect, though that is of small account at the front, where health is so good and indigestion hardly ever heard of. The open-air life, the regular and plenteous feeding, the exercise, *and the freedom from care and responsibility*, [my italics] keep the soldiers extraordinarily fit and contented.[5]

It was farcical; it was tragic. But the mood of the times was theatrical, and it worked.

In the first weeks of the war it was the British Expeditionary Force – the BEF – that crossed over to stand beside the French Army in defence of France. The BEF was originally planned to be 110,000 strong, and to consist of six infantry divisions and one cavalry division, all superbly trained. However, the 4th Division did not land in France until 23 August (just in time to join the Retreat from Mons) and the 6th Division did not reach III Corps on the Aisne until 16 September 1914. These few, then – a mere four divisions – fought the earliest battles of the war. It was at the Aisne, on 14 September 1914, that young Percy

Wyndham died. Two weeks earlier, two more members of the Coterie had also died, though with lofty scepticism Asquith refused at first to believe it, and wrote to Venetia: 'I should rather fear that John Manners and young Cecil may have been too impetuous and been taken prisoners. On the other hand they may be able to straggle back, as so many of the "missing" have done and are doing.'[6] His optimism was misplaced. They were both dead. Two platoons of the 2nd Grenadier Guards had been surrounded and, receiving no order to retire, fought on until everyone was either killed or wounded. John Manners and George Cecil, being young officers, did their expected duty by leading their men into these hopeless engagements, and both were killed. 'The Guards', commented Asquith, 'evidently had a rough time.'[7]

Even though these early deaths were more shocking than they later became to a nation practised in grief, families back home in England knew how to mourn with due pride and decorum. Billy Grenfell's letter, after visiting the Manners, 'Con' and 'Hoppy', in January 1915, observed: 'The Manners family are quite devastated, as one expected, but I never saw such Spartan and stoical bravery. It was both pathetic and uplifting to see them. If Con had six Johns she would give them all; she is a wonderful being. . . .'[8] Spartan; stoical; the classical models that the British upper classes had studied for so long were coming into their own. The public school ethos provided them with a shared language in which to speak of the war. The imagery of the games field, too, played an important part. Some even turned it to literal reality, dribbling a football across No Man's Land as they attacked the opposing German trenches. At this early stage of war there could still seem a gaiety in fighting, a gentlemanly pride in playing the game with high spirits. And for a few, there was a savage pleasure too.

Julian Grenfell, who had grown several skins over his earlier sensitivity, was one of those who gloried in battle and killing. He was one of the very few who would creep out alone, at night, to seek out Germans and shoot them point-blank – for the reckless excitement of it and because he hated them. On 15 October 1914, he wrote home from Flanders:

> The guns go on all day and most of the night – of course it is very hard to follow what is going on; even the squadron leaders know nothing; and one marches and countermarches without end, backwards and forwards, nearer and further, apparently without object. Only the Christian virtue of Faith emerges triumphant. It is all the most *wonderful* fun; better fun than one could ever imagine. I hope it goes on a nice long time; pig-sticking will be the only possible pursuit after this, or one will die of sheer ennui. The first time one shoots at a man one has the feeling of 'never point a loaded gun at anyone, even in fun'; but very soon it gets like shooting a crocodile, only more exciting, because he shoots back at you.[9]

One searches for irony; but there is none. Julian, who had been killing animals with gleeful bloodlust ever since he was a small boy; who had reported round for round his victories in the boxing ring; who had glorified violence for so long because it was one of the ways of being acceptable to his mother; Julian had ended by discovering that his mask had become reality. He really did enjoy killing Germans, and – unlike Rupert Brooke, who never had a chance to practise – he had become very good at it. In the New Year's Honours List of 1915 it was announced that he had won the DSO. At last Ettie could feel uncomplicated maternal pride. 'One loves one's fellow-man so much more when one is bent on killing him,'[10] wrote Julian, and his mother would have understood. She, too, was an arch-destroyer of the men she loved, not least her son.

By the winter of 1914 both sides had dug in for the cold, dark months. Germany had clearly failed in her early initiative to sweep through northern France and take Paris. The battles of the Marne, of Mons and of the Aisne had taught her respect for the courage and tenacity of the British troops, if not for the strategy of their leaders. Neither side could outflank the other, and so they settled down to a period of trench warfare: though nobody dreamed, at this stage, how long it would last.

The Germans, with customary thoroughness and discipline, constructed a superb system of trenches. They made the most of their initial advantage, control over the terrain, to seize the high ground. This was crucial. It meant that the water table lay at a level many feet below the bottom of their trenches, and that they could stay relatively clean and dry even in foul weather. It meant that they could build their trenches deep, floor them with slatted wooden duckboards, and reinforce the sides without fear of them collapsing as the wet seeped through. It meant that they could even be furnished with beds and tables and electric light. They cannot have been luxurious; but they were reasonably comfortable; and compared to the British trenches they were palatial.

The British in the trenches lived below ground, like rats in a latrine. Living in mud, which stuck to their boots and clothes and left mustard-coloured streaks on everything. Wading through yellow water that seeped through the duck-boards on the floor of the trench, and in wet weather reached up to the ankles and sometimes the knees. The trenches zigzagged, twisting and turning every few yards like an undulating caterpillar. This was to prevent an attacker shooting down them in a straight line. Their sides were made of earth, slippery and cold in winter, steamy in summer, with steps to enable men to climb out more easily. Every few yards there would be a shelf called a fire-step, on which the men used to sit, stand, play cards, spread out maps or eat meals. Above the surface sandbags were stacked, covered with hessian and filled with earth, the shape and colour of giant turds. Inside these trenches men were cramped together in their roofless burrow. Only the sky overhead was normal – except at night, when it might be lit up by flares or artillery barrages. For much of the time the noise around was deafening.

Above the ground, in front of the trenches, was a line of barbed wire defences and then the expanse of No Man's Land, perhaps fifty yards wide, perhaps twelve hundred. Beyond that the German trenches aimed death, day and night. A head raised above the parapet of the trench was likely to be blown open by a sniper's bullet.

From this refuge the men had to be ready to charge with pennants flying like the giant heroes of legend and history. Never throughout the course of the war did any British troops disobey the order to go 'over the top'.

The British, although they now knew the war would not be over by Christmas, could not believe that it would last beyond the summer. Their trenches were not built for a long stay. Their defences were inadequate, and so, often, were their communications. The British generals had discouraged the building of solid defences in the belief that, if the soldiers once got too comfortably entrenched, it would prove difficult to shift them.

The poets were not yet writing about the squalor of the trenches. The language of war was still the language of chivalry. Herbert Asquith – 'Beb', the Prime Minister's second son – wrote an inspiring verse about a volunteer, a dingy City clerk,

> His lance is broken; but he lies content
> With that high hour, in which he lived and died.
> And falling thus he wants no recompense,
> Who found his battle in the last resort;
> Nor need he any hearse to bear him hence,
> Who goes to join the men of Agincourt.[11]

These deaths were still untouched by horror. 'Brave little mothers' (a favourite phrase) held their heads high, with brimming eyes and patriotic hearts. Mothers – and fathers, too – knew nothing yet about the trenches.

British casualties by the end of 1914 were a fraction of those suffered by the French and the Germans. The British had 86,000 killed, wounded or missing; the French 850,000 – nearly ten times that number – and the Germans 650,000.

The men in the trenches settled down sombrely for the first winter. Their freezing vigil was broken by the spontaneous Christmas truce of 1914, when both sides met in No Man's Land, exchanged gifts of drink and cigarettes, and sang carols. But senior officers believed that such fraternization was dangerous. It would sap the men's fighting spirit if they realized that they had more in common with enemy soldiers in the opposite trenches just a few hundred yards away than they ever felt with the generals situated miles behind the lines. Yet just this feeling was widespread, though rarely expressed at the Front (certainly not during the first couple of years) and never at home, where the Souls would have regarded it as treachery. It is significant that David Jones's *In Parenthesis* – the most vivid account of trench life to have been written – is dedicated in part to 'The enemy front-fighters who shared our pains against whom we found ourselves by misadventure.'[12] At any rate, in future years no Christmas truce was permitted, on pain of court martial.

Officers below the rank of brigadier-general actually lived at the front, where they ate much the same food and shared the same dangers and discomforts as the men. Their life was brightened by a more regular and plentiful supply of whisky and gin (the men had SRD, which was believed to stand for Service Rum, Diluted) and parcels from home which often contained a wide range of home-made or luxury foods. These, however, were often shared out among the men. Certainly the Grenfells' letters home ask constantly for food and cigarettes with which to mitigate the hardships of their troops.

Many of the senior staff officers seldom if ever went near the trenches. They were based at Corps or Army HQ, usually billeted in large country houses. A Corps HQ had to accommodate nearly a hundred officers and men, along with fifty-one horses, as well as cars, vans and of course telephone lines. Life here was safe and in many cases more luxurious than anything they had known in peacetime. They often requisitioned historic French châteaux (or indeed, were sometimes given the use of them voluntarily) including their wine cellars, their kitchen gardens, and a skeleton staff which might include a chef. But senior officers also lived in breweries, schools, convents, even museums and seminaries – since the supply of large country houses in convenient proximity to the Front was limited. From here they planned the intricate, and often illusory, strategies that would win the war. The men at the Front executed them.[13]

Staff officers' lives were too valuable to be put at such risk. They would have heard the sound of artillery fire – indeed, it could be heard across the Channel, in Kent – but they were very rarely exposed to it. Immaculate in their tailored uniforms, swagger stick laid nonchalantly across gleaming knee-high boots, they experienced a war that had little to do with mud and blood and rain and cold. How else would it have been possible for a brigadier, inspecting a regiment out of the line in a rest area, to express displeasure because the cords on the men's *waterbottle corks* were not pipe-clayed (that is, whitened)? Presumably it was believed that such attention to detail maintained morale. It must also have evoked contempt and suppressed fury.[14]

Senior officers vied for the privilege of entertaining the young Prince of Wales, who tried persistently and unsuccessfully to persuade his father, King George V, to allow him to join his regiment, the 1st Battalion Grenadier Guards, in the front line, and share with them the experience of danger under fire. He was popular with the men because he used to visit the trenches, where he would hand out Abdullahs: cigarettes of the finest quality. Nominally attached to the staff of Field-Marshal Sir John French, Commander-in-Chief of the British Expeditionary Force, the young Prince was skilfully used to bolster the morale of the troops whenever conditions at the Front were safe. He was shrewd enough to perceive the immense difference between the soldiers' view of the war and that enjoyed from General Headquarters:

> We were about thirty miles from the front line, out of earshot of all but the heaviest artillery bombardments. Sir John French had surrounded himself with older officers and friends who instinctively thought of fighting in terms of the tactics of the Boer War. They liked their food and their comforts, and in the opinion of the men in the trenches were quite out of touch with what was actually happening in the line.[15]

Back home in England during the first winter of the war, public confidence in Lord Kitchener and Sir John French remained absolute. Criticism would have been unpatriotic, and in any case the propaganda machine afforded no basis for criticism. Newspaper accounts always erred on the side of optimism. Photographs of the trenches were staged so as not to show the real truth. It was months before any awareness of the enormous losses suffered by both sides began to filter through.

At this early stage, individual deaths were still regarded as a combination of exceptional bravery and appallingly bad luck. People had not yet realized that this war would mean slaughter on a huge scale. Yet from the first, the older generation saw the younger in terms of glory and courage and ultimately – if needs be – of sacrifice. From the day that war was declared, all young men could have only one rôle and one wish: *action*: to enlist, and to get to the Front as quickly as possible. Raymond Asquith ridiculed the mood prevailing in the first month of the war in a letter to an old friend from Balliol, Conrad Russell:

> There is a feeling in the air that everyone ought to make a fuss of some kind. I went up to London last week & found it seething with futility. I flung myself with gusto into the maelstrom of misdirected effort and ostentatious altruism. I put my name down for an organisation wh. Lovat & Desborough are promoting for drilling middle-aged breadwinners out of school hours. Probably the W.O. [War Office] will stop it, and quite right too. Then I went to the office of the National Service League, where an enormous staff is employed in rejecting the applications of well-meaning idiots for inappropriate positions – Boy Scouts with fixed bayonets see that one comes to no harm in the lift, and old women fill in innumerable printed forms which old men in other parts of the building tear up. The nett result of my activities was to reject an application by Evan Charteris to be an interpreter. . . .[16]

Within a very few months, such levity would become dangerous. At the end of the year Evan Charteris (then aged fifty) told Patrick Shaw-Stewart 'in no measured terms' that he and Raymond Asquith had been 'thought ill of in connexion with this war'. Evan could have meant that he disapproved of their flippancy; or have been referring to the fact that neither had immediately joined up. Yet Raymond had a busy law practice, a particularly happy marriage, and two young children; while Patrick – though only twenty-six – was an active director of Baring's Bank. Evan, a lifelong admirer of Ettie, might have been unconsciously motivated by jealousy of a rival half his age; but his attitude was universal. Three-quarters of a million had joined up within two months of the outbreak of war. The readiness of the upper classes to send their young heroes to the Front showed no signs of abating. In the first week of January 1915 Raymond Asquith enlisted with the Queen's Westminsters, while Patrick bowed to the inevitable and by March was on his way to Gallipoli. His companions there, among others from the Coterie, would be George Vernon and Charles Lister.

The campaign in Gallipoli was a reflection of the fact that the Great War was also an imperial war. Turkey had entered it on the side of Germany in October 1914, and the Turks, as lords and masters over most of the Middle East, had long been a thorn in the imperial flesh. Gallipoli was the Turkish peninsula that thrust along the eastern side of the Dardanelles straits, which led to Constantinople, guarding the Bosphorus and the Black Sea. It was the only channel through which Russia could approach the Mediterranean. If the British Navy could force the Dardanelles, then Constantinople could be captured – Turkey humiliated – and our Russian allies given an all-the-year-round sea route. Germany would be threatened, and Britain would hold the vital lands linking her Indian possessions with countries like Egypt and Aden where she already ruled. The prospect cannot ever have looked easy, but with so much at stake it was tempting – especially to the forty-year-old firebrand who was First Lord of the Admiralty: Winston Churchill.

The Dardanelles fiasco was basically devised by him, with Kitchener. It was seen as a universal panacea that would shorten the war. This was why a combined British and French naval force landed nearly half a million troops on Gallipoli. The plan was immensely ambitious. It failed catastrophically. The

British (including contingents from Australia and New Zealand) lost 205,000 men between April 1915 and January 1916: very nearly one in ten of all British casualties throughout the war.

On the Western Front, the battle of Neuve Chapelle in March 1915 resulted in 11,652 casualties, including over four thousand from the Indian Corps (another reminder that this was an imperial war). This battle gave the British public its first real intimation of the scale of the losses to come. Yet a popular song of the time boasted mindlessly:

> We licked 'em on the Marne
> And whacked 'em on the Aisne,
> We gave 'em hell at Neuve Chapelle
> And we'll bloody well do it again!

At its best, this confidence could take the form of high courage against suicidal odds. At its worst, it resulted in crude jingoism on the Home Front, an uncritical acceptance of the distortions of the propaganda machine, and the sadistic handing of white feathers (for cowardice) to any young male civilians who were not flagrantly wounded, or in some obvious way incapacitated from fighting. Now, as throughout the war, people at home were blind to the conditions at the Front.

At the highest level of society, although the war and the exploits of their sons remained the dominant topic of conversation, social life for the older generation continued relatively undisturbed. Magazines like *The Queen* reflect this. Interspersed with grieving notices of deaths were articles on how to cope with the increasing problem of entertaining. Food was sometimes in short supply, and becoming more expensive. Servants were harder to get hold of, and more demanding. Paris no longer inspired such frivolous new fashions. The callousness was surely unconscious; but it was there. Mothers grumbled to one another about how impossible their daughters had become. The custom of chaperonage, which had survived as the last anachronism protecting the reputations of upperclass virgins, was now almost abandoned. Yet the parents of these young women fought to maintain what had been the essential qualities of a marriageable daughter, regardless of the fact that the conditions of life were changing convulsively.

The young were determined to enjoy the time that was left to them, despite all the efforts of their elders to stop them. The Coterie had never been so bitterly disapproved of. Its members plunged into frenetic, hysterical gaiety, above all in organizing entertainments for those who were on leave from the Front. These were castigated as 'dances of death' by their scandalized parents. Duff Cooper wrote:

> How splendidly our youthful spirits resisted the gloom and terror which that shadow [i.e. of death] is wont to cast! It may well be that the near presence of death enables us to form a truer estimate of its importance. . . . We did not feel our losses the less because we wore our mourning more lightly. Among my own friends it became a point of honour never to show a sad face at the feast.[17]

By the beginning of 1915 almost every man from the Coterie was in some regiment, either in training; or abroad; or briefly back home on leave. The

exceptions were Duff Cooper, who could not be released from his work as a
Foreign Office clerk, and Alan Parsons, whose chronic asthma prevented him
from being eligible. Young women, since the deaths in the battle of Neuve
Chapelle, now lived on a high wire of tension, knowing that news might come at
any moment – by post, by a telegram or phone call, or (worst of all) accidentally
overheard – that a young man they loved was dead. They endured that fear; men
endured the risk – and the fear too, for their contemporaries. No wonder they
celebrated a few days of safety! Their wild, anaesthetizing lifestyle, that so
shocked their parents, was one way to make the tension bearable: at any rate,
outwardly. The older generation were spectators to these circus antics, alternately thrilled by the danger and horrified by the show of indifference to it. But
the young were performers. They knew that, far below the glitter and unholy
sparkle of the tightrope they were walking, there waited almost certain death.
And so they urged one another on to wilder and wilder extravagance:
champagne, and gambling, and drugs, and the beginnings of jazz, and disgraceful dancing, and staying out late, until they had scoffed at all society's taboos.
Lady Diana Cooper wrote about those decadent, death-defying nights:

> Looking back on those nightmare years of tragic hysteria, it is frightening to
> live them again in memory. . . . The young were dancing a tarantella
> frenziedly to combat any pause that would let death conquer their
> morale. . . . Wine helped, and there was wine in plenty – it was said too
> much. George Moore's dances of death flowed with the stuff. They became
> more frequent as leave became regular from the training centres and the
> trenches of France and the Middle East. The parties were left to the Coterie to
> assemble. Parents were excluded. We dined at any time. The long waits for the
> last-comers were enlivened by exciting, unusual drinks such as vodka or
> absinthe. The menu was composed of far-fetched American delicacies –
> avocados, terrapin, and soft-shell crabs. The table was purple with orchids. I
> always sat next to the host, and the dancing, sometimes to two bands, Negro
> and white (and once to the first Hawaiian) so that there might be no pause,
> started immediately after dinner. There were not more than fifty people. We
> kept whirling to the music till the orchids were swept away. . . .[18]

The men went back to the trenches; the women, many of them, went back to
the rigid, gloomy hospitals where they nursed. They had fought to overcome
their parents' stubborn resistance because they wished to share something of the
ordeal endured by husbands, brothers and friends at the Front. The Duchess of
Rutland opposed her daughter's desire to be a nurse, and beseeched friends to
reinforce her fearful warnings. One of them, recalled Lady Diana Cooper, was
Lady Dudley: 'She explained, in words suitable to my innocent ears, that
wounded soldiers so long starved of women, inflamed with wine and battle,
ravish and leave half-dead the young nurses who wish only to tend them.'[19] Not
even this deterred Lady Diana, and eventually she got her way and started as a
VAD probationer at Guy's Hospital. She was dressed in a hideous, starched
uniform, 'cut to deform the figure' and left to savour her triumph. 'No smiles. A
training hospital in 1914 was as inhuman as the army. No speaking to superiors
before being spoken to. All these rules had to be learnt by trial and error, as I
found out when next day I said "Good morning" to Matron.'[20] Yet she made a
success of nursing, and stayed at Guy's until recalled by her mother, ostensibly to

supervise the setting up of a hospital in a château at Hardelot in France. When that plan failed to materialize, the Duchess opened a small, and very select, hospital in her own London house at 16 Arlington Street, and here, in a more desultory fashion, Diana continued her nursing by day and her revelry by night.

She was only one among many who took up nursing. Within the first months of the war, Lady Angela Forbes (the mistress of Hugo Elcho) began by nursing, but in November 1914 opened a military canteen at Boulogne. (It fed 4½ million men in the course of the war, despite official disapproval.) Millicent, Duchess of Sutherland, also ran a hospital under the auspices of the Red Cross, and so did the Duchess of Westminster (at Le Touquet), Lady Norman (at Wimereux) and – for all her vivid fears of rape – Lady Dudley.

For young women like Monica Grenfell the war offered liberation from their parents' rule. She, and many of her friends, welcomed the opportunity to break away from the monotony of their home lives with 'enthusiasm, even exultation'. But there was also a genuine and humble desire to serve, as their brothers were doing. Aristocratic young women abased themselves to perform for strangers tasks that had always been done by servants – emptying chamber pots, changing soiled sheets, washing and bandaging the wounded. Monica trained for three months at the Whitechapel Hospital in the East End of London – in itself an area where she had probably never ventured before – and with this rudimentary initiation went confidently, even happily, off to France. Angela Manners* (whose brother John had been one of the first of the Coterie to be killed) went to Belgium. Lady Helen Vincent, one of the Souls, actually qualified as an anaesthetist, and served close to the fighting Fronts in France and Italy.

There were many more. Cynthia Asquith (Mary Elcho's eldest daughter, now married to 'Beb' Asquith and the mother of two little boys) was a VAD at Winchcombe, while her sister-in-law Letty Charteris and her younger sister Mary (Blunt's natural daughter) both followed the men they loved – Ego Charteris and Tom Strickland – to Egypt in 1915, and took up nursing there, at the Deaconess Hospital in Alexandria.

The older generation, too, played their part in what Ettie called the 'War Effort'. Her *Family Journal* recorded: 'The Working-Party at Taplow Court sent 955 garments to the hospitals and soldiers abroad, up to December 11th. On December 12th, Monica and her parents went over to France, and Monica took up her work at the British Hospital. Monica was then the only Probationer, all the rest of the staff were fully trained. There were 123 beds.'[21] A letter which Ettie wrote from Wimereux in December 1914 records her first impressions of the war with a characteristic blend of realism and 'stubborn joy':

> There are eight hospitals in and about this small village. The ambulances go off at break-neck speed to the Railway Station, three miles away, and come back very, very slowly. No mud ever encountered before seems real: here it permeates all life, with a cold clinging persistence, and penetrates into the houses and up the creaky wooden stairs. 'The trenches' everyone says and thinks all day long. . . . [The nurses'] courage and cheerfulness are absolutely amazing, never does the dark side of life even obtain a hearing. The same ubiquitous spirit possesses the patients. 'I feel a treat today,' said a boy who had his leg off yesterday. Another, very ill, said 'I am just like a king in here,

*Sister of John Manners, not of Lady Diana.

my wife would jump right up in the air to see me.' One man was too ill to speak, but held out a picture-postcard of his wife and baby, with indescribable happiness. . . .[22]

Julian, and later Billy, visited Monica in Wimereux several times from the Front, but, if she sent any letters home containing her own impressions of nursing, Ettie did not judge them worth quoting. Julian was beginning to experience that ambiguity which had plagued him several years before, when he could not reconcile his own truthful emotions and what his mother wished to hear. In mid-February 1915 he wrote home: 'You should have seen our men setting out from here for the trenches. Absolutely radiant with excitement and joy, at getting back to fight again! I do love fighting. . . .'[23] Yet a poem he wrote that spring reveals a strain of bitterness. It also shows he had mastered the art of saying what was acceptable to his mother while meaning almost the opposite.

> *Prayer for Those on The Staff*
>
> Fighting in mud, we turn to Thee,
>   In these dread times of battle, Lord,
> To keep us safe, if so may be,
>   From shrapnel, snipers, shell, and sword.
>
> But not on us, for we are men
>   Of meaner clay, who fight in clay,
> But on the Staff, the Upper Ten,
>   Depends the issue of the Day.
>
> God help the Staff – especially
>   The young ones, many of them sprung
> From our high aristocracy;
>   Their task is hard, and they are young.
>
> *O Lord, who mad'st all things to be,*
>   *And madest some things very good,*
> *Please keep the extra A.D.C.*
>   *From horrid scenes, and sights of blood.*[24]

The final stanza (the italics are Julian's own) may well have been a reference to the Prince of Wales, for in Julian's covering letter to his mother, dated 7 March 1915, he wrote, 'Don't shew it to ——': presumably the Queen, since on 1 March Ettie went to London, to take her turn on the rota as lady-in-waiting for a fortnight.

At the end of April 1915, Julian left the trenches and took a weekend's leave in Paris. He wrote about it to his mother with unforced enthusiasm. For once, he did not have to dissemble:

> I cannot imagine how I have lived so long without being there. I was absolutely fascinated by the whole thing. I had two divine Spring days there. Isn't it gloriously light and gay and beautiful? . . . What I liked most about Paris was the light-heartedness of it all, the complete joie-de-vivre of the place and the people. They are so much lighter of heart than anything of ours, and really much more natural: and such artists in fun.[25]

After this, Julian's few remaining letters revert to the taut antithesis of exultation and horror which characterized, more and more, letters home from the

Front. This last one ends: 'I went into one of the "forward dressing stations" that night when I stayed with the horses. A tiny hovel of a farm, 5 doctors, and the bad cases coming in and going out on the stretchers, everything chock-a-block. How *marvellously* brave and cheerful the wounded English Tommy is.'[26]

The chasm between what men experienced in the trenches and while fighting, and the idealized and distorted images of battle that were received by those back home, put an intolerable strain on the language the troops used in trying to write about what was happening. In the end, they evolved two quite separate languages. One, the language of letters home, relied on conventional, anodyne phrases that expressed only what the recipient could bear to hear. The other, the language of the trenches, became a masculine jargon of crude, abbreviated directness. French placenames were anglicized; bombs and shells were given nicknames, as were officers and generals; until in the end an idiom had evolved that defined the private experience of trench warfare much as the élite vocabulary of the Souls had once bemused the world outside their exclusive circle.

The need to blunt reality was shared by both officers and men. The ordinary soldiers' letters home were whittled down to a few stock phrases, meaningless beyond the reassurance that the writer was still alive. At the end of September 1915 Yvo Charteris, Mary Wemyss's youngest son, managed to get to France with the 1st Battalion Grenadier Guards. Barely nineteen, he had been longing to take part in the war, and brought a fresh eye to bear on what he found. Within three weeks he was writing to his sister, Cynthia Asquith: '. . . people at home in London are a great deal more real than this war, which seems weary of its own melodrama but does not know how to give it up.'[27] Few writers expressed so clearly the unconscious imagery of the 'theatre of war'. It was valuable because of the need to distance oneself from the intolerable reality of the fighting. A fortnight earlier, he too had been telling his mother about the mail he had to censor:

> The men have some wonderful conventions in their letters: there are two alternative ways of beginning, either 'Darling, just a line to answer your welcome letter, hoping this will find you as it leaves me' or more frequently, 'Just a line to say I am still in the pink' – (unless they have been properly bad, when they are generally 'getting on famously now'). If it is to their sweetheart they go on to ask her not to forget that there is 'someone somewhere in France', and they end up by reflecting that 'the best thing to do is to trust to the one above'.[28]

For men who were incapable even of writing this much (injury was the most frequent reason) there was a printed form available. Called Form 2042, but known as a 'Whizz Bang', or 'Quick Firer', it conveyed the minimum necessary information in short, colourless sentences, the user crossing out those which were not applicable. The most poignant is the last: 'I have received no letter from you lately/for a long time.'[29] The language used by those in the trenches varied from self-mocking domesticity – like christening a dug-out 'Cosy Nook Villas' – to brutal harshness. Much of it was very funny, and some has survived today. Bureaucratic paperwork was referred to disparagingly as 'bumf', because the soldiers called it 'bum fodder' and used it as lavatory paper. In outrageously extraordinary circumstances, such as those of trench warfare, the ordinary language of peacetime daily life soon becomes inadequate. Every other word used by soldiers was a four-letter obscenity. It had no meaning; it was part of a litany, a ritual incantation to express a constant state of nerves and fears that were inexpressible.

Inspired in the first place by the inability to pronounce local placenames (few ordinary soldiers had been far from home before, let alone abroad; while foreign languages were not taught except at public school: and not much even there) the men soon devised an imaginative set of anglicized names for the French towns and villages where they found themselves. These soon became so universal that they were used by field and even staff officers, and ultimately crossed to people back at home in England: such as 'Wipers' for Ypres, at the beginning of the war. In the later period it was known as 'Eeps'. Foreign names were defused of their strangeness by being turned into ingenious English versions of themselves. Auchonvillers was 'Ocean Villas'; Foncquevillers was 'Funky Villas'; while *estaminet* – a café where one could grab a quick meal or something to drink – was turned brilliantly into 'just a minute'! The trenches were given English street names, which helped to locate them quickly and correctly. Battalions were nicknamed affectionately to suggest their origins: Glasgow Boys' Brigade for the 16th Highland Light Infantry, or the ubiquitous 'Pals' or even 'Chums'. These names created a sense of fellowship as well as legitimizing the emotion – intense but rarely erotic – which men in the trenches felt for their fellow soldiers and brother officers.

The alternative to obscenity or cosiness was euphemism; and the officers, schooled in a literary and classical tradition, cloaked the reality of their lives in a comprehensive vocabulary of euphemism, suggestive of chivalry or legendary battles. In this way they could describe the fighting in terms that protected the innocence of their families. A whole list can be compiled of these necessary circumlocutions . . . *steed* or *charger* for horse; *foe* for enemy; *peril* for danger; *gallant* for earnestly brave; *plucky* for cheerfully brave; *staunch* (slightly derogatory) for stolidly brave. Those dead on the battlefield were called *the fallen*, while to die was to *perish* and one's death was one's *fate*. Some of the words from the games field came in useful, too: the objective of an attack was the *goal*; to be unpretentiously enthusiastic was to be *keen*; to move fast was to be *swift*.[30] Seen in this light, the poetry and letters of the First World War take on a new level of meaning. The stumpy Anglo-Saxon words used by soldiers among themselves were too coarse for the elevated emotions which those at home needed to disguise the brutal truth.[31]

One can select at random almost any letter by one of the Coterie to their parents and find this 'sentimentalization' of their experience. The two following were written by very young men, newly arrived at the Front, and serving so close to one another that they sometimes met. The first is by Yvo Charteris:

The place is riddled with communication-trenches which have very good names. It is pleasant to leave the security of one's ruin and listen to the 'sharp rattle of musketry' and the wailing of shells and watch the bursting shrapnel and flares going up in the evening. A flare is exactly like a Roman Candle, and a shell sounds very like a rocket. I don't know what is going to happen to our Brigade these next few days, I expect it will rest here a bit. We have got a delightful sight in our graveyard here, from one of the graves the tombstone has been laid open by a shell – the coffin-lid has been torn off showing the skeleton of a man – a toad is sitting on his chest and little brown mice are playing on his bones – R.I.P. says the tombstone.[32]

He had been at the Front for barely a fortnight, but already has learnt to obscure the horror of his surroundings with language that combines irony with childish references to fireworks, and the little brown mice of a children's nursery book. His mother, Mary Wemyss, would have needed insight and steely determination to read the true message behind this letter: I feel like a frightened small boy in the midst of death. He did, and he was.

The second letter was from Edward Wyndham Tennant – 'Bim' or 'Bimbo' to his mother, whom he worshipped. He too was very young when he arrived in France. He joined the Grenadier Guards at seventeen and was just eighteen when posted to France in August 1915. So tender-hearted that he once wrote home saying 'I think I shot a German the other day – if I did, God rest his soul',[33] he too devised for his mother a language that mitigated the atrocity he describes:

> I write to you from the dug-out which Osbert[†] and I share in the support trench immediately behind our front line. . . . It is rather exciting and I always wear my steel cap, night and day. . . . We came in last night, and had not been in long before a Scots Guards Officer told us there were two wounded men between the lines. We made him mark the place, and after dark we sent out the stretcher-bearers, who I rejoice to say found the men, who had been lying in a shell-hole, foodless, for six days and five nights! They had been afraid to crawl up to this trench, because they weren't sure it wasn't occupied by Boches, and they quite wisely preferred to risk dying of exposure than risk giving themselves up to them by mistake. They were terribly weak, and the sergeant told me it was like carrying a child to lift them, so light were they. But a small amount of food and tea, and a little rum strengthened them greatly. . . . Both are certain to recover, they tell me, for which I am very thankful; it was heart-rending to see them when they carried them in, just like very tired children.[34]

Again, the event is converted to something tender and pitiable which a mother could understand. The wounded and dehydrated men are described as 'very tired children', and the story is given a happy ending.

It was nearly always the case that sons wrote least honestly to their mothers – believing them to be most in need of protection from the truth. When writing (much more rarely) to their fathers, a certain manly gusto comes in which allows them to seem more direct. Letters to wives, though still careful, are often more truthful still; while letters to women who have experience of nursing, and need not be bamboozled about the appalling effects of shell wounds or the mental breakdown caused by nervous strain under fire, are the most factual of all. Later on in the war soldiers became more disillusioned with their superior officers, whose inefficiency or complacency – they felt – had led to many unnecessary deaths. Their letters became less protective. They began to want people at home to know the truth. Few heard.

The final phase of open warfare (when there was some chance of a break-

---

[†]Osbert Sitwell, who served in the Grenadier Guards from 1912–19. He was never part of the Coterie, but both Yvo Charteris and Edward Wyndham Tennant had known him slightly before the war.

through by either side) ended in late November 1914 when the last gap was closed at the First Battle of Ypres. During the winter, both sides sat freezing in their trenches while the High Command reconsidered tactics. In the spring of 1915 the British attacked first, at Neuve Chapelle, followed on 22 April by the German assault at Ypres. With the return to aggressive tactics, the number of deaths began to rise. There had been casualties throughout the previous months, but these were due to individuals shot by snipers or caught in a desultory bombardment, rather than to an organized attack. But as young officers were once again called upon to lead their men 'over the top', the sons of the Souls, even more than the ordinary soldiers whom they led, suffered a high casualty rate.

The first victim was Edward Horner, the tall, good-looking brother of Raymond Asquith's wife Katharine. To him, in a sense, the war must have seemed a godsend. Indeed, he celebrated its outbreak by ordering a special pair of riding boots in which to ride into Berlin! He lacked the intellectual calibre that distinguished so many of his friends in the Coterie, and although by 1914 he was a well placed young barrister in F. E. Smith's chambers, his nature was more satisfied by physical action and adventure. Within a few days of war being declared he had rejoined his territorial regiment, the North Somerset Yeomanry. What he expected war to be like can be deduced from the fact that he took with him his elder sister's two best hunters, his valet and a cook! On first arriving at the Front he cannot have been too disappointed, for he wrote home asking for a gold tiepin for his soldier servant. (To which Raymond Asquith riposted: 'Your letter asking for a gold pin for your servant does you great credit. May I send you out an emerald ring for his nostril?')[35] Also typically, his next concern was whether the King's call for temperance was likely to meet with universal approval? His brother-in-law was able to reassure him.

Edward Horner had been deeply if fitfully in love with Lady Diana Manners. When he was badly wounded in May 1915 she turned for help to George Moore – who was also besotted with her, and glad to use his influence with the Commander-in-Chief, Sir John French, on her behalf. Within hours, Moore had organized transport and a special pass to enable Edward's parents, and his sister, and a leading surgeon, and a nurse, *and* Lady Diana herself, all to go over to the hospital at Boulogne where he was lying. Lady Diana recalled:

> The scene is marked in memory's eye like a familiar picture – outside the station, pencils of searchlights and a procession of stretchers that seemed never-ending to me, looking at each sick face for the one I sought. And there it was – very, very ill and looking ecstatic. The bearers broke the procession and laid the stretcher down, and round we crowded, crying with relief, to see our precious Edward alive and due to recover.
> 'O darling, this is heaven,' he said.[36]

This story, and the emotional charge it carries, add credence to the notion that Lady Diana might well have married Edward Horner, had he survived the war.

Immediately after this came the news that Julian Grenfell, too, had been wounded: though it seemed at first as though his injury was only slight. Julian was with his regiment, the 1st Royal Dragoons, in the trenches near Ypres. Ahead of them was a small hill: Julian called it 'the little hill of death'.[37] At first light on Thursday 13 May, the Germans had begun shelling their position. The Royals were ordered to use the little hill as a lookout post from which to observe the enemy, and give warning if they tried to press the attack further forward. The hill was under very heavy shell fire, but Julian strolled nonchalantly over it, undeterred by the fact that he had already been hit once, though only enough to tear his coat and bruise his shoulder. His courage was so extraordinary that everyone remarked on it. He seemed quite impervious to danger. He insisted on returning over and over again to 'the little hill of death'. Finally, just after noon, when he and the general in charge of the Brigade were watching the German attack together, a shell landed very close to them, and both were hit. Julian himself knew at once that his injury was fatal. He had been struck on the head, and he said to the general (whose wound was not serious), 'Go on down, I'm done.'[38] When he reached No. 10 casualty clearing station he said again to a brother officer, 'Do you know, I think I shall die.'[39] Yet the bloodstained note which he scribbled in pencil to his mother the next day said only: 'We are practically wiped out, but we charged and took the Hun trenches yesterday. [This was not strictly true.] I stopped a Jack Johnson‡ with my head, and my skull is slightly cracked. But I'm getting on splendidly. I did awfully well. Today I go down to Wimereux, to hospital, shall you be there? *All all* love, Julian of the 'Ard 'Ead'[40]

The letter arrived on Sunday 16 May 1915: by chance, the very day that Billy was due to leave for France. It had already been arranged that his brother Ivo, who was sixteen and still at Eton, should come over to Taplow and spend Billy's last day with him. When the note first arrived, the family was upset and shocked, but not seriously concerned. Then at four o'clock in the afternoon came a telegram from the hospital in Boulogne: 'Your son here wounded in head. Better come. Use this as permit.'[41]

The Desboroughs, like the Horners, pulled all possible strings, and with the help of friends in the Admiralty were able to travel that same night on an ammunition boat which arrived at Boulogne at 5 a.m. They went straight to the hospital, and on arrival found Julian's sister Monica there already. (She had been nursing at Wimereux, a few miles away.) It was by now 17 May. Julian took ten days to die.

Billy arrived in France on the Thursday, as planned, and went first to the hospital where Julian lay. His brother's condition, and his mother's reaction to it, can be gauged from the letter that Billy wrote her directly afterwards, when he got to the Front:

> It was a joy to see you yesterday, so wonderfully brave and calm and strong. One feels that Judy [i.e. Julian] must repose now on the strength of those who love him as much as on his own, and that all the strangling influence of fear or misgiving should be cleared away from him. It was sad to see his 'dear, delightful head' brought so low, but I *really do* feel the most complete confidence and trustfulness.[42]

But Ettie's stubborn refusal to admit the reality of death could not save her son. Further inflammation of the brain was diagnosed; an operation was performed;

‡A 5·9 German shell that gave off thick black smoke, and was called after the negro boxer who was world heavyweight champion 1908–15.

Julian grew weaker. He was in terrible pain. Forty-eight hours before he died, he said: 'I've never been so well and I've *never* been so happy.'[43] At last he had learned to stand language on its head, as his mother had always wished, and to state the exact opposite of the truth. He pleased her almost as much by alluding to the classical models that she had always longed for him to emulate . . . Hippolytus, and Phoebus Apollo, the sun god. Ettie recalls proudly in her *Journal*: 'The thought that he was dying seemed to go and come, but he always seemed radiantly happy, and he never saw any of the people he loved look sad. Never once through all those days did he say one word of complaint or depression.'[44] Until finally, 'He knew them to the very end, and moved his mother's hand to his lips. At the moment that he died, he opened his eyes a little, with the most radiant smile that they had ever seen even on his face.'[45]

Thus, at last, on his deathbed, Julian Grenfell became the apotheosis his mother had always desired. Smiling, joyful, happy, *radiant* . . . did she ever wonder whether this was really a normal way for a young man to die, or his mother to watch it?

Julian was not the only one to die in that encounter: out of his fifteen brother officers who were alive when it started, only three survived.

A fortnight later, Mary Wemyss visited the bereaved Desboroughs: '*June 12th*. I went to Taplow and saw Ettie in her sitting-room. She was quite wonderfully calm, and upheld by a sense of Julian's continued presence and love. . . . I had tea with Willy; my heart aches for him, he looked so crushed, so seared, so patient and so brave.'[46]

It was not over yet. On 30 July Billy, too, was killed. He had been leading his platoon in a charge near Hooge. He died instantly, and his body was never recovered.

Ettie was not unique in her contradictory attitude to death and her denial of sorrow. The letters of condolence she received from her friends show that many shared it: unless like her sons they were deliberately tailoring their sentiments to meet her wishes. Lady Frances Balfour (whose son Oswald was wounded several times, though he survived the war), wrote: 'There is something very wonderful in motherhood today. We have given our children at a time when they would be ready to fight the good fight.'[47] Arthur Grenfell, a senior member of Willy's family, carried the sporting metaphor to its furthest extreme when he wrote of his concern for the continuance of the line:

> I wish I knew Ivo. I would try and show him that his duty lies in carrying on your work at home, and not abroad. We all liked playing flying-man, but some had to play back-up post, and some goals, in order to win the match, and we must play the game for the side. I am certain that his proper job is to prepare himself to take over your responsibilities, and assume the leadership of the family.[48]

The belief, firmly held by the British upper classes, that proportionately more of their sons died than those of other classes was not just an arrogant illusion. It was true. Junior officers tended overwhelmingly to come from the public-school- and university-educated sons of the aristocracy and the landed or moneyed gentry. Their rôle was to lead their men into battle, and to undertake some of the most dangerous and exposed tasks in war, like reconnoitring, conducting night raids, or mending the barbed wire defences in front of the trench. It was a matter of honour to carry out these duties personally, without delegating; just as it was a source of pride to be seen setting an example by leading their men 'over the top' and being first in the attack across No Man's Land. Inevitably, those in the forefront were often the first to be killed. Billy and Yvo Charteris and Ego and Raymond and 'Bim' and Julian Grenfell and countless others like them died because they consciously put themselves in the place of greatest risk. Analysis of the deaths among officers compared with those in the ranks shows beyond doubt that the social élites from which officers were largely recruited suffered disproportionately heavy losses.

There were other reasons, too. Many of the working-class men who wanted to enlist not merely at the outbreak of war but throughout its four years simply did not reach the necessary levels of fitness required for active service. All men volunteering were placed into four categories – Grade I, men without any disability; Grade II, men with minor disabilities, but capable of considerable physical exertion; Grade III, men with 'marked disabilities', best suited to clerical work rather than physical effort; and Grade IV, men totally unfit for military service. The overwhelming majority of upper-class men fell into categories I and II, and were thus the first to be sent to the fighting Fronts. But the standards of health were so low in many urban working-class districts that, ironically, the lives of many men were saved by the fact that they were not passed fit enough to go and die. Over one million men examined in 1917–18 alone were found to be unfit for combat duty. In the poorest industrial areas, about seven out of ten men would be found unfit. Most shocking of all are the figures relating to 210 eighteen-year olds from Lancashire and Cheshire who were placed in Grade IV. Their *average* measurements were: height, 4 feet 9 inches; weight, 84 lb (or 6 stone); chest, 30 inches. It is a particularly striking proof of the inequality that prevailed in the country during the 'golden era' of the last two decades before the war broke out. The consequence was that, the humbler a man's social origins, the less likely he was to see active service. The privileged social élites were the ones with the best chance of being healthy enough to die.

The earlier in the war a young man joined up; the younger he was at the time; the better educated and the more nobly born . . . the more certain it became that he would die. A few statistics[49] prove this. In the first year of the war, 33,393 officers were serving in the British Army. By September 1915, 5,233 officers – or 6.2 per cent of the total number – had been killed in action, died of wounds, or were missing, presumed dead. But if we take the percentage of serving officers in regiments that were in action between 1 October 1914 and 30 September 1915, the proportion of officers killed rises to 14.2 per cent, against 5.8 per cent from other ranks. This is out of all proportion to the 3.55 per cent of the Army who were officers.

Analyzing the deaths according to Oxbridge graduates, the statistics show an even higher death toll: 3,216 Oxford graduates who matriculated between 1910 and 1914 served in the war, and 942, or 29.3 per cent of them, were killed. The number is almost as high for Cambridge, proving that the Oxford figures were no fluke of mischance: 4,358 Cambridge men who matriculated during those years served in the British forces, and 1,138, or 26.1 per cent of them, were killed. If we take the complete Oxford figures, for all graduates serving throughout the war, we find that 13,403 served, and 2,569, or 19.2 per cent of them, were killed. Together, the dead from Oxford and Cambridge totalled 4,933 men who could, with partial justification, be described as 'the brightest and best' of their contemporaries. Hence the prevalent myth of an entire 'lost generation' that grew in strength during the post-war years.

The same heavy losses can be seen reflected still on the Roll of Honour board at any English public school. Here the influence of the OTC – the Officers' Training Corps – was paramount. Every public school, as well as most grammar schools and universities, had its OTC before the war. In consequence, most upper- and middle-class young men had some experience of military life and the actual duties of a junior officer before the war began. This, together with their fitness, and the early shortage of trained troops, ensured that they were quickly posted to the Front. It was taken for granted, by their parents, their schoolmasters and the younger boys still at school, that anyone from the OTC would rush to serve. The result was that English public schools lost about one former pupil out of every five who served: in striking contrast to the national average of one man killed for every eight who served.

The higher up the social ladder one climbs, the more the mortality figures rise too. Taking peers and their sons under the age of fifty in 1914, 18.95 per cent of those serving were killed. Not since the Wars of the Roses had the English aristocracy suffered such losses as those which they endured during the Great War. It is noticeable how many titles, after the war, passed direct from grandfather to grandson, while others – like that of Willy, 1st Baron Desborough – died out altogether.

The courage of these young sons has never been questioned. But there is an unforgiving irony in the fact that the British ruling classes, who alone had the political power to avert the war, also suffered the greatest losses as a consequence of it. Their ideology of glory, of sacrifice, inculcated at home, at school, at chapel, at university, on the playing fields and the grouse moors and around the dinner table – had its culmination in the sacrificial deaths of their sons, leaving them to reflect as best they might on the glory.

During the first year after the outbreak of war 5,233 officers died, 4,303 of them in France. Among them were several members of the Coterie: John Manners (Con and Hoppy's son, not Diana's brother), Percy Wyndham, George Cecil and the Grenfells. But the following year (which included part of the ghastly carnage on the Somme) the total was nearly three times as high. The rage that these young men began to feel (first guiltily, and in secret, and later on openly) at the waste of their youth and, indeed, the rest of their lives at the behest of the politicians – old men whose own lives were never in danger – and to a lesser extent the generals, was voiced by Wilfred Owen. The following poem is made more savage by being placed within the Old Testament context much favoured by those preaching the need for sacrifice:

The Parable of the Old Man and the Young

So Abram rose, and clave the wood, and went,
And took the fire with him, and a knife.
And as they sojourned both of them together,
Isaac the first-born spake and said, My Father,

Behold the preparations, fire and iron,
But where the lamb for this burnt-offering?
Then Abram bound the youth with belts and straps,
And builded parapets and trenches there,
And stretched forth the knife to slay his son.
When lo! an angel called him out of heaven,
Saying, lay not thy hand upon the lad,
Neither do anything to him. Behold,
A ram, caught in a thicket by its horns;
Offer the Ram of Pride instead of him.

But the old man would not so, but slew his son,
And half the seed of Europe, one by one.[50]

The Battle of Neuve Chapelle in March 1915 had been answered by the German offensive at Ypres, which began the following month. Edward Horner was wounded and the Grenfells killed in skirmishes that were a small part of this battle. The Allies retaliated throughout the summer of 1915, attacking at Aubers Ridge, Festubert and Loos, as well as in Gallipoli. By 30 September 1915 there had been a further 2 million casualties. British casualties in France *alone* were 318,853 of whom 72,593 had died. The combatants faced another enervating winter. Both sides were too tired, too cold, and too short of ammunition to summon the energy for the *coup de grâce*. At the end of 1915, Asquith replaced Sir John French with Sir Douglas Haig as Commander-in-Chief. French's incompetence was not disguised by public support. Kitchener's was. To people at home he remained an idol, and Asquith, although he could dilute Kitchener's powers, could not risk removing him. Many soldiers were beginning to feel alienated from civilians, with their glamorized images of the war, the simplified, black and white stereotypes that made all British soldiers heroes and all German ones degenerate cowards. Sassoon wrote savagely:

I'd like to see a Tank come down the stalls,
Lurching to rag-time tunes or 'Home Sweet Home',
And there'd be no more jokes in Music-halls
To mock the riddled corpses round Bapaume.[51]

The autumn and winter of 1915 saw its quota of Coterie dead. The first was Charles Lister – the son of Lord Ribblesdale and Margot's sister Charty. Charles had been the only one of his group to espouse socialism: and then only for a time. More intellectual than the others and more serious, he had been Julian Grenfell's best friend at Balliol. Julian had written of him admiringly: '. . . the best of all, a wild mind absolutely and wholly uninfluenced by contact with civilisation or people.' Charles had been sent with the Royal Naval Division to Gallipoli, and there, after being wounded three times, he finally died on a hospital ship on 28 August 1915. In his last letter to his sister Laura he had written: 'I now know that I shall not die. This does not mean that I may not be killed.'

Already the Coterie were becoming inured to the deaths of those they loved. Cynthia Asquith wrote in her private diary, with crucifying honesty: 'I am full of self-contempt at being able to think of myself. . . . I begin to feel a horrid numbness creeping over me. The Tragedy is so spendthrift. Either Billy's

[Grenfell] or Charlie's [Lister] death a year ago would have absorbed one's thoughts for ages.'[52] And two days later: '*Divine*, sunny, warm day and I felt quite well and happy.'[53]

The next to die was her own brother, Yvo Charteris, and his death was harder to bear. He was the Wemyss' youngest son, and he had insisted on going to fight even though he was not quite nineteen. His mother travelled with him by train to Gosford, the Wemyss family seat in Scotland, just a few days before his departure for France. During the journey through the night she had a premonition: 'I made him lie full length and he slept. He looked so white and still, and though I said to myself, he is still safe, he is still alive and under my wing, yet all the time as I watched him sleeping so peacefully there lurked beneath the shallow safety of the moment a haunting, dreadful fear, and the vision of him stretched out cold and dead.'[54]

Yvo's beloved sister Mary – so close to him in age that they often felt like twins – was at Gosford, too, for that visit. She remembers poignantly how the two of them walked for the last time through their old haunts in the surrounding woods. Yvo said to her, 'You know I probably shan't come back?' and she answered 'Oh *don't* say that!' He knew – they both knew: they only didn't know how soon.

Yvo arrived in France on 12 September 1915. His first experience of life at the Front thrilled him. He loved the night marches – 'one's legs swung onwards by a thousand singing men'[55] – and courted danger at night by going right across No Man's Land to look at the German trenches. For him it was all still novelty and adventure. His friend Edward Wyndham Tennant – the Glenconners' son 'Bim' – was nearby with his regiment. They met and compared notes, and the reality still bore some resemblance to their vivid expectations.

Within a week that was changing. Yvo wrote to his sister, Cynthia:

> The life is an exact inversion of what is natural to man – one lives as much as possible below one's element [i.e. underground] – one does all one's work at night sleeping at odd intervals in the day, and the meals are purely arbitrary. . . . The noise of a machine gun in the distance is the most sinister thing in the world, it is like the death-rattle of a giant – and a shell leaving a gun is an incomparably dreary sound, rather human – as though it loathed its mission.[56]

On 6 October – his nineteenth birthday – Yvo was made a platoon commander, the lowest rank for an officer in the Army. His regiment, the 1st Battalion Grenadier Guards, was now entrenched near Loos, and the action was almost continuous. Already the situation was becoming clear to him. He wrote to his sister on 7 October:

> It is I think beyond question always possible for either side to take the first *line* of trenches by a furious bombardment, of say a week (which makes the enemy retire to his dug-out, and upsets his nerve, as it inevitably must if kept on long enough) batter his trenches and machine-gun emplacements and cease only a few seconds before the infantry charge the trench; but only to take the first line is not worth the loss involved, as the first line can generally be won back by counter-attacks. I don't see that there is any military advantage in the line being a mile nearer Berlin, unless a gap is made through which troops can be poured to stop the enemy establishing himself in a second

line. . . . The Germans have dug-outs 27 feet deep, with a long periscope going up the trench with a machine-gun run up and down on a winch and fired by means of a periscope at the bottom (at least so they tell me), so they don't stand to lose many men, even in a bombardment. . . . [57]

If this simple analysis of the situation was obvious to a boy of nineteen who had been in France less than a month, why did it take so long for the generals running the war to become aware of it?

On 19 October the family received news that Yvo had been killed. He had been sent to rally his men, who were holed up in a shallow trench and not anxious to launch a fresh attack that they knew must be suicidal. Yvo showed the patrician disregard for danger that was expected of him, and in leading his men 'over the top' was hit by four bullets and died (or so at least his mother was told) instantly. It was a typical, and typically pointless, young officer's death.

His family were overcome with grief, and asked the usual futile questions, felt the futile waste: 'How can one believe it, that it should be the *object* to kill Yvo? That such a joy-dispenser should have been put out of the world on purpose. For the first time I felt the full mad horror of the war. . . .'[58] wrote Cynthia; and the next day she felt the pain even more keenly:

> Somehow with the others who have been killed, I have acutely felt the loss of them but have swallowed the rather high-faluting platitude that it was all right for them – they were not to be pitied, but were safe, unassailable, young, and glamorous for ever. With Yvo – I can't bear it for him. The sheer pity and horror of it is overwhelming, and I am haunted by the feeling that he is disappointed. It hurts me physically.[59]

Her father Hugo (now the Earl of Wemyss), who was normally indolent and easy-going, content so long as he had his good meals and a study to retreat to, was devastated: 'Poor Papa is most piteous – heartbroken and just like a child – tears pouring down his cheeks and so naively *astonished*. I think he really loved Yvo the most of his children, and was so proud and hopeful about him.'[60]

After a year of war and over half a million casualties, with no apparent gains achieved, people were less willing to swallow the 'high-faluting platitudes' – the rhetoric of sacrifice and heroes and eternal peace. Only Mary Wemyss (Elcho) could still write in the language of Ettie: 'Many a brave boy died thus gallantly, flinging to his country the gift of his life. They felt they owed this debt of honour, and though they hated war, to their way of thinking there was no alternative. They did not hesitate, they rushed with all the exuberance of inspired youth . . . we must not pity them, for they had the glory and the glamour in their hearts. . . .'[61]

The campaign in Gallipoli was also taking its toll of dead. Little George Vernon, the darling of the Coterie, spoilt and pleasure-loving and childish, died humiliatingly of dysentery at Suvla: not much 'glory' for him! He had loved Lady Diana Manners, who had never loved him in return, though she cherished and petted him; so she was surprised to find how much his death hurt: 'It's eleven and for two hours I can't stop crying,' she wrote to Duff, soon after hearing the news. 'O Christ the misery and the morphia not working. O Duff save yourself – if you die, where shall I be – my *poor* George. If only I could stop.'[62] Even she, the idol of her circle and beyond, was gradually coming to realize just how many young men of her generation had already died, and were yet to die. Who were they to marry, these aristocratic young women whose lives had looked so carefree just a couple of years ago? Whose children were they to bear? The possibility of reluctant spinsterhood was – to them – a spectre. Suddenly it seemed that it would become a reality. How was the ruling class to perpetuate itself, if all its young scions were killed? Yet the ruling class had, by definition, been responsible for the imperial cast of mind that led to a confrontation between the Great Powers. The ruling class had acquiesced in the war; they even glorified it, with their talk of 'high deeds' and 'noble hearts' and 'willing sacrifice'. Now, the young felt cheated. *Their* lives and *their* future were being disposed of in the name of ideals they had not shaped. It was all very well for the older generation: they were safe. They had found husbands and wives, made marriages, borne children. Their sacrifices were vicarious. Lady Diana's anguish was more immediate. One by one her 'best young men' – in Edwardian phrase – were going. First Julian (whom she never much liked) and then Billy Grenfell (whom she did); now George; what of Patrick Shaw-Stewart, in Gallipoli, and Edward Horner, now recovered from his fearful wound but back at the front, at his own insistence; what of Raymond Asquith who, although married, was her dearest love; what of Duff, safe for the time being? Would *any* of them survive the war?

The Germans had learnt their lesson at the Battle of Neuve Chapelle. They were determined that never again would they be taken by surprise. In 1916 they attacked first: at Verdun, in the bitter month of February. The battle lasted right through into the spring and summer. Once again, a flurry of activity was followed by a long period of attrition. The men at the Front knew that entrenched positions were by now virtually impregnable, whatever resources of human courage or artillery were hurled against them. But the generals did not know. The French, already at a low ebb, suffered terrible losses. But despite over 315,000 casualties, they did not yield. However, the British Army were forced to advance their next major offensive, which was to take place on the Somme, originally planned for August. The Regular Army – the British Expeditionary Force – who had been first in France when war was declared, had by now almost been wiped out, as had the Territorial Force, the Indian Corps and the Canadians who held the line with them. Their replacement, Kitchener's army of eager volunteers, still coming forward at the rate of a hundred thousand a month, was not yet fully trained. They badly lacked experienced officers. But there was no time to remedy these faults. The Germans must be distracted from Verdun, or the French Army would be annihilated.

Meanwhile, many British troops were being wastefully deployed, among them the force keeping control in Egypt. This was an area of British influence that had to be retained. It was here that Ego Charteris, now Lord Elcho, the son and heir of Hugo and Mary Wemyss, had spent the months fretting at his distance from the front line. His nearest friends were in Gallipoli; but he felt his place was in France. His wife Letty – Diana Manners's elder sister – was glad that he seemed to be stationed a safe distance from the fighting. How the world had been transformed! The frivolous make-believe of pre-war life must have seemed like a childish fantasy in which they had all aped the one-dimensional characters of history and literature. Now, more Shakespearian than they had foreseen, the stage in the final act was becoming strewn with corpses. Which of the players would be next? Exactly five years previously Mary Elcho had described the Shakespeare Ball:

> Ego went as the Marquis of Dorset in black velvet and crimson satin with a collar of snow-leopard (copied from Holbein's *Ambassadors*), Letty as the Marchioness of Dorset wore a dress of red and gold brocade (copied from Holbein's *Anne of Cleves*). Marjorie Manners came in looking charming as Anne Boleyn. I took Bibs, Squidge and Nannie to see some of the others . . . George Vernon as Henry VIII, Edward Horner as Buckingham, Raymond Asquith as Thomas Cromwell. . . . [63]

How thrilling it had all seemed, as the curtain rose upon the melodrama. How sickening the plot was turning out to be. How fast the dénouement was approaching.

Ego had joined the Royal Gloucestershire Hussars, and embarked with his regiment in April 1915 for Egypt, followed by his sister Mary and his wife Letty, both of whom found work as VADs in Alexandria. The first year did indeed turn out to be, for them, a relatively 'cushy' war. They went sightseeing around the Pyramids in big, jolly parties; Mary got married to Tom Strickland, also a serving officer, and Letty did her best to make it a 'proper' wedding, even though she was so far from home. They had Egyptian cooks and servants, and a thoroughly colonial lifestyle. 'We seem likely', wrote Ego reassuringly to his mother, 'never to hear a shot fired in anger.'[64] In August 1915 his regiment was sent to Gallipoli, but without Ego, who as senior subaltern was left behind in charge of the depot: 'This nearly broke his heart.'[65]

Gallipoli made him realize, from first-hand accounts, that all was not well with the conduct of the war. In September 1915 he wrote to his mother – hoping, perhaps, that she would pass the information on to Arthur Balfour –

> Gallipoli seems the last word in hell. The winter campaign – sitting in trenches won't be much fun, constant shell-fire, wherever they are, day and night – no water – and black pessimism. . . . You never hear of anything but bungling and ghastly casualties. It is no fun being killed when you feel it is just hopeless waste. From Generals downwards everybody talks in the same strain.[66]

He was stunned by the news about Yvo – the little brother who had so suddenly grown up and died – and wrote to his mother: 'To write down everyone one loves as dead – and then if any of us are left we shall be surprised. . . . I am so awfully sorry for Papa who loved him. . . . He must write his sons off and concentrate upon his grand-children, who thank God exist.'[67]

During the night of 22 April 1916, Mary Wemyss dreamt vividly of her eldest son:

> The atmosphere of the room seemed to quiver with excitement – I felt the stress and strain and *saw*, as if thrown onto a magic lantern sheet, a confused mass of black smoke splashed with crimson flame: it was like a child's picture of a battle or explosion. The flames and smoke were high up to the right of the picture and to the left I saw Ego standing, straight and tall.
>
> I felt that something had happened, but I knew not what, it was below the level of consciousness.[68]

Two days later *The Times* confirmed that Ego's regiment had indeed seen action east of the Suez Canal, at Katia. A couple of days later, the family at Stanway received news from Letty that Ego had been slightly wounded, and taken prisoner. They were dismayed; but reassured to know that he was still alive.

But they were wrong, and Mary's dream had been prophetic. Ego *had* been killed, leading his troops into action at last: the moment of glory, for which he had waited a year. It was not until July, after weeks of rumours confirmed, contradicted or denied, that they eventually received definite news of his death. At a London dinner party, Mary had overheard Mrs Keppel say that a syce (Arab servant) had sworn that after the battle he had watched by Lord Elcho's body for hours. But it seemed just a wild story and could not be checked. Letty came back from Egypt, to wait with the family for the best – or worst. Finally, however, they received word from his regimental sergeant-major: 'Lord Elcho wounded twice then shell blew out chest, *acted magnificently*, left dead at Katia.'[69] The truth could not be staved off any longer.

After so many weeks of hope, imagining him safe, picturing his return, Letty, his wife, went almost mad with grief. She had worshipped her husband, quite literally: 'Ego is my religion.'[70] Her younger sister, Lady Diana Manners, was summoned to try and bring her safely through the first excesses of grief. The family feared that her mind might crack under the strain of such long delayed sorrow, for Letty had not the intellectual resources nor the circle of close friends that sustained her mother-in-law, Mary Wemyss, and her sisters. Diana wrote helplessly:

What the despair is like you cannot think. 10,000 times would I sooner bear it, or see you or any of us (except Katharine) in such torture than poor darling Letty. She lies still all day and night moaning gently and with the prettiest babble – 'Sweet, sweet Ego. How can I face the long years? What shall I do with all his clothes? What does one do?' – till I feel more desperate than her and would love her to die. I know in her mind she is dreading herself, dreading never knowing love again, never having more children. . . .[71]

Two years later, Ego's soldier servant came to Stanway, to visit Mary and Letty. The two men had become very close during the months they had served together, and 'Scorgie' found it difficult to speak of that last encounter. Mary made notes of his conversation with them:

Scorgie was severely wounded and unable to return to the fight. Later on Ego came back to the tent where Scorgie lay. He had his coat off, and his wounded arm tied up in a scarf. He was wounded a second time, and returned to the tent to have his wound dressed. Scorgie said, 'Oh Sir, why do you not retire, you are twice wounded?' But Ego said he thought his presence might give courage to some of the young fellows there, and he went back to the firing line. Scorgie never saw him again. Fighting had begun about 5 a.m. and they held the Turks back till about 4 p.m., and the temperature would probably have been about 120°. Scorgie lay in the desert until the Australian Light Horse arrived some two or three days later. He asked for a whisky and said: 'There is a young man lying out there who is heir to great possessions – Lord Elcho – he may be alive, search, oh search, everywhere, please go and search until you find him.' But they could not find him.[72]

The biblical cadences of this story, its desert setting, and the heroism of both men, make it hard to read without tears. A far cry from the gaudy fancy dress balls of the last summers of peace: one more pointless death, in a particularly pointless battle, part of an increasingly pointless war.

– 11 –
Help Me to Die, O Lord

July–September 1916

Poem Before Somme

I, that on my familiar hill
    Saw with uncomprehending eyes
A hundred of Thy sunsets spill
    Their fresh and sanguine sacrifice,
Ere the sun swings his noonday sword
    Must say good-bye to all of this!
By all delights that I shall miss,
    Help me to die, O Lord.

That poem was written by William Noel Hodgson, MC, Bombing Officer of the 9th Devons, the day before the Somme offensive began, on 1 July 1916.

The failure of the Gallipoli offensive, and of the British attack on the Eastern Front, highlighted the urgent necessity for a major breakthrough. The Battle of the Somme was designed to boost morale among troops and civilians (not that the latter had a very realistic grasp of the progress of the war), to cripple the seemingly impregnable German Army, and to relieve the French. So confident were the British High Command of victory that, as Raymond Asquith told his wife on 11 June 1916, 'An order has just come to say that there is to be no cheering in the trenches when peace is declared. No-one can say that our Generals don't look ahead.'[1]

By now even the young officers at the Front had abandoned any illusions about the splendour and nobility of this war. At first, on arriving in France, Raymond had written to Katharine with weary resignation: 'The monotony of life is really rather appalling and even in this short time the noise of the guns has become as idiotic and tediously irritating as the noise of motor buses in London.'[2] But after six months he could no longer maintain his flippancy. At the beginning of June 1916 he wrote to a friend, Sybil Hart-Davis, 'Now that the Huns have conquered Italy and Greece and sunk all our ships and killed all our Canadians and all but taken Verdun I suppose it will be the turn of the British Army next. Well, well, there is much to be said for being quietly under the sod.'[3] It is dangerous to make such jokes in wartime.

Two months earlier, in April, his son and heir had been born. After a brief spell of leave, Raymond returned to the Front, scorning suggestions that he might now take a 'safe' job behind the lines . . . the sort of job that could easily have been arranged for the Prime Minister's son. But his letters to his wife continue to be cries of anguished tenderness. He longs to be with her and their two little girls and the new baby; yet, knowing her sensitivity and her fears, he does not allow himself to describe the worst that he is enduring.

To Lady Diana Manners, however, he is different. Her febrile courage and defiant pursuit of pleasure or oblivion among the carnage of her friends and of everything that had spelled normality may have scandalized her parents and their contemporaries, but Raymond understood her refusal to play the simple patriot. The older generation believed still that their values were best defended by war. The young, who had *seen* war, were beginning to think that if those values required defending in that way, then there must be something wrong with the values: for such a war *could not* be right.

On 23 June 1916, he gave vent both to his disgust at the war and also to his passion for Lady Diana (which in no way modified his deep love for Katharine) in a letter which is among the most visceral expressions of loathing of war. He was describing what he had seen on the front line at the places the troops called Maple Copse and Sanctuary Wood:

> Another night I was in a much worse place than this – the most accursed unholy & abominable place I have ever seen, the ugliest filthiest most putrid and most desolate – a wood where all the trees had been cut off by the shells the week before, and nothing remained but black stumps of really the most obscene heights & thickness, craters swimming in blood and dirt, rotting & smelling bodies & rats like shadows, fattened for the market & moving cunningly & liquorishly among them, limbs & bowels nestling in the hedges, & over all the most supernaturally shocking scent of death & corruption that ever breathed o'er Eden. . . . The only dug-out turned out to be a 'dirt trap' if not a death trap, awash with sewage, stale eyeballs, & other debris, so I spent 2 days on a stretcher in a shell hole in the gutter certainly, but looking all the while at the stars with which you have so richly studded my memory.[4]

The language of Arthurian romance had turned into that of Jacobean tragedy. It is as bestial as *The Duchess of Malfi* or *The Revenger's Tragedy*, and with the same disturbing note of intense eroticism to illuminate the horror. Raymond could not write thus to his wife; much less to his father. The War Committee cannot have known that conditions in the front line had deteriorated and come to *this*. On their rare visits, they were shown only the best trenches, the sprucest troops. And so, they finalized their plans for the rout of the Germans at the Battle of the Somme.

Lord Kitchener's death, when the ship that was taking him to a meeting with the Russians was blown up by a mine and sank, caused a great deal of consternation (not least to Margot Asquith, who heard the news midway through the christening of Raymond Asquith's baby son, and interrupted the service with her raucous whispers) but it did not make any real difference to the conduct of the war. Kitchener was perhaps even lucky, in a sense, to die as he did. He was the only outstanding military leader who could be said to have died 'in action', and he was, after all, sixty-six: three times the age of most of the

young men who died squalidly in trench warfare. Lloyd George succeeded him
at the War Office, and the cumbersome strategy of the war continued to take its
course: superb in detail (the trench maps, for example, are masterpieces of
cartography, constantly updated), brilliantly administered, but completely out
of touch with the facts of trench combat.

The main part in the attack on the Somme was to be played by the newly
formed 4th Army of more than half a million men, under General Sir Henry
Rawlinson: a man so invulnerable to self-questioning that before the battle he
issued a directive to the effect that 'All criticism by subordinates . . . of orders
received from superior authority will, in the end, recoil on the heads of the
critics.'[5] Since Rawlinson himself recognized no 'superior authority' except Haig,
this meant that he was, by his own instructions, infallible.

The men had rehearsed the battle for weeks, in stylized parodies of advance,
attack and capture that bore as much resemblance to the real thing as the model
trenches laid out for an admiring British public in the midst of leafy Hyde Park.
Most of the troops were untried; few had ever seen battle before; and they were
optimistic and sometimes even eager for the experience. Despite poor rations (a
loaf sometimes had to be shared among ten men and suffice as a day's food in the
trenches; though supplies of tea seldom failed, and the daily tot of rum was still
to be relied on) and heavy loads, the men were in surprisingly good heart as
rumours grew in the weeks before the 'big push'. One private recalled: 'I was
very pleased when I heard that my battalion was to be in the attack. I thought
this would be the last battle of the war, and I didn't want to miss it. I remember
writing to my mother, telling her I would be home for the August Bank
Holiday.'[6] His optimism was fully shared by General Rawlinson. Some brigade
commanders were even more sanguine: like the brigadier-general whose
instructions to the Newcastle Commercials were: 'You will be able to go over the
top with a walking stick, you will not need rifles. When you get to Thiépval you
will find the Germans all dead, not even a rat will have survived.'[7] And finally,
another brigade commander's Part Two Orders to the 1st London Rifle Brigade:
'Success is assured and casualties are expected to be ten per cent.'[8]

The reason for this confidence was the unprecedented artillery barrage that
was loosed upon the German trenches for a full seven days before the planned
attack. The sound of this bombardment could be heard in England: indeed, the
Prime Minister heard it in Downing Street.

Edward Wyndham Tennant, the eldest son of Lord Glenconner (Margot's
brother) and Pamela, whom Harry Cust had loved and lost, was one of the eager,
trusting junior officers taking part in the Battle of the Somme. In June 1916 he
had written a poem called 'The Mad Soldier'. Only thus, distanced by the
vernacular, could he allow his true feelings to be heard:

> I dropp'd here three weeks ago, yes – I know,
> And it's bitter cold at night, since the fight –
> I could tell you if I chose – no one knows
> Excep' me and four or five, what ain't alive.
> I can see them all asleep, three men deep,
> And they're nowhere near a fire – but our wire
> Has 'em fast as fast can be. Can't you see
> When the flare goes up? Ssh! boys; what's that noise?

Do you know what these rats eat? Body-meat!
After you've been down a week, an' your cheek
Gets as pale as life, and night seems as white
As the day, only the rats and their brats
Seem more hungry when the day's gone away –
An' they look as big as bulls, an' they pulls
Till you almost sort of shout – but the drought
What you hadn't felt before makes you sore.
And at times you even think of a drink . . .
There's a leg across my thighs – if my eyes
Weren't too sore, I'd like to see who it be,
Wonder if I'd know the bloke if I woke? –
Woke? By damn, I'm not asleep – there's a heap
Of us wond'ring why the hell we're not well . . .
Leastways I am – since I came it's the same
With the others – they don't know what *I* do,
Or they wouldn't gape and grin. – It's a sin
To say that Hell is hot – 'cause it's not:
Mind you, I know very well we're in hell. –
In a twisted hump we lie – heaping high,
Yes! an' higher every day. – Oh, I say,
This chap's heavy on my thighs – damn his eyes.[9]

This poem was written at Poperinghe, and sent to his mother, with an oblique appeal for her praise ('I believe I shall be quite angry if nobody likes my poems!'). Evidently she did like them, for soon afterwards he wrote, 'I was jubilant at getting your letter, and your praise.'[10] There is nothing to show that Lady Glenconner was able to comprehend the full horror contained in her son's evocation of madness and hell. His letters reverted to jokes and reassurances and nostalgic queries about Nanny and the family. He consoles himself by reading 'Non Nobis Domine', the poem Harry Cust had written to her over twenty years ago. The gulf between what those in the trenches could tell those who were not was as unbridgeable as ever.

At exactly 7.30 a.m. on 1 July 1916, the first wave of troops went over the top. For hundreds of yards they marched steadily into the line of German fire, mostly uphill and across rough ground, carrying 60 lb packs on their backs, falling wounded and dying, getting caught on the barbed wire, dying there, and being followed remorselessly by another and another wave of Gadarene soldiers. In the first hour thirty thousand infantrymen were killed or wounded. On the first day there were 57,470 British casualties, of whom 19,249 died. Of those, 993 were officers. This was almost the same number of deaths as the 22,000 in the whole $2\frac{1}{2}$ *years* of the Boer War. But then, only about one out of every eleven casualties died. On the first day of the Somme, only one in four of the officers who had gone 'over the top' were unhurt at the end of the day's fighting. For every yard of the 116-mile Western Front, there were two British casualties. The Germans lost one man for every seven British casualties. The British Army's losses on this single day easily exceeded the combined totals in the Crimean War, the Boer War and the Korean War.

When the Battle of the Somme ended, 140 days later, they were still four miles short of Bapaume. They had advanced, in all, six miles. The British suffered over four hundred thousand casualties. The total loss for all combatant armies was over one million, three hundred thousand men. The best of the British troops, officers as well as men, were the first to die on the Somme. The bravest, the most selfless, those most committed to their comrades and their country, ran most eagerly into the attack, and were consequently the first to be killed. Their loss was a blow which it seemed the country would never recover from and never forget; though realization of the full extent of the carnage was slow in coming. The British newspapers continued with their work of propaganda, minimizing the British casualties, exaggerating the German ones, and never giving their readers any inkling of the conditions of trench warfare. The strategy justifying the Somme was scarcely questioned by anyone. The fighting continued inter- mittently throughout July, August, and into early autumn, though never with the same senseless squandering of men's lives as on that first day.

Nobody who had seen it could have any illusions about the splendours of war again. Raymond Asquith wrote vitriolically: 'A blind God butts about the world with a pair of delicately malignant antennae to detect whatever is fit to live and an iron hoof to stamp it into the dust when found. . . . One's instinct that the world (as we know it) is governed by chance is almost shaken by the accumulat- ing evidence that it is the best which is always picked out for destruction.'[11] By now he could no longer even shield his beloved wife Katharine from the disgust which he felt. She too was clearly unable to hide her bitterness from him, for he wrote: 'I agree with you about the utter senselessness of war. . . . The suggestion that it elevates the character is hideous. Burglary, assassination and picking oakum would do as much for anyone.'[12] On 25 July he wrote to her:

> Do you know that today is the anniversary of our wedding? Nine years it is, as nearly as I can reckon. They seem very short and wonderfully pleasant as one looks back on them. You are sweeter and more lovely even than you were then, my Fawn, and I adore you a million times more and I am not sorry, not a bit. Give my love to Trim [short for Trimalchio: Raymond's nickname for his baby son, Julian].[13]

Although loyalty prevents him saying as much, Raymond Asquith must have brooded – as he sweltered in the trenches during the hot and dangerous summer of 1916 – upon the actions of the older generation who had brought him to this; the more so as his father was the Prime Minister who had declared war, and was still ultimately responsible for the running of it. To his wife he only said savagely, 'If Margot talks any more bosh to you about the inhumanity of her step-children you can stop her mouth by telling her that during my 10 months exile here the P.M. has never written me a line of any description. I don't see why he should. He has plenty of other things to do; and so have I. . . .'[14] To Lady Diana Manners he was more specific – as so often happened when he had something to say that would distress his painfully sensitive wife. Lady Diana had evidently written to him complaining that her mind was atrophying, and social pleasantries were becoming more and more of an effort. He replied:

> I know, no one better, the feeling of effort of which you speak. But our minds are not asleep because they do not wink and chatter all the time. Better a Lapland night than the dance of St Vitus. Think for one moment of those who find it no effort to talk. Their minds are almshouses where outworn notions

Arthur Balfour photographed outside the House of Commons at the turn of the century, just before he became Prime Minister, in the full flower of his political and personal influence as leader of the Conservative Party and the Souls.

Above: *Taplow Court on the Thames near Maidenhead. With its red brick and tidy lawns there is something curiously suburban about the Grenfell family house where Ettie entertained her many friends and admirers.*

Below: *A typical page from the Taplow Visitors' Book, with its clutter of celebrated signatures, amateur sketches, and the shadowy frown of a previous visitor (left) whose photograph has pressed upon the closed page for so long that its blurred image has been transferred to it.*

Above, left: *A snapshot from the Taplow Visitors' Book of Willy in 1909 standing beside a statuette of himself.*

Above, right: *By 1905 the Grenfell family was complete. Willy (now Lord Desborough) holds Imogen, born that year, on his lap, flanked by Julian and Monica; Ettie stands behind next to Billy; and the girlish figure sitting cross-legged in front is in fact Ivo.*

Right: *Archie Gordon, the charming and personable young man who loved Ettie and whose anxiety to please her she contrasted with her son Julian's obdurate nature.*

Opposite, above: *The young Lady Diana Manners, just into her teens, taken at about the time she first met and was dazzled by the young men of the Coterie.*

Opposite, below: *The same Lady Diana only a few years later, photographed in a state of daring undress by – she insists – her brother John.*

Above: *Lady Violet ('Letty') Manners in about 1910, just before her marriage to the Elchos' eldest son, Ego Charteris, and showing her distinctive profile. The exotic feathered hat was the height of fashion.*

Left: *Raymond Asquith photographed at about the time of his marriage, in his late twenties. He gave a copy of this picture to Ettie for her to paste into her Visitors' Book, as was the custom.*

Below: *Lady Granby's drawing of Katharine Horner, done in 1905 (two years before her marriage to Raymond Asquith) and emphasizing the huge dewy eyes that he said had enchanted him.*

Margot Asquith with her baby son Anthony. This studio portrait must have been taken in about 1903, when Margot was in her late thirties and had been married for nine years.

Venetia Stanley, the young woman whom Asquith loved, photographed in about 1914 when his obsession and her beauty were at their height. (Compare her dress and pearls with those of Lady Diana in the same year.)

H.H. Asquith, then Prime Minister, photographed just before the outbreak of the First World War. Despite his rather stolid appearance he was a man of strong sensual passions.

Below: Margot Asquith at about the same time, in her late forties, with her son Anthony. Although she knew of her husband's love for Venetia, her loyalty was unchanged and she was unforgiving towards anyone who criticized him.

Left: *Lord Kitchener, recalled from Egypt at the beginning of the war by public demand and created Earl Kitchener of Khartoum. By adding his pointing finger he made, said Margot, 'a lovely poster'.*

Below: *Lord Curzon in 1914. Widowed and denied high office, his face betrays the disappointment and grief of the last ten years.*

Opposite: *George Wyndham, still handsome, hair and moustache still worn in the style of the late Victorians, and only his eyes revealing something of the disillusionment in the last years of his life.*

Some of the young men who died . . . . Ego Charteris, killed in Egypt in 1916 . . . .

. . . . and his younger brother Yvo, killed when he was just nineteen years old.

Edward Wyndham Tennant ('Bim') survived a few months longer, but he too died on the Somme in September 1916.

Julian Grenfell, drawn here in peacetime by the Duchess of Rutland, died slowly from a head wound in May 1915.

Patrick Shaw Stewart, drawn by the Duchess of Rutland and looking more Rupert Brooke-ish than his red hair and pallid skin warranted in reality. He was loved by Ettie and was the shooting star of the Coterie – but he was killed on the last day of 1917.

Above: *Lady Diana Manners in 1914, when she was nearly twenty and already a dazzling beauty. In the next four years almost all the young men she loved were to be killed.*

Opposite, above: *Edward Horner, the brother of Katharine Asquith, was massively tall, handsome and debonair. It was widely rumoured that Lady Diana would have married him if he had survived the war . . . but he did not.*

Opposite, below: *Duff Cooper, whose post as a Foreign Office clerk kept him from the Front until 1918, which almost certainly accounts for his survival. After the war he married Lady Diana.*

Above: *Arthur Balfour
in old age – venerable,
distinguished,
statesmanlike.*

Right: *Margot Asquith
after the war. Her clothes
were still formidably
stylish, her wit was
sharper than ever; but
her happiness had gone.*

and wrinkled phrases and a host of dilapidated pensioners flaunt their threadbare fustian in the sun, and fight their burlesque battles with purblind eyes and blunted swords over the shadow of a shade of nothing. We do not hunt the carted hares of 30 years ago. We do not ask ourselves and one another and every poor devil we meet 'How do you define Imagination?', or 'What is the difference between talent and genius?', and score an easy triumph by anticipating the answer with some text-book formula, originally misconceived by George Wyndham in the early eighties at Glen, and almost certainly misquoted by Margot at the borrowed house of a Frankfort baronet, not because it was true or witty or even understood, but because it was a sacred obligation to respect whatever struck the late Sir Charles Tennant as a cut above what he had heard in the night school at Paisley where they taught him double-entry. . . . [15]

It is a swingeing indictment of that once-brilliant circle from a young man as brilliant as any of them had once been, but now grown callous, and a bleak insight into how their wit and vigour had degenerated to the point where it was just ritual mouthing of old jokes and stale squibs. The Souls refused to see that their attitudes to the world and to the war were now hopelessly inadequate, and had almost destroyed them. Their young heroes had turned to corpses, but in acknowledging the corpses they had to disavow the heroism; so they clung to the ashes of the heroism and glorified the decaying corpses. Raymond commented unsympathetically on this in a letter to Katharine. Ettie Desborough had spent much time in 1916 soliciting tributes to her dead sons from among their own generation, and also from her friends. These were later published at the end of her *Family Journal*, where they form more than seventy fulsome pages. The practice was not uncommon, but Raymond disliked it. The few of their sons who remained alive watched this process of self-deception with cold fury. Some of them could occasionally put it into words. Others, like 'Bim' Tennant, could not. Raymond was now almost forty, and knew himself to be more perceptive than his father had ever been. But Bim was still his mother's doting son, who would suppress almost anything that might cause her pain.

He wrote home every two or three days, long, nostalgic letters, full of childhood memories and nursery words. 'Do you remember when . . .?' was interspersed with dutiful enquiries after a tribe of Tennant and Wyndham relatives. His sweet nature and homesickness shine through their pages. He seldom mentioned what he was doing, unless to report an hour lying in a field bordered by poplars, or make jokes about the weather. His letters provided him with a fantasy of escape, and his mother – one must hope – with a rosy picture of her beloved son's life. 'They are going to do their best to finish the War this year, from all one hears. I pray we may,'[16] he wrote, with a touching faith in 'them' that was by now shared by few of his fellow soldiers. Finally, he was sent up to the front line at the beginning of September, in the third month of the Battle of the Somme. He sent a hurried line to reassure his mother: 'I hope that when you get this we shall have had our little show; and I shall still be all right. There is nothing to say except that I am in capital spirits, and thinking of you very much.'[17] Over the next week he saw so much of death that his own fears could not any longer be entirely suppressed. His letter ended: 'I am longing to see you. God grant it may be soon. I will write to you whenever I get the chance, but no-one knows what may happen in the next day or two. I pray I may be all right, but in any case "Where is Death's sting?" '[18] Just a year earlier, an exuberant boy had written: 'I wouldn't be anywhere but here for the world, darling Moth', I am on the high-road of my life!'[19] Now, a deeply shaken young man was writing: 'Thank Heaven I have come safely out of this battle after two days and two nights of it.'[20] He went on to describe the attack, briefly, minimizing his own part and his courage, and then ended; 'Darling Moth', I am so thankful to be alive; I suppose you have heard who are dead? Guy Baring, Raymond Asquith, Sloper Mackenzie, and many others. It is a terrible list. Poor Olive will be heart-broken – and so will Katharine. Death and decomposition strew the ground. . . . I must tell you of other things.'[21]

Bim Tennant and Raymond Asquith were brother officers in the Grenadier Guards. They must have fought, that day, within a few hundred yards of one another. Raymond was killed – it hardly needs to be spelled out – leading his men into the attack, that 15 September, advancing from Ginchy on Lesboeufs. The attack was hopeless, as all the officers must have been aware. Raymond was hit by a bullet in the chest. So as not to alarm his men, he lit a cigarette before being given morphia and carried to the dressing station. He died before he got there.

Lady Diana Manners, who had loved him with passion, said only 'I cannot write about Raymond.'[22] His wife Katharine was crushed in the darkness of a merciless grief. But she lived on; few people literally die of grief, especially when they have three small children. The rest of her life was spent chiefly in London and later at Mells, her family's home in Somerset, until her death in 1976. She did not re-marry.

Raymond Asquith is buried in the cemetery on Gommecourt Road, close to where he fell. On his tombstone is carved the regimental insignia of the Grenadier Guards, then his name, and below that the words:

> Small time, but in that small
> Most greatly lived
> This star of England.

Just four or five graves along lies Edward Wyndham Tennant. He died a week after Raymond, on 22 September. His last letter to his mother was written two days previously. He knew he was going to be killed. He knew she would read and re-read his final words, and so he phrased them carefully, weighing every sentence:

To-night we go up to the last trenches we were in, and tomorrow we go over the top. Our Brigade has suffered less than either of the other two Brigades in Friday's biff [15 September], so we shall be in the forefront of the battle. I am full of hope and trust, and pray that I may be worthy of my fighting ancestors. The one I know best is Sir Henry Wyndham. . . . We shall probably attack over about 1200 yards, but we shall have such artillery support as will properly smash the Boche line we are going for. And even (which is unlikely) if the artillery doesn't come up to our hopes the spirit of the Brigade of Guards will carry all resistance before it. The pride of being in such a great regiment! The thought that all the old men, 'late Grenadier Guards', who sit in the London Clubs, are thinking and hoping about what we are doing here! I have never been prouder of anything, except your love for me, than I am of being a Grenadier. Today is a great day for me. That line of Harry's rings through my mind, '*High heart, high speech, high deeds, 'mid honouring eyes.*' I went to a service on the side of a hill this morning, and took the Holy Communion afterwards, which always seems to help one along, doesn't it? I slept like a top last night, and dreamed that someone I know very well (but I can't remember who it was) came to me and told me how much I had grown. Three or four of my brother-officers read my poems yesterday, and they all liked them very much which pleased me enormously. I feel rather like saying 'If it be possible let this cup pass from me,' but the triumphant finish 'nevertheless not what I will but what Thou willest,' steels my heart and sends me into this battle with a heart of triple bronze.

I always carry four photies of you when we go into action, one is in my pocket-book, two in that little leather book, and one round my neck, and I have kept my little medal of the Blessed Virgin. Your love for me and my love for you, have made my whole life one of the happiest there has ever been; Brutus' farewell to Cassius sounds in my heart: 'If not farewell; and if we meet again, we shall smile.' Now all my blessings go with you, and with all we love. God bless you, and give you peace.

Eternal Love,
from Bim.[23]

Edward Wyndham Tennant held fast to all the old icons of his class – family tradition, religious faith, pride in his regiment: even the old men sitting in the London clubs; Shakespeare's *Henry V*, and the Bible, and the photographs of his mother – and they all betrayed him in the end. Raymond Asquith had discarded most of them, caring only for the love of his wife and friends and yearning to be with them; and that hope, too, was disappointed. The Battle of the Somme ended a month later. But the men in the trenches no longer believed the war would ever end.

Of the Battle of the Somme Oliver Lyttelton later wrote:

The 15th was the most wonderful day of my life. I drank every emotion to the dregs and I was drunk. It was superbly exhilarating. Our casualties have been frightful but that was a matter for the next day – that day we had joy in battle and felt the passions of hate and fear and grief and anger and pain and fatigue – it can be a passion to wish to sleep – and gratitude and prayer and peace.[24]

His survival was indeed extraordinary. By all the odds he should have been dead. Every statistical indicator was against him. A junior officer, in a conspicuous regiment, who had been in the trenches since February 1915 . . . yet Oliver Lyttelton lived through the Germans' first gas attack at Ypres, the Battles of Neuve Chapelle and Loos as well as the Somme, and in the course of all these experiences hardly ever failed to write a weekly letter to his mother. She kept them all. They are edgy, ebullient, and occasionally critical: 'Do we not all know that to be successful the soldier must carry: one rifle, one bayonet, one entrenching tool, 170 rounds of ammunition, six bombs, one pair of wire cutters, two days' rations, six sandbags, one coil of French wire, five pickets, one roman candle, one red parasol and a toothpick? Weight 840 lbs.'[25] The final weight is an exaggeration, of course: but it was true that soldiers were supposed to cross No Man's Land and go into the attack carrying equipment that weighed at least 60 lb. Civilians like H. G. Wells favoured the addition of heavy tin helmets (which were introduced) and a large body shield (which was not).

The ordinary soldiers in the trenches grumbled too, though rarely in letters home, but they knew they would not be listened to. Oliver Lyttelton, and for that matter Raymond Asquith, must have hoped that somehow their complaints would filter back to their parents and be translated into action. No one listened, and for a further two years nothing happened to put an end to the colossal killing. The weight of public opinion was against any breath of criticism, no matter how well-founded. By midway through the war the propaganda machine was working full blast. The Germans were 'degenerate Huns' who were either raping and torturing innocent civilians, or on the verge of turning tail and fleeing from our clean-limbed lads at the Front. All disbelief was suspended in the name of patriotism.

The Souls had always set themselves a little apart from – and *above* – the rest of their class, the ruling class. They claimed keener intellect, better judgment, greater social audacity, a defiance of conventions imposed by others. They prided themselves on a certain disengagement from their kind. In their early days, when they still formed a distinct and cohesive group, they were even regarded as a sort of fifth column within the aristocracy. Twenty or thirty years later, some of them still claimed the privilege of difference. Margot, with her abrasive candour; Ettie, with her devoted young men, did not willingly subject themselves to the petty rules of the establishment.

Thus it was that, when the war came, the Souls were uniquely placed to use that independence. They had accumulated power and influence. One of them – Asquith – was Prime Minister. Another – Balfour – had been a member of the War Council since 1914, and both he and Curzon became members of the coalition cabinet in 1915. At last they had the opportunity to use their prestige to curtail what was plainly a military stalemate, and devise an acceptable peace formula. Given that trio inside the cabinet, and the weight of support they might have mustered outside it, the Souls could have justified their privileged lives by proving that privilege can be put to good use. They did not.

They were fragmented as a group, ossified by eminence, and tired by the onset of old age. To question the strategy and conduct of the war was tantamount to treason. Some brave and outspoken individuals did it nonetheless, but not Asquith, nor Balfour, nor Curzon, nor any of their old playmates. They renounced their former superiority to stand foursquare behind the generals whose pig-headedness was killing their sons and nephews, and the sons of their friends, and the young men who would have inherited their privileges. Politicians and High Command alike clung to the belief that if they hurled their infantry against the Germans' strongest positions for long enough, the Germans must eventually surrender. Hundreds of thousands of lives were lost so that old men need not lose face. Young men died, and their elders were stoically philosophical: 'To live greatly and die soon is a lot which all of us must admire and some of us must envy; indeed to my thinking it cannot be bettered.'[26] wrote Arthur Balfour, himself aged sixty-seven, to Ettie, on hearing of the death of Julian. Rudyard Kipling wrote more bitterly after the death of his only son,

> If any question why we died
> Tell them, because our fathers lied.[27]

But he was unusual.

By 1916 the homogeneity of the British ruling class was being broken up by the war. A whole generation of young men and women began, for the first time, to share experiences and beliefs that were totally unlike anything their parents had lived through or considered. The junior officers often felt closer to their men in the trenches than to their own caste back home. Finding themselves, for the first time in their lives, the anonymous victims of a chain of command that cared little for them *en masse*, and only rarely saw them as individuals; that neither consulted nor listened; they began to understand something of the deep social resentment felt by men below them in the hierarchy: the hitherto anonymous working class. These undercurrents were rarely articulated on either side, and many who thought like this died before they could act upon their new perceptions. Others reverted, in peacetime or middle age, to the attitudes of their parents. But the broad social front presented by the upper classes was no longer unanimous.

The war did not only kill people. It also changed them. Above all, it changed the British aristocracy forever.

– 12 –
Quietus

1914–1918

Before 1914, members of the aristocracy were of more or less ancient lineage and combined landed wealth with political influence and local patronage. This gave them a predictable set of values and certain recognized obligations: described (often euphemistically) as 'a duty to serve'. They certainly believed they had a right to be served.

Their families had intermarried so closely and for so long, within their own charmed circle of eligible people, that *Debrett's Peerage* was a complicated web of cousinage and blood lines. They all knew one another. Along with these characteristics went a number of others less easily identified, and often the product of wishful thinking. Certain tribal attitudes and pastimes, it is true, were common to all the landed aristocracy. Less infallibly, they prided themselves upon a certain kind of looks: elongated in feature and limb, the sort of looks that are thought to go with 'breeding' and are called 'patrician'. Such fine-boned elegance as Lord Ribblesdale (the archetypal patrician) possessed was in fact as rare among the upper classes as any other: why, if not, the tribes of maiden aunts, so plain as to be unmarriageable despite their good connections?

After 1918 many of the distinguishing characteristics of the aristocracy changed forever. The old substructure of land and estates began to be divided up and sold off even more drastically than in the agricultural depression of the 1890s. The Duke of Rutland sold about half his Belvoir Estate in 1920, and received £1½ million for 28,000 acres. Many titles became extinct for lack of an heir (as had the Cowper earldom); or passed to an heir so remote that the link of blood was all but broken. Three years after Harry Cust's death, his uncle the 3rd Earl Brownlow died too. The earldom became extinct. The contents of Ashridge were dispersed, though much of the best furniture was moved to Belton for safe keeping. (In 1983 Belton itself had to be broken up to meet death duties and in 1984 its contents were sold by Christie's in a three-day auction.)

The effortless luxury provided by a hierarchy of indoor and outdoor servants, the carefully observed degrees of local and noble relationships, the leisure and security and amiability and affluence . . . all had begun imperceptibly to flow from the upper globe of the social hourglass into the lower globe and 1914 was the turning point. At the time no one was aware that a turning point had been reached, least of all those who were engrossed in the daily conduct of the war. For the Prime Minister, Asquith, life continued much as before and his obsession with Venetia Stanley still dominated his thoughts. He wrote to her in cabinet meetings, during sittings of the House, in his study, in his bedroom, in cars and on trains. One, two, sometimes three letters a day were urgently entrusted to messenger boys and postmen, while in return he begged for an hour-by-hour account of how her time was spent.

A private source suggests that Asquith had not the temperament for unconsummated love – certainly not for platonic love. He was too full-blooded to have been a Balfour, palely loitering; especially as Margot became disinclined for sex after twenty years of marriage. 'As women soon found out, to be left alone with him was to invite immediate and bold approaches, admittedly playful to begin with, for hand-holding, touching, fondling and kissing. He was, simply, an importunate lecher . . . if he found no resistance to his advances – or even active encouragement – he would take the relationship to its fullest conclusion.'[1] One cannot know for certain whether Venetia offered resistance or encouragement to the Prime Minister's advances; or, if the latter, how far she permitted his caresses to go. One can only recall that men in positions of power and influence are often sexually attractive; and Asquith in his sixties was still a handsome, virile-looking man. Venetia was twenty-eight when she married, and Edwin Montagu was certainly not her first lover. In the highly charged atmosphere of the war years, virginity was no longer a *sine qua non*. The rest is surmise.

The Prime Minister was not alone in this craving for emotional escape, away from the world of men and fighting and strategic planning and casualty lists. Many war leaders found a woman to idolize, as an escape when the grimness of reality all but overwhelmed them. Lloyd George, at this same time, was immersed in his secret love for Frances Stevenson, the secretary who later became his second wife; while over in France the diminutive General Sir John French was writing passionate love letters to Mrs Winifred Bennett. 'Like all our returned warriors [Sir John French] looks younger than when he went out, and in the best of condition'[2] wrote Asquith. In his midnight letter to Venetia on New Year's Eve, 1914, he continued, with blinkered perception: 'This year [1914] has been in the fullest sense what the Ancients used to call "annus mirabilis" . . . to you and me . . . it has been a succession of marvellous experiences. . . . You have sustained and enriched every day of my life.'[3] A fortnight later he demonstrated yet again her primary position in his world:

> When I got your letter . . . I at once postponed my interview with the King until noon, that we might have the hour 10.30–11.30 together. But you had already made your appointment with Violet and I can see that was difficult to change. . . . I wanted so much at the earliest opportunity and while the impressions were still fresh, to talk to you, & get your opinions about today's War Council.[4]

Venetia Stanley had become essential to him. Lady Diana Cooper – another of 'the Prime Minister's little harem', as Margot used to describe the younger women whom he liked to see around himself in the earlier, happier days before Venetia – believes that their relationship must have included some sexual contact.[5] The surviving letters do not provide evidence of this; but all Venetia's letters have disappeared, and we know not how many of Asquith's have gone as well. It is possible that at some stage they were selected, that any 'incriminating' letters were destroyed, and only the ambiguous ones remain.

Venetia certainly fulfilled a rôle as sounding board and critic that neither the Prime Minister's wife nor, apparently, any of his old friends were suited for. Her power over Asquith, and thus indirectly over the conduct of the war, is awesome; the responsibility she carried must have been a burden to her. Asquith wrote to her:

> You know how I value your judgement: I put it *quite first* among women, and there are only 2 or 3 men to my mind in the same class. And you have now shared my utmost confidence for so long and with such unsurpassable loyalty that I can speak to you really *more freely* about the most important things than I can to any other human being. It is a wonderful & I believe a unique relationship. Of course now that you are so hustled for time you can't write much about these things, tho' I hope you will give your view whenever you can. But it is a real necessity to me to see you, especially just now when things are trembling in the balance.[6]

The anxiety that runs between the lines of this, and many, letters, was justified. Flattering as it undoubtedly was to be the repository of the War Council's secrets, Venetia Stanley was now past her girlish years and, like her friend Lady Diana, she observed that the young men of her acquaintance were either marrying or dying. Beautiful, well-connected and intelligent she knew herself to be, but she did not yet live in an age when a woman might make a respected position in the world without the security of a husband.

At the beginning of 1915 a former suitor returned to court her. Ironically, he was the Prime Minister's private secretary, Edwin Montagu. He possessed almost every advantage. He was immensely rich; devoted to Venetia; moved in the highest circles of London society; and was intelligent and cultivated like herself. He was never likely to have to enlist; and, after all, if she did not marry him, who was there? He offered the prospect of escape from the Prime Minister's importunities, and perhaps also from the harshness and discomforts of nursing; and once the war was over she would have an assured position in society. Venetia succumbed. She must have known she did not love him, but he loved her, and she had grown used to one-sided worship. By the end of April 1915 she had agreed to become his wife. She knew the blow to Asquith would be overwhelming.

The relevance of this young woman's tangled and selfish emotions is that they involved the Prime Minister at a crucial point in the Great War and must have impaired his capacity to handle the great responsibilities entrusted to him. Normally balanced, imperturbable, objective, Asquith became emotionally distracted for several weeks, if not months. His wife Margot was now so unstable herself that he could derive little comfort from her, though her loyalty and discretion remained absolute, and she would pretend pitifully to friends that, of course, her husband showed her all Venetia's letters. At the moment of greatest strain Margot wrote a remarkable letter to Edwin Montagu. Her honesty shines through its disguised appeal:

> I had thought him [i.e. Asquith] just a little rough in answer when I asked him

if he was tired or cold Monday evening – this was all – but I was terribly out of spirits & tho' to him I may be cocky, snobby, anything you like – I am *fundamentally* humble & without any form of vanity (I know as well as Blanche that tho' I'm well made & have got an alert expression I'm plain, severe, crisp & candid). I have as you know often wondered if Venetia hadn't ousted me faintly – not very much – but enough to wound bewilder & humiliate me – (I have been chaffed about her more than once).[7]

The letter was evidently designed to persuade Edwin that *she* was the Prime Minister's first concern, and so he could safely marry Venetia. Unfortunately, she was wrong: at least for the time being.

It cannot have been coincidence that while this was taking place behind the scenes, Asquith's government was increasingly losing the confidence of Parliament. There were already complaints that the progress of the war was being hampered by a shortage of shells and ammunition. Kitchener even made the ludicrous suggestion that, in between attacks, British troops should go into No Man's Land and retrieve unexploded shells. On the basis of an inconclusive assurance from Sir John French, Asquith told the House of Commons and the country that the supply of shells was adequate. It was a lie. Everyone at the Front knew it to be a lie; and so did many of his parliamentary colleagues. Its effects were so damaging that they set in motion the revolt whereby Asquith was forced to surrender his party's control of the war.

On Tuesday 11 May 1915, Asquith wrote Venetia what was to be almost the last of the 560 letters he sent her between January 1912 and May 1915. It is entirely typical of most of the others, in its combination of fulsome concern for her and a gossipy, minute account of his own doings:

I have just come back from dining with Revelstoke at Carlton House Terrace – the Bencks [Count & Countess Benckendorff, the Russian Ambassador and his wife], E. Grey, Lady Desborough & Mrs Leo Rothschild. Quite 'nice' & peacable, & a little mild Bridge. I am not sure that you know him – John Baring? He has been now, to my knowledge, for over 20 years more or less in love with Ettie: as has been (for about the same space of time) Evan Charteris. The years have rattled by, & every kind of water has passed under the bridge: but *plus ça change, plus c'est la même chose* – an almost unique instance of *double* constancy.[8]

The following day he learnt of Venetia's imminent marriage. He sent her a cry of anguish – his last:

Most Loved –
As you know well, *this* breaks my heart.
I couldn't bear to come and see you.
I can only pray God to bless you – and help me.
Yours.[9]

Five days later, on Monday 17 May, it was agreed between Asquith, Lloyd George and Bonar Law that the government should be reconstructed as a coalition for the remainder of the war. Without Venetia's support, and the safety valve of his confidential letters to her, the Prime Minister could not go on.

On 26 July Venetia and Edwin Montagu were married. Their future life together was not to prove entirely happy; but, for the time being, the comfort and hospitality of their house in Queen Anne's Gate provided an ideal refuge for members of the Coterie. Edwin was a generous host who loved to surround himself with people whose own sparkle would make up for his lack of it. From mid-1916 onwards, his home became the accepted meeting place for men on leave from the Front, and they all – the younger generation of Asquiths, Charterises, Tennants and Manners – made it their focal point, in the increasingly rare hours of escape from the war.

The loss of the woman he loved was not, of course, the only reason why Asquith's government fell. Lord Northcliffe's propaganda sheets had whipped up anti-German feeling to unprecedented heights, while at the same time implying that Asquith and his colleagues were less than resolute in their conduct of the war. Sir John French began clandestinely to feed his complaints about Asquith to the daily newspapers, and a number of well-informed and highly critical articles appeared in *The Times, The Morning Post*, and *The Observer*. This last was the sin that Margot could not forgive. French admitted later, in his war memoirs, that he had resolved to bring about Asquith's fall: 'I determined on taking the most drastic measures to destroy the apathy of a Government which had brought the Empire to the brink of disaster.'[10] This, together with Northcliffe's determination to see Lloyd George in charge of the government, meant that forces were ranged against Asquith which at his best he could hardly have withstood. At his worst and most distraught, he could not even summon the energy to try.

His government was doomed when, after Kitchener's death in June, in the sinking of the *Hampshire*, he had replaced him as Secretary of State for War and leader of the War Council with the aggressive, ambitious and ruthless Lloyd George, eleven years younger than the premier. The damaging comparison between the two men could not be ignored. Asquith was supplanted because he lost the confidence of his colleagues. Had he retained it, no press campaign could have shifted him: and no press baron would have tried. Lloyd George's vigour contrasted all too favourably with Asquith's lethargy and depression – a depression accentuated when he heard the news of Raymond's death in mid-September. 'My husband', wrote Margot in the bellicose imagery of the time, 'fell on the battlefield surrounded by civilians and soldiers whom he had fought for, and saved, some of whom owed to him not only their reputations and careers, but their very existence. Only a handful of faithful men remained by his side to see whether he was killed or wounded, and on the 7th December Mr Lloyd George became Prime Minister.'[11] Asquith had been Prime Minister for more than eight and a half years.

To Asquith's disappointment and Margot's fury, Balfour became Foreign Secretary. Curzon, who had acted less than straightforwardly during the crisis by allowing Asquith to believe that he would never consent to serve under Lloyd George, then went on to do precisely that. He was one of the five members of a new, pared-down war cabinet, and President of the Air Board. (He too incurred Margot's venom. Nine years later he invited her to dinner, that the two old friends might be reconciled; but he died on the very day they were due to meet.)

Balfour was ill in the crisis week, and had to be consulted on his sickbed. He was nearly 70, and the lifelong affectation of languor, that had long concealed his secret pleasure in taking the centre of the stage, was becoming genuine at last. Nevertheless, the position of Foreign Secretary was not one he could resist.

Margot launched a series of hysterical letters and wild attacks, so that, when Balfour was forced to meet her, he reported afterwards that she seemed quite mad. The long association of the Souls was ending in bitterness and the particular pain of rejection by those who have been friends since the glorious days of youth.

Six days after Lloyd George became Prime Minister, Germany made the first formal approach towards peace. It consisted of little more than a veiled attempt to elicit the minimum terms on which the Allies would consider ending hostilities; but the fact that any approach at all was made is proof that the Germans had realized, like the British and French, that they were locked in a stalemate that was costing lives and making no progress. But the Allies insisted that Germany must concede much of her territory, and accept terms which would ensure that military aggression by the Central Powers (that is, Germany and her allies) would be impossible for many decades to come. These intransigent demands were far too severe, considering how finely balanced were the relative strategic positions of the combatants; and the German peace feelers were withdrawn. Britain would settle for nothing short of a total and humiliating defeat; Germany did not yet believe that so decisive a victory had been achieved. And so the war dragged on for nearly two more years.

Responsibility for the success or failure of the British response to the next peace initiative rested with Balfour more than any other member of Lloyd George's cabinet. In April 1917 he crossed the Atlantic to meet President Wilson at first hand, to enlist the whole-hearted support of the American public, and to discuss the options that lay ahead of the Allies. He spent a month there, and his celebrated charm dazzled the Americans. He was invited to address Congress and given a reception by the Senate, and the visit culminated in a benefit performance for the British Red Cross at Carnegie Hall. It was a typically American occasion, and Balfour rose to it. An American friend said in a letter to A.J.B.'s family at Whittingehame:

We had worked ourselves – the six thousand of us – to a pitch of enthusiasm which knew no bounds. Then there was a momentary hush, and all eyes turned to the hitherto unoccupied box; then there came shouts from all over the house, repeated over and over again: 'Balfour!'. . . . We just stood up and roared at him, and roared and cheered again and again. And then the orchestra struck up Rule Britannia, and we sang it with all our might, and defiantly. . . .

And bye and bye, when Choate waved his hand for silence, Balfour spoke to us, as we stood stock still, hardly breathing, – spoke as friend to friends. . . . We all of us, every one, came away satisfied and content in mind and heart, resolved, determined more absolutely than ever that 'this world must be made safer for Democracy'.[12]

He had scored a stupendous success: but it was no more than he needed. By the middle of 1917 Britain's situation was becoming desperate. Germany's submarines were sinking Allied ships at a rate that was running out of control, causing losses to merchant ships and supplies that the country could not afford. The food shortage was acute: bread in short supply; flour almost unobtainable. Meanwhile the economic situation was equally critical. The practical financial support of the United States was urgently needed. Balfour's telegram to a trusted American friend in Washington was little short of panicky:

> We seem on the verge of a financial disaster that would be worse than defeat in the field. If we cannot keep up exchange, neither we nor our Allies can pay our dollar debts. . . . A consequence which would be of incalculable gravity may be upon us on Monday next if nothing effective is done in the meantime. You know I am not an alarmist, but this is really serious.[13]

Something effective *was* done. America undertook to lend Britain $185 million a month, and $135 million within the week. Balfour's uncharacteristic flirtation with democracy at Carnegie Hall had served its purpose.

H. G. Wells was a perceptive critic of Balfour at this stage in his career, when his lifelong tepidness had been cooled still further by the onset of old age:

> Balfour might perhaps have been a very great man indeed if his passions had been hotter and his affections more vivid. The lassitude of these fine types, their fastidiousness in the presence of strong appeals, leave them at last a prey to the weak gratifications of vanity and a gentle impulse to pose. . . . As the war went on his poses became more and more self-protective.
>
> Amidst the clamour and riot of the war he faded away from power to eminence.[14]

Wells was proof against the power of the Balfour charm and the Balfour myth. In a brilliant juxtaposition, he realized that:

> while Lenin was using Marxism to make things happen because he was under the urgency of change, Balfour was using Christianity and Christian organisation, to resist changes that, whatever else they did, were bound to disturb the spacious pleasantness of his life. . . . If in 1912 I could call Balfour 'beyond question great', it seems almost my duty here to put that flash of enthusiasm in its proper proportion to what I think of the Russian. So let me say in all deliberation that when I weigh the two against each other it is not even a question of swaying scale-pans; Balfour flies up and kicks the beam.[15]

Herein lies the crux of the matter. Balfour was by nature, upbringing and self-interest a Conservative, the very opposite of an innovator; and he had been a poseur for so long that, together with many other Souls, they had all become like a group of children playing Statues: frozen in attitudes.

One exception to the prevailing support for the establishment and the status quo was a momentous breakthrough, and one with which Balfour's name would forever be associated. Ironically, in view of the anti-Semitism almost universal at this time among the British upper classes, it was to prove one of the cornerstones for the future state of Israel. The Balfour Declaration, signed by Balfour and addressed to Lord Rothschild in November 1917, affirmed the cabinet's sympathy with Zionist aspirations and declared itself to be in favour of establishing 'a national home for the Jewish people' in Palestine.

The most scathing indictment of his long career came from an old friend, now enemy, George Curzon. Curzon would never forget how Balfour had reneged on him during the crucial battle with Kitchener in India; and it must have caused him melancholy satisfaction when Kitchener's high-handed intransigence during the war proved Curzon to have been right about his old adversary. Towards the end of his life Curzon was embittered by grief, pain from his chronic back trouble, and the consciousness of being ill used. Much of his resentment was lanced in a long memorandum he wrote (for posthumous publication) in 1922 about Balfour, and though evidently biased, it contains much that is true:

> I regard him as the worst and most dangerous of the British Foreign Ministers with whom I have been brought into contact in my public life. His charm of manner, his extraordinary intellectual distinction, his seeming indifference to petty matters, his power of dialectic, his long and honourable career of public service, blinded all but those who knew from the inside to the lamentable ignorance, indifference and levity of his régime. He never studied his papers; he never knew the facts; at the Cabinet he had seldom read the morning's F.O. telegrams; he never got up a case; he never looked ahead. . . .
>
> The truth is that Balfour with his scintillating intellectual exterior had no depth of feeling, no profound convictions, and strange to say (in spite of his fascination of manner) no real affection.[16]

'No real affection': would Mary Wemyss, who as Mary Wyndham and Mary Charteris and Mary Elcho had loved him for so long, have agreed with that? It takes a remarkable woman to inspire an *amitié amoureuse* that lasts a lifetime; and perhaps a lack of virility in a man to sustain it without ever seriously distressing her husband or threatening her marriage. Yet, perhaps not. As a young bachelor, Balfour could have married Mary, but the death of his first love, May Lyttelton, was still too recent for him to feel free to propose marriage to someone else without a sense of disloyalty. Being supplanted as her suitor by Hugo Elcho was perhaps the ideal solution for all three of them. Their *ménage à trois* lasted for the greater part of half a century. It enabled Hugo to indulge guiltlessly in his physical infidelities; it gave Mary an emotional sustenance that her husband could not have supplied; and it provided Balfour with a lifelong alibi against prospective wives. In 1912 she wrote to him, 'although you have only loved me a little yet I must admit you have loved me long.'[17]

Curzon, for all his enamelled demeanour, was a man of physical passions. Platonic relationships were not to his liking, and nor was chastity, although he was faithful to Mary, his wife, throughout their marriage. After her death in 1906 he must have been emotionally as well as sexually lonely. It was two full years before he entered into another relationship. Astonishingly, the woman he chose as his mistress for the next eight years was the romantic novelist, Elinor Glyn. She had slanting green eyes and copper-coloured hair and nobody could have doubted her allure for a moment; but as a partner for the formal, intimidating Lord Curzon she must have seemed the least likely choice.

In fact she consoled him well, if clandestinely – for she was still married. Her temperament resembled that of her own heroines. She was fiery, passionate and unpredictable, a *femme fatale* and a submissive handmaiden by turns. Above all, she worshipped Curzon. Possessed of greater intelligence than her novels would suggest; an independent streak which was expressed in her love of travel (she was a *succès fou* at the Russian Imperial Court); and powerful erotic attraction; she proved the perfect mistress for Curzon. He invited her to stay with him and his three daughters at Crag Hall in Derbyshire, and she also helped him with the restoration of Montacute House in Somerset, which he rented in 1914 because he could not resist this poetic and fantastic Elizabethan house. In 1915 Elinor's husband, Clayton Glyn, who had been a gambler and an alcoholic for years, finally died. She must have hoped that Curzon would now marry her; but Curzon did not in the end prove to be the stock romantic hero, prepared to set the world's opinion at naught for the sake of true love.

On 10 December 1916 he joined Lloyd George's war cabinet, and all his hopes of high office were revived. On 11 December, without a word of warning from Curzon to Elinor, *The Times* carried the announcement of his engagement to a wealthy and beautiful American widow, Mrs Alfred Duggan. Here was a consort who could fittingly stand beside a future Foreign Secretary; even, perhaps, a Prime Minister. Curzon's callous abandonment of Elinor Glyn is one of the most discreditable episodes in his life. He tried to obliterate her name from his visitors' books (though here and there he overlooked the modest initials E.G.) and he never communicated with her again. In the course of their relationship he had written her (she said) nearly five hundred letters. Elinor burnt every one.

His second marriage was not to repeat the idyllic pattern of the first. 'Gracie' Curzon was, for all her beauty, charm, and gifts as a hostess, a spoilt and selfish woman. Curzon still longed for a son and heir, but no children were born to them, and Gracie, who was thirty-nine at the time of their marriage, may have been secretly relieved. Within three years, her infatuation with 'Scatters' Wilson was already common knowledge, and must have wounded Curzon's pride intolerably. 'Scatters' flirted with every pretty woman he met, and was described by Cynthia Asquith as 'a funny ebullient bounder, with his blue eyes and hoarse whisper'.[18]

George Curzon's father lived to extreme old age, and did not die until 1916, when his son at last inherited Kedleston. He spent much of the rest of his life restoring its cold, crumbling splendour, and longed for Gracie to share the task with him (as Elinor had so willingly done at Montacute). In 1921 he wrote to her, 'All ask for Gracie and want to see the beautiful lady. One day you will take up your duties as chatelaine of this place. . . . The old tradition still survives in this untarnished spot, and the people are single-minded and respectful.'[19] It was as close as he could get to pleading. She was unmoved: 'Kedleston, I would so much rather not go at all – there is nothing for me to do there – after all, one's home is where one's heart is.'[20] She could not have said more plainly that her heart was not with him.

Curzon's old age was poignantly unlike his glorious youth. Then, he had been the darling of the Tennant sisters, the adventurous hero of the Souls, the cynosure of London society. Rapid, brilliant, energetic, sought after; inwardly planning to marry Mary Leiter, outwardly flirting with every marriageable young woman. His life was the fullest and most perfectly balanced of any of the Souls. His old age was bedevilled by disappointment, loneliness, pain and the hurtful absence of those who had once been his dearest friends. Even the premiership finally eluded him, going instead to a man he knew to be his inferior: Stanley Baldwin. His belated earldom – in addition to the marquessate he inherited – turned to dust, for he had no son to whom he could pass it on. The only consolation this gave him was the thought that he also had no son to die in the war.

For meanwhile, of course, the deaths continued. The war went on. During the winter of 1916–17 the two sides sat at an impasse, through months of cold and weariness, killing each other from time to time but never achieving any real advance. 'Winter Warfare' was written after the war by a man who, aged just 18, had fought on the Western Front: Edgell Rickword.

> Colonel Cold strode up the Line
>   (tabs of rime and spurs of ice);
> stiffened all that met his glare:
>   horses, men and lice.
>
> Visited a forward post,
>   left them burning, ear to foot;
> fingers stuck to biting steel,
>   toes to frozen boot.
>
> Stalked on into No Man's Land,
>   turned the wire to fleecy wool,
> iron stakes to sugar sticks
>   snapping at a pull.
>
> Those who watched with hoary eyes
>   saw two figures gleaming there;
> Hauptmann Kälte, Colonel Cold,
>   gaunt in the grey air.
>
> Stiffly, tinkling spurs they moved,
>   glassy-eyed, with glinting heel
> stabbing those who lingered there
>   torn by screaming steel.[21]

Wilfred Owen arrived at the Western Front in the winter of 1917, and recorded in horror-struck letters his first impressions:

> It is pock-marked like a body of foulest disease, and its odour is the breath of cancer. I have not seen any dead. I have done worse. In the dank air I have *perceived* it, and in the darkness, *felt*. No Man's Land under snow is like the face of the moon, chaotic, crater-ridden, uninhabitable, awful, the abode of madness. . . . The people of England needn't hope. They must agitate. But they are not yet agitated even. Let them imagine 50 strong men trembling as with ague for 50 hours![22]

The politicians at home in warm, safe England (where, however terrifying these may have been, there were only 5,611 civilian deaths resulting from enemy air raids throughout the four years of the war) bickered and jostled for position and calculated the precise degree of humiliation that could be exacted from Germany. Meanwhile the young men in cold and cratered France fought and froze and died. The entry of the United States into the war on 6 April 1917 had the effect of ensuring that it would be more prolonged, for they injected fresh supplies of money and materials together with yet another brand of idealism – President Wilson's – that would sacrifice more young men in the cause of a more durable peace eventually. Furthermore the French were now under the command of a new Commander-in-Chief, and one who was alleged to have the secret formula for success in beating the Germans. His name was General Robert Nivelle. He was sixty-one but still handsome, energetic, glib, confident – and his appointment spelled certain death for thousands more. He promised miracles, but what he delivered was the Battle of Arras, in April 1917. It resulted in a quarter of a million casualties, 150,000 of them British. It was followed by the Battle of the Aisne, which Nivelle had assured the French would enable them to advance six miles. They moved 600 yards. At last the French troops had had enough. The French Army mutinied: fifty-four divisions refused to obey orders, and thousands of men deserted. Mass court martials restored order, and fifty-five men were shot for desertion *pour encourager les autres*.

The summer of 1917 was the Allies' lowest point in the war. Haig was still the British Commander-in-Chief, still convinced that the next offensive would be the one to bring victory. What he had in mind was the Third Battle of Ypres, otherwise known as Passchendaele. The groundswell for peace which was taking hold in the workshops and factories and front parlours of ordinary people all over Europe was ignored. It was largely a socialist groundswell, and so of course it was of no significance to the men in power. Passchendaele would answer all those faint-hearted, unpatriotic doubters. Haig was convinced that an all-out assault in Flanders was his last chance to win the war before the American reinforcements arrived to steal his thunder. The war cabinet, however, had its doubts: and Lloyd George in particular. On 16 July 1917 Haig was summoned from France to explain his strategy, his reasons, and his expectations of success, in person to the war cabinet. But at this late stage, barely two weeks before the offensive was due to be launched, Haig would brook no interference; and Lloyd George lacked the certainty or the decisiveness – despite his grave misgivings – to overrule him.

When the attack was duly launched on 31 July 1917 the Germans were well forewarned and well prepared, with a million men securely installed in the Flanders plain, many of them in solid concrete defences known as 'pillboxes' that were proof against the most courageous attack. What no one could have anticipated was that the August of 1917 was to be one of the wettest ever known, with rainfall at double the average level. The low-lying ground quickly became a swamp of mud and clay, churned up by the boots of the men and impeding the movement of both men and equipment. It was like fighting in slow motion, or in the agonizing lethargy of a nightmare. Every effort was doubled and redoubled by the weight and suction of the mud.

Haig saw no need to alter his plans, and was enraged by the growing talk of peace: the response of ordinary people in England and elsewhere to horrors which not even the propaganda machine could keep from them. In a personal letter to Robertson he stated his opinion revealingly:

> In this Army we are convinced we can beat the enemy, provided units are kept up to strength in men and material. . . . In my opinion the War can only be won here in Flanders. . . . Personally I feel we have every reason to be optimistic; and if the War were to end tomorrow, Great Britain would find herself not merely the Greatest Power in Europe, but in the World. The chief people to suffer would be the Socialists, who are trying to rule us all, at a time when the right-minded of the Nation are so engaged on the country's battles that they [the socialists] are left free to work mischief.* But whatever views

---

*The International Socialist Conference was taking place in Stockholm at this time. The Socialists were notorious for their pacifism.

may be held on the Socialist problems, there is only one possible plan to win the war and that is to go on attacking in Flanders until we have driven the German Armies out of it.[23]

And so, to defeat Germany and socialism, men continued to drown in mud, choke in mud, suffering a horror which outdid the hitherto unsurpassable horror of the Somme. The casualty rate was lower than it had been then because the mud rendered many shells harmless, as well as clogging up guns so that they could not be fired. Yet there were half a million casualties nonetheless, and in those conditions of primeval slime, even the lightly wounded often died. The distance from the fighting front to the casualty clearing stations was about 4,000 yards, and each man on a stretcher required sixteen bearers, battling through the mud in four relays of four men each, instead of the two that were sufficient in normal terrain. In such circumstances, many wounded men received no medical attention. A combination of several factors – their already weakened condition; the cold, wet, hunger and thirst they endured as they lay half-drowned in shell-holes; and their exposed and vulnerable position, an immobile target for German snipers – meant that only the strongest or luckiest survived.

By now everyone – Lloyd George in particular, and the war committee as a whole – could see that the Flanders offensive had become a hideous mistake. Everyone except Haig, who remained stubbornly convinced that the battle was being won and the price of victory was not too high. (No wonder that, almost seventy years later, men still write letters to the papers on Armistice Day complaining that the hated name of Haig is embossed in the centre of every commemorative poppy.) Haig's will prevailed. The fighting went on. It got worse. Then, in mid-October, the weather finally began to improve. For ten days the rain stopped. Haig wrote confidently to his wife, 'I expect we will have Passchendaele village today all right.'[24] He was wrong by almost exactly a month.

The Germans now introduced a new horror. They began to bombard the British front line with shells containing mustard gas, which caused blisters all over the body and damaged the eyes. On 7 November 1917, after thirteen weeks of fighting, the village of Passchendaele was finally taken by the British. It was by then a waterlogged, deserted heap of rubble.

The Third Battle of Ypres had cost 244,897 British casualties,[25] of whom 35,831 were killed. The German Army, over a similar period, had suffered 217,000 casualties, including 35,000 dead. This battle, more than any other in the Great War, was responsible for the growing disillusionment with generals and politicians. People were sickened by the casualty lists that made long columns in their daily newspapers, and gave the lie to glassily optimistic propaganda. The image of British troops fighting at Passchendaele, lumbering through rain, caked in mud, cold and hungry and unprotected, inflicted a traumatic wound on public consciousness.

The first evidence that the tide had, imperceptibly, turned and was flowing away from the lust for war, towards the longing for peace, came in the form of the Lansdowne Letter. Lord Lansdowne, the Conservative Leader in the House of Lords, wrote to the *Daily Telegraph* on 29 November 1917 in an attempt to make people understand that the time had now come for the Allied Powers to start considering the terms of a negotiated peace. It was a calm, reasoned, balanced letter. Lansdowne saw that the humiliation which the British and French dreamed of imposing upon a cowed and beaten Germany was a fantasy. They would have to settle for less:

> We are not going to lose this war, but its prolongation will spell ruin for the civilised world, and an infinite addition to the load of human suffering which already weighs upon it. In my belief, if the war is to be brought to a close in time to avert a world-wide catastrophe, it will be brought to a close because on both sides the people of the countries involved realise that it has already lasted too long.[26]

And then he uttered the phrase that brought down the greatest vilification upon him: 'We do not desire the annihilation of Germany as a Great Power.'

The gutter press next day excelled itself. Lansdowne was called a 'shirker' and a 'funk'. Pictures of his house were juxtaposed with pictures of starving children. He was ostracized by most of society, including members of his own family. Only the Asquiths – now that Henry was safely out of office, and need not translate his opinions into practical terms – publicly supported him. 'It is surprising,' said Margot drily, 'how easily non-combatants get acclimatised to Death.'[27]

The people might have been ready for peace. The troops had certainly had enough. Margot Asquith had been assured by her footman of that on his last home leave before he went back to the Front to die. She recalled: 'When my footman said goodbye he told me with bitterness how much he and his brother soldiers loathed the war: how they neither wanted to kill, or be killed; and implied that he would be only one more corpse to heighten the heap in the interval, before anyone of sufficient courage would come forward to suggest a truce.'[28] But the politicians, the press barons and the profiteers wanted the war to go on; and their views prevailed. The battle between the cabinet and the High Command ricocheted between France and England, fought with letters and memoranda and committee meetings. Lloyd George and Haig detested and distrusted one another. Both sides held passionate convictions, but the controversy was conducted in a gentlemanly fashion and there were no casualties.

On the Western Front, the heap of corpses grew. In November came a death that touched the Coterie at its very heart. Edward Horner, who had been critically wounded three times and each time had survived, and always insisted on going back to the Front, was killed on 21 November, leading the attack on a village near Cambrai. Lady Horner, like so many mothers of dead sons, published a book of family reminiscences after the war, clinging to the old and happy times. He was her only son, and after him, everything else took on an elegiac note: 'With him perished the last hope of direct male succession in an ancient and honourable English house. And there passed too a gay, sunny and adorable nature, the love of which made life sweeter and will keep it permanently sweeter for many.'[29] Duff Cooper wrote in his diary:

> By his death our little society [i.e. the Coterie] loses one of the last assets which gave it distinction. And I think we have paid more than our share. To look back now on our Venice party, only four years ago, is to recall only the dead. The original four who motored out there together were Denny [Anson], Billy [Grenfell], George [Vernon] and Edward, of whom not one remains. The

most precious guests, in fact the only ones that I can remember while I was there, were Raymond [Asquith] and Charles [Lister], both dead. . . . Only Patrick and I remain. We can make no new friends worthy of the old ones. . . . I begin to feel that the dance is already over and it is time to go.[30]

A few days later Duff met Patrick Shaw Stewart, briefly home on leave, and together these two, last of the inner circle of the Coterie, 'agreed that there was so little left in life that we had lost all reluctance to dying'.[31] That was at the end of November 1917, and before the year was out Patrick, too, was dead. Patrick had been to the Coterie, in a sense, what Curzon was to the Souls. Like Curzon, he had carried off every academic honour at Eton and Oxford, including being elected a Fellow of All Souls. Like Curzon, he was attractive to women, energetic, ambitious, witty. He lacked Curzon's autocratic sense of duty, and could never conceal the irreverent side of his nature. His friends knew that he had not gone to war out of any inflamed patriotism: he would far rather have stayed with Baring's Bank and made money and had fun and remained the spoiled protégé of Ettie Desborough. He went because his friends went. His sense of duty was to them, rather than to any large abstraction called England or Duty. Not that it mattered *why* Patrick, or Edward, or any of them had gone to fight; they were all faceless, anonymous, without identity to the enemy, and they were all killed regardless.

Ettie bore the news of his death with her usual wonderful stoicism. The few of the Coterie who now remained – Diana and Duff, Diana Wyndham (widowed now for over three years), and a few other young women – had been invited to Taplow for the weekend. They went, wondering if Ettie had heard the news, or whether they would have to break it to her. But she knew already. Duff's diary continues:

January 5th (1918) Lady Desborough came down to breakfast and held the table as gallantly as ever. A pleasant morning spent playing with ponies and donkeys and sitting about. I went for a walk . . . before tea – the same walk that we went only a month ago when we were lamenting Edward. We had not had time even to find new words for our new sorrow. . . . I played bridge until dinner. I sat between Lady Desborough and Ivo. We talked about the past. It is my favourite subject now.[32]

By now it was not only footmen who were disillusioned and war-weary. Duff's class and generation were labouring under a burden of grief and guilt that shadowed the rest of their days, and could only be lightened by resorting to a communal fantasy. This fantasy took two forms. The first believed that a whole generation had been wiped out – and the brightest and best of them at that (two statements that are self-evidently contradictory). The glamour of the young dead was never tested against mature achievement, let alone the disillusionment of failure and old age. Their early deaths spared them that. The second was the lengthening shadow of a former golden age, represented by the Edwardian era. Against it, all post-war life looked mean and graceless. Yet who remembers that there were 870 separate strikes in 1911, the last year of good King Edward's reign – so deep was social unrest in that golden era? Life cannot have been golden for the puny, stunted youths who were not even good enough for cannon fodder; nor for the endless supply of working-class adolescent girls who were deflowered by 'gentlemen' in the belief that taking a girl's virginity cured venereal disease. Only the golden days and the golden lads were remembered after the war. Everything else was suppressed. A society, like an individual, cannot go on behaving normally if the burden of guilt is too great.

Already within a couple of years the lament for the flower of British youth had begun. An article entitled, 'Those Balliol Men!', taken from *The Saturday Review* of May 1920, was reprinted in a slim, privately circulated memorial volume compiled for Patrick Shaw Stewart by his brother:

> It is one of the heaviest charges which we bring against our governors that, owing to their lack of preparation, the flower of our youth were sent out in the first year of the war, untrained and unsupported by adequate numbers, to be mown down by the enemy's guns. The best of a generation have been sacrificed, and they cannot be replaced. It is largely to the slaughter of the best of our young men that we ascribe the loss of mental and moral balance, the depravity – no milder word is possible – of the generation that is rising in their place. The example of young men like Patrick Shaw Stewart is worth a king's ransom to a nation. We may be sure that our sons, when they attain to years of judgement, will not forgive the Governments of 1900 to 1912 for the recklessness which issued in the losses of 1914 and 1915.[33]

How quickly the disgraceful decadence of the Coterie had been canonized into matchless brilliance! Yet in the end Patrick's bravery *was* Homeric. The Balliol War Memorial Book records: 'In the early morning of December 30, as he was going round the line, the Germans put up a barrage. Patrick refused to send up the S.O.S. rocket and though hit in the ear by a bullet, carried on, and was finally killed by a shell which burst on the parapet.'[34]

By the beginning of 1918 the Souls no longer existed, not even in name. Old friendships had been fragmented, sometimes broken off altogether, by the political divide that in their youth they had so effortlessly crossed. The critical year was 1911: when female suffrage, the constitutional row over the House of Lords, and civil war in Ireland had first set old friends against each other. The war, if anything, united them temporarily; they all shared in one another's bereavements. The straitened round of country house visits carried on, deprived of its former sparkle and assignations. In 1917 Harry Cust – dilettante, raconteur and ladies' man – had died suddenly of pneumonia, finding himself at the last in the arms of his wife. He had waited a lifetime – fifty-six years – to inherit Belton and the Brownlow title, only to die in the end *before* his uncle, the childless Earl. For all its early brilliance, his had been an unsatisfactory life, leaving behind, like a tendril of expensive cigar smoke, only the ephemeral trace of charm, wit and worldliness . . . and a legendary reputation as the father of numerous aristocratic bastards.

Without Harry, and without the young cavaliers lost in the war, who could provide the women of the Souls with that glinting edge of flirtation that had sharpened their wits and brightened their eyes? Besides, they were growing old. Wilfrid Scawen Blunt, in the privacy of his secret diary, wrote a last portrait of the once lovely and recklessly passionate Duchess of Rutland: 'With his [i.e. Cust's] old love I had some talk during the evening. She is grown terribly old and haggard. She smiled and was pleasant while we were talking but something interrupted our conversation and the smile vanished and her face dropped and she became suddenly a quite old woman.'³⁵ By 1918 she was in her sixties; Ettie was fifty-one, Margot fifty-four and Mary Wemyss fifty-seven. Balfour was seventy, Curzon fifty-nine and Asquith sixty-six. Suddenly they all looked older than their years. The war had aged and tired them. They still had their exquisite, outmoded courtesy but they were faded, pallid, like pot-pourri; their vitality buried with their lovers and sons. By 1918 the existence of a group called the Souls was only a memory.

The Coterie, for all their youth, had disappeared too. Fourteen of their number – out of a tightly knit circle of no more than thirty or forty – had been killed. Newly married Percy Wyndham had been the first to die, on 1 September 1914, while the insouciant bachelors Patrick and Edward survived another three years before they died too.

There is, perhaps, just one sense in which the deaths of 37,452 officers in the war were more shocking to their class than were those of the other 710,000 ordinary soldiers who were killed. The officers came from an upper class which was, by its very nature, intimate. This meant there was every possibility that dozens, even scores of those who died were known to one another's families. It made the sense of loss very much greater. At the end of the book which she wrote to commemorate her sons, Ego and Yvo Charteris, Mary Wemyss compiled a list of the young men of their circle and generation who had also died. Some fourteen were Coterie members; but aside from these, she names eleven others. Twenty-five young men, the sons of her friends, the friends of her daughters, they had all been known to her personally since they were little boys. Except for her son Ego, and Raymond Asquith, they were all under thirty when they died. It would indeed have seemed as though a generation had been wiped out.

Practically the only survivors were those who, like John Granby, the Rutlands' heir, had been deliberately kept away from the fighting front; or those like Duff, who had simply got there too late to be killed (though not too late to distinguish himself and win the DSO for gallantry); or, finally, those like Alan Parsons, who was categorized Grade IV because of his asthma, and never given a chance to enlist at all. Out of all the sons of the Souls who went to fight, only one – Oliver Lyttelton – returned after four years without having suffered a major wound.

Nineteen-eighteen was the year in which, thanks to the utter exhaustion of the German Army, and the arrival in June of one and a half million fresh, fit American troops, the war finally ground to a halt. On 4 October Germany formally requested an Armistice. They no longer believed they could win; they scarcely even wanted to. The fighting troops on both sides longed for an end to the war; but the politicians prolonged it for a little while yet, as they haggled over terms; long enough for the death of the poet, Wilfred Owen, to be added to the list of those killed. He died on 4 November, just a week before the ceasefire became reality. He had moved from compassion to deep pessimism. Like most of the men who had experienced the worst of the fighting, he could no longer believe their deaths had any meaning at all.

The same division between what those at home, and those who had fought for it, felt about the Armistice, is sharply etched in their recollections of 11 November 1918:

It was past eleven o'clock when we reached Liverpool Street, the armistice had been signed and the town was in an uproar. As we drove from the station I felt unable to take part in their enthusiasm. This was the moment to which I had looked forward for four years, and now that it had arrived I was overcome by melancholy. Amid the dancing, the cheering, the waving of flags, I could think only of my friends who were dead.[36]

That was Duff Cooper; and Oliver Lyttelton said much the same: 'So it was all over. I had expected riotous excitement, but the reaction of everyone, officers and men, seemed the same – flat depression.'[37] Margot Asquith's experiences at home in London were different:

While reading the newspapers, odd noises from the streets broke upon my ears. Faint sounds of unfinished music; a medley of guns, maroons, cheering, and voices shouting 'The British Grenadiers' and 'God Save the King'. I looked out of the window and saw elderly nurses in uniform, and stray men and women clasping each other round the waist, laughing and dancing in the centre of the street. It was a brilliant day and the sky was light. . . . Flags, big and little, of every colour and nationality were flying from roofs, balconies and windows. The men who were putting them up were waving their caps at each other from the top of high ladders, and conventional pedestrians were whistling or dancing breakdowns on the pavement; a more spontaneous outbreak of simple gaiety could hardly have been imagined, and I have sometimes wondered if any of the Allies on that day gave way to such harmless explosions of innocent joy.[38]

For others, the long pent-up tension, at last released, was more than they could bear. Waiting for peace had been like waiting for normality to resume. But life would never be normal – in the way it had been before the war – ever again. Lady Cynthia Asquith, on the verge of a nervous breakdown, wrote this final entry in her diary of the war years:

I am beginning to rub my eyes at the prospect of peace. I think it will require more courage than anything that has gone before. It isn't until one leaves off spinning round that one realises how giddy one is. One will have to look at long vistas again, instead of short ones, and one will at last fully recognise that the dead are not only dead for the duration of the war.[39]

Epilogue

Patrick Shaw Stewart to Ettie Desborough, August 1915:
'If Edward, George, Raymond, Ego and I are left, we can yet reconstruct a makeshift universe. But I suppose at least one more of us is bound to be killed.'
They were all killed.

Duff Cooper to Lady Diana Manners, 21 January 1918:
'Our generation becomes history instead of growing up.'[1]

Plaque in Hôtel de Ville, Albert (where much of the heaviest fighting took place), describing the appearance of the town at Armistice:
'Il ne subsiste alors que le nom, la gloire, et les ruines.'

H. H. Asquith, 2 November 1918:
'It is not too much to say that it [i.e. the Great War] has cleansed and purged the whole atmosphere of the world.'[2]

The Lord Mayor of Birmingham, 11 November 1918:
'Today is the greatest day in the history of our country, and it marks the beginning of a new era in human development. . . . We must take care to use this great opportunity aright so that the world may be better and not worse by the overthrow of the old order.'[3]

Lloyd George, on the Dissolution of Parliament, 1918:
'What is our task? To make Britain a fit country for heroes to live in.'[4]

Duff Cooper to Lady Diana Manners, April 1918:
'Think of Julian growing more like Lord Desborough. . . . and oh, what would have happened to Denny [Anson]? However it is a profitless speculation and cold comfort. And it is better to be a live Lord than a dead Lieutenant.'[5]

A. J. Balfour to Lady Wemyss (formerly Mary Elcho) on the night before he left London for the Paris Peace Conference of January 1919:
'As I have always told you, it is not so much the War as the peace that I have always dreaded.'[6]

Eight and a half million people were killed during the First World War: 745,000 young Englishmen were dead, and 1.6 million were wounded. This was approximately 9 per cent of all men under the age of forty-five.

From the Prologue to *Death of a Hero*, by Richard Aldington:
'The casualty lists went on appearing for a long time after the Armistice – last spasms of Europe's severed arteries. Of course, nobody much bothered to read the lists. Why should they? The living must protect themselves from the dead, especially the intrusive dead. But the twentieth century had lost its Spring with a vengeance.'[7]

Lady Mary Lyon, formerly Lady Mary Strickland, formerly Lady Mary Charteris, daughter of Lady Elcho . . . in conversation with the author, 17 February 1984, aged eighty-nine:
'When the War ended I felt it was marvellous, but of course what one also felt was that one missed one's brothers and all the people who had been killed. The War changed everything, though we didn't realize it at the time. For my parents life became more difficult in every way, because they couldn't get servants. For me – well, my husband came back from being a prisoner of war in Turkey and we had to pick up our lives again. We had been married for four months and then suddenly he'd been captured and was away for two and a half years. That was very strange: an extraordinary situation, really. But I started a child almost at once and that was my son, Guy. He was killed in the Second World War, in the RAF, aged twenty-two. He was reported missing for a year and then presumed dead. After the war they found a farmer in Schleswig-Holstein who remembered seeing his plane shot down. The whole bomber crew were all killed. It was a Stirling bomber. His name was Guy, Guy Strickland. I often feel life's not worth living any more.'[8]

Appendix I

PURCHASING POWER OF THE £ (1914=100p)

Year	Value	Year	Value	Year	Value	Year	Value
1825	65·08	1865	83·75	1905	118·33	1945	—
6	75·04	6	83·75	6	110·00	6	37·91
7	75·04	7	85·04	7	105·00	7	35·04
8	83·75	8	85·08	8	116·25	8	32·91
9	85·04	9	86·25	9	112·08	9	32·08
1830	83·75	1870	88·75	1910	108·75	1950	31·25
1	82·50	1	85·04	1	105·00	1	28·75
2	87·08	2	78·75	2	100·00	2	27·08
3	90·08	3	76·66	3	100·00	3	26·66
4	87·08	4	82·91	4	100·00	4	26·25
5	85·00	5	88·75	5	81·25	5	25·04
6	73·75	6	89·16	6	68·33	6	24·16
7	80·08	7	90·04	7	56·66	7	23·33
8	80·08	8	97·50	8	44·16	8	22·91
9	76·66	9	102·50	9	46·66	9	22·91
1840	77·91	1880	96·25	1920	40·00	1960	22·50
1	79·16	1	100·00	1	44·16	1	22·08
2	90·04	2	100·08	2	54·58	2	21·25
3	96·25	3	103·33	3	57·50	3	20·08
4	98·33	4	112·08	4	57·08	4	20·04
5	92·50	5	118·33	5	56·66	5	19·58
6	92·50	6	112·50	6	58·33	6	18·75
7	87·08	7	124·16	7	59·58	7	18·33
8	100·00	8	121·66	8	60·04	8	17·50
9	105·00	9	118·33	9	60·08	9	16·25
1850	105·00	1890	118·33	1930	63·33	1970	15·83
1	102·50	1	118·33	1	67·91	1	14·58
2	105·00	2	124·58	2	69·58	2	13·33
3	92·50	3	124·58	3	71·25	3	12·29
4	82·50	4	135·00	4	70·08	4	11·25
5	85·04	5	135·00	5	70·00	5	9·37
6	82·50	6	140·00	6	67·91	6	8·33
7	79·16	7	135·00	7	65·00	7	5·90
8	88·75	8	133·33	8	64·16	8	5·83
9	88·33	9	124·58	9	—	9	5·62
1860	85·04	1900	112·91	1940	—	1980	4·58
1	86·25	1	121·66	1	—	1	4·16
2	83·75	2	122·50	2	—	2	3·54
3	82·50	3	122·50	3	—		
4	80·08	4	121·66	4	—		

Compiled by: E. Barry Bowyer

George Curzon's Speech at the Hotel Cecil Dinner,

9 December 1898

Envelope superscribed: 'Lady Ribblesdale, 20 Cavendish Square, W', and inscribed (all in Curzon's handwriting): 'Copy of my speech at the Dinner given to us on Dec 9 1898 written down by me from memory on Dec 10 for Lady R'.

[page 1] Lord Elcho and friends of both sexes –
Assuredly this banquet has, at any rate in our eyes, who are your guests, many justifications – Not the least among them is the fact that it has tempted from a retreat which has been so protracted as almost to become indecent, the 'halting orator', as he has called himself, the timid rhetorical recluse, to whom we have just listened.* Tonight Lord Elcho has once more given to this party that which he has too long selfishly withdrawn from mankind; and the humour and the wit, not wholly destitute of preparation, which on one occasion drove the whole House of Commons, with their entire consent, to attend the Derby, and on another occasion, compelled the whole House, greatly against their will, to stay away – have flashed their most brilliant coruscations around our approaching departure. Lord Elcho commenced by deploring the fact that Lady Ribblesdale who [page 2] was the spokesman – for I decline in this context to use the word spokeswoman – of the company at our last dinner 8 years ago, has not fulfilled the same functions tonight. To some extent I share his sorrow; for I doubt not that Lady R had she spoken would have acquitted herself with a vitality not unworthy of her unconquerable sire.† But we may encourage Lord E by the assurance that she could not have delivered a speech more masculine in its effrontery, more feminine in the delicacy & subtlety of its compliment, than that which has just fallen from his own lips.

Lord Elcho then went on to pay to Mary and me many compliments. I understood him to say that those only had been invited to this banquet who were distinguished [page 3] by virtue and intelligence. But I also understand that Mary and I are the only guests this evening; and that all the rest of you are hosts. I

*Lord Elcho, who proposed the toast to the Curzons.
†Charles Tennant.

accept the compliment therefore as perfectly true in both particulars. I represent the virtue, and Mary the intelligence.

Lord E next compared me to Louis de Rougemont; and again I accept the compliment; for a man of more wonderful imagination or more startling performance has never been seen. But at this point there occurred a hiatus in his argument which he made no attempt to fill; for he did not go on to inform us who was the Yamba who is to share my 5 years sojourn in the desert wilds.

Finally Lord E proceeded to pay compliments to Mary and to speak of her as typifying the Anglo-American alliance. [page 4] I care not tonight to speak of the alliance of nations or of the national flag. All I know is that the American flag for me is all stars and no stripes. Enough for me is the alliance of individuals – that alliance by which I have now been honoured for nearly 4 years – an alliance which in its wider manifestations has added to English society many of its greatest ornaments, and has endowed a number of English husbands with the most incomparable of wives. And now I think I have exhausted Lord Elcho! But there is another justification for this banquet – and that is the graceful poem that was read out at an earlier stage of the evening by Mr G.W. [George Wyndham]. Who else could have done it? Poet, statesman – warrior – Adonis – [page 5] there has been no-one like him since Sir Philip Sidney. May he enjoy a similar fame! May he escape a similar fate!

Tonight is a night that I can never forget. Surfeited as I have been with the public demonstrations of the past few weeks, squeezed dry as I am of the last platitudes about India, it is with positive relief that I find myself in the wholly frivolous and utterly irresponsible society that is collected round these tables. For here I see about me the friends, and sometimes the critics, of a tumultuous but absolutely unrepentant youth – the comrades of a more sober and orderly middle age – and when I return 5 years hence, what I hope may be the props and the solace of dull and declining years. Lacking, as I am popularly supposed to be, [page 6] in most of the adornments and in many of the requisites, of a gentle and diffident personality, and of a modest and alluring career – there is one commodity in which I have never been wanting – and that is in the possession of whole-hearted and loyal friends. May I be permitted to say in the presence of Mary – since it has already been said by Hugo, which encourages me to repeat it – that since I married her, or since she married me – whichever be the formula best adapted to this vulgar age of emancipation – the number of those friends has greatly increased instead of diminishing; matrimony having gathered around us an ever-swelling band of those who have been more [page 7] attracted by her personality than they have been repelled by mine. So that it is amid a Macedonian phalanx of men with the hearts of women, and of women with the heads of men, that we now start forth upon our Asiatic venture. Of one thing you may be sure – that as our ship steams further and further away from these shores, as the sun rises daily more burning and nearer upon our course, often shall we look back upon this glorious evening, upon this memorable feast, upon this unique collection of all that makes life worth living.

There is only one additional favour that you can render us. Mary and I will often be rather lonely in India. We invite you – we supplicate you – nay, [page 8] we use our new-born prerogative to command you – with all the authority of the Great Mogul – to come and cheer us in our solitude. We will give you all that we can. The wealth of Ormuz and of Ind shall be laid at your feet. Lord Elcho shall satisfy his desire. He shall shoot tigers from the back of elephants, or elephants from the back of tigers, whichever he prefers. You shall see the eastern sun gild the eternal crests of the Himalayas in the morning, and sink to rest behind the boundless Western plains – You shall be serenaded by *bulbuls* – if you know what that is – in gardens of roses. George Wyndham shall compose a sonnet in the groves of the Taj; and the lady, or the ladies, who [page 9] accompany him shall respond in a manner appropriate to the occasion and the locality. Above all, we will give you an English welcome in an Indian home; and you shall realise that, behind the starch of a purely superficial solemnity, there lurk the same incorrigible characteristics which you have alternately bewailed and pardoned here. And therefore it is that we bid you goodbye, oh you queens among women, and oh you kings among men! We take to our hearts your tender and affectionate farewell. We thank those who have organised this never to be forgotten entertainment; and happy will be the dawn of that day that brings us back and reunites us all once more.

Houses in which the Souls Lived and Entertained

16 ARLINGTON STREET. London house of the Duke and Duchess of Rutland.

ASHRIDGE PARK. Country house in Hertfordshire belonging to the Brownlow family.

AVON TYRRELL. New Forest home of Lord and Lady Manners.

BELTON HOUSE. Ancestral home since the early seventeenth century of the Earl of Brownlow, near Grantham, Leicestershire. Much used by Harry Cust, who did not live long enough, however, to inherit it.

BELVOIR CASTLE. Near Grantham, Leicestershire. Principal seat of the Duke and Duchess of Rutland.

CLOUDS. Light and spacious country house at East Knoyle, near Salisbury, built in the 1880s by Detmar Blow for Percy and Madeline Wyndham.

DUNROBIN CASTLE. Country seat of the Duke of Sutherland at Golspie.

EASTON GREY. Wiltshire home of Thomas and Lucy Graham Smith.

GLEN. Scottish baronial mansion built by Sir Charles Tennant for his family near Innerleithen, Peeblesshire.

GOSFORD. Scottish ancestral home of the Earl of Wemyss in East Lothian.

40 GROSVENOR SQUARE. London house bought by Sir Charles Tennant in 1881.

HAGLEY HALL. Family home of the Lytteltons at Stourbridge, Worcestershire.

HATFIELD HOUSE. Ancestral home of the Marquess of Salisbury and the Cecils since Elizabethan times.

HEWELL GRANGE. Worcestershire home of Lord and Lady Windsor (later Earl and Countess of Plymouth).

KEDLESTON HALL. Seat of Lord Scarsdale in Derbyshire, later inherited and renovated by his son, Lord Curzon.

MELLS PARK. Manor house near Frome, Somerset. Home of the Horner family for four centuries.

PANSHANGER. Home of Lord and Lady Cowper in Hertfordshire; inherited in 1913 by their niece, Lady Desborough.

QUEEN ANNE'S GATE. London house belonging to Edwin Montagu and head-quarters of the Coterie during the war.

ST FAGAN'S CASTLE. Romantic, austere castle built for Lord and Lady Windsor near Cardiff.

STAFFORD HOUSE. Palatial London home of the Duke and Duchess of Sutherland, where they lavishly entertained both the Souls and the Marlborough House Set.

STANWAY. Gloucestershire home of the Charteris (Elcho) family for four centuries.

TAPLOW COURT. Vast Victorian pile on the Thames near Maidenhead where the Grenfells (later the Desboroughs) lived and entertained famously.

WADDESDON MANOR. Palatial Buckinghamshire house built for Ferdinand de Rothschild in 1881.

WHITTINGEHAME. Huge Scottish estate owned by Arthur Balfour.

WILTON HOUSE. Home of the Earl and Countess of Pembroke, near Salisbury.

WREST PARK. Home of the Earl de Grey, later 1st Marquess of Ripon, in Bedfordshire.

Notes

1. All Souls

1. H. G. Wells, *Experiment in Autobiography*, Vol. II, p. 635
2. Margot Asquith, *Autobiography*, Vol. I, pp. 174–5
3. Letter from George Curzon, 23 July 1882; quoted in Lord Ronaldshay, *The Life of Lord Curzon*, Vol. I, p. 62
4. George Cornwallis-West, *Edwardian Hey-Days*, p. 43
5. Lady Frances Balfour, *Ne Obliviscaris*, pp. 55–7
6. Letter to *The Times*, signed 'X', from Lady Desborough, 21 January 1929
7. George Cornwallis-West, *Edwardian Hey-Days*, p. 132
8. *The Whitehall Review*, 21 November 1891
9. *The World*, 16 July 1890
10. British Library Additional Manuscripts Wentworth Bequest 53926, 8 October 1883; cited by Elizabeth Longford, *A Pilgrimage of Passion*, p. 244

2. Their Own Good Hearts

1. Mary Wemyss, *A Family Record*, pp. 9–10
2. Margot Asquith, *Autobiography*, Vol. I, p. 6
3. H. J. Tennant, *Sir Charles Tennant*
4. Margot Asquith, *Autobiography*, Vol. I, p. 18
5. *Ibid*, p. 31
6. Mary Gladstone (Mrs Drew), *Diaries & Letters* (ed. Lucy Masterman), p. 268
7. Edith Lyttelton, *Alfred Lyttelton: an Account of His Life*, p. 126
8. A. G. C. Liddell, *Notes From the Life of an Ordinary Mortal*, p. 228, and Lord Chandos, *From Peace to War*, p. 27
9. Margot Asquith, *Autobiography*, Vol. I, pp. 35–6
10. From Laura Tennant's unpublished diary, 30 July 1882
11. Lady Frances Balfour, *Ne Obliviscaris*, p. 392
12. Margot Asquith, *Autobiography*, Vol. I, pp. 173–4
13. Mary Gladstone (Mrs Drew), *Some Hawarden Letters*, footnote to p. 173
14. From Laura Tennant's unpublished diary, 19 November 1879
15. *Ibid*, September 1884
16. Lady Frances Balfour, *Ne Obliviscaris*, p. 393
17. Margot Asquith, *Autobiography*, Vol. I, pp. 27 and 29
18. From Laura Tennant's unpublished diary, 31 December 1883
19. A. G. C. Liddell, *Notes from the Life of an Ordinary Mortal*, p. 227
20. From Laura Tennant's unpublished diary, 28 October 1884, her 22nd birthday
21. From A. G. C. Liddell's unpublished diary; quoted in D. D. Lyttelton's unpublished memoir, *Interwoven*, and in Lord Chandos, *From Peace to War*, p. 28
22. From Laura Tennant's unpublished diary, 28 October 1884
23. *Ibid*, 22 November 1884
24. *Ibid*, 30 November 1884

25. Mary Gladstone (Mrs Drew), *Some Hawarden Letters*, p. 147
26. Margot Asquith, *Autobiography*, Vol. I, p. 36
27. From Laura Tennant's unpublished diary, 12 January 1885
28. Lord Chandos, *From Peace to War*, p. 21
29. Betty Askwith, *The Lytteltons*, p. 165; taken from Lavinia Lyttelton's diary, 9 November 1866 (Hagley Papers)
30. Lord Chandos, *From Peace to War*, p. 16
31. Edith Lyttelton, *Alfred Lyttelton*, p. 128
32. From Laura Tennant's unpublished diary, 19 November 1879
33. From A. G. C. Liddell's unpublished diary; quoted in Lord Chandos, *From Peace to War*, p. 29
34. *Ibid*, p. 30
35. From Laura Tennant's unpublished diary, Christmas night 1884
36. *Ibid*, 12 January 1885
37. *Ibid*
38. From A. G. C. Liddell's unpublished diary; quoted in Lord Chandos, *From Peace to War*, p. 30
39. From Laura Tennant's unpublished diary, 12 January 1885
40. From A. G. C. Liddell's unpublished diary, 3 January 1885; quoted in Lord Chandos, *From Peace to War*, p. 31
41. From Laura Tennant's unpublished diary, 12 January 1885
42. Letter from Laura Tennant to Alfred Lyttelton, April 1885; quoted in Edith Lyttelton, *Alfred Lyttelton*, p. 140
43. Letter from Alfred Lyttelton to Laura Tennant, January 1885; quoted in Edith Lyttelton, *Alfred Lyttelton*, p. 140
44. From Wilfrid Scawen Blunt's secret diary, 21 May 1885, MS 333, p. 9, Fitzwilliam Museum, Cambridge
45. Margot Asquith, *Autobiography*, Vol. I, p. 40, and Edith Lyttelton, *Alfred Lyttelton*, p. 143
46. Edith Lyttelton, *Alfred Lyttelton*, pp. 145–6, and Margot Asquith, *Autobiography*, Vol. I, pp. 44–5
47. Mary Gladstone (Mrs Drew), *Some Hawarden Letters*; letter from E. Burne-Jones, 1 May 1886
48. Mary Gladstone (Mrs Drew), *Her Diaries and Letters*, p. 387
49. Wilfrid Scawen Blunt, *My Diaries, 1888–1914*, p. 57; entry for his first visit to Glen, 20 September 1891
50. Lady Frances Balfour, *Ne Obliviscaris*, p. 391

3. The Marlborough House Set

1. Margot Asquith, *More Memories*
2. *The Greville Memoirs, 1817–60*, 22 January 1848; quoted in Elizabeth Longford, *Victoria RI*, p. 217
3. *Ibid*, p. 277; letter from Queen Victoria to Princess Frederick William ('Vicky'), 27 April 1859
4. Letter from Queen Victoria to Princess Victoria, November 1862
5. A. L. Kennedy (ed.), *My Dear Duchess: Letters to the Duchess of Manchester*, p. 214
6. Margot Asquith, *More Memories*, pp. 234–7
7. *Ibid*
8. Rev. John Neale Dalton; quoted in Philip Magnus, *King Edward the Seventh*, p. 158
9. O. R. Macgregor, *Divorce in England*
10. Countess of Antrim, *Recollections*, p. 221
11. Georgina Battiscombe, *Queen Alexandra*, p. 194
12. From Wilfrid Scawen Blunt's secret diary, 4 June 1909, MS 9, Fitzwilliam Museum, Cambridge
13. *Ibid*
14. *Ibid*
15. *Ibid*, 28 January 1902, MS 273
16. *Ibid*, 7 February 1909
17. Letter from Queen Victoria to the Lord Chancellor, 21 February 1870; quoted in Philip Magnus, *King Edward the Seventh*, p. 108
18. Roger Fulford (ed.), *Your Dear Letter: Private Correspondence of Queen Victoria and the Crown Princess of Prussia, 1865–71*, pp. 262–3
19. Giles St Aubyn, *Edward VII: Prince and King*, p. 169
20. E. F. Benson, *As We Were*, p. 101
21. Wilfrid Scawen Blunt, *My Diaries, 1888–1914*, 2 June 1891, p. 53
22. Margot Asquith, *More Memories*, pp. 240–1

4. 'King Arthur' or 'The Adored Gazelle'

1. Max Egremont, *Balfour*, p. 29
2. Quoted in Piers Brendon, *Eminent Edwardians*, p. 80
3. Max Egremont, *Balfour*, p. 29
4. *Ibid*, p. 23
5. *Ibid*
6. A. J. Balfour, 'The Palm Sunday Case', from the *Proceedings of the Society for Psychical Research*, Vol. 52, p. 170; quoted in Max Egremont, *Balfour*, p. 199
7. Arthur James, First Earl of Balfour, *Chapters of Autobiography*, pp. 68–9 and 84–6
8. Max Egremont, *Balfour*, p. 37
9. Piers Brendon, *Eminent Edwardians*, p. 70
10. Margot Asquith, *Autobiography*, Vol. I, p. 167
11. Letter from A. J. Balfour to W. S. Churchill, 1 February 1904; quoted in Lord Chandos, *From Peace to War*, p. 60
12. A. J. Balfour, *Chapters of Autobiography*, pp. 93–4
13. The Balfour Papers (74), Whittingehame; quoted in Max Egremont, *Balfour*, p. 72
14. A. J. Balfour, *Chapters of Autobiography*, editor's note, p. 133
15. Max Egremont, *Balfour*, p. 64
16. A. J. Balfour, *Chapters of Autobiography*, pp. 209–10
17. *Ibid*, pp. 230–2
18. *Ibid*, p. 231
19. *Ibid*
20. Letter from Mary Elcho to Arthur Balfour, 12 June 1896
21. Max Egremont, *Balfour*, p. 68
22. Lord Chandos, *From Peace to War*, p. 58
23. Letter from Laura Lyttelton to Lady Frances Balfour, 5 October 1885
24. Max Egremont, *Balfour*, p. 70
25. Cecil, *Life of Lord Salisbury*, Vol. III, p. 347; quoted in Max Egremont, *Balfour*, p. 83
26. Max Egremont, *The Cousins*, p. 114
27. Piers Brendon, *Eminent Edwardians*, p. 92
28. Max Egremont, *Balfour*, p. 70
29. *Ibid*, p. 83
30. Blanche Dugdale, *Arthur James Balfour*, p. 110
31. *Ibid*, p. 113
32. Kenneth Young, *Balfour*
33. Elizabeth Longford, *Pilgrimage of Passion*, p. 230
34. From Wilfrid Scawen Blunt's secret diary, September 1887; quoted in Max Egremont, *The Cousins*, p. 119
35. Elizabeth Longford, *Pilgrimage of Passion*, p. 246
36. *Ibid*, p. 248
37. Max Egremont, *The Cousins*, p. 120
38. *Ibid*, p. 119
39. Letter from A. J. Balfour to Lady Elcho, 27 October 1887
40. Letter from Lord Salisbury to A. J. Balfour; quoted in Max Egremont, *The Cousins*, p. 130
41. *Ibid*, p. 130
42. Elizabeth Longford, *Pilgrimage of Passion*, p. 307
43. *Ibid*, p. 310
44. Wilfrid Scawen Blunt, *Secret Memoirs*, 14 January 1895, MS 34
45. *Ibid*, 4 May 1895, MS 34, p. 70
46. *Ibid*
47. *Ibid*, 2 February 1895
48. *Ibid*, 16 February 1895; quoted in Elizabeth Longford, *Pilgrimage of Passion*, p. 313
49. *Ibid*, 21 February 1895, p. 313
50. *Ibid*, 26 February 1895
51. Elizabeth Longford, *Pilgrimage of Passion*, p. 283
52. Wilfrid Scawen Blunt, *Secret Memoirs*
53. *Ibid*, 30 March 1895; quoted in Elizabeth Longford, *Pilgrimage of Passion*
54. Letter from Hugo Charteris to Wilfrid Scawen Blunt; quoted in Elizabeth Longford, *Pilgrimage of Passion*
55. *Ibid*, p. 315

56. *Ibid*, p. 317
57. Wilfrid Scawen Blunt, *Secret Memoirs*, 14 January 1895, MS 34
58. Elizabeth Longford, *Pilgrimage of Passion*, p. 319
59. Wilfrid Scawen Blunt, *Secret Memoirs*
60. Letter from Mary Elcho to A. J. Balfour, 12 June 1896; quoted in Max Egremont, *Balfour*, p. 118
61. *Ibid*, 12 June 1896
62. Letter from Mary to George Curzon; quoted in Kenneth Rose, *Superior Person*, p. 289
63. Nigel Nicolson, *Mary Curzon*, p. 146
64. Letter from George to Mary Curzon, 1901; quoted in Nigel Nicolson, *Mary Curzon*, p. 147
65. *Ibid*
66. *Ibid*, p. 149
67. *Ibid*
68. *Ibid*
69. Max Egremont, *Balfour*, p. 103
70. Max Egremont, *The Cousins*, p. 249
71. *Ibid*, p. 265

5. But Not as Equal Souls

1. Nigel Nicolson, *Mary Curzon*, p. 94
2. Letter from Lord David Cecil to the author, 7 April 1983
3. Frances, Countess of Warwick, *Life's Ebb and Flow*, p. 80
4. *Ibid*, p. 72
5. Wilfrid Scawen Blunt, *Secret Memoirs*, 2 June 1891
6. Many of those interviewed by the author who knew Willy Grenfell insist that he was a scholar and took a First at Balliol. College archives, however, show that he in fact obtained a Second. The mythical First may well have been an example of Ettie's ability to make things happen simply by wishing they had – with such intensity that she convinced herself, and then others, that her version was the truth.
7. Mary, Countess of Wemyss, *A Family Record*
8. Lady Desborough, *Pages from a Family Journal*
9. *Ibid*
10. *Ibid*
11. Lord David Cecil in conversation with the author, 1983
12. *Ibid*
13. Philip Ziegler, *Diana Cooper*, p. 2
14. From Wilfrid Scawen Blunt's secret diary, 16 October 1893; continued on 9 November 1893
15. Quoted in Max Egremont, *The Cousins*, p. 163, and seen by him among the Grosvenor Papers
16. From Wilfrid Scawen Blunt's secret diary, 20 May 1894
17. Robertson Scott, *Life and Death of a Newspaper*, p. 371; quoted in Kenneth Rose, *Superior Person*, p. 153
18. Margot Asquith, *Autobiography*, Vol. I, p. 260
19. From Wilfrid Scawen Blunt's secret diary, 26 July 1892, MS 32, p. 42
20. *Ibid*, 3 August 1892
21. *Ibid*, MS 32, 26 July–27 August 1892
22. *Ibid*, 31 August 1892
23. From Margot Tennant's unpublished diary, 5 December 1891, written at Assiount in Egypt.
24. From Wilfrid Scawen Blunt's secret diary, 2 June 1894
25. From Laura Tennant's unpublished diary, 1 April 1884, at Mells Park
26. *Ibid*, 10 February 1885 (one month after her engagement)
27. From a letter sent to Wilfrid Scawen Blunt in 1912 by a woman whom he does not name, and copied by him into his diary. Internal evidence shows that she is *not* Margot Asquith.

6. Souls at Play

1. Lady Desborough, essay on 'Play' from *Flotsam and Jetsam*
2. Harold Nicolson, *Sir Arthur Nicolson, Bart*, p. 7; quoted in J. A. Mangan, *Athleticism in the Victorian and Edwardian Public Schools*
3. Cotterill, *Suggested Reforms in the Public Schools*, p. 177
4. Christopher Hassall, *Rupert Brooke*, p. 61
5. Edith Lyttelton, *Alfred Lyttelton*, p. 46
6. Letter from Arthur Balfour to George Curzon, 16 April 1896; quoted in Kenneth Rose, *Superior Person*, p. 179

7. Lord Ronaldshay, *Life of Curzon*, Vol I. p. 158
8. Letter from Margot Tennant to George Curzon, September 1887
9. Maurice Baring, *The Puppet Show of Memory*, pp. 167–8
10. Letter from A. G. C. Liddell to Constance Wenlock, 2 July 1893
11. From Margot Tennant's unpublished diary, 20 October 1893
12. Lord Longford in conversation with the author, April 1983
13. Margot Asquith, *Autobiography*, Vol. I, p. 31
14. Kenneth Rose, *Superior Person*, p. 182
15. Lady Angela Forbes, *Memories and Base Details*, p. 130
16. Lord Longford, in conversation with the author, June 1983
17. Philip Magnus, *Gladstone*, p. 447
18. Frances, Countess of Warwick, *Afterthoughts*, p. 126
19. Letter from Lord David Cecil to the author, 26 April 1983
20. Lady Desborough, *Pages from a Family Journal*, p. 87
21. *Ibid*, p. 248
22. *The World*, 1893
23. *Ibid*
24. Lady Desborough, essay on 'Play', from *Flotsam and Jetsam*
25. Daisy, Countess of Warwick, *Life's Ebb and Flow*, p. 38
26. *Ibid*, p. 176
27. Vita Sackville-West, *The Edwardians*, pp. 26–7
28. Mary Gladstone, *Her Diaries and Letters*, p. 321
29. Anita Leslie, *Edwardians in Love*, p. 272
30. *Ibid*, p. 277
31. Frances Horner, *Time Remembered*, p. 155

7. Iron in the Souls

1. *The Times*, 26 December 1889
2. Margot Asquith, *Autobiography*, Vol. I, p. 174
3. Letter from George Curzon to Margot Tennant, 18 November 1889; quoted in Lord Ronaldshay, *Life of Lord Curzon*, Vol. I, p. 150
4. Nigel Nicolson, *Mary Curzon*, p. 38
5. Quoted in Nigel Nicolson, *Mary Curzon*, p. 40
6. *Ibid*, pp. 56–7
7. *Ibid*, p. 164
8. *Ibid*, p. 65
9. Lord Ronaldshay, *Life of Curzon*, Vol. I, p. 208
10. Letter from George Curzon to Wilfrid Scawen Blunt, 1894
11. Lord Ronaldshay, *Life of Curzon*, Vol. I, p. 224
12. Nigel Nicolson, *Mary Curzon*, p. 72
13. Quoted in Kenneth Rose, *Superior Person*, p. 283
14. Letter from George Curzon to Cecil Spring-Rice, 28 November 1895; quoted in Kenneth Rose, *Superior Person*, p. 289
15. *Ibid*
16. Nigel Nicolson, *Mary Curzon*, p. 83
17. Letter from Margot Tennant to George Curzon, 26 February 1892, previously unpublished. This extract quoted by kind permission of Lord Crathorne for the Tennant family.
18. Quoted in Nigel Nicolson, *Mary Curzon*, p. 84
19. *Ibid*, p. 100
20. Quoted in Lord Ronaldshay, *Life of Curzon*, Vol. I, p. 269
21. Quoted in James Morris, *Farewell the Trumpets*, p. 108
22. *Ibid*
23. Quoted in Kenneth Rose, *Superior Person*, pp. 322–3
24. *Ibid*, p. 324
25. *Ibid*; letter from Queen Victoria to Lord Salisbury, 27 May 1898
26. *Ibid*, p. 327
27. Nigel Nicolson, *Mary Curzon*, p. 103
28. *Ibid*, p. 105; letter dated 18 September 1898
29. Quoted in Kenneth Rose, *Superior Person*, pp. 337–8
30. From Rudyard Kipling's *Recessional*, 1897
31. Lord Ronaldshay, *Life of Lord Curzon*, Vol. II, p. 27

32. Quoted in Nigel Nicolson, *Mary Curzon*, p. 118
33. Letter from C. E. Dawkins(?) Esq., 24 May 1901, in India Office Library, MS Eur F 111
34. Nigel Nicolson, *Mary Curzon*, p. 146
35. *Ibid*, p. 146
36. *Ibid*
37. *Ibid*, p. 143
38. *Ibid*, p. 151
39. The former Evelyn Baring was a distinguished Colonial civil servant who was private secretary to the Governor-General of India for 4 years and Consul-General in Egypt from 1883. He was created First Baron Cromer for his services in 1892
40. Letter from Lord Esher to his son, 2 December 1901; from *Journals and Letters of Reginald, Viscount Esher*, Vol. I, p. 321
41. Letter from George Curzon to George Wyndham, 7 May 1902; from Curzon MS in India Office Library
42. Letter from A. J. Balfour to George Curzon, 12 December 1902; quoted in Kenneth Rose, *Superior Person*, p. 353
43. Letter from Sir Arthur Godley to George Curzon, 1 January 1904; quoted in Kenneth Rose, *Superior Person*
44. Quoted in Leonard Mosley, *Curzon: The End of an Epoch*, p. 99
45. Quoted in Nigel Nicolson, *Mary Curzon*, p. 163
46. *Ibid*, pp. 109–10
47. *Ibid*, p. 171
48. *Ibid*, pp. 176–80
49. Letter from George Curzon to Lord Northcote, 9 December 1904; from collection in India Office Library
50. Letter from Mary to George Curzon; quoted in Nigel Nicolson, *Mary Curzon*, p. 184
51. *Ibid*, p. 186
52. Quoted in Max Egremont, *Balfour*, p. 174
53. Letter from A. J. Balfour to George Curzon, 23 August 1905; quoted in Kenneth Rose, *Superior Person*, p. 365
54. Nicholas Mosley, *Julian Grenfell*, p. 104
55. Earl of Winterton, *Pre-War*, p. 20
56. Wilfrid Scawen Blunt, *Secret Memoirs*, 19 December 1905
57. Quoted in Lord Ronaldshay, *Life of Lord Curzon*, Vol. III, p. 30
58. Oscar Wilde, *Lady Windermere's Fan*, 1891
59. Lady Alexandra Metcalfe in conversation with the author, July 1983
60. Nigel Nicolson, *Mary Curzon*

8. Country House Weekend

1. Lady Cynthia Asquith, *Remember and Be Glad*, p. 64
2. *Ibid*, p. 6
3. Margot Asquith, *Octavia*, Cassell 1928, p. 33
4. Margot Asquith, *Autobiography*, Vol. I, p. 190
5. Cynthia Asquith, *Remember and Be Glad*, p. 44
6. *Ibid*, p. 45
7. *Ibid*, p. 46
8. *Ibid*, p. 27
9. *Ibid*
10. From Wilfrid Scawen Blunt's secret diary, 3 September 1887
11. From *Nineteenth Century* for October 1881, p. 474; quoted in Heather A. Clemenson, *English Country Houses and Landed Estates*
12. Lady Cynthia Asquith, *Diaries 1915–18*, Introduction, p. xii
13. Max Egremont, *Balfour*, p. 311
14. Bagehot, *The English Constitution*, Introduction
15. Quoted in Brian Masters, *Great Hostesses*, p. 19
16. Earl of Midleton, *Records and Reactions*, p. 51
17. Lord David Cecil in conversation with the author, 18 March 1983
18. Lady Desborough, *Pages from a Family Journal*, pp. 90–1
19. *Ibid*, p. 85
20. Bagehot, *Physics and Politics*, 1872
21. Quoted in Clive Aslet, *The Last Country Houses*, p. 97

22. *Ibid*, p. 98
23. Lord Chandos, *Memoirs*, p. 28
24. Readers who are interested in learning more about the lives of servants in great houses are referred to – among others – Carol Adams, *Ordinary Lives*; Caroline Davidson, *A Woman's Work is Never Done*; and Mark Girouard, *Great Country Houses*
25. This reminiscence comes from the late Lady Hardinge, First Baroness of Penshurst, born a Cecil and brought up in Hatfield
26. George Cornwallis-West, *Edwardian Hey-Days*, pp. 132–3
27. *Ibid*
28. Lord Ernest Hamilton, *The Halcyon Era*

9. Second-generation Souls: The Corrupt Coterie

1. Philip Ziegler, *Diana Cooper*, p. 18
2. Lady Diana Cooper, *The Rainbow Comes and Goes*, p. 78
3. Letter from Raymond Asquith to John Buchan, 19 December 1901; quoted in John Jolliffe (ed.), *Raymond Asquith: Life and Letters*, p. 86
4. *Ibid*, p. 141; 20 March 1906, letter to Aubrey Herbert
5. *Ibid*, p. 34; letter to H. T. Baker
6. *Ibid*, p. 49; letter to H. T. Baker, 1 October 1898
7. *Ibid*, p. 70; letter to H. T. Baker, 15 July 1900
8. *Ibid*, p. 80; letter to H. T. Baker, 1 August 1901
9. *Ibid*, pp. 114–15; letter to Katharine Horner, 23 July 1904
10. *Ibid*, p. 120; letter to Katharine Horner, 21 November 1904
11. *Ibid*, p. 155; letter to Lady Horner, 30 July 1907
12. Lady Cynthia Asquith, *Diaries 1915-1918*, 15 September 1915
13. Lady Diana Cooper, *The Rainbow Comes and Goes*, p. 73 (Penguin edition)
14. Nicholas Mosley, *Julian Grenfell*, p. 146
15. Letter from Archie Gordon to Lady Desborough, 12 April 1908; quoted in Nicholas Mosley, *Julian Grenfell*, p. 146
16. W. S. Gilbert, *Iolanthe*, 1885
17. Mary, Countess of Wemyss: *A Family Record* (no page number)
18. Quoted in Lady Desborough, *Pages from a Family Journal*, May 1910, p. 188
19. *Ibid*
20. *Ibid*
21. Apsley Cherry-Garrard, *The Worst Journey in the World*, p. 598 (Penguin edition)
22. *Ibid*, p. 606
23. Wilfrid Scawen Blunt, *My Diaries, 1888–1914*, 16 April 1912, p. 800
24. Letter from Julian Grenfell to Marjorie Manners, December 1909; quoted in Nicholas Mosley, *Julian Grenfell*, p. 166
25. Lady Desborough, *Pages from a Family Journal*, pp. 161–2
26. *Ibid*.
27. Quoted in Nicholas Mosley, *Julian Grenfell*, p. 169
28. Lady Desborough, *Pages from a Family Journal*, p. 167
29. Lady Diana Cooper, *The Rainbow Comes and Goes*, p. 97 (Penguin edition)
30. *Ibid*, p. 94
31. *Ibid*, pp. 94–5
32. *Ibid*, p. 100
33. Osbert Sitwell, *Great Morning*, p. 239
34. Margot Asquith, *Autobiography*, Vol. II, pp. 217–18
35. Lady Desborough, *Pages from a Family Journal*, pp. 438–9
36. Edith Lyttelton, *Alfred Lyttelton*, p. 368
37. *Ibid*, p. 336
38. Quoted in Max Egremont, *The Cousins*, p. 279
39. Osbert Sitwell, *Great Morning*, pp. 235 and 242
40. Lawrence Jones, *An Edwardian Youth*; quoted in Michael and Eleanor Brock, *H. H. Asquith: Letters to Venetia Stanley*, Introduction, p. 5
41. Lady Diana Cooper in conversation with the author, March 1983
42. Michael and Eleanor Brock, *H. H. Asquith: Letters to Venetia Stanley*, letter 101, 20 July 1914, p. 108
43. Letter from Margot Asquith to Lady Desborough, 21 March 1914
44. Michael and Eleanor Brock, *H. H. Asquith: Letters to Venetia Stanley*, letter 106, 27 July 1914, p. 128

45. *Ibid*, letter 108, 28 July 1914, p. 130
46. *Ibid*, letter 109, 29 July 1914, p. 132
47. *Ibid*, letter 110, 30 July 1914, pp. 136–7
48. *Ibid*, letter 112, 1 August 1914, p. 139
49. Lady Desborough, *Pages from a Family Journal*
50. Letter from Julian Grenfell to Lord Desborough, August 1914, quoted in Lady Desborough, *Pages from a Family Journal*
51. Letter from Julian Grenfell to Lady Desborough; quoted in Nicholas Mosley, *Julian Grenfell*, p. 230
52. Rupert Brooke, *Peace*
53. Mary, Countess of Wemyss, *A Family Record*, p. 235
54. *Ibid*

10. Dances of Death

1. Gilbert Murray, *How Can War Ever Be Right?*, pp. 24–7
2. Quoted in Christopher Hassall, *Rupert Brooke*, p. 471
3. *Ibid*, p. 480
4. Letter from Julian Grenfell to Lord Desborough; quoted in Lady Desborough, *Pages from a Family Journal*
5. Lord Northcliffe, 'What to Send Your Soldier'; from *Lord Northcliffe's War Book*, p. 53; quoted in Paul Fussell, *The Great War and Modern Memory*, p. 87
6. Michael and Eleanor Brock, *H. H. Asquith: Letters to Venetia Stanley*, letter 148, 9 September 1914, p. 227
7. *Ibid*, letter 145, 3 September 1914, p. 222
8. Letter from Billy Grenfell, January 1915; quoted in Lady Desborough, *Pages from a Family Journal*
9. Quoted in Nicholas Mosley, *Julian Grenfell*, pp. 236–7
10. *Ibid*, p. 241
11. E. L. Black (ed.), *1914–18 in Poetry*
12. David Jones, *In Parenthesis*, 1937
13. I am grateful to Mr Peter Scott, Hon. Editor of *Stand To!*, the Journal of the Western Front Association, for most of the facts and figures in the previous paragraphs
14. I am grateful to Major J. R. St Aubyn for this reminiscence, which he was told as a schoolboy by his father
15. *A King's Story: the Memoirs of HRH the Duke of Windsor*, p. 111
16. John Jolliffe (ed.), *Raymond Asquith: Life and Letters*, p. 192
17. Duff Cooper, *Old Men Forget*, p. 51
18. Lady Diana Cooper, *The Rainbow Comes and Goes*, p. 129
19. *Ibid*, p. 105
20. *Ibid*, p. 107
21. Lady Desborough, *Pages from a Family Journal*
22. *Ibid*, pp. 494–5
23. Nicholas Mosley, *Julian Grenfell*, p. 247
24. Julian Grenfell, *Prayer for Those on the Staff*; quoted in full in Lady Desborough, *Pages from a Family Journal*, p. 505, and also in E. L. Black (ed.), *1914–18 in Poetry*, p. 102
25. Lady Desborough, *Pages from a Family Journal*, p. 541
26. Julian Grenfell's last letter home, 8 May 1915
27. Letter from Yvo Charteris to Cynthia Asquith, 7 October 1915
28. Letter home from Yvo Charteris, 20 September 1915; quoted in Mary, Countess of Wemyss, *A Family Record*, p. 316
29. Paul Fussell, *The Great War and Modern Memory*, p. 182
30. *Ibid*, p. 22; these words are selected from a longer list
31. It is interesting to note that when the Falklands War broke out in April 1982, the *Guardian* commented on exactly the same transmutation of language occurring almost immediately:

> The last few days have turned up a list just as impressive as Fussell's Great War catalogue. . . . The Union Jack is *The Flag of Freedom*; the South Atlantic is the *cruel waters*; British soldiers are *our brave boys*; British commandos are *our tough guys*.
>
> The language is unashamedly discriminatory. British casualties tend to be the *price of victory*, which doesn't seem to be true of Argentine casualties. Sea Harriers tend to be *lost* or *shot down*; while Mirages and Sea Hawks are, as a general rule, *blown out of the sky*. Argentine gun boats, by the same formula, are *blasted to smithereens*, while British ships are generally *sunk*. Britain's 'brave planes' carry out bombing raids or strafe enemy ships; Argentine pilots, by contrast, embark on *desperate suicide missions* or carry out *merciless air onslaughts*. And talking of 'brave planes' you may

have noticed that *HMS Antelope* (alias *HMS Valour*) was a *brave little frigate*, not so much blasted to smithereens as *stricken*. (From the *Guardian* Diary, Thursday 27 May 1982.)

32. Mary, Countess of Wemyss, *A Family Record*, p. 320
33. Pamela Glenconner, *Edward Wyndham Tennant*, p. 167
34. *Ibid*, p. 142
35. John Jolliffe (ed.), *Raymond Asquith: Life and Letters*, p. 197
36. Lady Diana Cooper, *The Rainbow Comes and Goes*, p. 131
37. *Ibid*, p. 259
38. *Ibid*
39. *Ibid*, p. 260
40. Lady Desborough, *Pages from a Family Journal*, p. 546
41. *Ibid*, p. 548
42. *Ibid*, p. 550
43. *Ibid*, p. 553
44. *Ibid*, p. 554
45. *Ibid*, p. 556
46. Mary, Countess of Wemyss, *A Family Record*, p. 289
47. Letter from Lady Frances Balfour; quoted in Lady Desborough, *Pages from a Family Journal*
48. *Ibid*, p. 622. Ettie and Willy evidently agreed, and their youngest son was never sent to fight. However, my borrowed copy of Enid Bagnold's *Diary Without Dates* originally belonged to him; his name is written in the front, in a surprisingly childish, stilted handwriting considering that he was twenty at the time: *Ivo Grenfell, Harrogate, May 1918*. Inside the book is a stiff square card bearing the address *Taplow Court, Taplow, Bucks*, and their telephone number, *75 Maidenhead*, beautifully engraved. On the reverse side someone – presumably Ivo himself – has scribbled a long list of voluntary organizations and their telephone numbers . . . Green Cross, Land Service Corps, Food Control Office. . . . He obviously longed to play some part in the war, feeling himself overshadowed, perhaps, by the lengthening myth that was being created around his brothers. In the end, his parents were not to see their line perpetuated. Young Ivo was killed instantly in a car crash in 1926. Willy was the first and last Baron Desborough.
49. Statistics taken from *Population Studies*, Vol. 31, no. 3, November 1977; J. M. Winter, *Britain's Lost Generation of the First World War*, pp. 449–66
50. Wilfred Owen, *The Parable of the Old Man and The Young*; from Dominic Hibberd (ed.), *Wilfred Owen: War Poems and Others*, p. 69
51. E. L. Black (ed.), *1914–18 in Poetry*, p. 105
52. Lady Cynthia Asquith, *Diaries 1915–18*, p. 79
53. *Ibid*, p. 76
54. *Ibid*
55. Mary, Countess of Wemyss, *A Family Record*, pp. 305–6
56. *Ibid*
57. *Ibid*, p. 306
58. Lady Cynthia Asquith, *Diaries, 1915–18*, p. 90
59. *Ibid*, p. 91
60. *Ibid*, p. 92
61. Mary, Countess of Wemyss, *A Family Record*
62. Artemis Cooper (ed.), *A Durable Fire: the Letters of Duff and Diana Cooper 1913–50*, p. 26
63. Mary, Countess of Wemyss, *A Family Record*, p. 166
64. *Ibid*
65. *Ibid*
66. *Ibid*, p. 347
67. *Ibid*, p. 352
68. *Ibid*, p. 372
69. *Ibid*
70. Philip Ziegler, *Diana Cooper*, p. 77
71. *Ibid*, p. 77
72. Mary, Countess of Wemyss, *A Family Record*, p. 393

11. Help Me to Die, O Lord

1. John Jolliffe (ed.), *Raymond Asquith: Life and Letters*, p. 268
2. *Ibid*, p. 217
3. *Ibid*, p. 266
4. *Ibid*, p. 270

5. Martin Middlebrook, *The First Day on the Somme*, p. 99
6. *Ibid*, p. 81
7. *Ibid*, p. 97
8. *Ibid*
9. Quoted in Pamela Glenconner, *Edward Wyndham Tennant*, p. 293; poem dated 13 June 1916
10. *Ibid*, p. 197
11. Letter from Raymond Asquith to Lady Diana Manners, 10 July 1916; quoted in John Jolliffe (ed.), *Raymond Asquith: Life and Letters*, p. 273
12. *Ibid*, p. 274
13. *Ibid*, p. 278
14. *Ibid*, p. 286
15. *Ibid*, p. 287
16. Pamela Glenconner, *Edward Wyndham Tennant*, p. 226
17. *Ibid*, p. 229
18. *Ibid*, p. 231
19. *Ibid*, p. 127
20. *Ibid*, p. 231
21. *Ibid*, pp. 231–3
22. Lady Diana Cooper, *The Rainbow Comes and Goes*, p. 89
23. Edward Wyndham Tennant's last letter to his mother, 20 September 1916; quoted in Pamela Glenconner, *Edward Wyndham Tennant*, pp. 234–5
24. Lord Chandos, *From Peace to War*, p. 163
25. *Ibid*, p. 158
26. Nicholas Mosley, *Julian Grenfell*, p. 265
27. Rudyard Kipling, *Common Form*; quoted in John Silkin (ed.), *The Penguin Book of First World War Poetry*, p. 131

12. Quietus

1. From a confidential letter to the author, 2 January 1984
2. Michael and Eleanor Brock, *H. H. Asquith: Letters to Venetia Stanley*, letter 230, 20 December 1914, p. 333
3. *Ibid*, letter 242, p. 347
4. *Ibid*, letter 259, p. 377
5. Lady Diana Cooper in conversation with the author, February 1984
6. Michael and Eleanor Brock, *H. H. Asquith: Letters to Venetia Stanley*, letter 275, 25 January 1915, p. 394
7. *Ibid*, letter XXI from Margot Asquith to Edwin Montagu, 16 April 1915, p. 546
8. *Ibid*, letter 424, p. 592
9. *Ibid*, letter 425, p. 593
10. Sir John French, *1914*, p. 356
11. Margot Asquith, *Autobiography*, Vol. II, p. 247
12. Blanche Dugdale, *Balfour*, Vol. II, pp. 151–2
13. *Ibid*, p. 155; telegram to Colonel House, 29 July 1917
14. H. G. Wells, *Experiment in Autobiography*, Vol. II, pp. 775–8
15. *Ibid*
16. Quoted in Kenneth Rose, *Superior Person*, p. 380
17. Letter from Mary, Countess of Wemyss to A. J. Balfour, 19 November 1912; quoted in Max Egremont, *Balfour*, p. 309
18. Lady Cynthia Asquith, *Diaries, 1915–18*, p. 300
19. Kenneth Rose, *Superior Person*, p. 10
20. *Ibid*, p. 11
21. Edgell Rickword, *Winter Warfare*, quoted in E. L. Black (ed.), *1914–18 in Poetry*, p. 57
22. *Ibid*, p. 50
23. John Terraine, *The Road to Passchendaele*, pp. 228–9
24. *Ibid*
25. *Official History of the First World War*, 1917, pp. 360–1
26. *Daily Telegraph*, 29 November 1917
27. Margot Asquith, *Autobiography*, Vol. II, p. 269
28. *Ibid*, p. 263
29. Tribute to Edward Horner by F. E. Smith; quoted in Frances Horner, *Time Remembered*, p. 226
30. Duff Cooper, *Old Men Forget*, p. 69

31. *Ibid*

32. *Ibid*, p. 71

33. *The Saturday Review*, 22 May 1920; reprinted in Memorial Volume for Patrick Shaw Stewart, pp. 21–3

34. *Ibid*, p. 44; reprinted from the Balliol College War Memorial Book

35. From Wilfrid Scawen Blunt's secret diary, 18 May 1904

36. Duff Cooper, *Old Men Forget*, p. 92

37. Lord Chandos, *From Peace to War*, p. 198

38. Margot Asquith, *Autobiography*, Vol. II, pp. 282–3

39. Lady Cynthia Asquith, *Diaries, 1915–18*, p. 480

Epilogue

1. Artemis Cooper (ed.), *A Durable Fire: the Letters of Duff and Diana Cooper, 1913–1950*, p. 45

2. Arthur Marwick, *The Deluge*, p. 261

3. *Ibid*

4. *Ibid*, p. 263

5. Artemis Cooper (ed.), *A Durable Fire: the Letters of Duff and Diana Cooper, 1913–1950*, p. 97

6. Blanche Dugdale, *Balfour*, Vol. II, p. 194

7. Richard Aldington, *Death of a Hero*, prologue, p. 3

8. Lady Mary Lyon in conversation with the author, 17 February 1984

Bibliography

ADAMS, CAROL, *Ordinary Lives a Hundred Years Ago*, Virago 1982

ALDINGTON, RICHARD, *Death of a Hero*, Chatto 1929

ASKWITH, BETTY, *The Lytteltons: a Family Chronicle of the Nineteenth Century*, Chatto & Windus 1975

ASLET, CLIVE, *The Last Country Houses*, Yale University Press, New Haven & London 1982

ASQUITH, CYNTHIA, *Diaries 1915–18*, Hutchinson 1968
    Remember and be Glad, James Barrie 1952

ASQUITH, MARGOT, *Autobiography Vol. I*, Thornton Butterworth 1920; *Vol. II*, 1922
    More Memories, Cassell 1933
    Places and Persons, Thornton Butterworth 1925
    Myself when Young, Muller 1938
    Off the Record, Muller 1943

BAGNOLD, ENID, *Diary without Dates*, Heinemann 1918
    Autobiography from 1889, Heinemann 1969

BALFOUR, ARTHUR JAMES, 1st Earl of, *Chapters of Autobiography* (edited by Mrs Edgar Dugdale), Cassell 1930

BALFOUR, LADY FRANCES, *Ne Obliviscaris*, Hodder & Stoughton 1930

BALSAN, CONSUELO VANDERBILT (CHURCHILL), *The Glitter and the Gold*, Heinemann 1955

BARING, MAURICE, *The Puppet Show of Memory*, Heinemann 1922

BATTISCOMBE, GEORGINA, *Queen Alexandra*, Constable 1969

BENSON, E. F., *As We Were: a Victorian Peep-Show*, Longmans, Green & Co. 1932
Dodo, Methuen 1893

BLACK, E. L., *1914–1918 in Poetry*, Hodder & Stoughton 1970

BLUNT, WILFRID SCAWEN, *My Diaries: Being a Personal Narrative of Events 1888–1914*, Martin Secker 1919
    Secret Memoirs, Diaries, Cahiers (MSS in Fitzwilliam Museum, Cambridge)

BONIFACE, PRISCILLA, *Hotels and Restaurants 1830 to the Present Day*, published for the Royal Commission on Historical Monuments at HMSO 1981

BRENDON, PIERS, *Eminent Edwardians*, Secker & Warburg 1979

BROCK, MICHAEL and ELEANOR (eds), *H. H. Asquith Letters to Venetia Stanley*, Oxford University Press 1982

BROOK-SHEPHERD, GORDON, *Uncle of Europe: the Social and Diplomatic Life of Edward VII*, Collins 1975

CAFFREY, KATE, *Edwardian Lady: Edwardian High Society 1900–1914*, Gordon & Cremonesi 1979

CAVENDISH, LADY FREDERICK, *Diary* (in 2 vols), John Murray 1927

CHANDOS, LORD, *From Peace to War: a Study in Contrast 1857–1918*, The Bodley Head 1968

    Memoirs, The Bodley Head 1962

CHERRY-GARRARD, APSLEY, *The Worst Journey in the World*, Chatto & Windus 1922; Penguin 1983

CLEMENSON, HEATHER A., *English Country Houses and Landed Estates*, Croom Helm 1982

COOPER, ARTEMIS (ed.), *A Durable Fire: the Letters of Duff and Diana Cooper 1913–1950*, Collins 1983

COOPER, DIANA, *The Rainbow Comes and Goes*, Rupert Hart-Davis 1958

COOPER, DUFF, *Old Men Forget*, Rupert Hart-Davis 1953

COOPER, NICOLAS, *The Opulent Eye: Late Victorian and Edwardian Taste in Interior Design*, The Architectural Press, London, 1976

CORNWALLIS-WEST, GEORGE, *Edwardian Hey-Days: a Little about a Lot of Things*, Putnam 1930

COWLES, VIRGINIA, *Edward VII and His Circle*, Hamish Hamilton 1956

CRATHORNE, NANCY, *Tennant's Stalk: the Story of the Tennants of the Glen*, Macmillan 1973

D'ABERNON, VISCOUNT, *Portraits and Appreciations*, Hodder & Stoughton 1931

DAVIDSON, CAROLINE, *A Woman's Work is Never Done: a History of Housework in the British Isles, 1650–1950*, Chatto & Windus 1982

DESBOROUGH, LADY, *Pages from a Family Journal, 1888–1915*, privately printed 1916

    Flotsam and Jetsam, privately printed 1949

DUFF, DAVID, *Alexandra, Princess and Queen*, Collins 1980

DUGDALE, BLANCHE (MRS ERNEST), *Arthur James Balfour: First Earl of Balfour KG, OM, FRS: Vol. I 1848–1905*, Hutchinson 1939; *Vol. II 1906–1930*, 1936

DUGDALE, JAMES, 'Sir Charles Tennant, the Story of a Victorian Collector', published in *The Connoisseur*, September 1971

EGREMONT, MAX, *Balfour: a Life of Arthur James Balfour*, Collins 1980

    The Cousins: the Friendship, Opinions and Activities of Wilfrid Scawen Blunt and George Wyndham, Collins 1977

ESHER, LORD, *Journals and Letters of Reginald Viscount Esher*, 4 Vols, Nicholson & Watson 1938

FIELD, LESLIE, *Bendor: the Golden Duke of Westminster*, Weidenfeld & Nicolson 1983

FIELDING, DAPHNE, *The Duchess of Jermyn Street: the Life and Good Times of Rosa Lewis of the Cavendish Hotel*, Eyre & Spottiswoode 1964

FORBES, LADY ANGELA, *Memories and Base Details*, Hutchinson 1921

    What I Remember, Hutchinson 1921

FORD, COLIN, and HARRISON, BRIAN, *A Hundred Years Ago: Britain in the 1880s in Words and Photographs*, Allen Lane, The Penguin Press 1983

FUSSELL, PAUL, *The Great War and Modern Memory*, Oxford University Press 1975

GIROUARD, MARK, *Life in the English Country House: a Social and Architectural History*, Penguin 1980

   The Victorian Country House, Yale University Press, New Haven and London 1979

   The Return to Camelot: Chivalry and the English Gentleman, Yale University Press 1981

GIRTIN, TOM, *The Abominable Clubman*, Hutchinson 1964

GLADSTONE, MARY (MRS DREW), *Her Diaries and Letters* (edited by Lucy Masterman) Methuen 1930

   Some Hawarden Letters, Nisbet & Co. 1917

GLENCONNER, PAMELA, *The Sayings of the Children: Written Down by Their Mother*, Blackwell 1918

   The White Wallet, T. Fisher Unwin 1912

   Edward Wyndham Tennant, John Lane, The Bodley Head 1919

GLYN, ANTHONY, *Elinor Glyn: a Biography*, Hutchinson 1955

GORE, JOHN, *Edwardian Scrapbook*, Evans Bros 1951

GRIGG, JOHN, *Nancy Astor*, Sidgwick & Jackson 1980

HARTCUP, ADELINE, *Children of the Great Country Houses*, Sidgwick & Jackson 1982

HASSALL, CHRISTOPHER, *Rupert Brooke: a Biography*, Faber & Faber 1964

HIBBERT, CHRISTOPHER, *Edward VII: a Portrait*, Penguin 1982

HORNER, FRANCES, *Time Remembered*, Heinemann 1933

HOROWITZ MURRAY, JANET, *Strong-Minded Women and Other Lost Voices from 19th Century England*, Penguin 1984

HOUSMAN, LAURENCE, *War Letters of Fallen Englishmen*, Gollancz 1930

HYDE, H. MONTGOMERY, *The Londonderrys: a Family Portrait*, Hamish Hamilton 1979

JENKINS, ROY, *Asquith*, Collins 1964

JOLLIFFE, JOHN, *Raymond Asquith: Life and Letters*, Collins 1980

JONES, DAVID, *In Parenthesis*, Faber & Faber 1937

JULLIAN, PHILIPPE, *Edward & the Edwardians: a Biography*, Librairie Hachette, England 1962

   Sarah Bernhardt, Editions Balland 1977

KEPPEL, SONIA, *Edwardian Daughter*, Hamish Hamilton 1958

LANG, THEO, *My Darling Daisy*, Michael Joseph 1966

LEJEUNE, ANTONY, *Gentleman's Clubs of London*, Macdonald & Jane's (date unknown)

LESLIE, ANITA, *Edwardians in Love*, Hutchinson & Co. 1972

   Jennie: the Life of Lady Randolph Churchill, Hutchinson 1969

LIDDELL, A. G. C., *Notes from the Life of an Ordinary Mortal*, John Murray 1911

LISTER, BEATRIX (ed.), *Emma, Lady Ribblesdale; Letters and Diaries*, privately printed 1930

LONGFORD, ELIZABETH, *A Pilgrimage of Passion: the Life of Wilfrid Scawen Blunt*, Weidenfeld & Nicolson 1979

   Victoria RI, Weidenfeld & Nicolson 1964

LORD, WALTER, *A Night to Remember*, illustrated edition, Allen Lane, Penguin Books 1976

LYTTELTON, EDITH, *Alfred Lyttelton: an Account of His Life*, Longmans, Green & Co. 1917

MAAS, JEREMY, *This Brilliant Year: Queen Victoria's Jubilee 1887*, Catalogue to exhibition at the Royal Academy of Arts 1977

MACCARTHY, DESMOND, *Portraits I*, Putnam 1931

MACDONALD, LYN, *Somme*, Michael Joseph 1983

MACLEOD, KIRSTY, *The Last Summer: May–September 1914*, Collins 1983

MAGNUS, PHILIP, *King Edward the Seventh*, John Murray 1964
    Gladstone: a Biography, John Murray 1954

MANGAN, J. A., *Athleticism in the Victorian & Edwardian Public Schools*, Cambridge University Press 1981

MARTIN, RALPH, *Lady Randolph Churchill: Vol. II 1895–1921*, Cassell 1971

MARWICK, ARTHUR, *The Deluge: British Society and the First World War*, Macmillan 1965

MASON, PHILIP, *The English Gentleman: the Rise and Fall of an Ideal*, André Deutsch 1982

MASTERS, BRIAN, *Great Hostesses*, Constable 1982

MAUROIS, ANDRÉ, *Disraeli: a Picture of the Victorian Age*, John Lane, The Bodley Head 1927

MIDDLEBROOK, MARTIN, *The First Day on the Somme: 1 July 1916*, Allen Lane, Penguin 1971

MIDLETON, EARL OF, *Records and Reactions 1856–1939*, Murray 1939

MORRIS, JAMES, *Pax Britannica; the Climax of an Empire*, Faber 1968
    Farewell The Trumpets: an Imperial Retreat, Faber 1978, Penguin 1979

MOSLEY, LEONARD, *Curzon: the End of an Epoch*, Longmans, Green & Co. 1961

MOSLEY, NICHOLAS, *Julian Grenfell: his Life and the Times of his Death 1885–1915*, Weidenfeld & Nicolson 1976

NEVILL, RALPH, *London Clubs*, Chatto & Windus 1911

NICOLSON, HAROLD, *King George V: his Life and Reign*, Constable 1952
    Some People, Constable 1927

NICOLSON, NIGEL, *Mary Curzon*, Weidenfeld & Nicolson 1977

OWEN, WILFRED, *War Poems and Others* (edited and with an introduction and notes by Dominic Hibberd), Chatto & Windus 1973

PARSONS, I. M. (edited and introduced by), *Men who March Away: Poems of the First World War*, Chatto & Windus 1965

PEVSNER, NICOLAS, *Victorian and After: Studies in Art, Architecture and Design*, Thames & Hudson 1968

PLESS, DAISY, PRINCESS OF, *By Herself*, John Murray 1928

PONSONBY, SIR FREDERICK, *Recollections of Three Reigns*, Eyre & Spottiswoode 1951

PRIESTLEY, J. B., *The Edwardians*, Heinemann 1970

QUENNELL, PETER (ed.), *Genius in the Drawing-Room: the Literary Salon in the Nineteenth and Twentieth Centuries*, Weidenfeld & Nicolson 1980

RIBBLESDALE, LORD, *Impressions and Memories*, Cassell 1927

RONALDSHAY, RT HON. THE EARL OF, *Life of Lord Curzon* (3 vols), Ernest Benn 1928

ROSE, KENNETH, *Superior Person: a Portrait of Curzon and his Circle in Late Victorian England*, Weidenfeld & Nicolson 1969
    King George V, Weidenfeld & Nicolson 1983

SACKVILLE-WEST, VITA, *The Edwardians*, The Hogarth Press 1930

ST AUBYN, GILES, *Edward VII: Prince and King*, Collins 1979

SANSOM, WILLIAM (introduction), *Victorian Life in Photographs*, Thames & Hudson 1974

SASSOON, SIEGFRIED, *The War Poems*, Faber & Faber 1983

SCOTT, PETER T. (Hon. ed.), *Stand To! the Journal of the Western Front Association*, *Vols 6–11*

SEWELL, LIEUT-COL. J. P. C., *Personal Letters of King Edward VII*, Hutchinson 1931

SHAW STEWART, BASIL, *Patrick Shaw Stewart: a Memorial Volume*, privately printed by Wm. St C. Wilson 1940

SILKIN, JON (ed.), *The Penguin Book of First World War Poetry*, 1979

SITWELL, OSBERT, *Left Hand, Right Hand!*, Macmillan 1945
   The Scarlet Tree, Macmillan 1946
   Great Morning, Macmillan 1948

SORLEY, CHARLES HAMILTON, *The Poems and Selected Letters* (edited and with an introduction by Hilda D. Spear), Blackness Press 1978

SPENDER, DALE, *Women of Ideas and What Men have Done to Them*, Routledge & Kegan Paul 1982

STORRS, SIR RONALD, *Orientations*, Nicholson & Watson 1945

STUART, DENIS, *Dear Duchess: Millicent Duchess of Sutherland 1867–1955*, Gollancz 1982

TAYLOR, A. J. P., *The First World War*, Hamish Hamilton 1963

THOMPSON, F. M. L., *English Landed Society in the 19th Century*, Routledge & Kegan Paul 1963

THOMPSON, PAUL, *The Edwardians: the Remaking of British Society*, Weidenfeld & Nicolson 1975

WARWICK, FRANCES, COUNTESS OF, *Life's Ebb and Flow*, Hutchinson 1929

WELLS, H. G., *Experiment in Autobiography* (2 vols), Gollancz 1934

WEMYSS, COUNTESS OF (MARY ELCHO), *A Family Record*, privately published 1932

WEST, REBECCA, *1900*, Weidenfeld & Nicolson 1982

WINGFIELD-STRATFORD, ESMÉ, *The Victorian Sunset*, Routledge 1932

WINTER, J. M., *Britain's Lost Generation of the First World War*, Journal of Population Studies, Vol. 31, Number 3, Nov. 1977

WOHL, ROBERT, *The Generation of 1914*, Weidenfeld & Nicolson 1980

YOUNG, KENNETH, *Arthur James Balfour: the Happy Life of the Politician, Prime Minister, Statesman & Philosopher, 1848–1930*, Bell & Sons 1963

ZIEGLER, PHILIP, *Lady Diana Cooper*, Hamish Hamilton 1981

Index

Horner, Lady Frances (1858–1940; *née* Frances Graham), 23 and n., 24, 25, 30, 91; biographical note, xvii; artistic ability, 8; and Laura Lyttelton's death, 31; appearance, 73; on marriage, 84–5; on Harry Cust, 101; art collection, 134; family reminiscences, 134; children, 149; at Mells, 151; and her son's death, 218
Horner, Sir John (1842–1927), 85, 149; biographical note, xvii–xviii
Horner, Katharine (1885–1976), 149, 151; biographical note, xxii; *see also* Asquith, Katharine
Hotel Cecil, London, 116, 128
Hôtel Vendôme, Paris, 109, 110
Hotel Weimar, Marienbad, 47
House of Commons, 54–5, 59, 113, 116, 138, 139, 164, 209
House of Lords, 54, 130, 139, 162, 170, 220
hygiene, 146

Imperial Russian Opera, 163
Impressionists, 56
Independent Labour Party, 86
India, 67, 158, 170; Prince of Wales' tour of, 44; Curzon's travels in, 108; Curzon as Viceroy of, 114–19, 121–5, 126–8, 130; First World War, 176
India Council, 122, 124
India Office, 114
Indian Corps, 192
Innerleithen, 18
Ireland: Home Rule, 54, 55–6, 164; Balfour as Irish Secretary, 59–61, 62–3; Blunt visits, 61–3; Sinn Fein, 139; civil war, 220
Irish Nationalists, 59, 61, 63
Ismay, Sir Bruce, 157
Italy, 29; First World War, 179, 196

James, Henry, 50, 61, 133, 135
Jekyll, Mrs Herbert, 24
jewellery, 99, 145
Jews, 49
Jones, David, 174
Jones, Inigo, 57, 136
Jones, Lawrence, 163
Jowett, Benjamin, 134

Kabul, 110
Karsavina, Tamara, 163
Katia, 194
Kedleston Hall, 5, 106, 131, 138, 214, 229
Kent, 175
Keppel, Mrs, 37, 42, 194
Kipling, Rudyard, 50, 51, 83, 205
Kitchener, Lord: in India, 122–3, 124–5, 127, 212; in First World War, 170, 175, 176, 189, 192, 209, 212; death, 197–8, 210
Knowsley, 98
Korean War, 199

Labour Party, 86
Lamb, Lady Caroline, 77, 97
Lancashire, 187
Lancers, 123–4
The Lancet, 40
land ownership, 136–8, 206
Langtry, Lillie, 37
language: Souls' private use of, 94–7; of warfare, 181–3
Lansdowne, Lord, 165, 217–18
Lansdowne Letter, 217–18
Lascelles, Charles, 23
Lasselle, 84
Latimer, 57
Law, Andrew Bonar, 209
Le Nôtre, André, 92
Leconfield, Lord, 79, 162
Leicestershire, 81
Leicestershire Sunday School Union, 46
Leighton, Sir Frederick, 56
Leinster, Duke of, 78
Leinster, Hermione, Duchess of, 64, 66, 78, 93, 142
Leiter, Levi Z., 110, 111, 126
Leiter, Mary (1870–1906), 106–7, 108–11, 214; *see also* Curzon, Mary
Lenin, 212
Leopold, Prince, 73
Lesboeufs, 202
Le Touquet, 179
Lewis, Rosa, 142, 144
Liberal Party, 56, 59, 129
Liberty's, 15
Liddell, Adolphus ('Doll'; 1846–1930), 21, 23–5, 27–8, 91, 92, 95; biographical note, xviii
Lindsay, Norah, 94
Lindsay, Violet, *see* Granby, Lady Violet
Lister, Barbara, 149
Lister, Charles (1887–1915), biographical note, xxii; in the Coterie, 149; socialism, 152, 154; holiday in Venice, 159; in First World War, 176; death, 189, 190, 218
Lister, Diana, 149, 162–3; *see also* Wyndham, Diana
Lister, Laura, 149, 189
Lister, Susy, 91
Lister, Thomas, *see* Ribblesdale, Lord
literature, 133–4
Lloyd George, David, 162, 198, 207, 209, 210–11, 216, 217, 218, 223
Local Government Board, 55
London: clubs and restaurants, 6–7, 136; prostitution, 40
London Rifle Brigade, 198
Londonderry, Lady, 133
Londonderry House, London, 6
Longford, Lord (Frank Pakenham), 93, 95, 97
Loos, Battle of, 189, 190, 203
Lords, 90
The Lorettonian, 89

Credits

The publishers wish to thank the following for their permission to reproduce the photographs in this book: Lady Diana Cooper, Lord Crathorne, Milton Gendel, the Hon. John Jolliffe, Lady Mary Lyon, Lady Alexandra Metcalfe, the Earl of Oxford and Asquith, the Earl of Plymouth, the Taplow Visitors' Book by courtesy of the Hon. Nicolas Gage; the BBC Hulton Picture Library, *Country Life*, the Fitzwilliam Museum Cambridge, the Mansell Collection, Popperfoto.

The author and publishers are also grateful to Mr Mark Bonham-Carter for permission to quote from Margot Asquith's *Autobiography* and from H. H. Asquith's letters published in *H. H. Asquith Letters to Venetia Stanley*; to The Bodley Head for permission to quote from Lord Chandos, *From Peace to War*; to Rupert Hart-Davis for permission to quote from Lady Diana Cooper, *The Rainbow Comes and Goes*, and from Duff Cooper, *Old Men Forget*; to Hutchinson Books Limited for permission to quote from Cynthia Asquith, *Diaries 1915–18*; and to Oxford University Press for permission to quote from Michael and Eleanor Brock, *H. H. Asquith Letters to Venetia Stanley*.